CW01670429

Scottish Photography: A History

Scottish Photography: A History

TOM NORMAND

Luath Press Limited
EDINBURGH
www.luath.co.uk

for Carey

First published 2007

ISBN (10): 1-906307-07-5
ISBN (13): 978-1-906307-07-3

The publishers acknowledge the support of

Scottish Arts Council

towards the publication of this volume.

The paper used in this book is recyclable. It is made from low-chlorine pulps produced in a low energy, low emission manner from renewable forests.

Printed and bound by Grafo, Bilbao

Typeset in Quadraat by 3btype.com

The author's right to be identified as author of this book under the Copyright, Designs and Patents Act 1988 has been asserted.

© Tom Normand 2007

Contents

Acknowledgements and Photographic Credits

I am indebted to the generosity and assistance of those artist-photographers who have kindly supplied images and copyright permissions. I am delighted to acknowledge the copyright of the following individuals:

© Jane Brettle; Peter Cattrell; Colin Cavers, and commissioned by Fife Council Museums West; Chick Chalmers; John Charity; Calum Colvin; Thomas Joshua Cooper; Dalziel and Scullion; Robin Gillanders; Catriona Grant; Vaughan Judge; Stephen Lawson; Owen Logan; Patricia Macdonald; Calum Angus Mackay; Joseph McKenzie; Wendy McMurdo; Pradip Malde; Garry Fabian Miller 'Courtesy the Artist/ Ingleby Gallery Edinburgh'; Gunnie Moberg; Lida Moser; Ron O'Donnell; Rankin; Joe Rock; Glyn Satterley; David Shrigley and 'Courtesy the artist and Stephen Friedman Gallery, London'; Ian Stewart; Ruth Stirling; Maud Sulter; Wolfgang Suschitzky; Jeremy Sutton-Hibbert; Albert Watson; Andy Wiener; David Williams; Claire Wheeldon; Gus Wylie.

A number of Institutions and Artists' Estates have co-operated in providing images, reproduction permissions and copyright. I would like to acknowledge the rights of:

T & R Annan & Sons Ltd. [FIGS.9,21,23,68,83,106,107]; Aperture Foundation, Paul Strand Archive [FIG.38]; British Library [FIG.40]; Collection Centre Canadien d'Architecture/Canadian Centre for Architecture, Montréal, Canada [FIG.77]; City Library, Edinburgh and 'Courtesy of Edinburgh City Libraries and Information Services – Edinburgh Room' [FIG.137]; Estate of Alfred G Buckham [FIG.49]; Estate of Fay Godwin [FIG.40], George Eastman House [FIGS.109,139]; The Glasgow Police Museum and Heritage Society [FIGS.34,35]; Harappa Archive [FIG.58]; Hulton Picture Library [FIG.73]; Werner Kissling Estate courtesy of David Lockwood [FIG.92]; National Galleries of Scotland [FIGS.15,22,49,52,69,70,71,87,136]; The Trustees of the National Library of Scotland [FIG.67,82]; McManus Gallery in Dundee [FIG.76]; Margaret Watkins Estate courtesy of Joseph Mulholland [FIG.110]; Dr John Murray 'Courtesy of Lawrence and Sybil Hite' [FIG.57]; Notman Photographic Archives, McCord Museum, Montreal [FIG.62]; Oscar Marzaroli Trust [FIGS.10,75,84]; Orkney Public Library [FIG.93]; SCRAN [FIG.97]; Smith Archive [FIGS.88,89]; University of Aberdeen [FIG.103]; University of St Andrews and 'Courtesy of the University of St Andrews Library' [FIGS.1,3,6,7,13,16,17,18,29,39, 41,44,45,46,47,48,78,86,91,116]; George Washington Wilson Collection, University of Aberdeen [FIGS.30,42, 43,79]; Wellcome Library, London [FIGS.61,98]; and Private Collections.

The assistance of individuals has been invaluable and their specialist knowledge a treasured resource, I would like to thank:

Douglas Annan; Gloria Chalmers; Shona Corner; Alastair Dinsmor; Omar Khan; David Mackie; Richard Ovenden; Lori Pauli; Michael Russell; Eoin Shalloo; Mike Smith; Aaron Watson; Clara Young. And, of course, all at Luath Press.

Amongst my academic friends and colleagues I am indebted to the encouragement and support of:

Natalie Adamson; Annette Carruthers; Duncan Forbes; Cilla Jackson; Martin Kemp; Julie Lawson; Dana MacFarlane; Venda Pollock; Norman Reid; Larry Schaaf; Graham Smith; Sara Stevenson; Russell Young.

For guidance and inspiration I remain eternally grateful to Robert Bancroft and Michael Scott.

This book would not have been completed without the support of the University of St Andrews, and an award from the Arts and Humanities Research Council.

List of Illustrations

Introduction

CHAPTER FIVE: **Photography and Art**

CONCLUSION

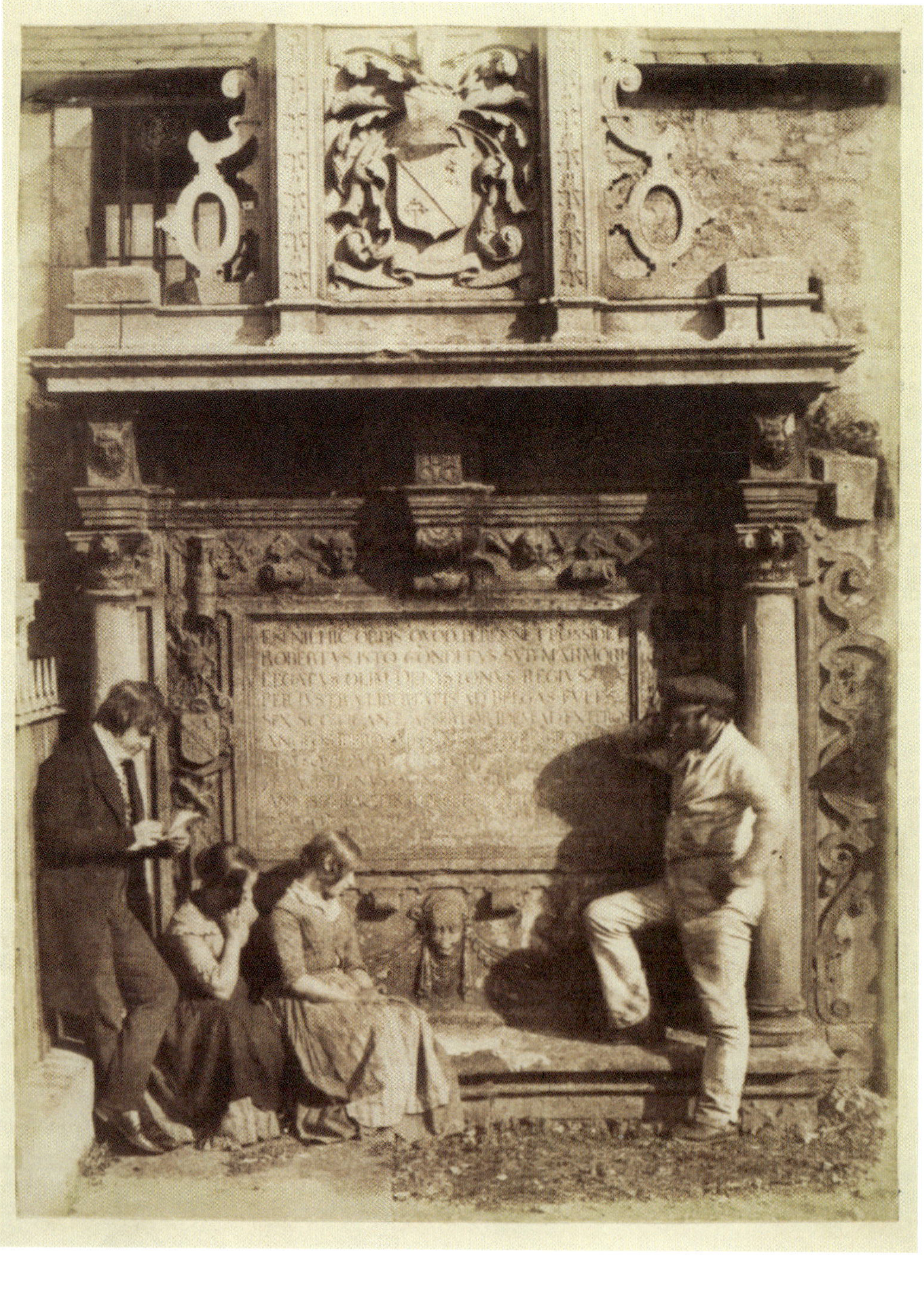

FIG.1
Hill and Adamson
Dennistoun Monument, Greyfriars Churchyard: 'The Artist and the Gravedigger'
1840s

Introduction

A history of photography from Scotland

The photograph is surely the visual form of our age. It gives shape to our collective and personal memory, records the major events and the intimate incidents of life, and distils experience. More than this, the photograph is freighted with the kaleidoscopic cargo of modern culture. It visualises the world in its infinite variety and diversity, realises every nuance of routine and change, and reveals each moment of destruction and creativity. And, of course, the photograph occupies every dimension of human life. From newspaper to album, magazine to billboard, postcard to pamphlet, archive to gallery, desktop to attic, the photograph inhabits every corner of existence. Paradoxically, the very universality of the photograph makes it near invisible, for the photograph is now so common as to be taken for granted and so habitual that it is mere custom. Yet to look at photographs is to see the fundamental matter of social life; history, culture, identity, consensus, conflict, self and others. To look at photographs, then, must surely allow us to condense experience and recognise our place in the world.

This book concerns 'a history of photography from Scotland', and undoubtedly that description requires some delicate 'unpacking'. The national dimension is, perhaps, the easiest to explain. While bookshops are adorned with histories of photography from France, America, Japan, Germany and England, no systematic narrative of photography from Scotland is given representation. There is some surprise in this, for Scotland took a lead role in the early development of photography and has occupied centre stage, at intervals, throughout the dramatic unfolding of its history. It was in Scotland that William Henry Fox Talbot found a sympathetic convert to his new technology in the commanding personality of the physicist David Brewster, and it was to Scotland that Talbot journeyed to create his seminal 'Sun Pictures' in 1844. Moreover, it was in the work of that esteemed photographic partnership, David Octavius Hill and Robert Adamson, that an apotheosis of 'the art of photography' was first reached. These principal characters in the established canon created, in Edinburgh and in St Andrews, a catalogue of works that remain the heart of photography's pulsating history.

There is a rationale and a logic to 'a history of photography from Scotland', then, but the proviso is surely held within the carefully placed indefinite article and the companion preposition; for this is 'a' history and it is not 'the' history, and it is 'from' Scotland rather than 'of' Scotland. If it is possible to forgive this sophistry then the explanation is helpful. It would be impossible, at this point in time, to write a definitive history of Scottish photography. Unlike the history of Scottish painting, or indeed the history of Scotland's literature and poetry, the archive of photography from Scotland is undernourished and incomplete. Despite sterling efforts from curators, academics, archivists and interested enthusiasts there remains a subterranean mass of undiscovered works in the cavernous labyrinth of Scotland's cultural treasure-house. Canonical figures have successfully surfaced from these deeps, but the work of noted professionals, once esteemed commercial studios, semi-professional and amateur devotees, photographic travellers and album-makers, institutionally assigned photographers, photographic journalists, and even the rising tide of young artists who are using photography remains veiled. Some of these are revealed in the pages that follow, but the mission is immense and remains open to every variety of researcher and enthusiast. This history, then, is circumscribed and partial, a first narrative account of Scotland's photography and a foundation for subsequent work.

The sense of a history of photography 'from' Scotland is equally as important. The photograph is universal and transcends national boundaries. While it is correct that a national photography may be the bearer of specific characteristics and may embody the marque of a nation's history, it is also the case that photographs and photographers, like nation-states, sit in dialogue. Scottish photographers have worked within Scotland, but they have also travelled to the corners of the globe and settled every continent. Moreover, the most esteemed of international photographers have journeyed to Scotland in order to undertake projects and create portfolios that reflect upon the nation's image. This history, then, is not solely concerned with those photographers who are Scottish by birth, or who work only in Scotland, but looks to the only meaningful sense of Scotland's photography, the establishment of a fruitful and vibrant international discourse.

From this perspective the taxonomy of photography from Scotland presents some interesting problems. While it is appropriate to dilute any overt national dimension, and to challenge the concept of a canon of 'great men' through the integration of amateur photographers and the vernacular genus, it is still necessary to structure the narrative. The approach here is thematic, and the chosen themes relate to the principal types of photograph created within the Scottish context. Portraiture, most obviously, for the concern with recording personality as evidenced in a 'real' face was a key moment in the early history of Scotland's photography. Landscape, indisputably, for the land has been viewed as the most important signifier of the nation's history and identity. Documentary, certainly, for this form became not only the most widespread and pervasive of photographic styles but also encompassed every aspect of the nation's culture. And, finally, the photograph as 'object' or artwork. This troubled concept, born of the original debate concerning photography's status as art or science, remains something of a challenge. However, the history of Pictorialism and the commitment of younger artists to the medium has dictated that this is one of the richest veins of photographic practice. These are the core themes of this study, and with each of these broad themes nuances of style, content, technique and intention are evidenced. These distinctions establish the unique characteristics of the individual photographer's work, and so the overall approach seeks to release the whole complex dynamic of Scotland's photography.

The deeper context of this thematic approach views photography from Scotland along three main trajectories; the photograph as memory and so as memorial, the photograph as document, and the photograph as object. This discussion of theoretical issues may best be illustrated in a practical study. Take, for example, Hill and Adamson's beautiful image of *The Dennistoun Monument, Greyfriars Churchyard*, pictured shortly after the establishment of the new medium of photography in the early 1840s. The photograph features one of the many imposing monuments in this ancient churchyard. The memorial inscription sits at the centre of the composition while the architectural embellishments of columns and carved insignia create an intriguing frame. A group of people rest at the monument. These have been identified as a self-portrait of the artist and photographer David Octavius Hill, two of his nieces, and one of the cemetery's gravediggers. The gravedigger would act as a guide to the monuments and stones, and indeed this photograph is sometimes recorded as *The Artist and the Gravedigger*.

In many senses Hill and Adamson have embodied the entire aesthetic of photography in this extraordinary and prescient image. The photograph is a document, certainly, in that it records a moment in time and lays this down for posterity. It acknowledges the undeniable fact of this event. Simultaneously, the figures sit in communion with a memorial, they reflect upon mortality and recognise fate. Consequently a complex web of memory is realised in this tableaux. This group, in the company of the gravedigger, will recall their life as memory while the photograph itself relives the frozen moment as a visual memory and as a memorial. Adding further levels of meaning, the artist stands in contrast to the gravedigger; creative life in juxtaposition to the surrender of eternal sleep. In this duel the artist claims a victory in the creation of the artwork, the object that is the photograph. And so, with this single image, Hill and Adamson have prophesied the very essence of photography, its unique character as memorial, document and object. It is these attributes that are revealed in this history of photography from Scotland, a history that echoes with the story of the nation and reverberates throughout the world community.

CHAPTER ONE

Memorial, Document, Object: The Photograph in Scotland

The photograph in Scotland embraces a host of sentiments and feelings. In this it is no different to the photograph in any other environment. However, in the Scottish context there exists a particular accent, a brogue that shapes themes and attitudes, ideas and emotions. The root of this is cultural, and culture is, of course, moulded by circumstance. It might be said that the unique history of modern Scotland has afforded ample range for a distinctive note in Scotland's photography. Here, the sentiment of memory, combined with the practical empiricism of the photographic document and the aesthetic appeal of the photograph as object have joined to create a striking chord. A chord that echoes the development of photography in all its variety yet reveals some unique and noteworthy characteristics. This triumvirate – the memorial, the document and the object – offers a passage towards a concrete and a conceptual understanding of the history of photography in, and from, Scotland.

Memorials

Memory as consciousness

There is an incident in W. G. Sebald's novel *Austerlitz* where the protagonist is confronted by a photograph. He reflects:

> I heard Vera again, speaking of the mysterious quality peculiar to such photographs when they surface from oblivion. One has the impression, she said, of something stirring in them, as if one caught small sighs of despair, *gémissements de desespoir* was her expression, said Austerlitz, as if the pictures had a memory of their own and remembered us, remembered the roles that we, the survivors, and those no longer among us had played in former lives.[1]

This reflection on the mystery of photography is resonant, for the photograph may be viewed as a special kind of memory. Memory, that is, as something that will 'surface from oblivion', in which there is 'something stirring' and which may release these 'small sighs of despair'. Everyone, perhaps, has photographs of family, and friends, and loved-ones, that are treasured as reminiscence, or as recollection. These are the transcripts of the generations, handed through families and groups to aid recall and to initiate storytelling. For the generality of people such photographs are recondite and perhaps meaningless, but for each possessor of the image they are particular and familiar and consequential [FIG.2].

Such photographs, then, are memory, and in many cases they take the place of memory. That is to say, the photograph becomes the recollection; for, if memory is conceived as something like a dream-world, fractured and surreal, then the photograph is a stable recollection, a truth. As Roland Barthes insisted, 'the very essence, the *noeme* of Photography... will therefore be: "That has been".'[2] This essential and provocative photographic truth then, this thing 'that has been', is held and retained as memory.

Many of the photographs we now venerate as art might be reclassified in this manner. The photograph, in its infant years during the 1840s and 1850s, was principally developed as a medium for the dissemination of the individual portrait. These portraits were both celebration and memorial. They offered a vision of the person and a testament to their character, while simultaneously presenting a memory of their being at a particular time, a memorial. Barthes, again, is helpful here for he insisted that 'however "lifelike" we strive to make it... Photography is a kind of primitive theatre, a kind of Tableaux Vivant, a figuration of the motionless and made-up face beneath which we see the dead.'[3] We may view Hill and Adamson's artful construction of, say, *Patrick Byrne* (c. 1797–1863), the eminent and blind Irish Harpist who visited Edinburgh in 1845, as precisely this dual configuration; recording Byrne's features and his status in a 'tableaux vivant', while

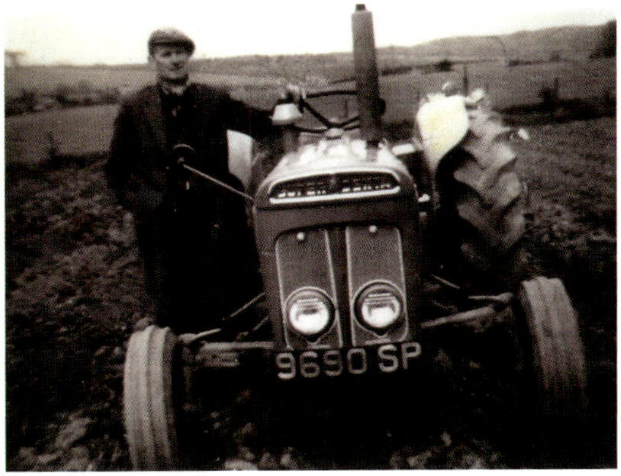

FIG.2
Anon.
Man and Tractor
circa 1963

simultaneously memorialising his life in this 'motionless' pose [FIG.3]. Of course, Hill and Adamson have also composed Byrne in the style of the mythic bard Ossian. The blind harpist is viewed in profile and decorated with a primitive plaid-like robe. The 'look' of the photograph has been designed to connote the famous image by the neo-classicist Alexander Runciman who created a sketch of *Ossian Singing* in 1772. Moreover, the setting of Byrne within this provocative context signals a conscious desire to connect with the memory of the fictional Celtic bard, James Macpherson's own Ossian. For all this the photograph remains as a memory and celebration of Patrick Byrne, a blind harpist, a bard, and it functions now as it did in the 1840s, as a testament and memorial.

FIG.3
Hill and Adamson
Patrick Byrne
1845

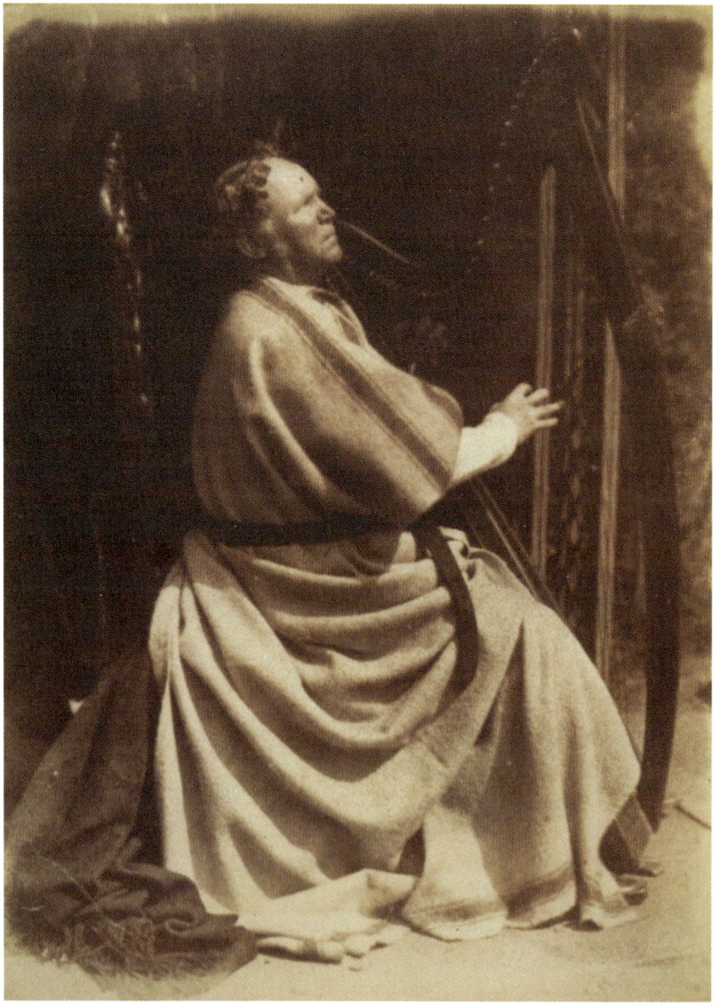

We can extend this sense of memory to contemporary portraiture in, for example, Robin Gillanders' evocative portrait of the artist *Ian Hamilton Finlay with Bust of Rousseau*, completed in 2004 [FIG.4]. Gillanders' work is, consistently, subtly crafted. He is a master of light and shade and is acutely sensitive to the nuance of these qualities in the portrait study. In *Ian Hamilton Finlay with Bust of Rousseau* the swathes of shadow and light are constructed to present a sense of drama, certainly, but also a kind of historical resonance; a memory of Finlay's being and life's work; almost, it might be said, the atmosphere of a mausoleum. Gillanders is conscious of the 'shadow' that sits in the background of each portrait study, and this is surely the shadow that Barthes recollects, that is, the spectre of mortality. The impression of dramatic contrast and the dark shadow-play of the photograph evoke the depth of mystery that allies this image not only to the realm of memory but also to the status of memorial.

Photographs, then, carry multiple and complex meanings all gathered under the banner of memory. It is these slippages of meaning that the contemporary Scottish photographer Calum Colvin consciously recalls in his portrait studies. Whether it is the constructed tableau of a contemporary portrait, as in the subtle iconography of his commissioned study of the composer *Portrait of James MacMillan*, 1996, or in the imagined world that he creates in commemoration of the national bard *Robert Burns* [FIG.5], 2002, Colvin is mixing memory and history and memorial. In all, these photographs become a kind of testament to an event that is passing or past. In this remarkable way, art, the photograph, represents life, but becomes death, or rather becomes memory and memorial.

This, of course, is the import of Barthes' remark that such images are '... a figuration of the motionless and made-up face beneath which we see the dead'. Less dramatically, perhaps, John Berger has offered a

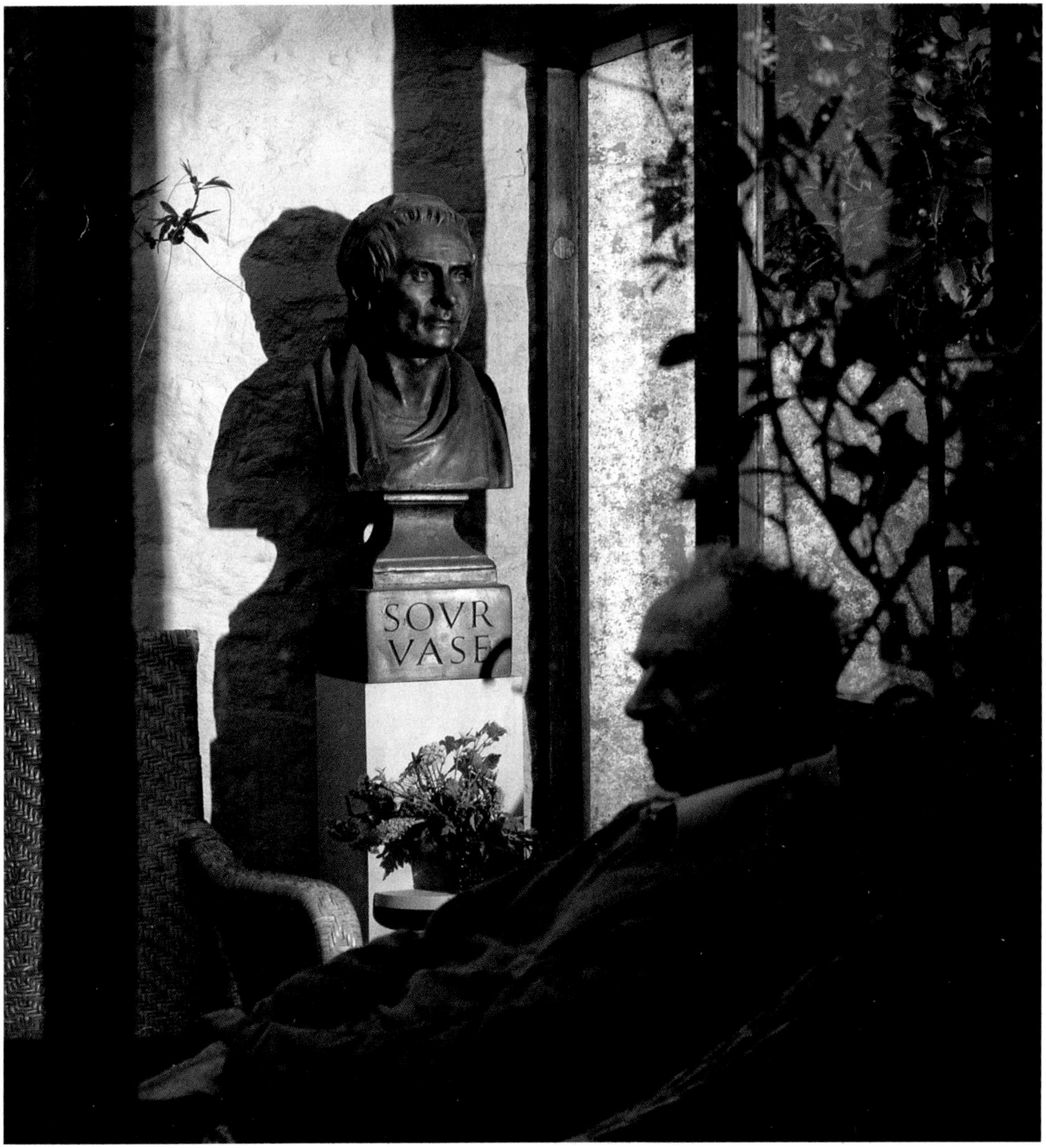

FIG.4
Robin Gillanders
Ian Hamilton Finlay with Bust of Rousseau
2004

comment based on the pragmatic use of the photograph. He writes:

> What served in place of the photograph; before the camera's invention? The expected answer is the engraving, the drawing, the painting. The more revealing answer might be: memory. What photographs do out there in space was previously done within reflection.[4]

The idea that the photograph, and photography, offers to the mind a space for reflection is seductive. In the case of the photograph that space is less an opening for the imagination, and more a room where memory is encountered. In this way the photograph represents, at the first level, memory as consciousness. The photograph is a recalled awareness, a remembered perception, one that opens the door into an individual's history. Moreover, this can remain the case whether the photograph is an 'artwork' recording a celebrated individual, or a 'vernacular' image, a personal snapshot.

FIG.5
Calum Colvin
Robert Burns
2002

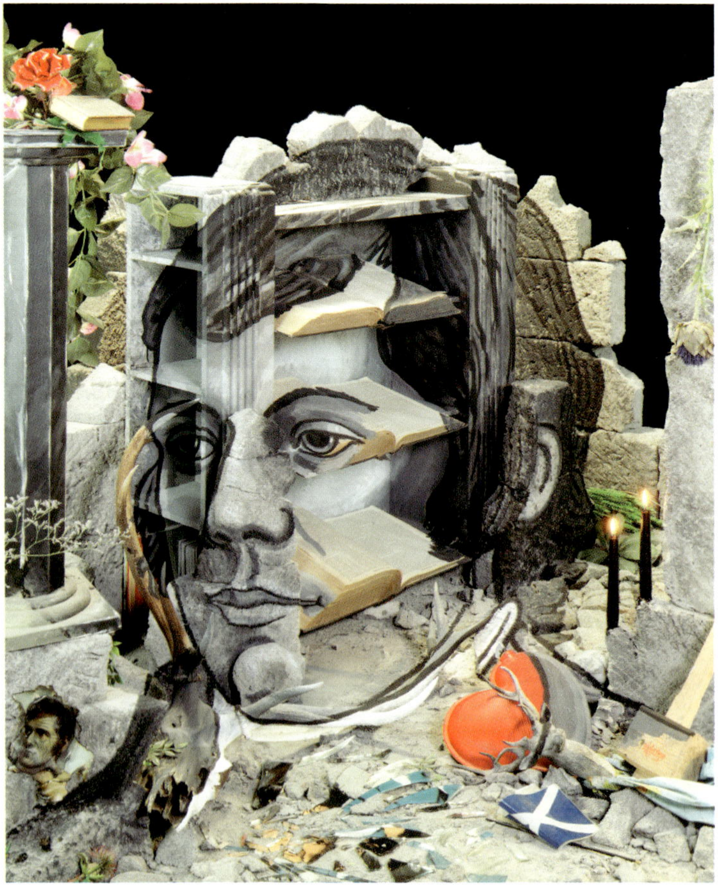

Memory as history

The photograph in this highly individualised sense is surely the common currency of the medium. This is the point at which everyone will engage with photography; this is personal. However, it is also appropriate to understand photography in an historical sense. Evidently, the photograph has documented the historical moment, and moments with which we are all familiar; from Desdéri's *Paris Commune: Bodies of Insurgents* to Hung Cong Ut's *Children Fleeing a Napalm Strike in Vietnam*. Photographs have both recorded and, it might be argued, changed history. But there is a more specialised sense in which the photograph engages history. It may be possible that the photograph can evoke a kind of historical memory, a site of collective remembering. In his introduction to Pierre Nora's epic intellectual adventure *Realms of Memory*, Lawrence D. Kritzman notes that:

> Pierre Nora's *Realms of Memory* (1984–1992)... seek[s] to locate the 'memory places' of French national identity... The history of memory is realised through the imaginary representations and historical realities that occupy the symbolic sites that form [French] social and cultural identity.[5]

These 'memory places' are, importantly, the loci of a collective psyche. Nora himself makes much of this difficult association of memory and history. He writes:

> Memory is life, always embodied in living societies and as such in permanent evolution, subject to the dialectic of remembering and forgetting, unconscious of the distortion to which it is subject, vulnerable in various ways to appropriation and manipulation, and capable of lying dormant for long periods only to be suddenly reawakened. History, on the other hand, is the reconstruction, always problematic and incomplete, of what is no longer... Memory is rooted in the concrete: in space, gesture, image, and object. History dwells exclusively on temporal continuities, on change in things and in the relations among things. Memory is an absolute, while history is always relative.[6]

Here, memory and history are juxtaposed in methodological terms, but it is possible to view this polarity as an interdependent project; history may be presented as an imagined projection based on memory. Most engagingly, it may be presented in this way in the photograph.

This sense of historical memory as something concretely embodied in symbolic sites has been a familiar trope of photography in general, and, in particular, of landscape photography; so that the history of landscape photography in Scotland has been marked by a constant reference to the 'landscape of association'. This is evidenced in the obsession that early commercial photographers, like George Washington Wilson and James Valentine, had with the landscape of the Scottish Highlands. Both these photographers celebrated the 'memory places' of Scottish history, scouring the Highlands for sites that resonated in the nation's chronicles. Here, photographs such as James Valentine's *Glencoe* [FIG.6] abound. These images are viewed simultaneously as an archetype of the 'land of the mountain and the flood'; as the site of the infamous 'Massacre of Glencoe' where individuals from the Clan Campbell, acting as agents of the crown, slaughtered the indigenous Macdonalds in 1692; and indeed, as the site of 'Ossian's Cave'. Evidently, throughout this trope, landscape becomes the very embodiment of history and of memory.

This approach is not simply the outcome of a sentimental Victorian romanticism. Indeed, in the 20th century it became marked in Robert Moyes Adam's evocative landscape images of mountains, castles, glens and lochs; like, for example, *Loch Ossian* [FIG.7], 1933; while, significantly, Calum Colvin would 'sample' Adam's Highland landscapes in a number of his own constructions, including references in *The Explorer*, 1985, and in *Jacob's Ladder*, 1989. Indeed there exists, even today, a veritable industry of Scottish landscape photography, one that forms the stock representations of picture calendars, postcards and decorated internet sites.

It is commonplace to contend that these panoramic landscape images were created for the developing tourist industry, one of those new social phenomena that came to define the distinctive character of modernity in the 19th century. In this frame they were the emblems of 'wilderness' and difference; a marked contrast to the 'civilised' urban environment that contemporary populations were coming to regard as a natural habitat. Here, the landscape photograph illustrated not just the tourist memento postcard or booklet, but a multitude of travel books and guides, and of course functioned as a formal memory of a tourist visit to some 'different' land. However, the selection of relevant sites was consistently determined by historical association. So the Pass of Killiecrankie, the Wade Bridges, the Glenfinnan Monument, the deserted crofts of Wester Ross, ruined brochs, carved Celtic crosses, and every kind of spectacular, austere, sublime castle; these were the stalking grounds of the landscape photographer. All such images allude to, and memorialise, the history, culture and identity of the nation and its people. Sites like these, then, provide what Kritzman has called a 'symbolic encyclopaedia' of the national identity. More powerfully, perhaps, photographs of these sites realise that symbolism in concrete form (Barthes' 'that-has-been') and preserve it as memory. In consequence history, now understood as memory, is released to a collective experience, a 'national identity', not purely through academic research, but through an immediate and largely unmediated visual experience. 'That-has-been' becomes 'this-is-us'.

Memory and myth

Of course, all of this assumes a settled, and an uncomplicated, sense of history and identity. In any nation this is not so, and it is certainly not so in Scotland. In fact these visual images, these photographs of symbolic sites, do not simply recollect collective memories, but *construct* a collective memory. That is, their presence acknowledges and reifies a national story that takes the form of a potent myth. Such a myth, while informed by history and at some level 'true', or at least accepted, is nevertheless a symbolic system, a 'constructed narrative'.

It is at this level, in the 'constructed narrative', that Calum Colvin's photographs express the idea of the photograph as memory and the photograph as myth. Colvin has long recognised that the photograph, even the most compelling documentary photograph, creates a kind of fiction. In every sense the photograph is a 'point of view'. His oeuvre is largely generated through a sense of the ways in which a photograph can appear to contain a settled subject, but will subtly

FIG.6
James Valentine
Glencoe from the Study
1878

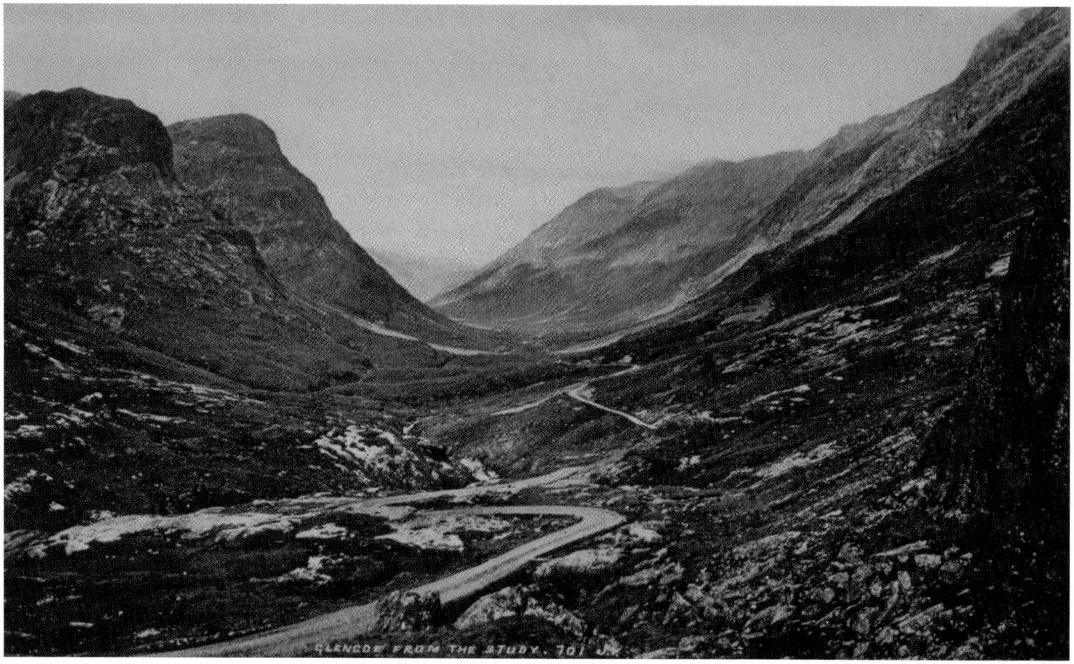

FIG.7
Robert Moyes Adam
Loch Ossian
1933

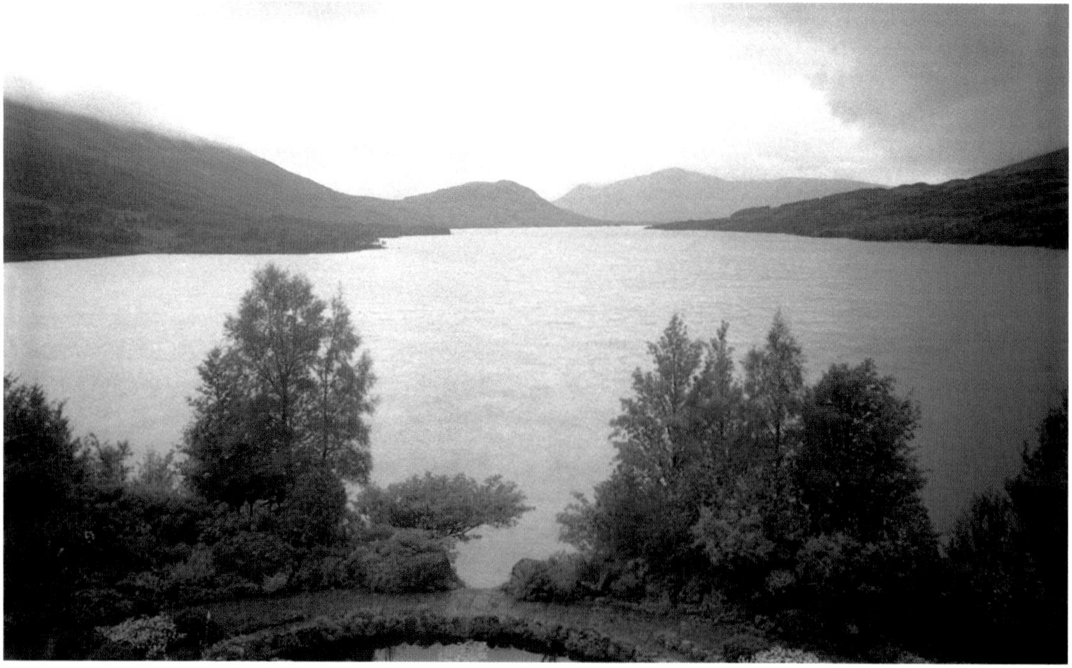

undermine that subject by introducing counter-point and challenge. Hence, the myth of 'Scottishness' is presented in terms of symbolic sites, recognisable narratives and cultural archetypes, but is disrupted by the inclusion of kitsch stereotypes and comic interventions. The 'realm of memory', then, is both recognised and reprised, yet is contested. In fact its nature as myth is explored and adapted in a way that reveals the functioning of cultural narratives *and* of photographic imaginings.

The recurring subject of Ossian is a case in point. Colvin completed an entire project on the history and myth of Ossian in 2004, but in doing this he was journeying on a path already well trodden by photographers of all kinds; Hill and Adamson, George Washington Wilson, James Valentine, Robert Moyes Adam, *et al*. For these photographers had all, in their various practices, touched upon the sites and symbols of the Ossian story. Importantly, there are devastating slippages of memory and meaning that run through the history of Ossian's presentation and reception. These begin with the febrile disputation regarding its authenticity following James Macpherson's 'discovery' of the 'Celtic Homer' in 1760, and continue to the present day. In many ways the story is both a mythic representation and its own myth. Moreover, the challenge to the work as 'truth' is a challenge also to the notion of an authentic national story, of a collective cultural memory, of a settled historical account, and, in the case of Colvin's imaginative constructions, of the veracity and 'integrity' of the photographic image.[7]

It might be suggested that MacPherson's Ossian was itself a response to the perceived loss of a national story, a Scottish national identity, in the period after the Act of Union in 1707. In other words, the desire for a mythic narrative emerged at the point where the practical history was subsumed. In another context, Kritzman, also, has reflected upon this idea:

> The creation of 'realms of memory' is the result of modern society's inability to live within real memory; the consecration of a 'realm of memory' takes place because real environments of memory have disappeared. The projection of a 'realm of memory' is therefore the sign of memory's disappearance and society's need to represent what ostensibly no longer exists.[8]

and:

> But for now, what remains of the idea of nationhood is engendered by a nostalgic reflection, articulated through the disjunctive remembrance of things past. In a way, one might argue that the quest for memory in the contemporary world is nothing more than an attempt to master the perceived loss of one's history.[9]

What is significant here is the notion that the return to 'realms of memory' (of which the photograph is one dimension) is a rational reaction to rapid change and development in the contemporary period. Hence the reflection on Macpherson's Ossian is pertinent because we live in a parallel, social and cultural universe. If Macpherson was responding to Scotland's incorporation within the larger project of the British Empire, then currently the concern with myth and memory may be viewed as a response to each nation's incorporation in a globalised culture and environment.

Recently Gilles Lipovetsky has called this new, globalised environment 'hypermodern'. This he views as a 'second cycle of modernity' and a stage beyond the 'postmodern'. Of this condition he notes:

> What defines hypermodernity is not exclusively the self-critique of modern institutions and forms of knowledge, but also revisionary memory... it is marked by the return of traditional landmarks and of ethnic and religious demands based on types of symbolic heritage that go back a very long way and stem from diverse origins. In other words, all the memories, all the universes of meaning, all the forms of collective imaginary that refer to the past and that can be drawn on and redeployed to construct identities and enable individuals to find self-fulfilment.[10]

If we accept this context, the memories, history and mythic stories presented in the world of photography, and the world of Scottish photography being observed here, become one site of this longing. More than this it is an irresistible site, one that functions in reaction to the repression of memory in the contemporary world. Lipovetsky, again:

> ... in celebrating the pleasures of the here-and-now and the latest thing, consumerist society is continually endeavouring to make collective memory wither away, to accelerate the loss of continuity and the repetition of the ancestral. The fact remains that, far from being locked up in a self-enclosed present, our age is the scene of a frenzy of commemorative activities based on our heritage and a growth in national and regional, ethnic and religious identities... a groundswell of memory.

This 'groundswell of memory', in all its complexity and with all its contradictions, is precisely what photography offers; and is the covert theme of a vast array of Scottish photography.

Memory and melancholy

This is not to say that these memories are unproblematic, nor do they exist as a salve to contemporary experience. In fact, these 'memory places' can be both disturbing and melancholic. Barthes, in *Camera Lucida*, consistently returns to the idea that the photograph embodies a kind of 'death'. His key phrase is 'the melancholy of the Photograph itself'.[12] Even Sebald, in *Austerlitz*, reflects on this unsettling character of photography. In the addenda to his first confrontation with the photograph of himself when young, he recalls:

> The picture lay before me, said Austerlitz, but I dared not touch it... hard as I tried both that evening and later, I could not recognize myself in the part. I did recognize the unusual hair line running at a slant over the forehead, but otherwise all memory was extinguished in me by an overwhelming sense of the long years that had passed.[13]

The photograph, it seems, impels the reflecting viewer towards a kind of tragedy. Its role as memory conjures up intimations of mortality and of loss. Interesting, then, that Calum Colvin should include *Scota 01* [FIG.8] in his assemblage of Ossian images, especially with its source in Durer's powerful etching *Melencolia I*. Here is the acknowledgement of the photograph, not only as memory, and history, and myth, but as the portent of melancholy. Always, the photograph is a kind of evidence of something 'that-has-been' and that is now lost. So that, even in the most casual of snapshots, there is the substantiation, and the memorial, to a moment. Or, as Sebald reflects, it is 'as if the pictures had a memory of their own and remembered us, remembered the roles that we, the survivors, and those no longer among us had played in former lives.'[14] Melancholy, it might be said, is the inevitable sensation of the photograph.

If this complex sense of memory may be regarded as the core value of the photography then the power of the photograph is clear; it presents the individual and the culture with an abstracted self-image. However, photographs also have a more practical significance, they provide an actual vision of the 'real' world, most especially in their manifest form as documents.

Documents

Collecting records of roles from former lives is, perhaps, the function that is most recognised in the annals of photography. The photograph is, irrevocably, a document. Interestingly, when Liz Wells introduced 'Documentary and Photojournalism' in her anthology *The Photography Reader*, she noted:

> The term 'documentary' was coined by Scottish film-maker John Grierson, in 1926, to designate work based upon the 'creative interpretation of reality'. However, documentary-style street photography dates from the mid-1860s (for instance Thomas Annan in Glasgow, John Thomson in London, Jacob Riis in New York).[15]

Documentary photography, by this projection, is rooted in the work of three Scots and a Danish emigrant to the United States. Certainly, Thomas Annan's fascinating photographs of 'The Old Closes and Streets of Glasgow' [FIG.9] are amongst the earliest documentary works, presaged only by Charles Marville's photographic record of Baron Haussmann's transformation of the city of Paris during the 1860s. Likewise, John Thomson's views of 'Street Life in London', and more particularly his 'Illustrations of China and its People', remain amongst the most of intriguing of 19th-century documentary images.

The attachment of Scottish photographers to the documentary project is certainly apposite, for documentary works are wholly compatible with the empirical and pragmatic turn of the Scottish Enlightenment sensibility. Equally, the scientific rationalism of the photographic technology, which correlated with the 'objectivity' of the documented scene, made an appeal to those intellects tempered by the methods of logical-positivism. In fact the photograph as document often overlapped with the idea of the photograph as memory. Annan, for example, was, in his 'Old Closes and Streets of Glasgow', creating a memorial to those streets about to be condemned by municipal improvement. Simultaneously, a cultural resistance to the photograph's intervention in the world of art was stimulated by the mechanical and recording, that is the 'documentary', nature of the medium.

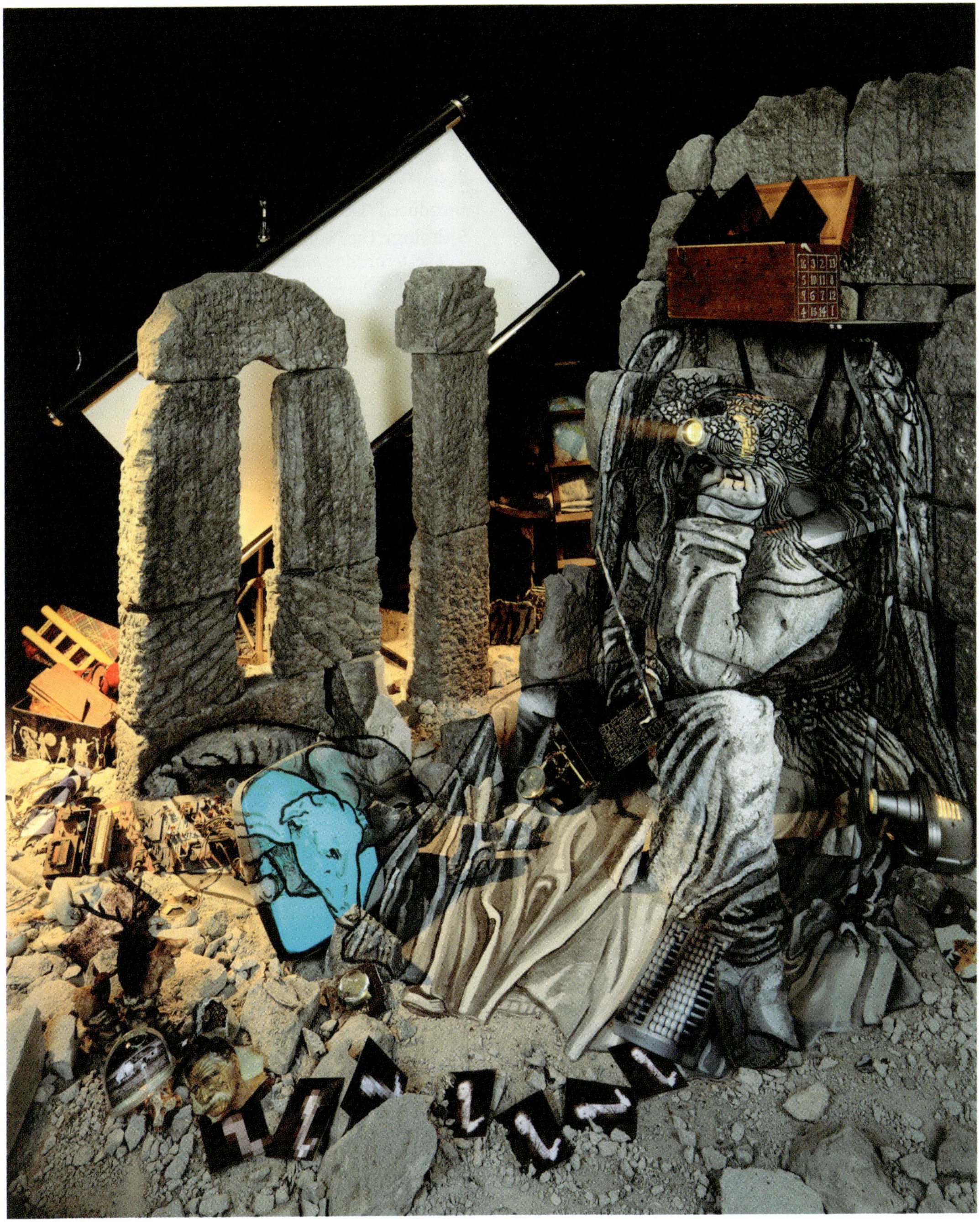

FIG.8
Calum Colvin
Scota 01
2004

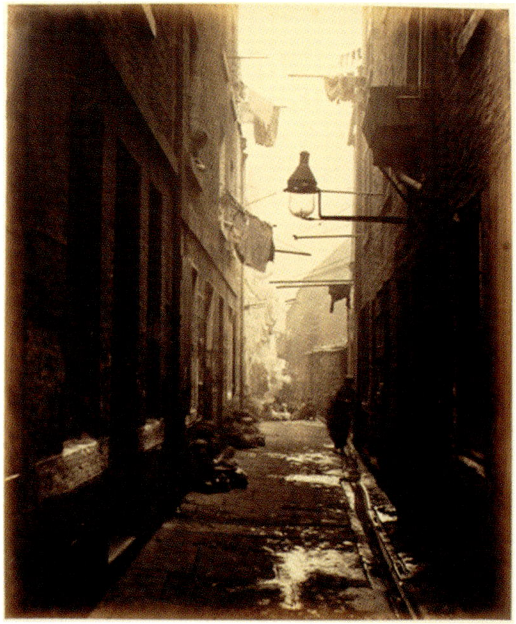

FIG.9
Thomas Annan
Close No.18, Saltmarket
1868

Document and artwork

The extraordinary strength and potency of the photograph as memory has been identified as its fundamental weakness, at least by Charles Baudelaire. Writing in *The Salon of 1859*, Baudelaire's irritation at the mechanical nature of photography spilled over into an attack on the democratisation of culture:

> If photography is allowed to supplement art in some of its functions, it will soon have supplemented or corrupted it altogether, thanks to the stupidity of the multitude which is its natural ally. It is time, then, for it to return to its true duty, which is to be the servant of the sciences and the arts... Let it hasten to enrich the tourist's album and restore to his eye the precision which his memory may lack... Let it rescue from oblivion those tumbling ruins, those books, prints and manuscripts which time is devouring, precious things whose form is dissolving and which demand a place in the archives of our memory... But if it is allowed to encroach upon the domain of the impalpable and imaginary, upon anything whose value depends solely upon the addition of something of a man's soul, then it will be so much the worse for us![16]

For Baudelaire the photograph released memory in only the most practical form, it provided empirical documentation of an external world. Its weakness, however, and the point at which it separated from art, was its mechanical means. The brief moment that was shaped by the opening and closing of the shutter was a description of the world in which the imagination was absent. Photography, here, was not the evocation of memory, but was, in fact, a moribund recollection; an empty vision, a mere record.

In some ways Baudelaire's jaundiced view of photography had been foreshadowed by Elizabeth Eastlake some two years previously, in 1857. Eastlake, an early and erudite champion of photography, nevertheless viewed the medium as a means for objectively recording the real world. The contemporary technological obsession with a sharply defined image distanced the medium from any sense of art. And so:

> The falling off of artistic effect is even more strikingly seen if we consider the department of landscape. Here the success with which all accidental blurs and blotches have been overcome, and the sharp perfection of the object which stands out against the irreproachably speckless sky, is exactly as detrimental to art as it is complimentary to science.[17]

For Eastlake, then, the irresistible destiny of photography was towards a documentary image; an accurate reflection of the external, the real, world. Indeed, in her meditation on this condition she profiles something of Baudelaire's politics:

> Thus the whole question of success and failure resolves itself into an investigation of the capacities of the machine, and well may we be satisfied with the rich gifts it bestows, without straining it into a competition with art. For everything for which Art, so-called, has hitherto been the means but not the end, photography is the allotted agent – for all that requires mere manual correctness, and mere manual slavery, without any employment of the artistic feeling, she is the proper and therefore the perfect medium. She is made for the present age, in which the desire for art resides in the small minority, but the craving, or rather necessity, for cheap, prompt and correct facts in the public at large. Photography is the purveyor of such knowledge to the world. She is the sworn witness of everything presented to view.[18]

The camera as 'witness' was lauded as a virtue within this paradigm, and as 'witness' it could not be 'art'. Most especially, its mechanical nature was deemed to set it outside the realm of 'feeling'; touch, mood, emotion.

These kinds of pressures were deeply influential in the Scottish context, so much so that the documentary image became a kind of norm. Certainly, there were those voices advocating photographic Pictorialism, James Craig Annan most famously. But the advocacy of photographic experiment, formalism, or indeed any aspect of modernism, was absent from the Scottish scene, at least until the late 20th century. In some senses the fundamental nature of photography, in Scotland, was defined by these absences. Unlike the history of the medium in France, or Germany, or the United States, the idea of the photograph as an independent and respected form was marginal to Scottish culture. Equally the notion of the photograph as an artwork, free from a recording or denotative function, was subsidiary. In this climate the photograph as record, notation, 'proof', became commonplace and hence the preponderance of 'documentary'.

The idea of a 'documentary' image, however, was not without its difficulties. Thomas Annan's 'Old Closes', for example, were evidently tidied-up and sterilised, in fact aestheticised, before being made available to the recording lens. Municipal pride may have demanded a record of the inner-city slums before their demolition, but equally that municipal pride demanded they were sanitised prior to the camera's intrusive and uncompromising stare. Fully 100 years later, in the civic regenerations of the 1960s, documentary photographers like Oscar Marzaroli and Joseph McKenzie would photograph children playing in the decaying streets of the Gorbals in Glasgow [FIG.10]. These photographs, full of energy and life, and a kind of homily to the disappearing notion of 'community', became emblems of the ways of life of a hitherto invisible class. In fact it was this propensity of the camera to act as an anthropological notebook that cemented its status as a 'scientific instrument' and compromised its potential within the fine arts.

Documentary projects were myriad and various in the history of photography from Scotland, and especially in the years between 1860 and 1960. Besides Thomas Annan's landmark work it is possible to catalogue George Washington Wilson's remarkable images of crofters in Skye, James Cox's photographs of rural poverty in the 1880s, Werner Kissling's recently

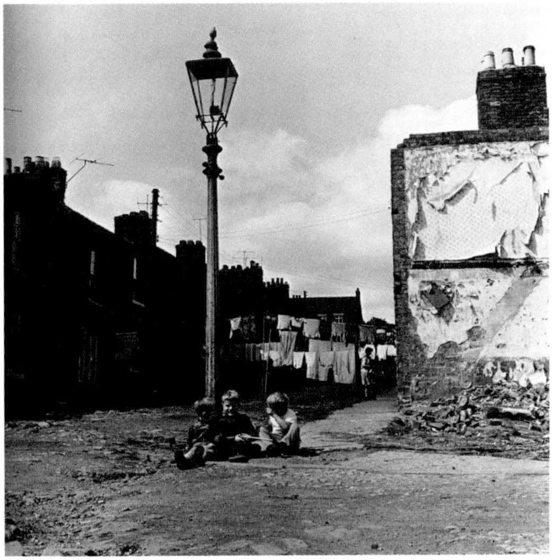

FIG.10
Oscar Marzaroli
Gorbals Children
1966

rediscovered photographs of life in Eriskay during the 1930s, Humphrey Spender's observations of the Gorbals in the late 1930s, and indeed Bill Brandt and Bert Hardy's sojourns into that same estate in the 1940s. It is possible to add to this list, though by no means to complete it, by noting Paul Strand's epic images of the peoples of South Uist, published as *Tir A' Mhurain* in 1962, and to complement this with John Charity's views of life in Wester Ross in the 1980s. These are all projects located within Scotland but equally many eminent photographers have gone from Scotland to document life in foreign parts. Hence the extraordinary images that John Thomson captured on his visit to China in the 1860s, William Carrick's provocative portraits of 'Russian types' taken in St Petersburg during the 1860s, and William Notman's studies of North American life witnessed after his emigration to Canada in 1856. In the contemporary period these types of project have been undertaken by photographers like Jeremy Sutton-Hibbert, whose sympathetic survey of Romanian gypsy culture emerged in the 1990s, and also by Ruth Stirling, whose study of contemporary Inuit culture was sponsored by the Canadian Science Council in 1988.

This basic catalogue of projects is partial and does not include the remarkable number of documentary endeavours that recorded industrial activity and the expanding cityscapes of modern Scotland. Indeed these are all projects that were centred on peoples, or indeed 'types', and notably upon those groups and classes of individual who were marginal to the developing culture and peripheral to the metropolitan core. This sense of 'documentary' focuses upon the point at which the method and medium become allied to anthropology. The camera records, as a privileged viewer, the life of the 'other'. This 'other' is, by definition, outside the officially-sanctioned 'core' civilisation; that is, the social group who own and control the camera as technology as well as the institutions that provide for the photograph's dissemination. The fascinating feature of this relationship is the parallel between the invention of the camera and the rise of the middle class. The camera appeared as both an invention of scientific and industrial capitalism and as an instrument of bourgeois practice; practice, that is, at the concrete and at the ideological level. In this event it is little surprise that a majority of 19th-century photographers were 'amateurs' in that they undertook the activity as a hobby, or 'professionals' in the sense that they established studios for commercial work. In both cases these were the activities of a committed Victorian middle class; intrigued by the new technology, enthusiastic in an entrepreneurial scheme, and enquiring in the manner of a social reformer or cultural voyeur.

This last point is often presented as a key value of the documentary photograph. Commentators have argued that the camera, and particularly the documentary project, was discretely constructed as an instrument for policing or social control. Within this frame Thomas Annan's view of the 'Old Closes' was not so much an exercise in documenting change as a mechanism for capturing the sites of social unrest and potential political conflict. Certainly there is a voyeuristic component to these middle-class safaris into the inner-city ghetto, but Annan was surely a social utilitarian and sympathetic to the idea of social improvement. Of more note, in this respect, is the use of photography in police files, institutional records and bureaucratic systems. However, the politics of documentary photography have been, generally, liberal and reformist. Sympathetic visions of the rural and the urban poor, heart-wrenching images of destitute and deprived children, desperate visions of 'outsiders' and the dispossessed, are often presented as a stock material of the documentary. The implied politics of these projects is a liberal identification with the pain and suffering of the 'other'.

This aspect of documentary has been the subject of considerable controversy. In 1975 the American critical theorist and photographer Allan Sekula first noted that:

> The celebration of abstract humanity becomes, in any given political situation, the celebration of the dignity of the passive victim.[19]

And subsequently the artist Martha Rosler has, more directly, suggested that:

> The liberal documentary assuages any stirrings of conscience in its viewers the way scratching relieves an itch and simultaneously reassures them about their relative wealth and social position.[20]

Later, she continued:

> The liberal documentary, in which members of the ascendant classes are implored to have pity on and to rescue members of the oppressed, now belongs to the past. The documentary of the present, a shiver-provoking appreciation of alien vitality or a fragmented vision of psychological alienation in city and town, coexists with the germ of another documentary – a financially unloved but growing body of documentary works committed to the exposure of specific abuses... Perhaps a radical documentary can be brought into existence. But the common acceptance of the idea that documentary precedes, supplants, transcends, or cures full, substantive social activism is an indicator that we do not yet have a real documentary.[21]

These are strong charges, though the case against traditional documentary made here remains 'not proven', at least within the Scottish context. In many cases the desire to photograph the poor was the result of a political identification with a dispossessed social class. Thomas Annan may be classified in this way, despite his aestheticisation of poverty, as might Bert Hardy's images, and certainly Paul Strand's epic photographs of his 'ideal' community in the Hebrides. In the period after the Second World War Oscar Marzaroli entered the Gorbals of Glasgow as an ally of the social class he photographed, and much contemporary work has eschewed the sadly maligned liberal idealism in favour of a nuanced realism.

The most interesting example of this new approach has been the work of the contemporary documentary 'realist' Owen Logan [FIG.11].[22] While accepting that 'documentary' has an identifiable history styled either as civic project, voyeuristic safari, politicised manifesto, 'subjective' documentation or aestheticised social concern, and while mindful of the critique of these approaches as a stylised and sanitised humanist conceit, Logan has looked to re-evaluate the 'realist' approach to documentary photography by creating a meaningful dialogue between photographer and subject. As Logan has put it, 'I try to underline how important it is to think about lens-based work from both ends of the lens.'[23] In this respect Logan has created 'realist' projects wherein he develops a neo-Marxist approach, one that seeks to lay bare the root causes of social circumstance while simultaneously offering proposals on the options for social change. In this way he rejects the empathetic and highly aestheticised approach of, say, a fashionable documentary photographer like Sebastiao Salgado. Moreover, he looks to view each project as a dialogue with the subject, one wherein the voice of those being surveyed is fully represented. In undertaking this programme, through his various documentary projects, he has further sought to undermine the role of authoritative institutions, galleries, museums and official platforms in the dissemination of his work. Herein, it appears, the potential for a genuinely radical and subversive form of documentary is revived.

These are all meaningful aspects of the photograph as document. Interestingly they all, in one respect or another, elide into the broader construct of the photograph as memory. These 'documents', after all, bring forward, no matter what their politics and ideological agendas, those numberless 'small sighs of despair'. They recall communities, events, meetings and festivities that are all too human. Such recollections are intense and haunting, indeed they are surely the very heart of culture. The power of the photograph to create such moments is, in part, a function of its unique 'realism', but it is also a quality derived from the photograph's valorisation into an exquisite and treasured 'object'.

FIG.11
Owen Logan
Bob Ballantyne's 'Inverted Coalmine', North Sea Oil Platform, UK *Sector,*
from 'Oil Lives'
2002

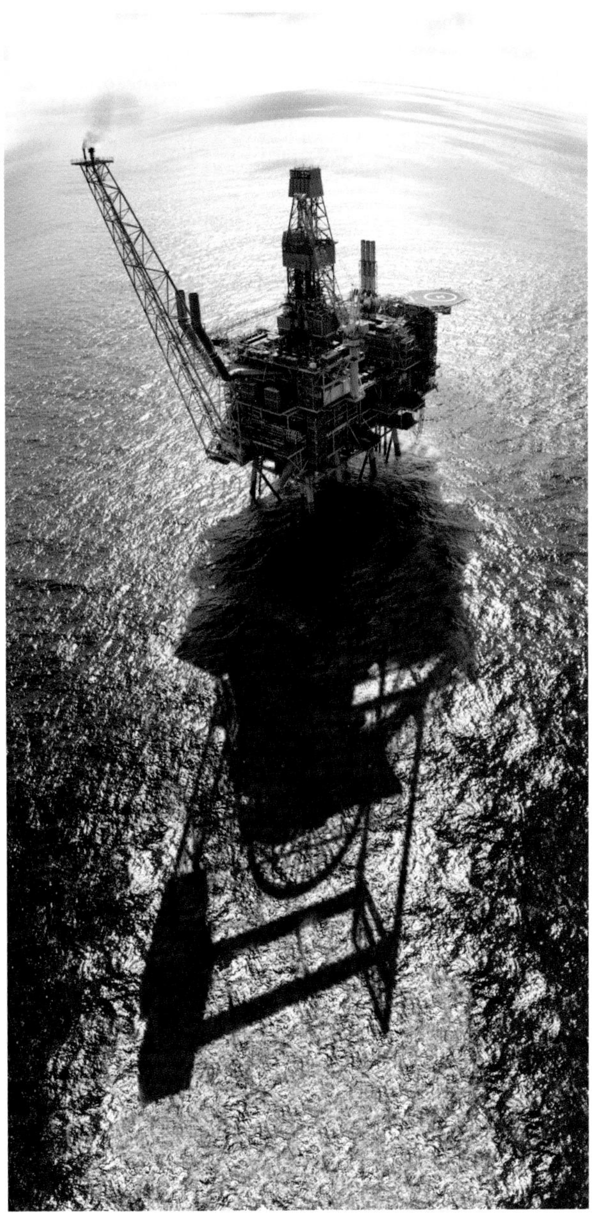

Objects

A great deal of contemporary photographic theory has seen fit to marginalise the photograph as object.[24] The photograph, because of its claim to the 'real', is often presented as a pragmatic artefact of cultural history, as 'indexical' of social negotiations and power relations, or more generally as a semiotic code. Within this context the photograph becomes a site for cultural, social and political skirmishing. In consequence its cultural framing and locus is viewed as being more important than its status as image. The photograph, then, is a 'representation' rather than an object. In part this has developed as a resistance to the antiquarianism of those photographic histories that concentrate on the early years of the medium. Also, it creates an opposition to the formalism of the first grand histories of photography, histories that concentrated upon the construction of an identifiable and authoritative 'canon'.[25] More particularly, perhaps, it is an attempt to rescue photography from the numbing grip of the institutions; museums, galleries, the marketplace; wherein its potency and promise might be compromised.

These are righteous concerns, but the photograph is, also, an object. It has a presence and integrity, a status and 'look', a virtue and often a beauty that relates to its quality as art. The redundant debate concerning photography's categorisation as art is now of little consequence, but the means by which it has been incorporated into bourgeois cultural practice remains significant. The fact that the most desperate of documentary images are presented, casually, on crisp, white gallery walls, and that the photographic portrait is now an esteemed constituent of all the national portrait galleries, is testimony to the institutionalisation of the medium. This very institutionalisation has served to sanctify the photograph's status as object, and, while recognising its authority as image, may yet have stolen its intrinsic power.

Salons, exhibitions and galleries

The early history of photography, in Scotland as elsewhere, was characterised by a twin momentum. Firstly, there was the need to refine the science and tune the technology. Generally this was embodied in an experimental investigation seeking to realise that elusive alchemical transformation, the creation of a negative image and its conversion into a positive photograph. Subsequent to this there was a further motivation to 'sharpen' and complete the photograph, to render the scene more 'real'. These magical goals were, of course, the territory of the first great pioneers of the medium, Niecephore Niépce, Louis-Jacques-Mande Daguerre, and William Henry Fox Talbot. In Scotland these investigations were enhanced, considerably, by individuals like David Brewster, a friend and collaborator of Talbot, and by the circle of scientists and photographic pioneers who surrounded Brewster in St Andrews and in Edinburgh.

Brewster would introduce the ever-enquiring minds of Edinburgh's professional classes to Talbot's 'calotype' process and, by 1843, the Edinburgh Calotype Club had been formed.[26] It is probable that this was the first photographic club established anywhere in the world and it is certainly revealing that its members consisted of professional gentlemen who approached the medium as a fascinating new science. It was a science, however, that produced not only empirical results but 'artistic' images and the institution of the club would soon elide into the fellowship of the salon.

Edinburgh became something of a centre for these first institutions of photography, largely because it was itself a centre of middle class life and the home of those advocates, academics and scientists who had the time and inclination to explore the new world of the photograph. Following the demise of the Edinburgh Calotype Club in the middle years of the 1850s, a passing occasioned by the fast developing science of the albumen and wet-collodian processes of printing, there emerged the Photographic Society of Scotland in 1856. This was followed by the establishment of The Edinburgh Photographic Society in 1861. The energy and experiment of these associations was largely focused on meetings and exhibitions. In effect they constituted the first salons of the new art. Edinburgh, in fact, had been the hub for important photographic exhibitions from the very dawn of photography. In December of 1839 five examples of the daguerreotype, as well as 'Twenty Photogenic Drawings' by Talbot, were shown in the Exhibition of Arts, Manufactures, and Practical Sciences held in the Assembly Rooms. In 1841 a further four daguerreotypes, by one D. Montreal, were displayed at the annual exhibition of the Royal Scottish Academy. Edinburgh was also the centre for the embryonic industry of the photographic magazine. The records of the Photographic Society of Scotland were published from its establishment in 1856, and were incorporated in a journal that also housed the minutes of the Manchester Photographic Society. In effect, then, the new art and science was coming to fashion an infrastructure of institutions that authenticated and endorsed the medium. Herein it began the process of establishing photography as a branch of official, high, culture.

It would be wrong to assume these events were peculiar to Edinburgh and its social establishment. The Glasgow Photographic Association was founded in 1855 and instituted with an exhibition, 'Photographs and Photographic Apparatus', in that same year. Earlier still, in 1853, the city of Aberdeen was to host the Society of Arts' First Touring Exhibition of Photographs. And, in 1854, an Exhibition of Photographic Pictures was put on display at the Central Library in Dundee. By this period photographic studios were becoming commonplace. James Valentine established his portrait studio in Dundee in the early 1850s. He would go on to create the Valentine firm, which became world-renowned for popular landscape images, though this was a field pioneered by George Washington Wilson of Aberdeen, whose first commercial venture was launched in partnership with John Hay in 1853. In Glasgow, Thomas Annan would move from lithographic printing to launch his esteemed photographic studio in 1855. These internationally recognised studios would be underpinned by myriad commercial practices springing into the bustling high streets of almost every town in the country.

Commercial studios represented a form of professional practice, though not a mode of artistic practice in the specialised sense of that term. The studio system existed to cater for a public need, and studio portraits and landscape works were not recognised as art objects until the development of a market for rare and precious vintage prints in the second half of the 20th century. The distinction between professional and amateur, then, was moot. Professionals, in the 19th century, were tradespeople while amateurs were those esteemed gentlemen who experimented with the new medium, or even hobbyists. As the 19th century gave way to the 20th this relationship was further complicated. The advent of 'halftone' photographic printing technology, in the 1890s, opened the way for photographs to be mass produced in newspapers, journals and books. The profession of photography was widened to include the 'photo-journalist' while simultaneously the photographic image became ubiquitous. However, the distinction between the commercial or illustrative photograph and the photograph as art object sharpened into a clear division during this period.

The clearest signal of this split was the founding of the Linked Ring in 1892.[27] This group was established in opposition to The Royal Photographic Society whose members championed the idea of scientific experiment leading to the most focused, well-defined and most objective of photographic prints. The 'art-photographers' of the Linked Ring desired a representation that would parallel painting in its more ethereal and mysterious evocations. Emerging in the period where symbolist aesthetics were ascendant amongst avant-garde artists, the members of the Linked Ring adopted the mantle and manner of their symbolist and neo-impressionist progenitors. Amongst the founding members, notably Henry Peach Robinson and George Davison, there existed a strong inclination towards the 'Pictorial' photograph; a photographic image taken, or manipulated, to give the appearance of a tonal picture. Accompanying this was a curious cabbalistic sensibility. The founding, and subsequent, members of the Linked Ring all adopted arcane nomenclature calculated to heighten the mysterious, almost occult, designation of the group.

A key figure in the Linked Ring was a son of Thomas Annan, James Craig Annan. Craig Annan, codename 'The Selector', was an outstanding advocate of the photogravure process and an exceptional 'Pictorialist' photographer [FIG.12]. A close associate of Charles Rennie Mackintosh and of the circle of Scottish engravers – D. Y. Cameron,

William Strang, James McBey, *et al.* – who would revolutionise printmaking at the dawn of the 20th century, the younger Annan was invited into the closed circle of the Linked Ring in 1894. He was closely involved in this group, especially during the later years of the 1890s, and, besides his extraordinarily evocative photographs, he championed an 'artistic' framing and hanging of photographic exhibitions.[28] In this ambition he was allied to the aesthetic philosophy of that behemoth of the American Photo-Secession, Alfred Stieglitz, and he would, in fact, become a significant collaborator with Stieglitz in the production of the groundbreaking journal *Camera Work*.

Craig Annan, then, was instrumental in a process that reconfigured the photograph as an art object. Here, the 'look' of the work, its framing, its hanging, the style of the gallery, the presentation of the show, was all designed to evoke the manner of an artwork. In effect the photograph progressed from the scientist's laboratory to the salon wall. With this development Craig Annan would become an esteemed exhibiter, and medal winner, at a host of national and international exhibitions, notably at the inaugural exhibition of the Photo-Club de Paris in 1894, and at the 'IV Fotograficheskaya Vyvstavka' in Russia during that same year. In 1897 he showed, triumphantly, on home ground at 'The International Photographic Exhibition' in Glasgow, and would see his works travel to the United States for 'The International Exhibition of Pictorial Photography' held in Buffalo. Glasgow, once again, would be the site of a major success when the Annan studio held sway over the 'International Exhibition' of 1901.

It is the case that Craig Annan's career ran parallel with the triumph of Pictorialism in photographic aesthetics, and with its demise, in the period of the First World War, he largely removed himself from the world of photography to become a dealer in etchings. In part it was the success of Stieglitz in promoting a 'straight' photographic aesthetic that brought about this change. Stieglitz, though a champion of Craig Annan, and in his early years an advocate of a modified pictorialism, nevertheless came to support a vision of photography that sponsored the idea of an unmediated image. That is, he inaugurated and encouraged the view that photography, as an art, should acknowledge its unique and essential aesthetic qualities. This vision encouraged a photographic formalism that presented an immediate and a direct image, neither 'retouched' nor in other ways manipulated, but which acknowledged the potential and the limits of the photographic image. At its finest this view became encapsulated in the work of Stieglitz's acolyte Paul Strand, who would be the subject of the final two editions of *Camera Work* in 1917.

There is little evidence of a self-consciously 'straight' photography, nor indeed of a formalist or modernist photographic vision, taking root in Scotland after this period, but the ethos of Craig Annan's salon-based aesthetic would survive in the activities of the Scottish Photographic Federation. Here again the issue of the professional and amateur photographer becomes moot. The Federation was established in 1903 and its membership consisted of those photographic clubs that would affiliate to the national body. These clubs were organised around towns and villages, in workplaces and amongst trades organisations, and through art clubs; the first President was Henry Coates of the Perthshire Society for Natural Science. The membership of each club was mixed, with a proportion of semi-professional and commercial photographers amongst the host of amateur enthusiasts. The Federation organised portfolio exhibitions, lantern slide shows, and lectures, all designed to 'promote co-operation between, and organise activities for the mutual benefit of Affiliated Societies as well as promoting the general advancement of photography'.[29] Each year a 'yearbook' of the Federation's finest pictures would be published, and these were selected from works exhibited at the annual photographic salon. The first of these salons was held in 1904 and was hosted by the town of Perth, and exhibitions have been held annually to this day with significant breaks only during the two world wars.

The quality of the work shown in these salons has been remarkable and remains testament to the passion and fascination which the photograph has inspired. The important aspect here, however, is the institutionalisation, at every level, of the photograph

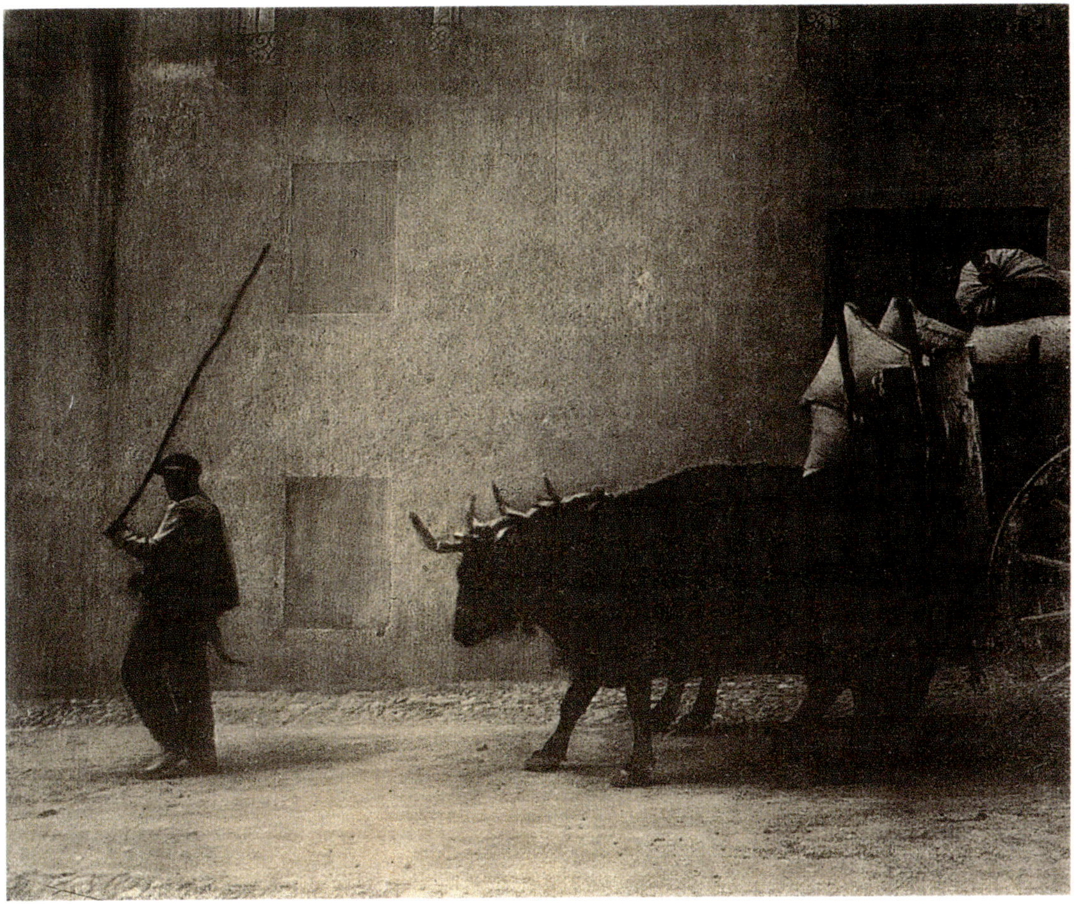

FIG.12
James Craig Annan
Bullock Cart, Burgos
1913

as an object. Craig Annan's salon presentation is echoed in the annual salons of the Scottish Photographic Federation, and the photograph as a form is valorised into a purely aesthetic object. In this event the vernacular, documentary, indexical, and the democratic dimensions of the medium are, it might be said, subtly diminished. Consequently, in the modern period the photograph has come to be presented and studied as a work of fine art. The success of the historical account, complete with its canon of great photographers and catalogue of definitive works, set the platform for the election of photography to the pantheon of official high culture. This election was confirmed by the success of historic photographs within the contemporary marketplace.

While this process began in America, and was extended throughout Europe, it was not until the later part of the 20th century that Scottish curators and academics became fully aware of the rich heritage in Scotland's photography and of the nation's important place in the history of the medium. The Scottish Photography Archive was established, within the august neo-gothic portals of the Scottish National Portrait Gallery, in 1984. In 1990 the National Galleries of Scotland held their first celebration of Scottish photographers with an exhibition of young contemporaries titled 'New Scottish Photography'. While this exhibition explored the modern scene the historical account was opened out some five years later in a landmark exhibition, 'Light From the Dark Room', of 1995. Further attempts to generate a momentum in photographic practice were presented in the festival 'Fotofeis', a biennial 'Scottish International Festival of Photography' which began in 1993, but was sadly abandoned in 1998.

This activity within the official cultural institutions was assisted by adventurous and forward-thinking initiatives in the subsidised private sector. In 1977 Stills Gallery was created, in Edinburgh, with a mission to show photographs from around the world in a dedicated photographic gallery. This became a focus for those contemporary photographers who would emerge in the 1980s, and a forum for a number of signpost exhibitions. During 1988 the Portfolio Gallery opened with a show of work by the experimental and documentary photographer Ruth Stirling, and continued to present ambitious photographic exhibitions until its closure in 2001. Like Stills, the Portfolio Gallery was situated in Edinburgh, but Glasgow too has had a dedicated photographic gallery in the form of Street Level Photoworks. As a background to these exhibiting galleries a few specialist journals have promoted contemporary and historical aspects of photography from Scotland. The demise of the Portfolio Gallery was, in a sense, illusory, for its activities were continued in the extraordinary photographic journal *Portfolio: Contemporary Photography in Britain*, which remains one of the most inspired photographic journals in print, and a weathervane for contemporary photographic debate. Meanwhile issues in the history of photography have been explored in *The Scottish Photography Bulletin*, later styled as *Studies in Photography*, produced from the expertise of the Scottish Society for the History of Photography.[30]

Given this infrastructure of organisations and institutions the photograph slips, in its discreet denotation, from representation to object; it does not only record the world, but reorders it as art. In the contemporary period most cultural practice, within the world of photography, has recognised this uneasy relationship. Simultaneously photographers have accepted the aesthetic power of the photographic image and embraced its ineffable presence. This is important, for photographs, even where they embody the burden of the real, can and do recall the ineluctable majesty of the visual. They are objects in the acute sense of distilling consciousness and recognising, memorialising, being.

The photograph in Scotland

All of this, memory, document, object, serves to reveal some of that complex set of mediations by which we understand the photograph and photography. The history of Scottish photography displays some of these features at all points and all of these features at some points. In realising these mediations it is best to approach the body of Scottish photography in a thematic fashion. Hence a concern with that first evidence of memory, the human face in the portrait study. Opening out this human presence into the landscape subsequently affords a sense of location and source. The broader spectrum of human activity, work, leisure, and relationship, as well as the colour and excitement of social life is captured in the lens of the documentary photograph, while the cultural nexus of the photograph is explored in its role as 'art'. This is the route map for what will follow, but throughout this voyage it is the compelling power of the photograph that acts as signpost and guide.

CHAPTER TWO

Portraits and People

Narcissus, it would appear, is the most appropriate deity in respect of the camera's art; for, if the camera is, famously, a 'mirror with a memory' then it is the echo of the ego that is released in the photograph. Nowhere is this more clearly revealed than in the photographic portrait. Barthes has remarked that 'Photography... began, historically, as an art of the Person; of identity, of civil status, of what we might call, in all senses of the term, the body's *formality*'.[1] He might equally have recorded its primary role as a ceremonial recognition of the human face.

Very quickly, after the technical problems of capturing the photographic image had been mastered, the camera was used to celebrate the individual personality in the form of the photographic portrait. In this venture it would emulate the manner and convention of painting, adopting 'sets' and backcloths, costumes and poses, that echoed the established customs of the traditional painted portrait. Its subjects too were, in the early years at least, traditional; sober studies of esteemed individuals whose social status and rank marked them out as worthy of a place in the permanent record of society's 'great and good'.

The camera and the photograph, however, would become a democratic and democratising medium. From the period after the announcement of photography, in 1839, until the appearance of the first 'snapshot' camera, George Eastman's hand-held 'Kodak' of 1888, the potential for a broader public to take and have taken portrait images developed at an exponential rate. Certainly the group most represented in this expansion was the dynamic and burgeoning middle class of the Victorian period, but it is also true that a wide cross-section of society would find their face captured in the portrait form. Besides the sensitive and sometimes mannered formal portraits of the early period the form would develop through the introduction of celebrity portraits; the fashion for the carte-de-visite in the period after 1854; the vogue for the 'family album' promoted by George Washington Wilson's portraits of Queen Victoria and her family at Balmoral, taken in the years after 1854; the emergence of that staple of the photographic studio, the Cabinet portrait in 1866; and, of course, the 'snapshot' portrait of the later 1880s. This list of portrait types is partial, however, for it omits the 'institutional' use of portrait photographs. Portraiture was never simply a means of recording significant persons, but was also a method of social recognition and social control. Hence, the archives of school photographs, records of army regiments, pageant assemblies of sporting clubs, and serried ranks of professional and workplace groups. At the official, bureaucratic, level the files of criminal records supported by photographic identification, the medical photographs, the authorised asylum records became the anthropological and ethnographic documentation that stands as testament to the taste for racial stereotype denoted by facial characteristics.

Yet for all the popularity of the portrait, and given its universality, it remains an ambiguous and mysterious form. At one level the portrait study is the most complete visual expression of the ideology of individualism. Conventionally, it is created to afford insight into the personality, and a glimpse of the essential character. In this sense it is often presented as a study in greatness. In the world of painting the artist's genius was marked by the ability to see inside the subject, to find the core being. Elizabeth Eastlake, in 1857, was quick to note this distinction between painting and photography in relation to the portrait:

> But let us examine a little more closely those advances which photography owes to science – we mean in an artistic sense. We turn to the portraits, our *premiers amours*, now taken under every appliance of facility both for sitter and operator. Far greater detail and precision accordingly appear. Every button seen – piles of stratified flounces in most accurate drawing are there – what was at first only suggestion is now all careful making out – but the likeness to Rembrandt and Reynolds is gone! There is no mystery in this.[2]

For Eastlake the very success of photography, in terms of verisimilitude, was a mark of its failure as 'art'. The photographic portrait was simply too 'real', or accurate, to allow for insight. Yet photographers were, and are, ever-conscious of the ways in which the photograph both denotes the person and connotes the personality. When Hill and Adamson posed their epic image of the stonemason-turned-geologist *Hugh Miller* [FIG.13], for example, they deliberately created a consciousness of his sculptural presence. They presented the pose of a man engaged in a science that was not only cerebral, but physical, and they caught his rock-like commitment. In this respect the photographic portrait was surely equal to the painted image.

In other ways the photographic portrait has proven itself capable of the most nuanced and complex associations. Take, as an example, Maud Sulter's (b. 1960) portrait photograph *Calliope* [FIG.14], from her 'Zabat' series of 1989. This image is a self-portrait.

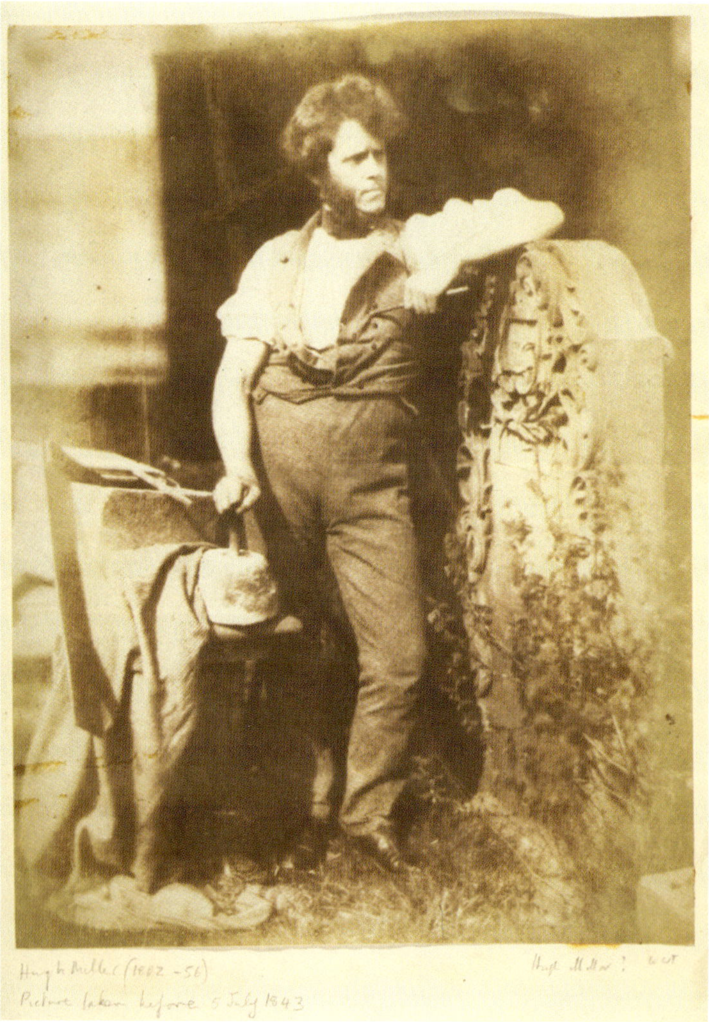

FIG.13
Hill and Adamson
Hugh Miller
1843

In its appearance it is rich and sumptuous, large-scale and intensely coloured, and presented in an ornate gild frame indicative of a classical artwork. It looks like an academic painting, but is manifestly a photograph. As a photograph it contains many, subtle, allusions. The image would appear to reference the great French photographer Gaspard Félix Tournachon, universally known as Nadar, and particularly his famed portrait study of the actress Sarah Bernhardt taken in 1859. Sulter's pose echoes the half-length torso of Bernhardt, and her robe references the casually thrown gown that exposes the actress's bare shoulder. In Nadar's finest image of Bernhardt she leans on a plinth or tabletop. This too is quoted in Sulter's *Calliope* though here the table contains a picture frame, in fact the presentation case for a daguerreotype. At one level, then, Sulter presents this portrait of herself in relation to a signature moment in the history of photography.

The portrait, however, is more nuanced than this straightforward allusion. *Calliope* belongs to a series of works, titled 'Zabat', in which Sulter posed eminent cultural figures, all of them black women, in the manner of mythic goddesses. Here she established a pantheon of muses that juxtaposed the Greek archetype. More pertinently still, she framed these figures within the context of the 'classical' tradition. That is, she established a visual context for these individuals that disrupted the paradigm of Western convention. Most tellingly, Sulter portrayed the writer and cultural commentator Bonnie Greer in the manner of a formal Gainsborough portrait. In doing this Sulter deliberately challenged racial assumptions, and particularly the ideological concept the 'English rose'.

This issue of race and ethnicity runs yet deeper in this project. Nadar was a friend and associate of Charles Baudelaire, indeed he completed the most esteemed photographic images of the poet. It is well known that Baudelaire is portrayed on the right-hand side of Gustav Courbet's famed allegory *The Painter's Studio* of 1855. Equally it is documented that Baudelaire, in a fit of pique, requested his companion Jeanne Duval be erased from his side in this painting. The 'ghost' of this portrait is there still. Sulter has long been fascinated with this erased, near invisible, black woman. She has subsequently portrayed herself as Jeanne Duval,[3] and there is a distinct allusion to the 'look' of Duval in her image of *Calliope*. In the self-portrait *Calliope*, then, the photographer is not simply portraying the self. Rather, the work alludes to personal identity, concepts of beauty and notions of creativity. More significantly, it opens out issues of power and representation, the ideological nature of female symbolism and the trauma of racial and racialist stereotype. Here, the portrait study becomes an ingenious manifesto in which the assumptions of conventional thought are comprehensively critiqued.

The photographic portrait, then, is a treasure-house of ideas and associations. It records a 'real' person, certainly, but it is equally as adept at penetrating the mask and revealing the character. At a deeper level it offers the potential to juxtapose the individual and the context so that discreet correspondences, tensions and pressures are revealed. At its finest it will open out the individual and explore the sitter's presence, their 'being', while revealing also their relation to the broader social discourse; Narcissus through a refracting mirror.

Reverend gentlemen and scientists

Narcissism, however, had no place in the early history of portrait photography in Scotland, for such pagan vanity was surely an abomination to the reverend gentlemen of the Church of Scotland. Of the many schisms and principled disruptions within the long history of the Church of Scotland, the deepest was surely the Disruption of 1843. At this time something over 470 ministers from an assembly of 1,200 left the official body of the Church of Scotland and formed the evangelically inclined Free Church of Scotland. The secessionists were protesting for the rights of Presbyterian governance and were led by the erudite and energetic academic and theologian Thomas Chalmers. Chalmers would become Principal of the Free Church College from its inception in 1843 until his death in 1847. Given the fundamentalism of the Free Church programme it is surprising that the event was to be commemorated in a 'graven image', but the Scottish painter David Octavius Hill (1802–70) was inspired to paint the group portrait of all the dissenting ministers. In this he was encouraged by Sir David Brewster, the scientist who would, amongst a sweep of other innovations, refine Sir Charles Wheatcroft's stereoscopic viewer. Brewster, who had been appointed Principal of the United College of St Salvator and St Leonard at the University of St Andrews in 1838, would introduce Hill to the pioneer photographer Robert Adamson (1821–48) and together they would undertake one of the most ambitious and significant projects in the history of photography.[4]

Hill, of course, was presented with the most difficult of challenges; how to incorporate some 470 recognisable portraits in a group composition. The completed work, all four square metres of it, now hangs in the offices of the Free Church in Edinburgh. By all accounts it does not include all of the

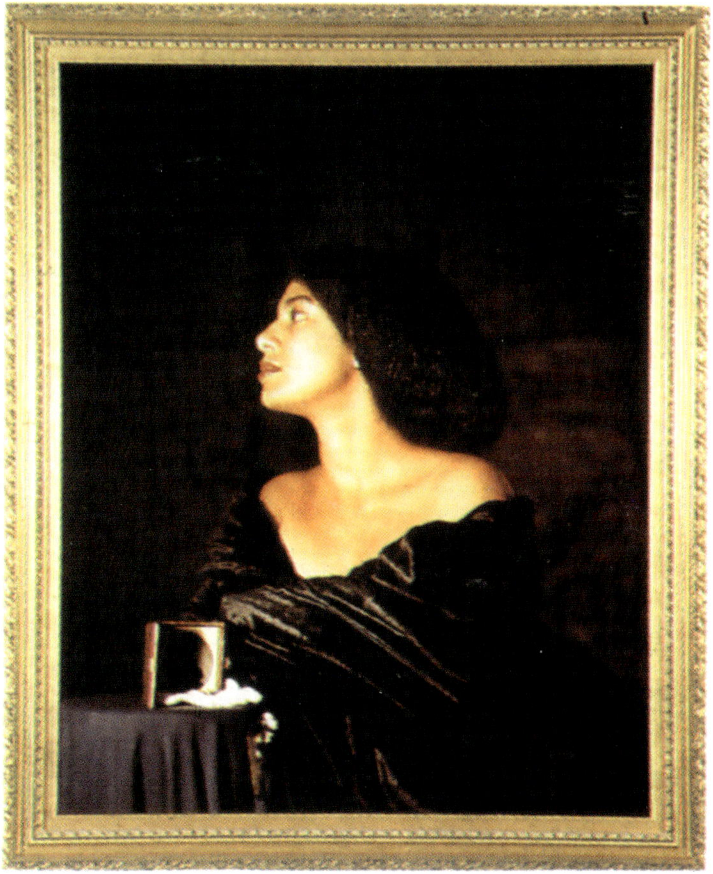

FIG.14
Maud Sulter
Calliope from
'Zabat' series
1989

secessionists, nor is it Hill's finest painting. However, it is a landmark creation in that each of the portrait heads was based on a calotype photograph of the sitter.[5] Brewster had served the introduction of Robert Adamson to Hill with the express aim of creating a photographic gallery of the dissenting ministers. These would act as a memory of each minister and the basis for the painted portraits. It is testament to the depth of this project that Hill and Adamson would become internationally recognised for their partnership as photographers, and that Hill, for all that he was an established academic painter, should be known to history as a founding father of photography. Indeed, Hill's painting of *The Signing of the Deed of Demission*, begun in 1843, would not be completed until 1866, some 18 years after the death of Robert Adamson.

The gallery of posed figures that Hill and Adamson completed assembled an impressive catalogue of individual types. It is generally assumed that Hill acted as an 'artistic director' and that Adamson was possessed of the technical knowledge. The calotype process, when successful, allowed for a subtle tonal image and a suffused light-filled photograph. Hill, the painter, was sensitive to lighting and pose and context while Adamson was master of the chemistry and could realise Hill's vision. The portraits of the Free Church ministers are archetypes of the 'Rembrandtesque' ambitions of these groundbreaking photographers at the dawn of the new medium, and none more so than the group portrait of *Dr Thomas Chalmers and his Family* from October 1844 [FIG.15]. This extraordinary photograph of the patriarch shows him surrounded by his kinsfolk, all women, and by his grandchildren. He, alone, looks directly at the camera in an attitude that seems to interrogate posterity itself. The strong sunlight falls from the left of the assembly, who are arranged in the manner of an informal tableaux, and bounces around inside the composition. In fact it sets Chalmers' white hair ablaze in stark contrast to his shadowed features. It is known that this image was taken in the grounds of Merchiston Castle School[6] and so the foreground holds an architectural decoration; a globe of carved rock. This rock seems to echo the solidity and steadfast character of the central figure and only named individual in the group, for Thomas Chalmers sits rock-like and imposing amongst his acolytes. Like all of Hill and Adamson's best work this is a remarkable portrait, informal yet arresting, objective yet moving. It is all the more remarkable that this partnership could create such consummate images while battling the science of the new technology.

Science and scientists were, however, the prime movers in the development of photography and it is their portraits that fill the pages of the earliest photographic albums. The most eminent of these figures, in Scotland, was surely Sir David Brewster (1781–1868). Brewster was primarily a physicist with a special interest in optics. He had invented the kaleidoscope in 1816, and refined the extant stereoscope through a development of lens refraction. From 1838 he was Principal of the United College at the University of St Andrews, and was a confidant of Fox Talbot, working with him at Lacock Abbey and corresponding on Talbot's experiments with the calotype process throughout the early years of its development. His presence made St Andrews a centre for research in this early phase of photography. Brewster, as Vice-President of the St Andrews Literary and Philosophical Society, which was established in 1838, was able to introduce Talbot's methods to a cohort of lively and enquiring professionals in the town. The experiments of his immediate circle, Dr John Adamson (1809–70), Thomas Rodger (1833–88), Hugh Lyon Playfair (1786–1861) and, of course, Robert Adamson, form the bedrock of photography in Scotland. While the earliest of these experiments was with the daguerreotype process, the greater flexibility of Talbot's process became the preferred method of the group once the problems of exposure time and focus were mastered. Given the inherent difficulties of Talbot's technology the earliest photographs tend to be topographical views of the town, but refinements, principally developed by John Adamson, allowed for the shorter exposure times that would permit successful portrait studies.

Among the most fascinating of these portraits are those where the pioneer photographers create personal studies of each participant in this magic circle; Hugh Lyon Playfair's portrait of David Brewster

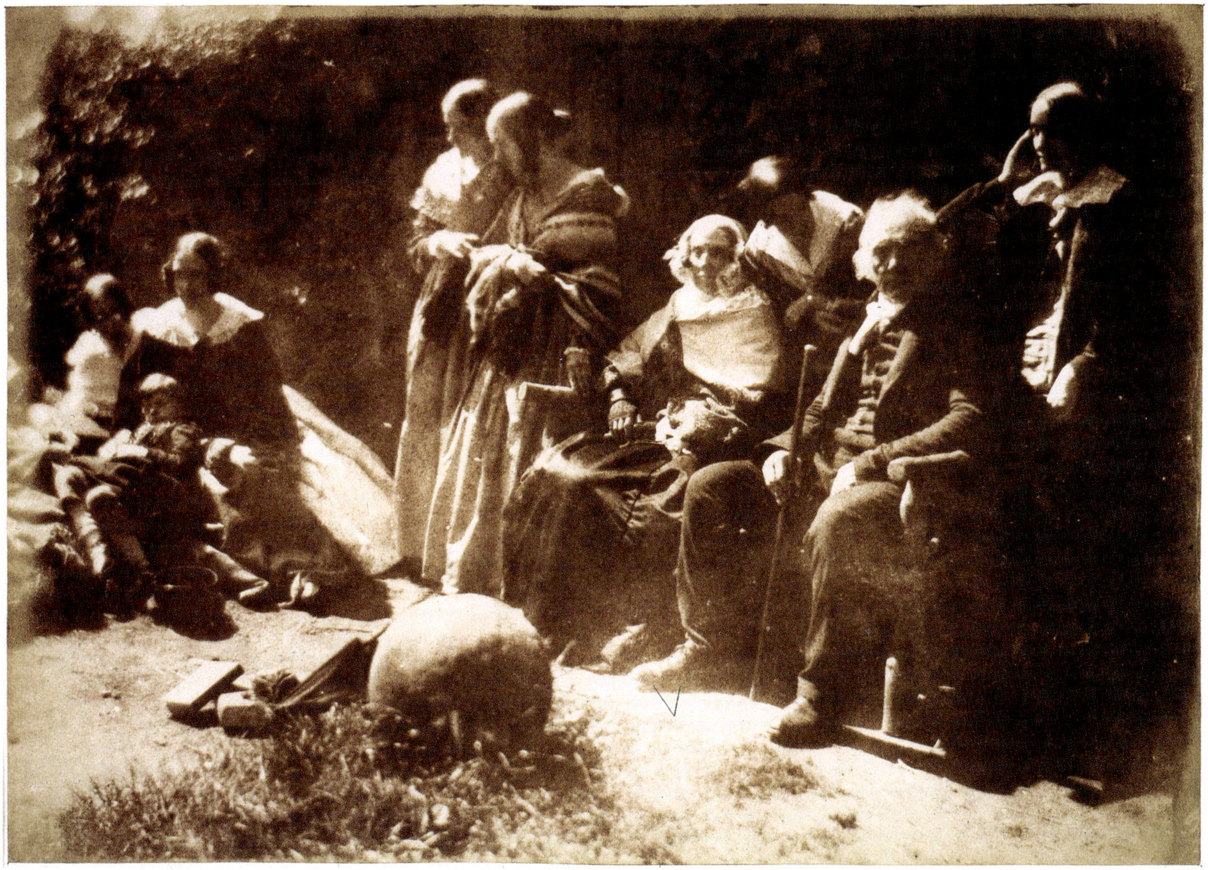

FIG.15
Hill and Adamson
Dr Thomas Chalmers and his Family
1844

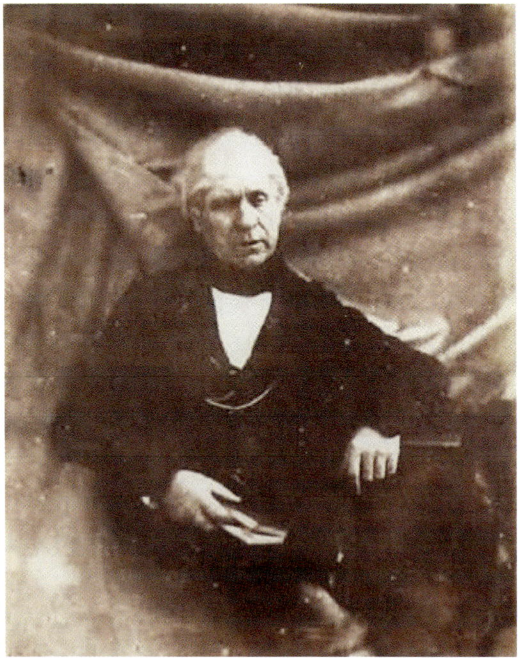

[FIG.16], John Adamson's study of Thomas Rodger [FIG.17][7] and Thomas Rodger's portrait of Hugh Lyon Playfair [FIG.18]. These works all date from the 1840s and demonstrate the refinement of the technology alongside a sensitivity to the requirements of portraiture. Brewster was photographed many times, by all of his associates, and Playfair's image is typical in the semi-formal pose of the academic, book in hand, set against a draped backcloth. The chiaroscuro effect was almost certainly a result of the necessity of using natural light, and the soft-focus an unintentional consequence of the calotype process. John Adamson, a physician in the town and doughty improviser of the calotype, produced an extraordinarily moody and 'romantic' portrait of Thomas Rodger. Rodger was the youngest of the group, and very much a student of John Adamson. He would, however, establish himself as a professional photographer in St Andrews, during 1849, and become the town's most celebrated 'photographic artist', with a career that flourished until his death in 1888. His portrait of Playfair, who was Provost of St Andrews

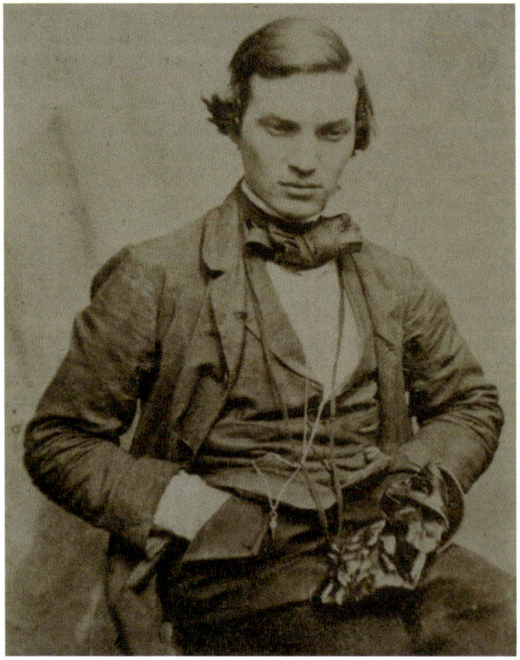

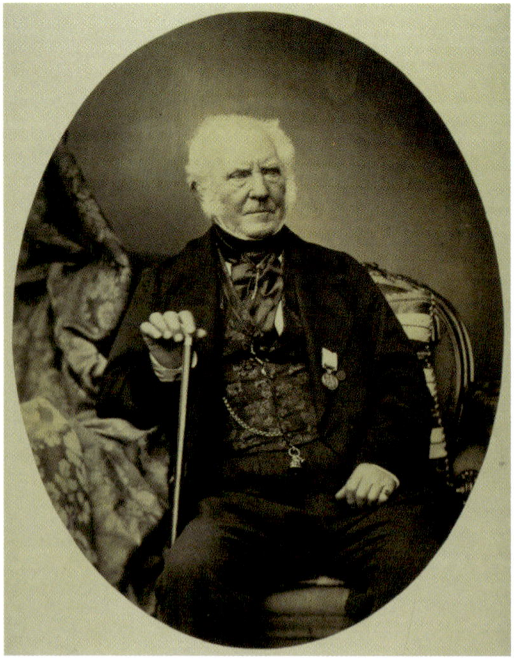

Top:
FIG.16
Hugh Lyon Playfair
David Brewster
n.d.

Bottom left:
FIG.17
John Adamson
Portrait of Thomas Rodger
1845

Bottom right:
FIG.18
Thomas Rodger
Hugh Lyon Playfair, Provost of St Andrews
circa 1849

from 1842 until his death in 1861, is a classic studio composition, deftly posed and subtly imposing.

Many of these St Andrews based scientists and gentlemen photographers would become associates of the Edinburgh Calotype Club when this was formed around 1843, notably Brewster, John Adamson, and also Playfair. In many ways this signalled the expansion of photography, as a realm of scientific enquiry, throughout the major centres of the country. Certainly, many of the participants remained professional individuals who engaged with the camera as an intellectual 'hobby'; so John Cay, Cosmo Innes, and John Francis Montgomery were all Advocates by profession, while James Calder Macphail was a Free Church minister, and George Moir a writer. Yet the association between the new 'art' and the rational enquiry of scientific experiment was binding. The camera was an instrument, a symbol almost, of that rapid expansion of technological practice that signalled 'modernity', and its links to a burgeoning entrepreneurial and innovative universe of change have been immutable.

In this respect there has been an affiliation between the camera and the world of science throughout its history. Evidently the photograph became one of the means through which experiment was recorded, documented and transcribed, while the camera has also served as witness and celebrant at the annunciation of scientific breakthrough. From an array of potential images it is possible to isolate Wolfgang Suschitzky's stirring *Portrait of Alexander Fleming*, taken in 1944 [FIG.19]. Suschitzky (b. 1912), an Austrian émigré to Britain, was steeped in the documentary tradition and took some remarkable photographs of street life in the city of Dundee during the 1940s. In this same period he was commissioned to photograph the Scottish scientist and discoverer of penicillin, Alexander Fleming. His portrait, a bravura image of the scientist at work in his laboratory, creates an arc back to the portraits of David Brewster fully 100 years before.

In Brewster's time the camera was both the recorder of the scientist's likeness and the subject of his experiment. In the contemporary period, with the advent of the digital camera and digitised imagery, this complex association has re-emerged. Wendy McMurdo (b. 1962) has been instrumental in exploring the territory opened out by the new technology of the digital revolution. During 1995 her series of photographs collectively entitled 'In a Shaded Place – the Digital and the Uncanny' set out to stretch the definition of the 'real', presented by the photographic image, through the manipulation of the digital representation. Subsequently McMurdo has consistently worked on the cusp of photographic technologies and pure-science innovation, often contesting the human dimension of scientific progress. In 2002 she was commissioned to create a portrait study of *The Scientists of the Roslin Institute* [FIG.20], who were then at the forefront of experimentation in molecular genetics and had successfully developed cloning technology in animals. This image, a digitally manipulated group portrait in four parts, fashions the photographs of the scientists within a manipulated or 'cloned' environment. This creates an image that is at once complete and comprehensible, but on analysis is constructed and manufactured. In this way McMurdo has allowed the science of the camera to evoke and emulate the science of these particular experiments.

There is little doubt that this world of science has

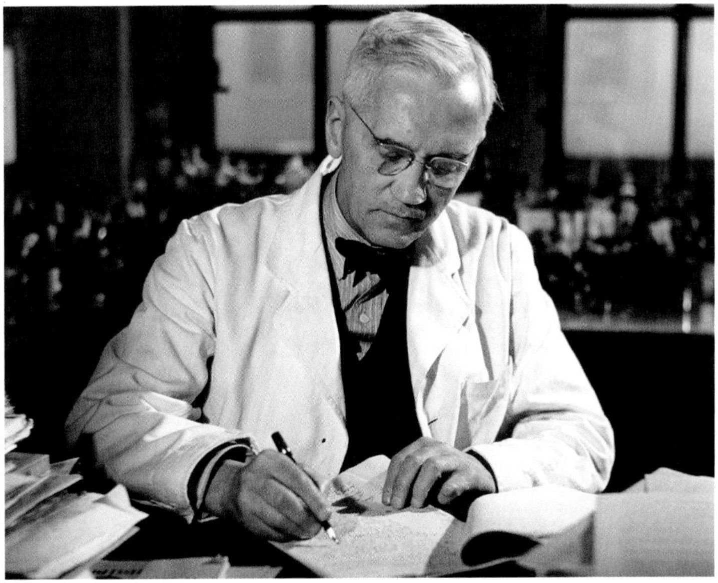

FIG.19
Wolfgang Suschitzky
Portrait of Alexander Fleming
1944

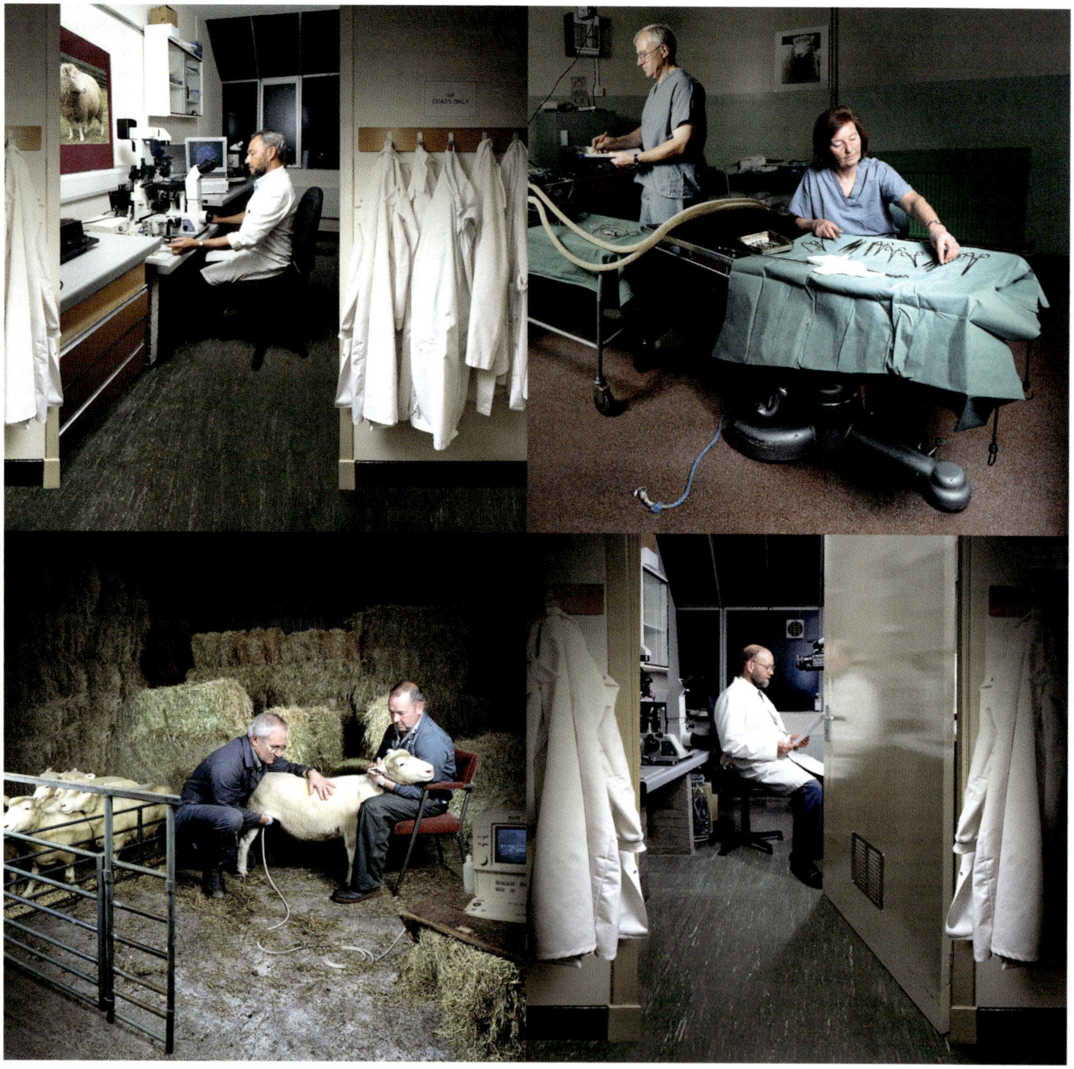

FIG.20
Wendy McMurdo
The Scientists of the Roslin Institute
2002

been crucial to the development of the photograph, and has been mirrored in the photographic portrait. But, always, this has been framed within the context of the world of art. There is little surprise, then, in the use of the camera in recording and immortalising the lights of this other realm, for the camera itself was christened the 'pencil of nature' and was destined to become an artist's tool.

Art and artists

The photograph is, evidently, a kind of 'print', and this aspect of photographic technology intensified the association with the world of art. Where artists were initially drawn to the photograph as a means of capturing likeness, they would also appreciate the link with printmaking, which was one of the most commercially viable means of trading in the visual

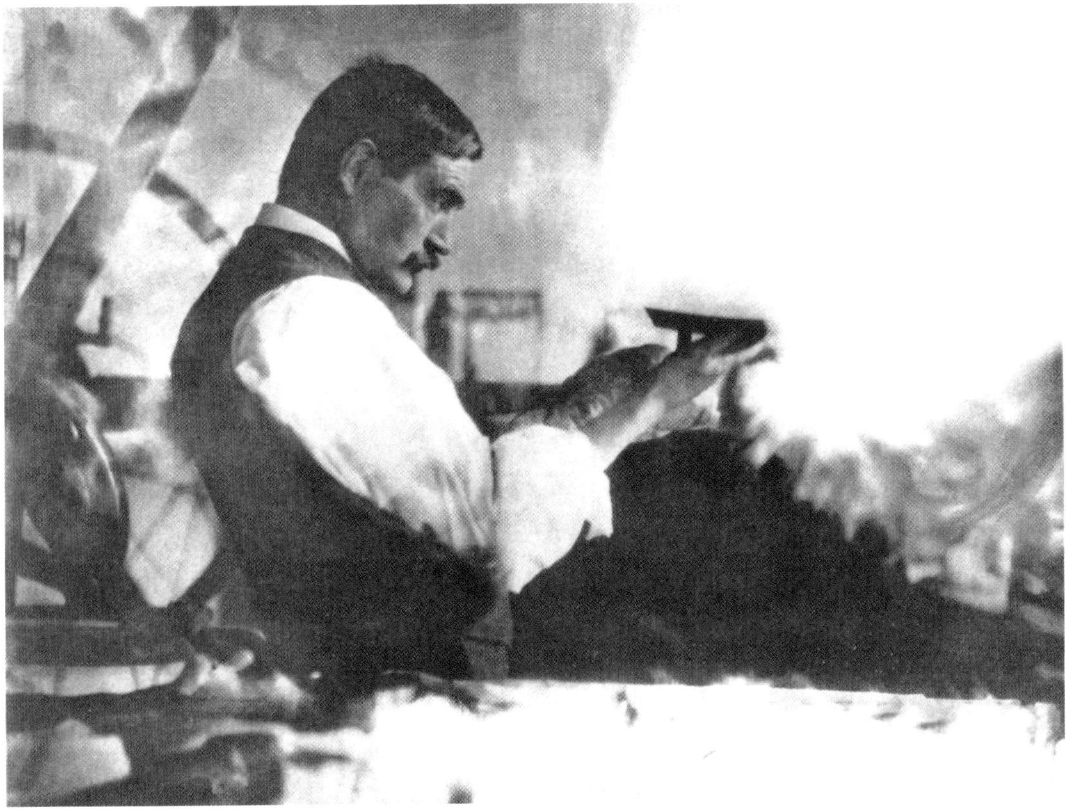

FIG.21
James Craig Annan
The Etching Printer – William Strang Esq. ARA
1902

arts. In 1902 James Craig Annan (1864–1946) would celebrate this alliance in his evocative portrait *The Etching Printer – William Strang Esq.* ARA [FIG.21], in which the artist is seen interrogating the gradations on a printing plate. Craig Annan was a friend and confidant of the most illustrious Scottish printmakers of his time, notably D. Y. Cameron, with whom he travelled to Venice in what was an homage to the individual who reinvented the etching print in the 19th century, James Whistler. At this technical level, then, there existed a clear correspondence between photographers and artists. However, there was a further association. A number of individuals who turned to photography had been, and remained, painters. David Octavius Hill is the most obvious example, but George Washington Wilson began his career as a portrait miniaturist, and the landscape photographer Robert Macpherson – who consistently styled himself an 'Artist-Photographer' – had an early career as a painter before creating his esteemed photographic panoramas of the city of Rome in the 1860s. These, among others, testify to the intimate links between artists and photographers, and given this association it is little surprise that the photographic portrait should have settled on images of artists.

David Octavius Hill, with his legion of friends and colleagues in the Royal Scottish Academy, naturally produced some of the earliest and most compelling images of artists. His individual portraits of Sir William Allan, history painter and President of the Royal Scottish Academy; Sir George Harvey, the landscape painter who would later be elected President of that august institution; William Borthwick Johnstone, the landscape painter and first curator of the National Gallery of Scotland; John Stevens, the portrait painter; David Scott, the history painter; David Roberts, the Orientalist and landscape painter; and George Meikle Kemp, the architect of the Scott Monument in Princes Street, Edinburgh were the perfect foil to the array of clergymen and professionals who were his principal subjects. Indeed, Hill and Adamson's signature study of the academician and landscape painter *Horatio McCulloch* [FIG.22] remains an archetype of the 'troubled' artist; brooding, intense and concentrating, he is shown on the cusp of creative flight with brush and palette in hand. These are homilies to a shared circumstance. The artist and photographer, in this period at least, is acknowledging a parallel search for the ineluctable image.

This intimacy of subject, calling and mission would run deep into the history of the photographic portrait in Scotland. James Craig Annan's most reproduced image is quite probably his romantic depiction of the symbolist painter and architect *Charles Rennie Mackintosh*, taken in 1893. Moreover, the gifted circle of artists around Mackintosh and the Glasgow School of Art, Margaret and Frances Macdonald, Jessie M. King, Anne Macbeth and others, were the natural confidants and subjects of a photographer whose role as artist was unchallenged. But in fact Craig Annan's assured portraits of young artists can be viewed as doubly intriguing; not only were they, in the main, portraits of women, but these were images of a self-conscious bohemian middle class. Unlike the professional artists depicted by Hill and Adamson, establishment figures to a man, here was the emergent avant-garde. Their dress was different, the environment 'modern', their attitude confident and assertive. These features were most ably demonstrated in Craig Annan's portrait study *East & West* [FIG.23], a symbolist image which was illustrated in Steiglitz's *Camera Work* in October 1910. In this photograph the female figure is dressed *à la mode* and is surrounded by austere and geometric art nouveau furniture that is

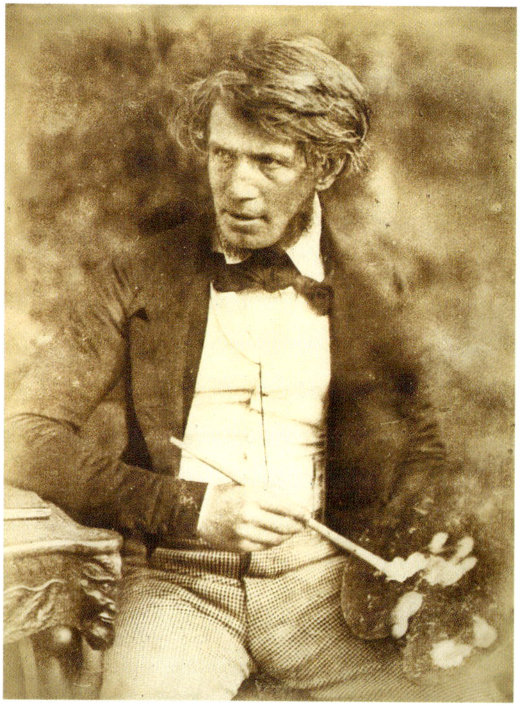

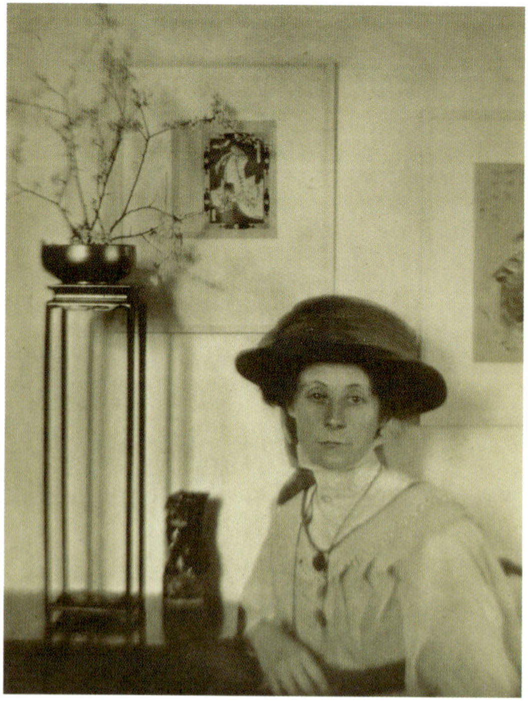

Left:
FIG.22
Hill and Adamson
Horatio McCulloch
n.d.

Right:
FIG.23
James Craig Annan
East & West
from *Camera Work*
1910

further complemented by a decorous *japonaiserie*. In many ways individuals like these were representative of a new Scotland. In 1888 the city of Glasgow held its first 'International Exhibition', a gala that eclipsed the exhibition held in Edinburgh during 1886, and set out to echo the success of the Great Exhibition of 1851. Glasgow's exhibition was a triumphal clarion of capitalism and empire, and this was a celebration of Scotland's place in that new world order. Yet the arts were at the centre of this extravaganza and were viewed as a corollary to industry and science.[8] Craig Annan himself was responsible for organising the photographic gallery and the artists in his portraits were the advanced guard of an insurgent 'modernity'.

The intrigue of 'modernity' would run into the 20th century, though Scotland's eminence as an industrial nation, the workshop of the world, would be crippled by economic crisis, slump and war. In the event of a contracted marketplace Scottish art, generally, suffered and photography, at least in its form as portrait art, was increasingly marginalised. In the revaluation of society and culture after the Second World War a renaissance of Scottish art was heralded by the inauguration of the Edinburgh International Festival of the Arts in 1947. Here, again, Scottish culture looked to secure an international profile and photography would act as handmaiden to the arts.

A young American, Lida Moser (b. 1921), had read of this new festival while living in New York and proposed a photo-article on Scottish cultural figures to the editor of *Vogue* magazine. Moser was then a tyro photographer who had trained under Bernice Abbott and was familiar with the documentary movement in New York City. She would go on to develop a career as a photojournalist and become a member of the Photo League in the United States, but this was her first prestige assignment. Commissioned for the photo-essay in 1949, Moser was introduced to those artists who formulated a Scottish avant-garde in the post-war period, as well as to the assembly of the Scottish Renaissance Movement who were gathered around the figure of Hugh MacDiarmid. Besides her austere and impressive portraits of nationalist intellectuals like MacDiarmid and Douglas Young, she would photograph the architect Basil Spence, the actor Duncan Macrae and the playwright James Bridie, amongst other luminaries. In the published article, her images were accompanied by a text, 'Scottish Talents', written by Eric Linklater, who was also one of her subjects.[9] The majority of her portraits, however, were of visual artists; the doyenne of Scottish modernism John Duncan Fergusson seen against a backdrop of 'Colourist' paintings, a quizzical William Gillies pushed to the edge of his portrait by one of his quasi-abstract still-life paintings, Anne Redpath seated with a painting as a foil, and a brooding bohemian *Portrait of William Crosbie* [FIG.24] caught leaning against a large 'advanced' canvas. Moser has remarked that she was familiar with the work of the Annans,[10] and there is a clear association between these portraits and the work of Craig Annan over half a century before. In both cases the photographer was displaying an affinity with the artist that ran counter to Elizabeth Eastlake's early insistence on their separate identities.

In the contemporary period this type of association would be reprised and confirmed. Robin Gillanders (b. 1952) has not only taken the most authoritative

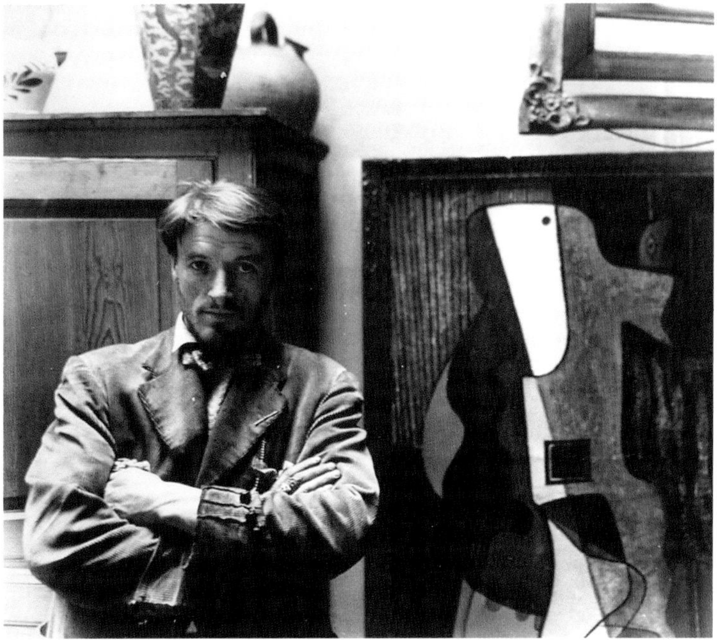

FIG.24
Lida Moser
Portrait of William Crosbie
1949

portrait photographs of the internationally acclaimed artist Ian Hamilton Finlay, but has collaborated in the dissemination of his work through his beautifully produced photobooks.[11] An early portrait of the artist-poet *Ian Hamilton Finlay, Little Sparta*, from 1996, shows Finlay in a tiny rowing boat in a small stretch of water at Little Sparta, the artist's 'philosophical' garden project. Gillanders has written of this portrait:

> My portrait of Ian Hamilton Finlay, with whom I have been collaborating over the last few years, was planned over about a year and very carefully constructed... I wanted to make a portrait of Ian that expressed my view of him as a relatively solitary figure within his own physical universe of the garden at Little Sparta, and to include reference to his fascination for boats and the sea. I wanted to put him in the smallest rowing boat he has, to attempt a reference to his boyish sense of play and humour. In retrospect it seems to suggest more extensive metaphors: his apparent marginalised status as an artist in Scotland and the fragility of his existence at Little Sparta.[12]

It might be argued that Gillanders' recent collaboration with Finlay has allowed for the fullest expression of both their arts; Gillanders' subtle, indeed magical and finely crafted, black and white photographs of Finlay's work providing an ingenious and worthy counterpoint to the artist-poet's constructions and plantings.

A similar association has existed between the poet George Mackay Brown and the Swedish photographer Gunnie Moberg (b. 1941). Moberg has been resident in the Orkney Isles since 1976 and there she became a collaborator with Brown, who was, and remains, indelibly inscribed on the islands' cultural history. Brown, a native of the Orkneys, produced poems, stories and novels that were deeply rooted in the landscape and folklore of his homeland. His work, by turns elemental, atavistic and religious, became a touchstone for Moberg's development from photo-journalist to landscape photographer. Within this process she completed a number of portrait studies of the poet, studies that fully recognise and assert Brown's remarkable physiognomy, most notably in the profile study *George Mackay Brown* [FIG.25], where the poet is crisply focussed against the hull of the Orkney ferry ship the *St Ola*. Moreover, the partnership composed an assembly of photobooks in which Moberg's photographs were complemented with lyrics specially composed by the poet. The most celebrated of these is *Stone*, a limited edition publication in the tradition of the 'artist's book', published in 1987. Here, the lyrical intensity of Brown's verse is set in harmony with the near-abstract formality of Moberg's images.

Evidently the links between photographers and artists spilled over into a close association between photographers and cultural figures generally. Additionally the respect accorded to the photographic portrait in the modern period, that is to say the recognition that the photographic portrait might parallel or indeed rival the traditional painted portrait, has resulted in a number of public commissions for photographic portraits. Amongst these the images of composers and musicians have been the most adventurous. David Williams (b. 1952) created his evocative, soft-focus portrait of the renowned Shetland fiddler *Aly Bain, Musician* in 1995 [FIG.26]. Williams, himself a musician, was fully aware of the sense of rapture and 'flight' occasioned in the throes of performance and looked to capture this elusive mood in his portrait. The result was an image that is itself 'musical'. Williams produced a portrait in tones of blue, a muted almost spectral image of the musician in performance. The sense of space and interval, shadow and light, pitch and timbre in the photograph is calculated to reflect the musician's rhapsodic recitation. Most

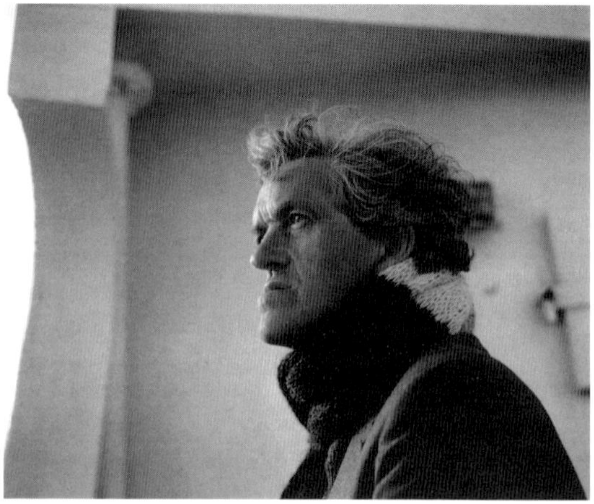

FIG.25
Gunnie Moberg
George Mackay Brown
1990

clearly, the dark and melancholic nature of the image echoes the sense of a threnody or lament in all its sorrowful despond.

There is an allusion here, and one that highlights the continuity between fine art and photography. Williams was, in part, referencing Sir Henry Raeburn's famous *Portrait of Neil Gow*, from circa 1793. This popular and exemplary portrait of 'the father of Strathspey and Reel players', who was famed also for his elegiac compositions, was a touchstone for subsequent portraits of musicians. In fact this idea is reprised in Calum Colvin's (b. 1961) commissioned portrait of the composer *James Macmillan*, from 1996 [FIG.27]. Colvin's constructed image, a three-dimensional stage-set subsequently painted upon with a portrait of Macmillan and finally photographed, contains a fiddle set in the lower left-hand corner of the work. Although the 'set' for this portrait

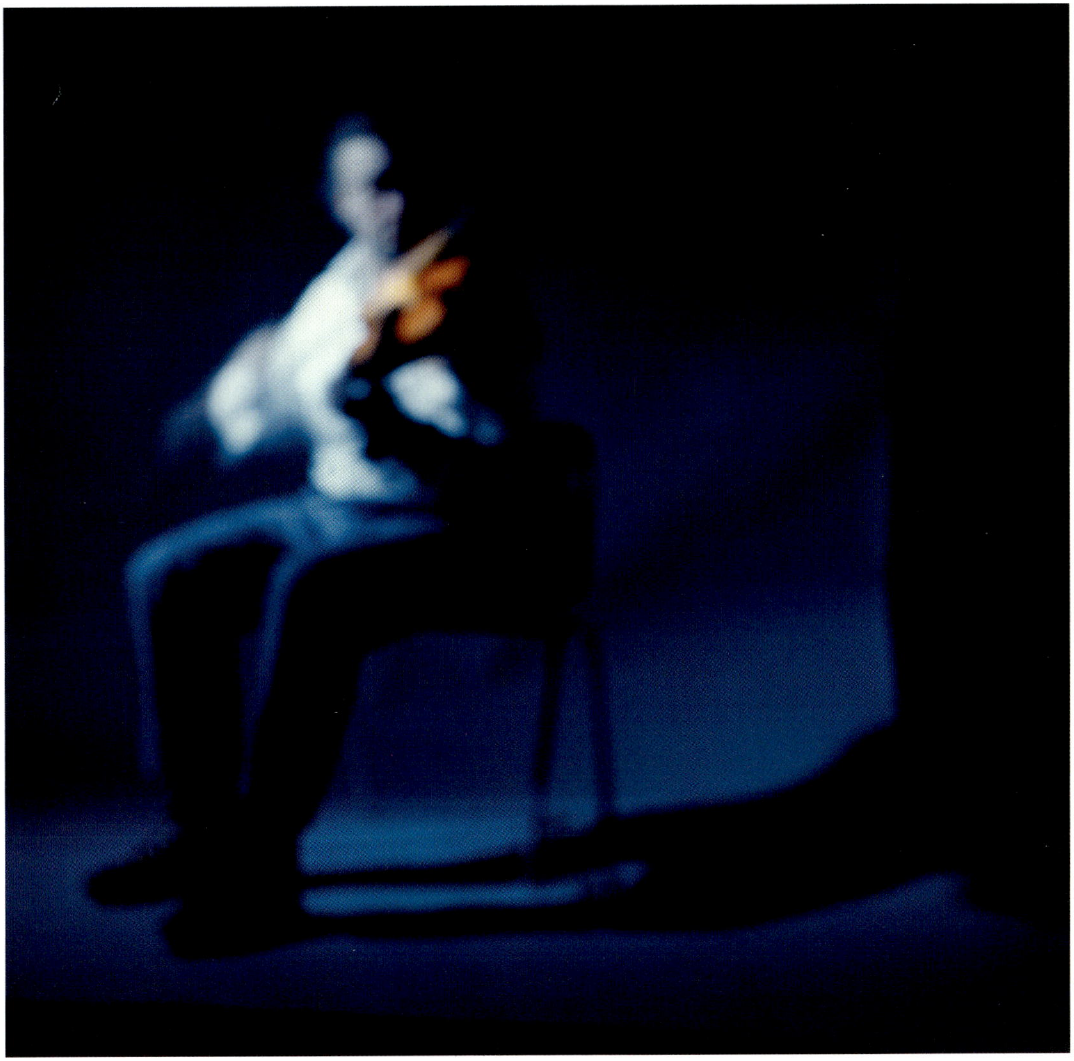

FIG.26
David Williams
Aly Bain, Musician
1995

is, nominally, Macmillan's writing desk and studio, the area is strewn with associated paraphernalia and related symbols. The fiddle is a direct reference to Gow's precedence as an eminent Scottish performer and composer, a position inherited by the esteemed subject of Colvin's portrait.

Portraying the social classes

Clergymen, scientists, artists – all are in some way connected to the history of the photograph and to photographic portraiture in Scotland. This lineage is insistent but it is partial. The real power of the photograph, even in its form as portraiture, was in the way it represented the social world.

FIG.27
Calum Colvin
James Macmillan
1996

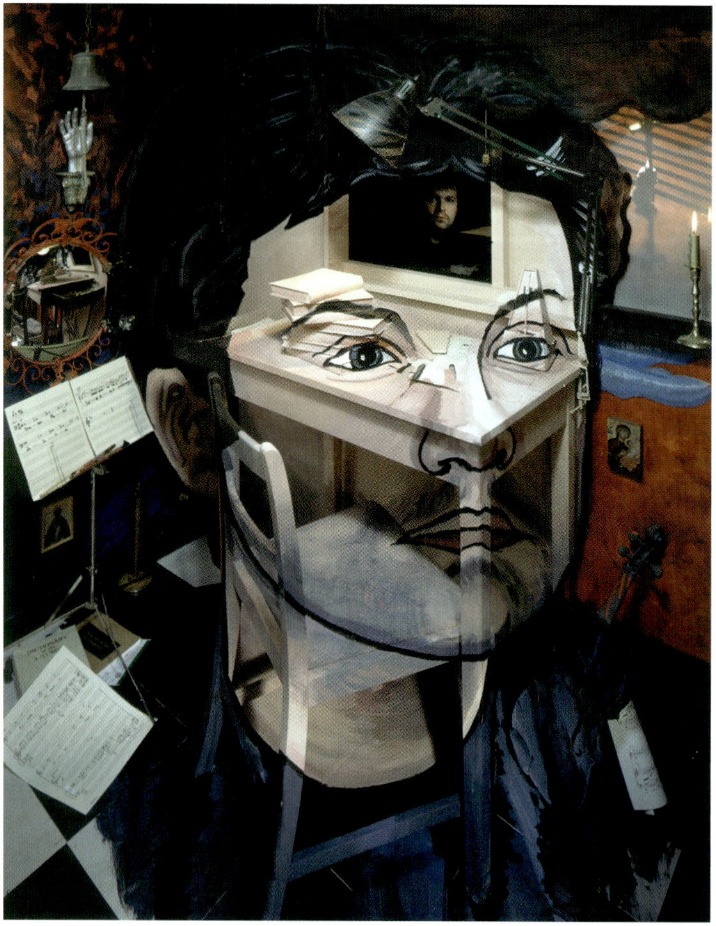

The photograph, evidently, was a visualisation of the modern world, and the modern world was characterised by social change. These changes were most apparent in respect of social class. At the birth of photography Scotland was developing as a nation actively engaged in the process of industrialisation and as an established partner in the colonial enterprise of the United Kingdom. Agricultural revolution had occasioned not only the Highland Clearances and the rationalisation of lowland farming, but also a gradual decline in the power of rural landowners. This was made manifest in the periodic slumps that plagued the agricultural industry throughout the 19th century and most especially after 1870. Heavy industry, while equally prone to periods of depression, nevertheless sustained an emergent bourgeois class of entrepreneurs and 'self-made men' while generating a bureaucracy of middle-class administrators and, of course, an army of working-class labourers. While the landed aristocracy would dabble in photography, even respecting this form as an ersatz version of the formal portrait in oil, it was the more dynamic middle class who would view it as a modern enterprise and art. In this respect photography was an absolute correlate of the democratisation of culture and a protagonist in the changes that defined the social world in the late 19th and early 20th centuries. Evidence of this social dynamic is marked in the wild expansion of photographic portraiture during this period.

Photography would become actively patronised by Queen Victoria, and most especially by her consort Albert, in the 1850s. In Scotland, it fell to George Washington Wilson (1823–93) to become the chief beneficiary to this patronage. Wilson, in 1854, was in partnership with John Hay in the photographic firm of Wilson and Hay in Aberdeen, and was invited to create a photographic record of the restoration of Balmoral Castle which was begun in 1853. The Balmoral Estate had been leased by Victoria in 1848 and would become her summer residence thereafter; a 'royal appointment' that led to the fashion for Highland chic and tourist pilgrimage throughout the coming century. Besides these recording duties Wilson, whose partnership with Hay ended in 1855, was commissioned to produce portraits of Victoria, Albert and their family, as well as studies of visiting dignitaries and even estate workers. Many of these works were commissioned for private albums and were in no sense 'official' portraits, but they undoubtedly helped establish the cultural currency of the photographic portrait.

In consequence of this the aristocratic classes began to show some interest in engaging photography as a technology and art. Horatio Ross (1801–86) is a fascinating example of this development. A landed aristocrat, Ross was the Member of Parliament for the Montrose district between 1832 and 1834 but was universally known as a sportsman and dilettante. He was a renowned horseman, yachtsman, angler and most famously, the first captain of the Scottish Match Rifle Team. Indeed Ross, and his sons, represented Scotland in the National Rifle Association championships of 1863. Amongst this glut of hobbies Ross took to photography in 1845, and he would help found the Photographic Society of Scotland in 1856, naturally becoming its first vice-president. Ross's subjects tended to be images associated with hunting, shooting and fishing; the everyday pastimes of his class. Interestingly he was an advocate of the daguerreotype process before experimenting with the calotype and collodian processes, and his signature photographs *Craigdacourt* of 1848 and *Hoddy and John Munro Fishing at Flaipool* from 1847 are in the medium of the daguerreotype.

Ross encouraged the prospect of outdoor photography and scenes from Highland life, and only nominally can these be described as portraits of his friends and family. However, there exists a fascinating portrait study of Ross himself, created by one of the most famous English photographers of the 19th century, Roger Fenton. Fenton had trained as an artist and had spent time in Paris during 1851, when he became familiar with the experiments of Daguerre. His reputation as a photographer was sealed when, in 1855, he was commissioned to take photographs of the Crimean War; in consequence becoming the world's first 'war photographer'. At the close of the Crimean conflict, in 1856, Fenton was sufficiently celebrated to be asked to photograph Queen Victoria and her entourage at Balmoral. In 1860, nine years before his death and one year before he mysteriously retired from photography, he shot a remarkable portrait of *Captain Horatio Ross* [FIG.28]. Ross is seen crouching on one knee, his left leg supporting a steadying arm while he shoulders his rifle and takes careful aim at an unknown target. The background is stark and bare, a shadowed building perhaps, and a parade ground. The lighting, from the left of the image, throws the long shadow of the marksman to the right of the picture and out of the shot. Evidently this is Ross the rifleman but the image remains contingent; like a portrait by Velasquez or one of Manet's realist manifestoes. In any event this is an extraordinary portrait; for all that Fenton's views of the Crimean War were sanitised and made acceptable for a patriotic Victorian public, he was aware of the power of a bullet. This portrait of Captain Ross subtly contains, and projects, that threat and deadly impetus.

It might be suggested that Ross's own work amounted to a kind of social diary, a memoir of his aristocratic lifestyle, family and friends. A more distilled version of this trope would become available in the photography of an individual who was one of Scotland's few 19th-century woman photographers, Lady Henrietta Gilmour.[13] Gilmour (circa 1850–1926) began taking photographs sometime around 1890, following the birth of her seventh child. With estates in Fife, and the summer's lease on hunting and

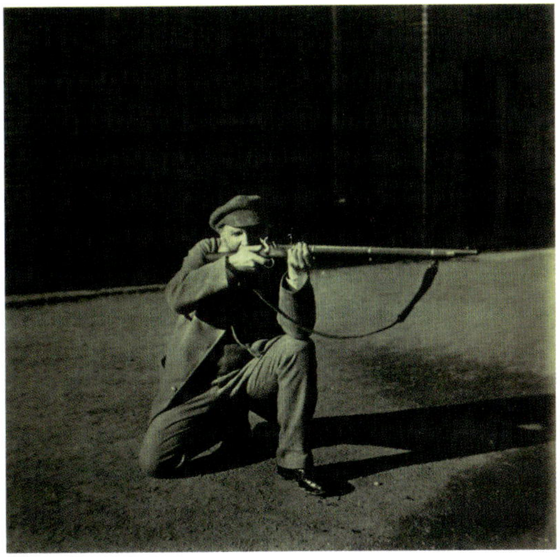

FIG.28
Roger Fenton
Captain Horatio Ross
1860

fishing estates in the north-west of Scotland, Gilmour's subjects were exclusively her family and their country pursuits. She had something of a passion for the formal portrait and the photograph *Netta in Grannie's Dress* [FIG.29], taken circa 1900, is a fair image of her youngest daughter presented in the classical manner of a painting by Ingres. The dress itself, a fine silk brocade, all folds and rich flowing pattern, is testament to a sumptuous and luxuriant social world. The broader context of this society is evidenced in Gilmour's other photographs; portraits of family and servants, hunting and fishing parties, fancy dress balls, and the panorama of estate and land. That photography was something of a hobby for Gilmour is evidenced in the fact that she tired of the occupation sometime around 1910, though she lived on until 1926. Her photographs, however, remain as witness to the compelling nature of the medium and the exclusive world of the landed classes.

There is, however, a case for arguing that photography is the art of the middle classes. It was born at the cusp of that massive industrial and commercial expansion that was initiated by the middle class; it recorded, in the most minute detail, the world created and explored and exploited by the middle class; and it presented an opportunity for the entrepreneurial investment so beloved of the middle class. More than that, it became the means through which this

Bottom left:
FIG.29
Lady Henrietta Gilmour
Netta in Grannie's Dress
circa 1900

Bottom right:
FIG.30
George Washington Wilson
Aberdeen Portraits
1857

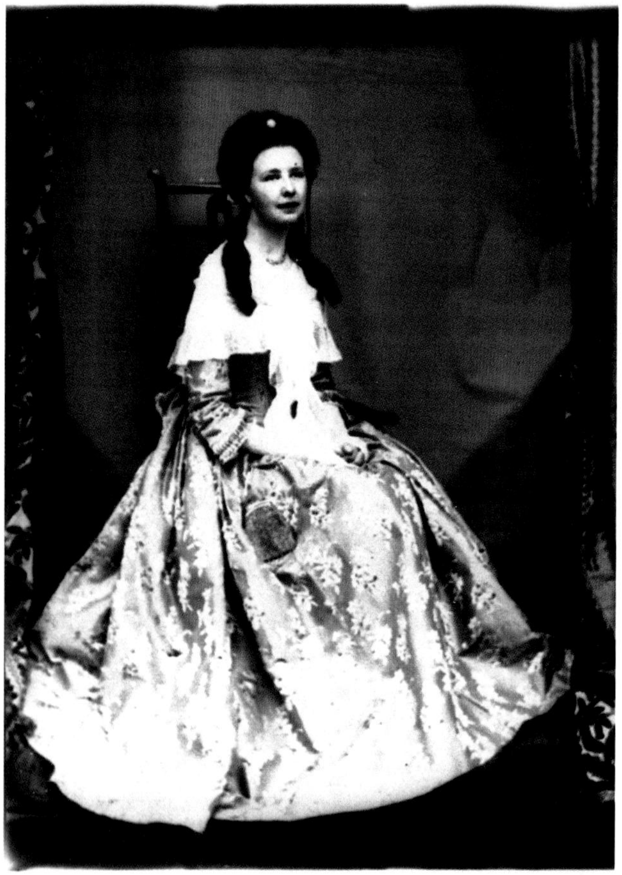

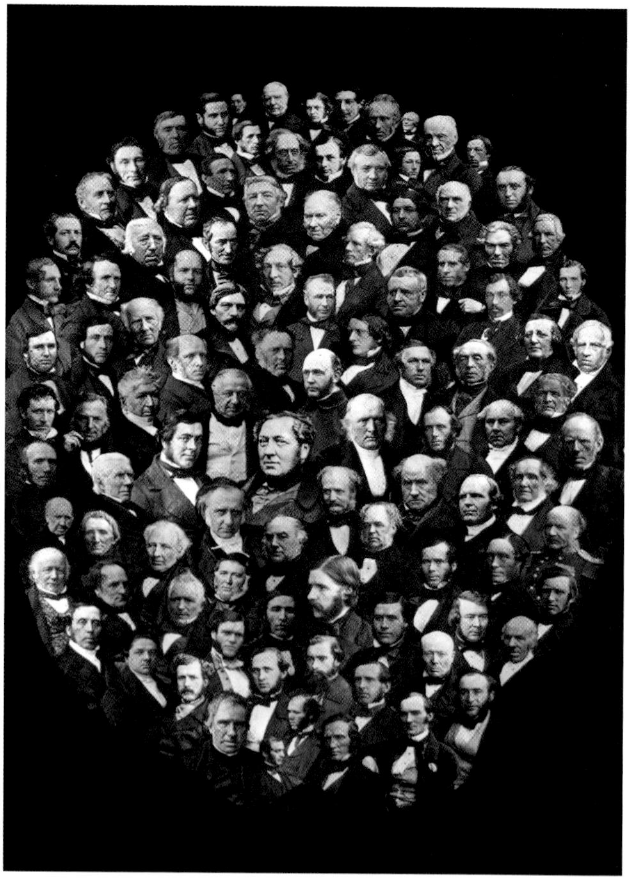

emergent bourgeoisie would find itself celebrated and immortalised in visual form, for the portrait photograph, at least in the 19th century, was overwhelmingly a middle-class affair.

In respect of this it is worth examining George Washington Wilson's advertisement for his photographic studio in Aberdeen. Roger Taylor has called this 'the world's first recorded use of photomontage' and it is certainly an impressive assemblage of portrait heads.[14] More than this, it was created fully six years before the French photographer, Desdéri, patented his 'mosaic' photographic format. Wilson, ever the entrepreneur, had a keen eye on his portrait market and chose to promote this aspect of his business with a hitherto untried 'combination' print. In 1857 he gathered his collection of negatives of Aberdeen's professional classes and grouped them in a single montaged photograph titled *Aberdeen Portraits* [FIG.30]. Taylor notes Wilson's discriminating sense of social status in assembling these heads:

> The size and placing of the heads take on a particular significance, and it comes as no surprise that the largest and centrally placed head belongs to the only titled person, Sir Thomas Blaikie. Around him are ranged the advocates, artists, bankers, professors, reverends and surgeons.[15]

As an advertisement this would have provided an arresting visual display; it might even have seemed 'magical'. The power of the image, however, resided in its potential to promote the immediacy, accessibility and commonality of the photographic portrait. Here were the middle-class denizens of Aberdeen society elected to the visual canon.

Wilson, by implication and by practice, was publicising the idea that this type of reification could be shared by all, or at least by those who could afford his 'six shilling' fee. In fact, very soon after Wilson's enterprising trick, the technology would develop such that the portrait photograph became affordable to a much wider group of people. Moreover, unlike the mass of whiskered faces in Wilson's manifesto piece, this group would include women and children.

The carte-de-visite became *the* fashion accessory, amongst the middle classes at least, very soon after its development in the 1850s. It was the ever-enterprising Frenchman André Desdéri who first filed the patent on this innovation, in 1854. Developments in the technology of the camera allowed for a multiplying of images on a single glass plate. These multiples, once developed, afforded sometimes as many as 10 photographic portraits to be reproduced, on a scale that paralleled the visiting card and at a cost that was easily affordable to the expanding middle class. Cut and mounted onto backing card, these portraits became a kind of cultural currency. They introduced a visitor in the most spectacular fashion, they offered a modest means of producing an album of family and friends, and they afforded a novel method by which the public could access the portrait of the celebrities of the period. Desdéri, famously, secured the popularity of his patent by persuading Napoleon III to have his portrait distributed in this form in 1859, while throughout Britain miniature images of Queen Victoria sold literally in their hundreds-of-thousands. Just as importantly the Scots exile Alexander Gardner (1821–82), famed for his photographs documenting the American Civil War, would produce Abraham Lincoln's carte-de-visite in the period circa 1862. He would also produce the last cabinet portrait of the doomed President, just four days before his assassination [FIG.31].

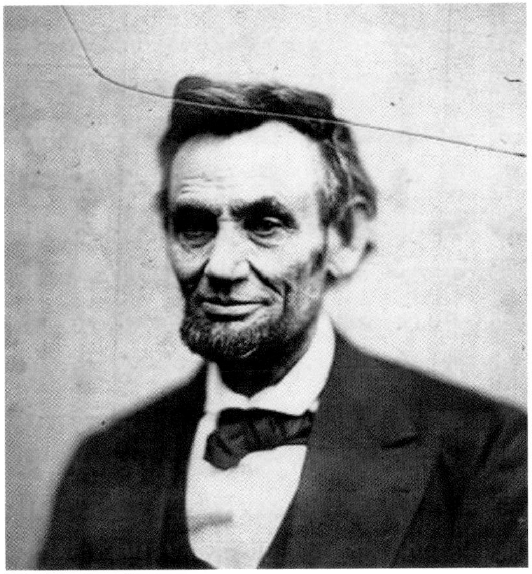

FIG.31
Alexander Gardner
Abraham Lincoln (Last Portrait)
10 April 1865

The carte-de-visite was introduced to England in 1857, and would become a commonplace feature of the middle-class home by the 1860s. In Scotland it led to a significant expansion in the number of photographers and photographic studios, whose businesses were suddenly peppering the high streets of even the smaller towns and villages. In the 1850s, for example, a modest burgh like Dunfermline in Fife could boast of only two photographic studios, one of which was styled as offering services in 'photography and bird stuffing'.[16] By the 1880s there were at least 15 studios catering to the needs of the town. The fact that the bulk of this business was generated by the low-cost carte-de-visite is evidenced in the number of such images that still rest, unvisited, in the backrooms of antique and curio shops. Firms included William Toddie 'Photographic Artist' of Bonnar Street, Alex P. Taylor of East Port, Handu Hardie & Federwitz 'Artists & Photographers' of North Station Road, The Fife Photo. Coy of Kirkgate, W. G. Mackie 'Portrait Group and Architectural Photography' of North Station Road and James Norval of North Station Road [FIG.32]. This small selection of photographers active in Dunfermline in the 1880s, many of them plying their trade in the same street and moving into and out from partnership with each other, gives a sense of the vigorous and vibrant nature of the industry. Multiply this throughout the country and something in the nature of a visual, and commercial, revolution was under way.

If, however, the number of portraits was increasing exponentially, the 'look' of the works remained within a tight aesthetic frame. Reduced in scale, industrially manufactured and low in cost, the portrait studies in carte-de-visite form echo the conventional portraits of the period, though perhaps with less artistry. Whiskered patriarchs posing stiffly at attention, frail and nervous-looking women seated amid domestic furniture, family groups staged as a formal hierarchy and children presented as miniature adults. This profoundly Victorian representation of middle-class life was the mainstay of the photographic studio. Such was its popularity that these images would be collected in customised albums, complete with tooled leather binding and heavy brass clasps.[17] These books, in style, emulated the portentous family bible and so completed the circle of an idealised and virtuous prosperity realised, therein, as a visual manifesto.

The era of the carte-de-visite was the 1860s, though its popularity remained, in Scotland at least, until the 1880s. Its gradual decline was hastened by the introduction of a further development in the photographic industry, the emergence of the 'Cabinet' photograph. The Cabinet photograph was larger in scale and might, therefore, be afforded a place on the family mantelpiece, or indeed the cabinet. George Washington Wilson had introduced this larger-scale image in 1862 as an appropriate size for his panoramic landscape photographs. In the world of portraiture, however, it allowed the studio photographer a greater scope in which to highlight his skills. In truth the Cabinet portrait photograph tended to echo the form of the carte-de-visite; it utilised a similar repertoire of set poses, clichéd props and stolid lighting. However, the larger scale allowed for the introduction of some novel refinements. Young gentlemen would be pictured leaning rakishly on the saddle of a gleaming bicycle [FIG.33], while older gentlemen might bring their loyal Labradors and a favourite shotgun into the studio. These images would become a common stock of the larger family album, which soon became a feature of the middle-class home. Symbolically, they were the signals of a certain social cache and status, indicating the 'worth' of these individuals which had been translated into a visual canonisation. Even after the introduction of Eastman's Kodak's No. 1 Brownie camera in 1888, complete with its simple operation and flexible roll film, photography remained a middle-class affair, for the price of this 'universal' camera, £2 and 2 shillings, lay outside the boundaries of the labouring man or woman.

It is interesting, then, to reflect on the whereabouts of the working class in this pantheon of portrait photography. In many ways they are distinguished by their absence, or rather by their presence elsewhere, for the working classes and the poor tend to be represented, anonymously, in documentary photography. Here, they were embodied in the nature of their labour and the conditions of their life. The notion that their face might be an important mark of

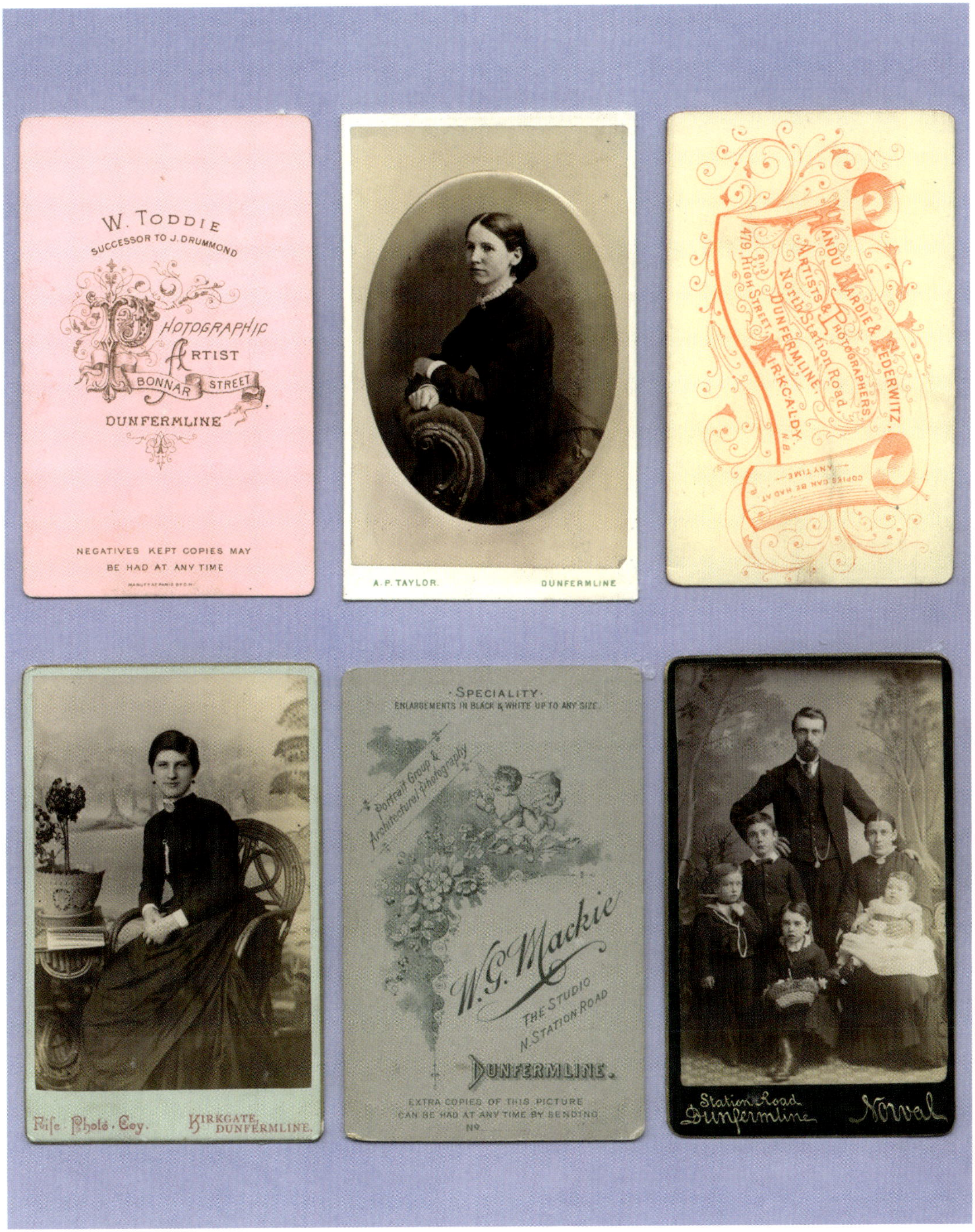

FIG.32
Dunfermline studios: William Toddie 'Photographic Artist' of Bonnar Street, Alex P. Taylor of East Port, Handu Hardie & Federwitz 'Artists & Photographers' of North Station Road, The Fife Photo. Coy. of Kirkgate, W. G. Mackie 'Portrait Group and Architectural Photography' of North Station Road, and James Norval of North Station Road

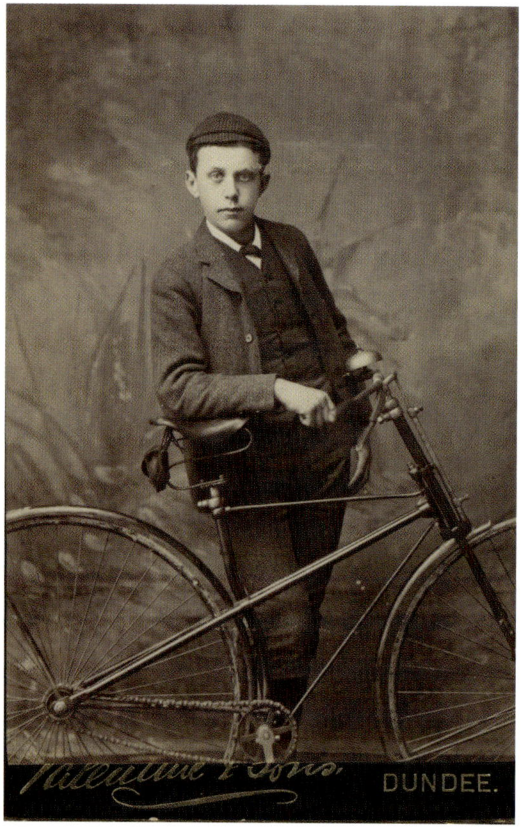

FIG.33
Studio Portrait
Young Gentleman and Bicycle
n.d.

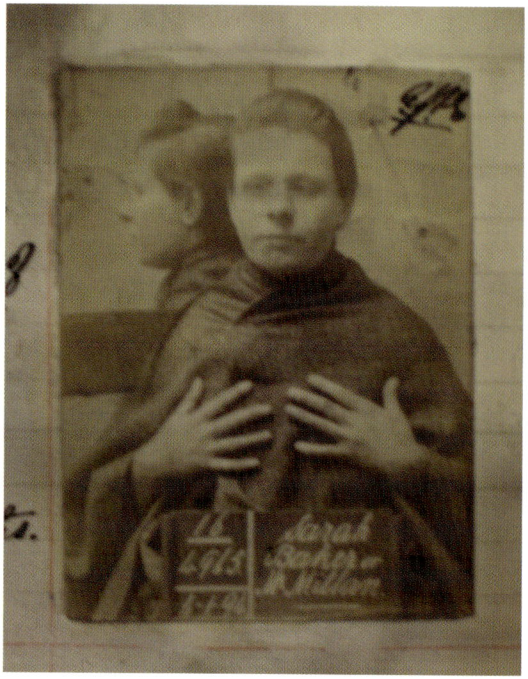

Right:
FIG.35
Police photographer
Sarah Baker or McMillan
1896

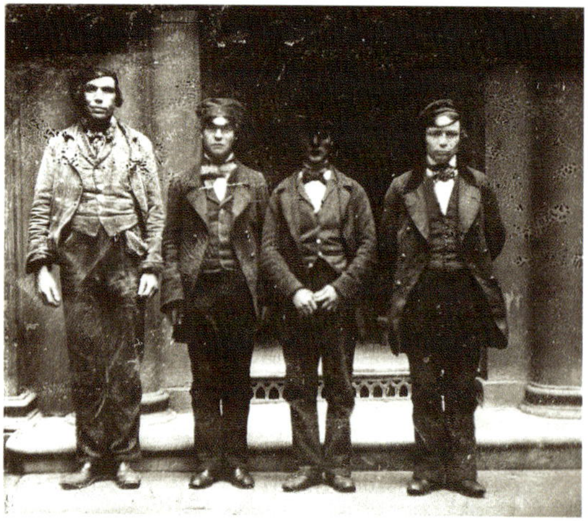

Below:
FIG.34
Police photographer,
inscribed 'from left to right – a dirty thief, a card sharper, a pickpocket and a tailor'
1863

their personality and character is lost; except in a few, revealing, instances. Portraits of labourers, the poor, the underclass were routinely taken from the 1860s onwards. Glasgow police, for example, began to take photographic records of prisoners from 1862, and by the turn of the 20th century held over 10,000 photographs in their records department. The Dundee police force seem to have begun to photographically document local criminals in the period around 1870. These photographs properly belong to that sub-section of photographic history that focuses on the nature of institutional records. But they are, evidently, portraits.

The photograph inscribed verso as, From left to right – a dirty thief, a card sharper, a pickpocket and a tailor, [FIG.34] was taken in the courtyard of the Central Police Office, Glasgow, in 1863.[18] It is, in many ways, an extraordinarily formalised group portrait; the participants stand, earnestly, to attention; they face front at an equal spacing and with a suitably resigned countenance. They are, in every sense, 'caught' by the camera. Yet they remain anonymous in this format.

This would not be the case once the procedure of the photographic police record was fully deployed. Herein, as is the case with *Sarah Baker or McMillan* [FIG.35], photographed in 1894, the individual is portrayed giving the fullest account of her identity. Sarah Baker is required to present her face full to the camera. Behind her, and obliquely at the appropriate angle, is a mirror that records her profile. In front of her a chalked board records her name(s) and identity number while, most disconcertingly of all, she flattens her hands across her breast in order to display her fingers, a primitive and abstruse form of the fingerprint.

In the 19th century photographic records like these were the albums of the poor, but the 20th century would see technological developments and the falling costs of photographic reproduction open out the portrait to an even wider populace. One of the first signs of this process was the emergence of the street photographer. The Edinburgh-born champion of the documentary image John Thomson (1837–1921) would celebrate this phenomenon in *Street Photographer* from 'Clapham Common Industries' [FIG.36], a photograph taken in 1877 and included in his illustrious photobook *Street Life in London*. Thomson shows the itinerant street photographer, plying his trade on the Common, taking portrait studies of promenading gentlefolk and their children. The centrepiece of his photograph is the wheeled 'studio' which displays examples of his work. In front of this the wooden chair is set out for the portrait

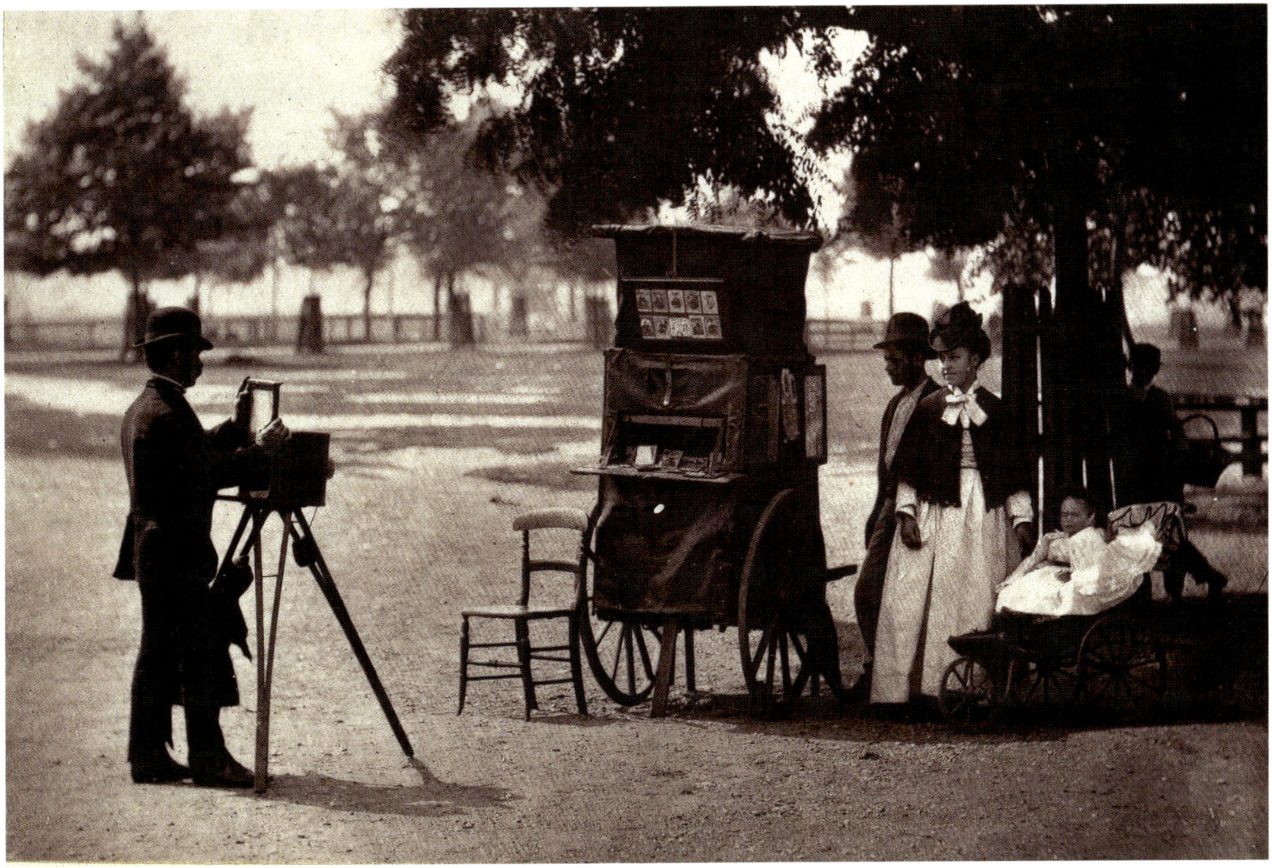

FIG.36
John Thomson
Street Photographer
from 'Clapham Common Industries'
1877

sitting. This genre of casual street photography would exist well into the 20th century, when photographers would turn up at fairs and festivals offering to take portraits of the revellers and holiday-makers. These figures would often bring exotic 'props', a parrot or a monkey [FIG.37], for the petrified model to hold and thereby add an element of novelty to the portrait. Following this brief 'sitting' the photographer would carefully note the name and address of the model, and collect his fee. Sometimes the photograph might even be posted and delivered to the poor deluded patron.

If this history of the photographic portrait locates its signature form in images of the aristocracy and the middle classes then it must be acknowledged that there would be a gradual shift in emphasis throughout the 20th century. In part this was occasioned by the falling costs of cameras and their related technologies, so that everyone might be represented in the 'snapshot' portrait. But, just as importantly, distinguished photographers began to recognise working people and their kin as individuals rather than as 'types'. The signal of this change, in Scotland, was fired by an outstanding American photographer, Paul Strand.

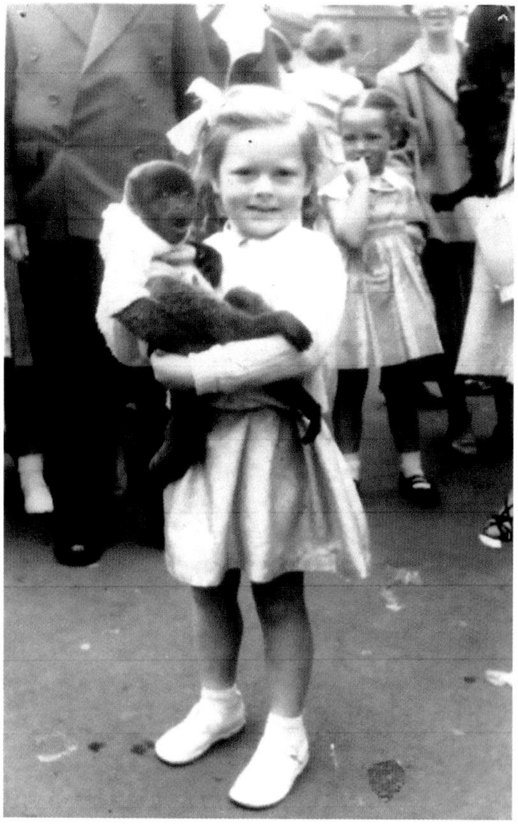

FIG.37
Street photographer
Young Girl and Monkey
circa 1960

Paul Strand (1890–1976) travelled to Scotland in 1954. Here, he photographed the people of Benbecula, South Uist and Eriskay in the Western Isles. This project was published in the photobook *Tir a' Mhurain: the Outer Hebrides of Scotland* in 1962. Strand, of course, was recognised as a pioneer modernist. A pupil of the committed documentary photographer Lewis Hine in the first decade of the 20th century, he became an associate of Alfred Stieglitz,[19] and subsequently a photographic formalist concentrating on sharply focused machine forms and quasi-abstract images. Strand would eventually be recognised as the prime mover in a new photographic realism, sometimes called 'straight' photography, which accented an unmediated approach to the image. This distinctively photographic aesthetic allowed him to produce works that eschewed 'pictorial' devices and concentrated on a forthright, objective depiction of the subject. John Berger has written that 'The photographic moment for Strand is a biographical or historic moment, whose duration is ideally measured not in seconds but by its relation to a lifetime',[20] and it is this sense of biography and history that Strand brings to his portraits of individuals in the Western Isles.

Strand's project in the Western Isles was a correlate of his photographic essays on small communities in New England, in France and in Italy. There is a strong case for arguing a political dynamic at work in all of these assignments.[21] Strand, ever-mindful of the political engagement of his first mentor, Lewis Hine, remained a fellow-traveller in Left causes throughout his career. His portraits of small villages and communities were, in many respects, visions of 'ideal' worlds; self-contained, communal, socially and ethically centred. Given this, his biographical and historically-orientated portraits existed as a kind of manifesto and required a heavily directed aesthetic. Berger, again, has offered the most convincing sense of this portrait aesthetic:

> In practical terms this means that he decides what he wants before he takes the picture, never plays with the accidental, works slowly, hardly ever crops a picture, often still uses a plate camera, formally asks people to pose for him. His pictures are remarkable for intentionality. His portraits are very frontal. The subject is looking at us; we are looking at the subject; it has been arranged like that.[22]

This uncompromising frontality, this 'straight' aesthetic, sits at the root of Strand's objectivity, and is the basis for his claim to a kind of 'truth'. He has presented his subjects in close-up, sharply focused and contained. He has allowed the camera, in its unique fashion, to record every feature of their physical 'look' and in doing so has released their core being; their 'realness'. Moreover Strand has insisted on that singular feature of their identity, he has named each of his sitters. This would be a required motif of the formal portrait, where those portrayed were the social elite, but Strand insisted on the democracy of the photograph. In this he required acknowledgement of a common humanity, and sourced this in the human face.

It is worth considering these portraits further, and viewing them from the point of view of the subject. Strand had travelled to the Outer Hebrides and into a culture that was marginal to industrial Scotland. The primary sign of this difference was language, for the first tongue of these people was Gaelic. In journeying to the Gàidhealtachd Strand was voyaging to a world that had been mythologised by the political centre, compacted to a culture of tartanry and residual customs, and categorised as a social anachronism. Strand, it appears, refused to recognise this derogation and the subjects of his portraits understood the respect he afforded to their individuality and their culture. Certainly this explains the compliance of his many sitters, and the esteem in which he is still held in the islands of South Uist and Benbecula. This compliance is remarkable for Strand's images were 'hard-won'. Donald John Campbell, the son of Strand's portrait subject *Neil Campbell* [FIG.38], has explained how Strand would insist on the conditions of the sitting.[23] Subjects were instructed not to smile, they were set to hold their pose until all the conditions of light and circumstance were correct, and they were drilled in their pose and props. *Neil Campbell*, for example, is pictured holding a cigarette in a style that echoes the pose of the universal working man, but he was not a smoker at this period and Strand is clearly creating a useful fiction. Likewise *Mary Campbell*, the young girl pictured in front of a window frame in Benbecula, has recalled Strand's requirements for a portrait study. Fourteen years old at the time when Strand encountered her as she hung out washing with her mother, she is pictured with her back pressed against the window frame in shelter from the gusting wind. Strand, nevertheless, waited an inordinate time before taking the photograph, carefully judging the changing light and mood.[24] He would then go on to photograph Mary's mother, and her grandmother.

The result of this uncompromising aesthetic is a gallery of faces that speak through the ages and are particular to a place. Margaret MacLean's penetrating stare, a contest with the camera's lens; Kate Steele's lined face and silver fringe of hair, eerily framed by her dark shawl; the stoical resignation of Norman Douglas's watchful gaze; the intensity of Ewan MacLeod's reciprocal glance, a counterpoint to his hard-set mouth; and, everywhere, the textures of the islands. These textures become a correlate of Strand's portrait subjects, lichen covered stone walls, sand and kelp, patterned peat stacks, striated rocks and rough grassland. Strand has set his subjects inside the landscape and reflects on their necessary relationship with the land, the shore and the sea. In this sense Strand's portraits are witness to the inviolable connection between person and place, being and culture.

Portraiture

Portraiture does not always demonstrate the sensitivity of Paul Strand's vision, for Strand saw the portrait as an exercise in the discovery of a common humanity. In doing this Strand was making a connection with a deeper Scottish tradition. Strand was a close associate of Stieglitz. Stieglitz, through his relationship with James Craig Annan, was familiar with the work of Hill and Adamson and had illustrated many of their photographs in *Camera Work*. While these tended to be portrait images of society figures, the October 1909 edition of the journal contained a photograph titled *Newhaven Fisheries*. In fact this was a photograph of fisherfolk in St Andrews, and is properly named *North Street, Fishergate, St Andrews; Baiting the Lines*. However, there is little doubt that Strand knew of Hill and Adamson's Newhaven images. Moreover, he would be familiar with the fact that the partnership, in the tradition of Scottish democracy and accountability, had named the individual sitters from this marginalised community of fishermen and women; hence, the gallery of portraits that would include the pensive *Elizabeth Johnstone Hall; a Newhaven Beauty*, and the weather-worn *Willie Liston; Redding the Line*. Strand's work in the Western Isles echoed the dialogue between portraiture and documentary that was first evident in the Newhaven photographs of Hill and Adamson. More particularly, he recognised the humanist dimension of this project and reflected this intent.

In the contemporary period the portrait form has become familiarised in the style of the celebrity photoshoot. This is, perhaps, a correlate to the studio portrait of the 19th century, though its relative sophistication of technique and conscious desire for the novel, 'edgy' configuration allows for a more striking image. Herein, Narcissus does reign supreme and unchallenged. Scotland has helped produce at least two celebrated celebrity photographers in Albert Watson (b. 1942) and John 'Rankin' Waddell (b. 1966), both of whom have produced impressive portraits of the world's glitterati. However, the portrait form, in its more modest and satisfying manner, remains a record of achievement and being, of memory and memorial, and even of social process and change. Beyond this, it sustains the fascination in the ineffable strangeness, and beauty, of the human face.

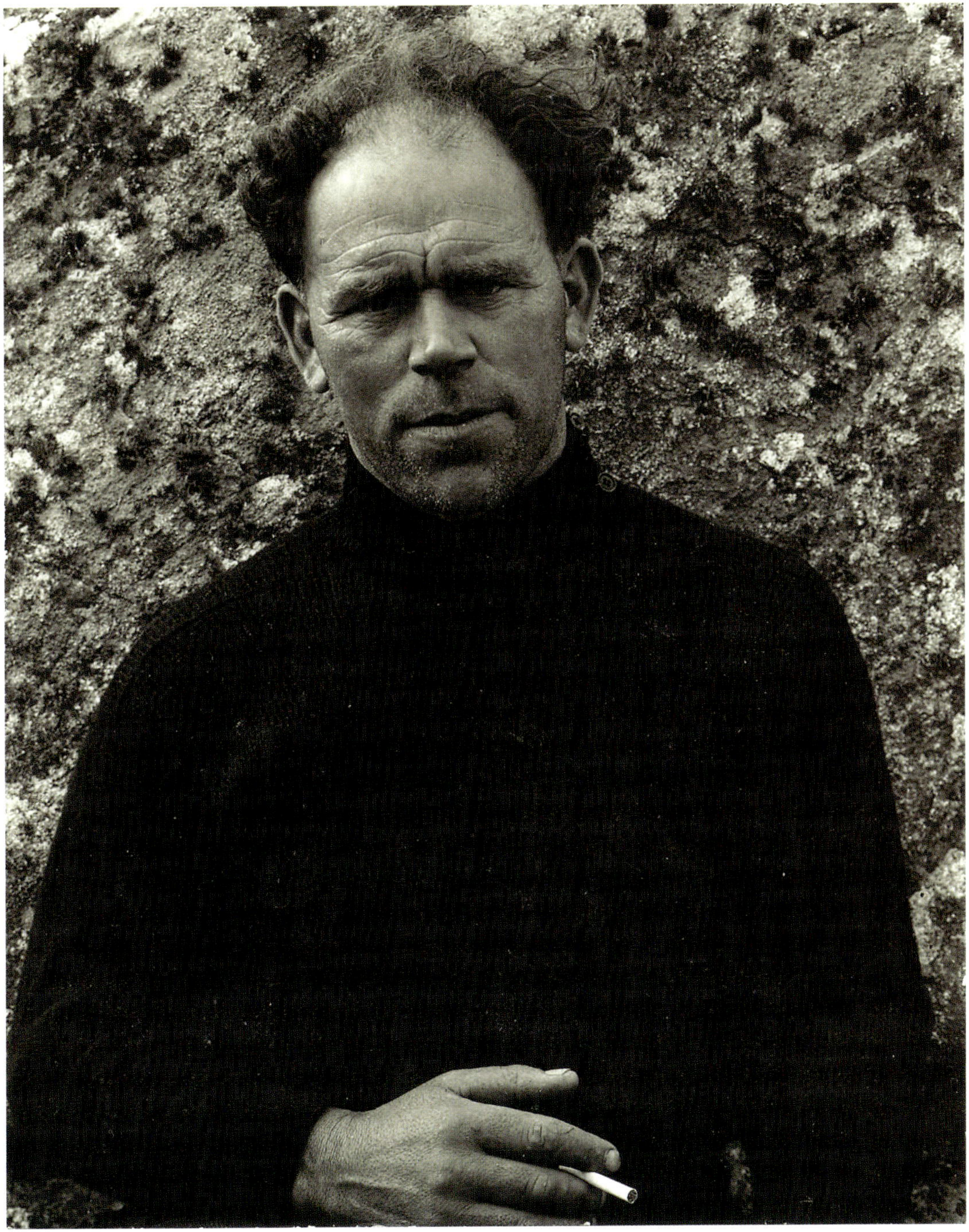

FIG.38
Paul Strand
Neil Campbell
1954

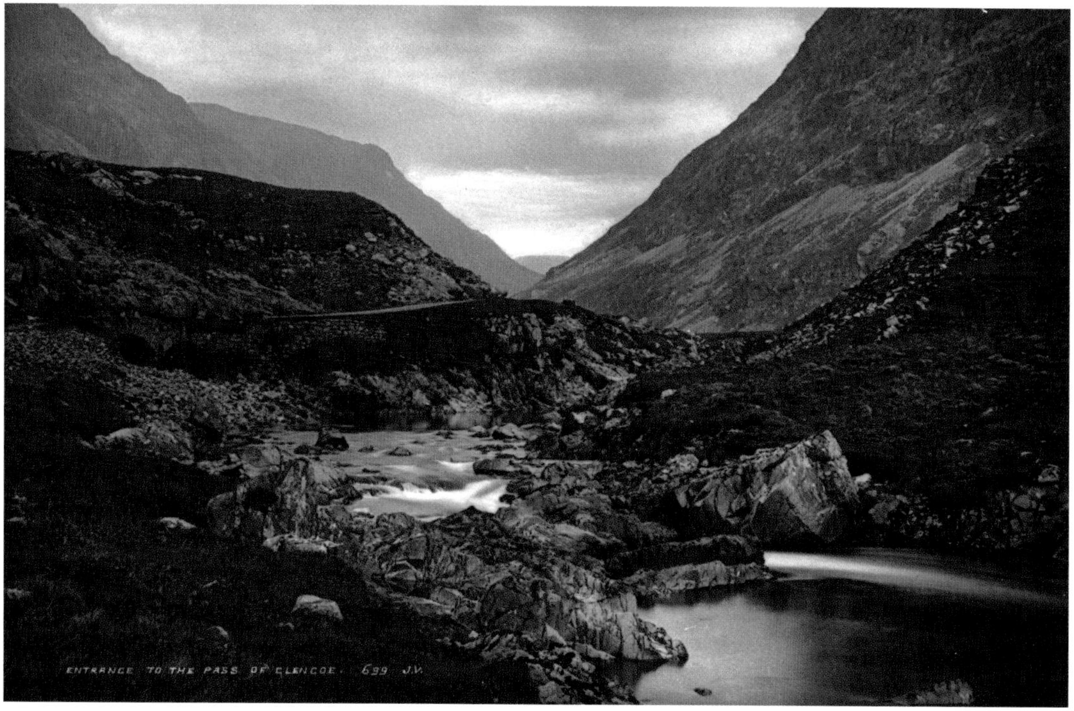

FIG.39
James Valentine
Glen Coe, Entrance to the Pass
1878

CHAPTER THREE

Land and the Landscape

Land and landscape may give rise to a host of atavistic emotions. It is not simply that the landscape will promote wonder, either in terms of the sublime or the beautiful, but that it is so often invested with 'identity'. Moreover this notion of identity is powerfully associated with a sense of nationhood, and consequently views the landscape as a substantiation of tribal tenure, historical connection and social incorporation. Landscape, then, is a special kind of memory; it is imbued with feelings and sentiments that seem to call up ancestral voices and pull at the collective consciousness. In this way landscape imagery will contain a complex set of meanings that are fundamentally ideological, and sometimes political. This would certainly be the case in 19th-century constructions of landscape, and sometimes also in 20th-century manifestations, but more enlightened views of the landscape have configured its role as natural environment. That is, the notion of ownership is overridden by the duty of custodianship; the land does not 'belong' to the group but exists independently as a natural force to be treasured and, sometimes, feared.

Landscape imagery, then, will carry these diverse and sometimes conflicting meanings. Certainly it can be viewed as the repository of a particular kind of memory, but it may also be presented as a poem to Nature, or be viewed as evidence for spiritual faith, or it may be that most deceptive thing, a 'window on the world'. However, it remains almost impossible to consider landscape images without a series of connections and relationships becoming manifest, and these are often, in the broadest sense of the term, 'national'. Historically, painters have been acutely aware of this, for landscape, whether classical, ideal, sublime, romantic, picturesque, modern or even abstract, has remained a loaded symbolic system created in order to trigger an almost primordial impulse. This is surely occasioned by the propensity of landscape imagery to help mediate the understanding of self, and self-consciousness, in relation to the exterior world. Through expansion and extension this fundamental self-knowledge metamorphoses into a kind of national self-consciousness. This has certainly been the case in landscape painting in Scotland. Whether in the romantic wilderness of Horatio McCulloch's Highland scenes, the flamboyant 'weatherscapes' of William McTaggart's Argyll, or the rural utopia that is James McIntosh Patrick's Angus, the 'sense of place' has been bounded by a sense of nation. Here, and throughout the tradition, it is not simply that the geography of these Scottish places is so distinctive, but that the ideological resonance of landscape necessitated a reflection also on history and ancestral 'presence'.

While these characteristics continued to tumble through the history of the painted landscape it might have been assumed that the invention of photography would realign this discourse. Photography was not simply a new medium but one that, potentially, gave access to a radicalised, democratic, 'realist' vision. The ideological aspect of the land and landscape could be opened up to a vernacular, politicised, indeed socialised survey. Consequently the elements of myth and identity might dissolve as the land became viewed as a political space wherein real social forces came into conflict. Within this paradigm the notion of 'ownership', for example, might become less a prerogative of race and more a consequence of social class. Equally, the sense of a shared history might be broken down into a fractured series of conflicts and tensions across political divides.

In fact the history of landscape photography, in Scotland and elsewhere, has demonstrated a curious resistance to the overturning of established ideological imperatives. Photography, as an aesthetic for image making, remained for decades after its invention a scion to the practice of fine art and the conventions of painting, most especially in the landscape photograph. In part this was determined by the fact that most early photographers, where they were not experimental scientists or enthusiastic amateurs of the new medium, were trained painters. Their vision, as it were, was shaped and conditioned by the customs of academic taste and sensibility. Moreover, the majority of early practitioners were closely attuned to the demands of the market. Even a new medium like photography would become filtered through a commercial system. Consequently the mass production of a particular photograph, while undermining the 'uniqueness' of the painted landscape image, nevertheless repeated, through emulation and imitation, its visual form and thereby its discreet ideological conditions.

Yet the new medium did afford significant opportunities for the disruption and interrogation of established cultural practice. Within the field of landscape some photographers would work at the edges of the established paradigm, most especially in the latter part of the 20th century and into the contemporary period. Here they began to re-evaluate the perception of landscape and the ideological imperatives present in the landscape image. Inevitably it was this work 'at the edges' that challenged the orthodoxies of landscape aesthetics and offered a quasi-political re-alignment of view, vista and scene.

Of course, sometimes a photograph is just a photograph and a landscape simply a landscape. Nevertheless, the most interesting aspects of landscape photography are revealed in those images that either wholly articulate the ideology of the form or open it out to challenge. Within the Scottish context both these options are in evidence and in abundance. Take, for example, James Valentine's (1815–80) photograph of *Glen Coe, Entrance to the Pass*, registered in 1878 [FIG.39], and compare this with Fay Godwin's (1931–2005) *Meall Mor, Glencoe*, taken in 1988 [FIG.40]. Valentine's Glencoe is every bit the 'land of the mountain and the flood'. It is a Highland archetype, steeply rising hillsides, rocky outcrops, a river of rapids and pools, with just the hint of a track or pathway. As a design it is set to connote the sense of wilderness and an awesome feeling for this barren, sublime beauty. Naturally

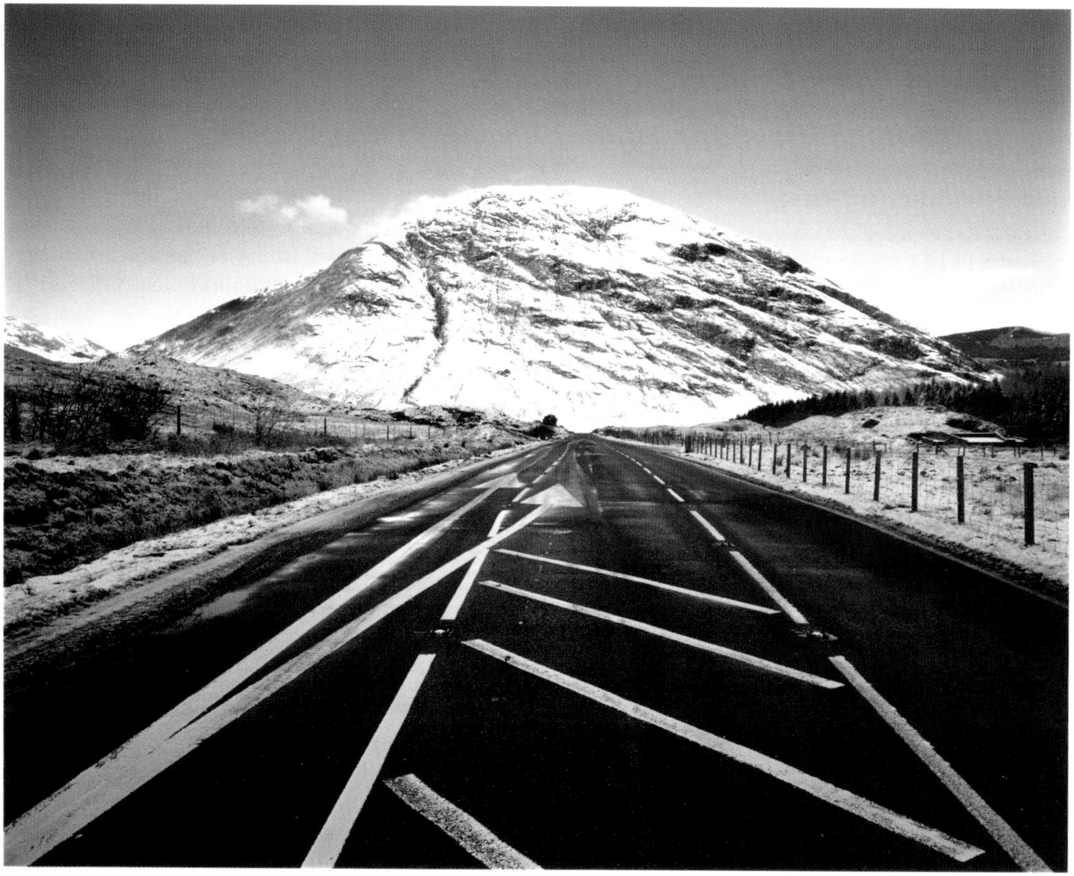

FIG.40
Fay Godwin
Meall Mor, Glencoe
1988

the historical associations are implicit, for this is the land of clannish dispute and 'Clearance', but the overriding mood is that of an untamed and untameable 'otherness'. This is the rhetorical flourish championed by painters like McCulloch and reinvented in acres of canvas adorning the walls of the Royal Scottish Academy throughout the 19th century. It is a memory of the physical geography that has defined and created Scotland's history and identity, or at least one aspect of that identity. Godwin's Glencoe is markedly different. She has focused her lens on Meall Mor, one of the many mountains in this range that has become a mecca for hillwalkers and ramblers. Godwin, who was born in Berlin, was an advocate for the right of access to the land and the need for environmental protection. Her photograph deliberately foregrounds the modern carriageway, and the roadside fence, that leads to the mountain. The tension here is clear, Godwin champions the majesty of nature while acknowledging the incursion of humankind. In this sense she reflects upon the dichotomy between the political necessity for open access and the potential harm to the landscape occasioned by that right. Throughout her work, in Scotland and elsewhere, this theme concerning the ethics of land and landscape remained a dominant interest.

Ethical concern was not, however, a marked note in more traditional landscape photographs. In fact the landscape photograph came to overreach the potential of the individual portrait as a commercial enterprise.

In this form it would illustrate tourist albums, picture books and every kind of popular journal. Consequently the panorama of the mountains and the countryside became a commonplace decoration of the Scottish home; a reminder of wild nature just beyond the edge of the expanding city.

Panoramas

Soon after its invention the new medium of the photograph was to be exploited as a necessary tool in the development of parallel new and burgeoning industries; leisure, travel and tourism. Importantly, the invention of the camera coincided almost exactly with the development of the railway system, and the railway system created a pathway for the modern industry of tourism. The first, local, railway lines began to emerge in Scotland during the 1830s, while the major Edinburgh and Glasgow line was opened in 1842. By the mid 1840s railway companies were expanding across the Scottish Lowlands, and the Highlands themselves were opened up from the mid 1850s. Railways, of course, were a necessary prerequisite of a successful industrial economy and an interconnected urban infrastructure. However, they also accommodated the related social processes of leisure, travel and sightseeing. In 1846 Thomas Cook was to organise the first 'package' holiday to Scotland. The new class of leisured consumers, anxious to experience the scenic splendours of the Highland wilderness, journeyed from the industrial and commercial centres to the 'untamed' lands already celebrated in academic landscape painting. A flight from the urban centre to the marginal wilderness was only complete when a souvenir marked the journey. Given the confluence of the new technologies it was inevitable that this marker would be the photograph, and thereby was established the commercial mass market for landscape photography.

This vigorous commercial market fed on a specific vision of Scotland chiefly informed by Romantic literature. Much has been written on Sir Walter Scott's role in constructing a vision of Scotland and 'Scottishness'. The success of the ballad poems 'The Lady of the Lake' (1810) and 'The Lord of the Isles' (1815), as well as the Scottish-based novels like *Rob Roy* (1818), helped to create a sentiment for national feeling based on an epic, and tragic, national history. More importantly, the majestic descriptions of landscape focused this history on the monumental panorama that is Scotland's Highland geography. In Scott landscape became, unequivocally and exceptionally, the repository of history and nation. The extraordinary international success of his writing created an archetype of 'Scotland' as a land of mountain and flood, hill and heather, loch and glen. A wilderness wherein nature lay untamed and the people adapted, imperfectly, to its violent tempers.

This association was marked at the very dawn of photography by the English claimant to the invention of the medium, William Henry Fox Talbot (1800–77). Talbot's second album of photographs was titled 'Sun Pictures in Scotland' and was published in 1845. This book consisted of some 'twenty-three photographic views... connected with the life and writings of Sir Walter Scott.'[1] Talbot had taken these photographs in 1844 and was paying homage to, and recognising, the immense popularity of Scott's work in the mid 19th century. Consequently he included images of Scott's home, Abbotsford House, and of Scott's resting place in Dryburgh Abbey. He also established something of a fashion for photographs taken in and around Loch Katrine [FIG.41], already made famous as the picturesque setting of Scott's landmark poem 'The Lady of the Lake'. Talbot was prescient in creating this album, for it was Scott's reputation, and the romantic vision of Scotland that he popularised, that would become the staple of landscape photographers for the ensuing decades and deep into the 20th century. Indeed Talbot's views of Loch Katrine, and there were seven of these produced in 'Sun Pictures', set the tone and established the paradigm for the Highland landscape photograph.

Talbot's vision of scenic grandeur, informed as it was by Scott's romanticism, could not be further from the industrialised, urbanised, modern Scotland of the 19th century, but this archetype was dominant. In part this process was assisted by Queen Victoria's residences in the Highlands, and the culture of 'Balmoralism' that flowed from her Highland holidaying. Victoria purchased the Balmoral estate, on the banks of the River Dee, in 1848 and set about having the castle restored. Subsequently it would be established

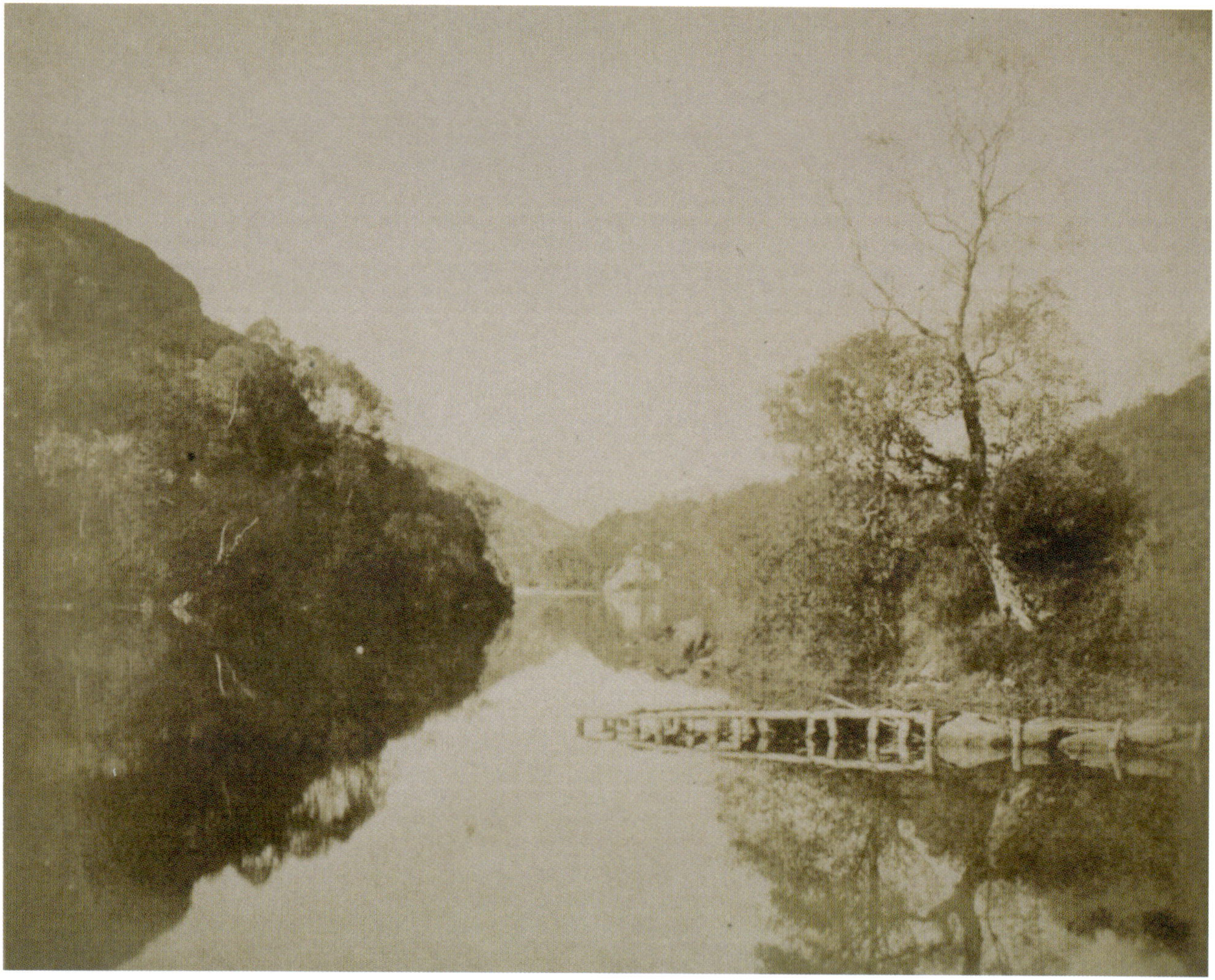

FIG.41
William Henry Fox Talbot
Loch Katrine from 'Sun Pictures'
1844

as a summer residence so that the fashionable middle classes would soon identify a Highland holiday as a privilege sanctioned and authorised by the aristocracy. Victoria's favoured photographer was George Washington Wilson, who was given exclusive access to the Royal Family at Balmoral, and who produced the iconic image of Victoria on horseback attended by her servant John Brown. From 1855 Wilson was a familiar figure at Balmoral, where he helped satisfy the Queen's enthusiasm for the new medium of photography by producing images of her family and her staff. Simultaneously he produced photographs that catalogued the rebuilding of the castle and documented the scenic splendours of the surrounding landscape.

It was these landscape photographs that became Wilson's signature form. While he remained a noted portraitist, and produced in his 'Highlands and Islands' series an intriguing document of peasant life in the Western Isles, his prestige and historical importance lay in the countless landscape images that were to decorate the travelogues, swell the treasured albums, furnish the stereoscopes and, eventually, accumulate in the curio shops of Scotland's back streets. Through the 1850s and beyond, however, Wilson presented Scotland to the world in a visual form that was uniquely accessible. Moreover, he was no journeyman photographer. His photographs, informed by a training in the fine arts, explored the full potential of the new medium such that a feeling for movement, natural light and spacial dynamics was balanced against a sense of composition, tone and harmony. Indeed, Wilson's technical skill in this respect was noted in the period. Writing in the journal *Photographic Notes*, dated 1 November 1860, the editor comments:

> You look at a hundred views by Mr. Wilson, and... there is in them a mellowness of effect, a tone over the sky and highest lights, and an amount of detail in the deepest shadows, which realise natural truth... In his instantaneous pictures Mr. Wilson has succeeded not only in getting the clouds, the ripple of the water, and figures in motion, but in combining in the same picture the full details of the shadow.[2]

Consequently, at his best, he produced some of the most skilled, dramatic and poignant images of the Highland landscape.

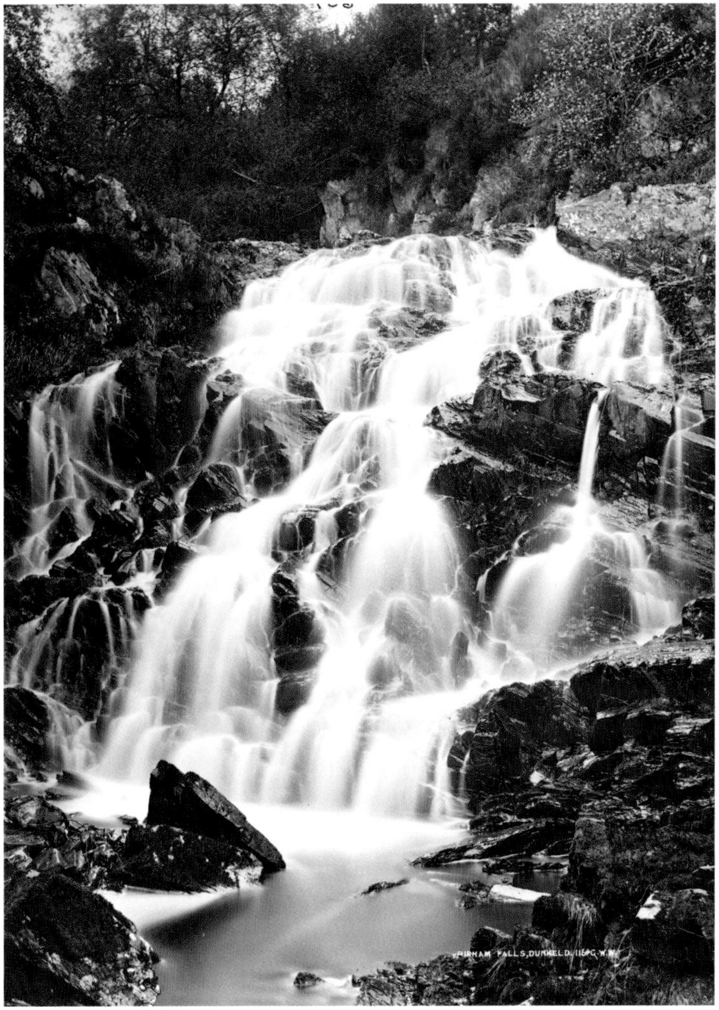

FIG.42
George Washington Wilson
Birnam Falls, Dunkeld
circa 1860

Amongst the many subjects and scenes that Washington and his company would photograph there is an interesting sub-set of waterfall images. His *Birnam Falls, Dunkeld* [FIG.42] is an attractive example of this theme. There is, of course, a subtle historical and literary allusion to Shakespeare's *Macbeth*, where 'Birnam Wood to high Dunsinane Hill shall come against him', but Wilson's concern was with the broken waters of the steep fall. At one level this is a study in nature's power; the foaming waters break

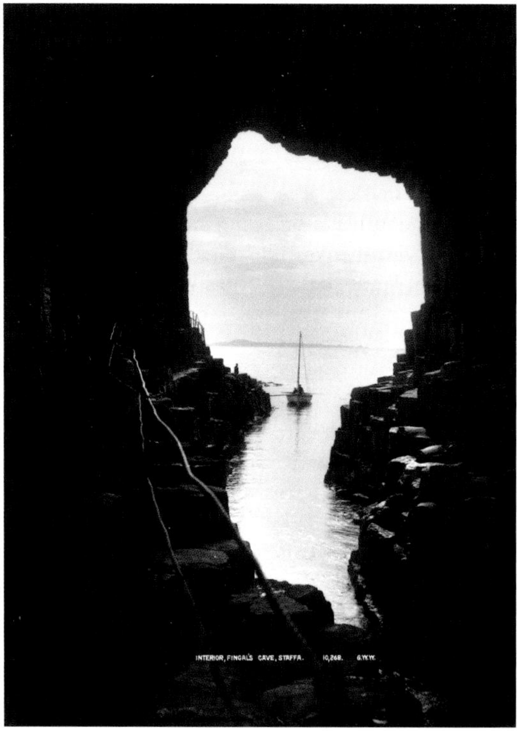

FIG.43
George Washington Wilson
Interior of Fingal's Cave, Staffa
after 1853

across the rocks and cut a serrulated path through the outcrops of stone. Simultaneously, this image allowed for an interest in textures and surfaces; the background foliage contrasting with the jagged rocks, the falling water eliding into the still pool. Above all, however, this is an example of the concern with time and movement. In the image of a waterfall the camera might perform its most novel trick, freezing the moment while allowing for the convincing impression of water in motion.

One other fascinating example of Wilson's talent is his image of the *Interior of Fingal's Cave, Staffa*, taken some time after 1853 [FIG.43]. The sea-cave itself, situated on the Isle of Staffa to the north of Iona on the west coast of Scotland, would become a landmark site in Scottish photography. Its unique stratification, formed from hexagonal columns of cooled tertiary basalt lava, lends it the air of a natural cathedral and so it became celebrated in painting and photography and, of course, in music, for Felix Mendelssohn's *The Hebrides: Fingal's Cave* would become a standard of the Victorian repertoire. Wilson, like other photographers, took images of the impressive cave entrance and the astonishing pillars that shaped the island's geography. It was possible for Wilson to sail into the sea-cave itself, and indeed to step across the hexagonal columns into the deep inner recesses of the cave. This he has done for his interior view, a remarkable photograph that is framed by the dark cave walls and looks outward to the fissure of light at the cave's entrance, a dramatic and early example of photographing a scene against the prevailing light. He has also, in the picturesque manner, allowed his transport, a single-mast fishing boat, to bob at the cave's opening and so complete a scene that is at once evocative and unsettling.

Yet it is inescapable that Wilson was nakedly commercial in his enterprise; his typical viewpoint was panoramic and he was implicitly romantic in his selection of subjects. His studio grew inexorably with the development of tourism and Wilson turned the production of photographic landscapes into a manufacturing industry. There is a famous photograph of his printing works in St Swithin's Street, Aberdeen. A long open courtyard furnished with wooden trestles, surrounded on each side with developing and printing sheds, and peopled by a host of women workers. It is a sunlit scene, for the women are engaged in the laborious process of setting out the printed sheets to develop in the natural daylight.[3] For all the world this was a rudimentary form of factory production. The intensive nature of this production was exacerbated by the difficulty in collecting the images. Each negative could produce only one contact print so that Wilson, having located his scene, was forced to take a number of identical exposures in order to fully satisfy the public demand. In these senses, at least, he was as much an entrepreneur as an artist.

Wilson's acute sense of commerce and trade in respect of the new medium was further highlighted by his choice of scene. He fed on images of royalty, but more significantly on the mythic vistas of Scotland's romanticised history. He specialised in ruined castles, historic battle sites like Killiecrankie and tragic memorials like the Pass of Glencoe. Naturally, he also explored those vistas closely associated with the literature of Sir Walter Scott. Hence his many views of 'The Silver Strand' on Loch Katrine and his emblematic views of Abbotsford. These are often stirring and evocative panoramas. Certainly, at their best, they are technical marvels, especially given the unpromising conditions of their production. However, it is their ideological and political properties that remain fascinating. In some degree Wilson was 'branding' Scotland for the tourist market. More significantly he was invoking a sense of 'nationhood' that splintered from the modern industrial Scotland of the central belt and asserted the dominance of a recidivist, politically inert sentimentalism.

None of this was unusual in Victorian culture. To a great extent Wilson was guilty only of democratising an aesthetic already established in the 'ben and glen' romanticism of the Royal Scottish Academy. His success, however, spawned a host of imitators, most notably the Dundee-based James Valentine, who is famously said to have wandered the Scottish countryside looking for the holes laid down by Wilson's tripod. Valentine, if anything, was the greater entrepreneur, establishing an industry that impinged upon Wilson's souvenir images and a company that very nearly cornered the market in picture postcards. To some extent these two pioneers were the progenitors of the entire commercial system in Scotland.

Like Wilson, Valentine was a master of the panorama. He looked to create a vision that was epic, heroic, aggrandising and perfectly attuned to the mythologies of Scotland's nationhood. And, of course, he looked to make this vision profitable. The Valentine company, which specialised in printing and lithography, had been established in the city of Dundee by John Valentine in 1825. James Valentine would develop the family business by moving into the new medium of photography, and he was first sent to Paris in order to learn the mysteries of the daguerreotype process in the 1840s. Subsequently he would have associations with that other colossus of commercial landscape photography, Francis Frith, who had set up studios in Reigate, Surrey, during the 1860s. The high point of James Valentine's involvement with photography was in the period after 1866 when he photographed landscape views in Scotland under the patronage of Queen Victoria. In 1878 the business was administered by one of his sons, William Dobson Valentine (1844–1907), and it was during this time that the engagement with the picture postcard market was established. All of these developments led to a thriving industry that published albums, view-books, illustrated tourist guides and individual landscape prints, as well as the profitable postcard and greeting-card images. Many of these were Scottish scenes, which were now taken by the host of journeymen photographers employed by the firm. Still more were works bought from other firms and photographers, including George Washington Wilson's own company.[4] Such was the ambition of the Valentine company, however, that they also produced scenic views from around the world. While most of this latter group were photographs purchased from indigenous firms and individuals there exists a fascinating group of landscape images of New Zealand taken by a younger son, George Dobson Valentine (1852–90), during a recuperative retreat to the antipodes in the period circa 1885.

This was a prosperous and expanding industry, and the Valentine archive holds images of every possible vista and view from throughout Britain, and some from around the world.[5] A typical Valentine picture of the Scottish scene might include a loch or sea, a castle or landmark, some mountainous or coastal terrain, and a big sky; in fact every cliché of the scenic backcloth. A typical example would be *Castles Sinclair and Girnigoe, Wick*, first registered by the company in 1891 [FIG.44]. This photograph of twin ruined castles in the far north of the country is interesting because of the way it melds historic time and geological time. The picture shows the remains of Girnigoe Castle, a 15th-century keep and the older of the two structures. Though within the county of Caithness, this was a fiefdom of the Earls of Orkney and when the older castle fell into disrepair a further structure, Castle Sinclair, was built on the same promontory in 1642. Cromwell's troops were garrisoned in this castle during the period of the interregnum and it became the focus for further

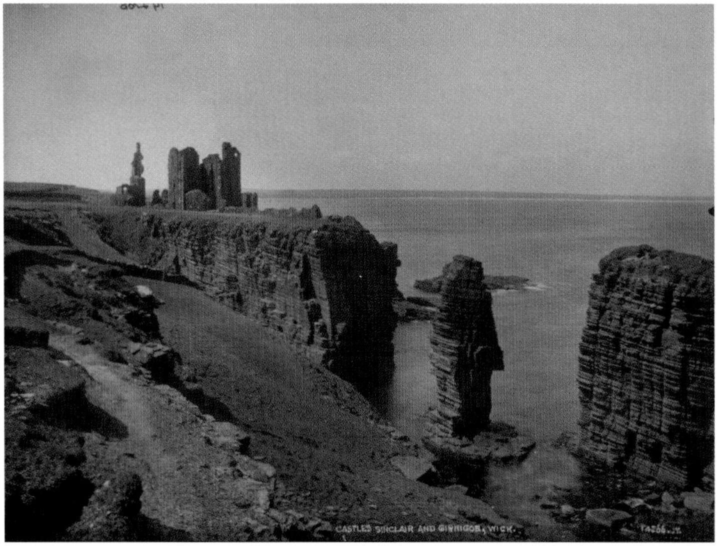

FIG.44
James Valentine
Castles Sinclair and Girnigoe, Wick
1891

conflict at the end of the 17th century. After this Castle Sinclair went the way of its predecessor, and now two ruins sit together on a headland that is gradually being eroded by the action of the turbulent North Sea. The image of these ruined castles, as portrayed by Valentine, was a poignant reminder of Scotland's troubled history, but the juxtaposition with the striated and fractured rock formations was doubly affecting. The twin castles were, here, mirrored in the dual sense of time; the one historic and human, the other geological and environmental. Moreover, the combination of these qualities produced an image that was, and remains, extraordinarily elegiac. Of course it is unlikely that Valentine's photographers were fully conscious of these esoteric nuances, but they were an endemic part of the sentiment of Scotland's landscape photography and the best of Valentine's images are replete with such references.

The best of Valentine's photography was, however, an increasingly rare commodity as the company grew exponentially and the production of photographs became industrial in scale. This industry remained prolific throughout the first half of the 20th century, eventually being bought over in the early part of the 1960s. Valentine's company, and the company history, remains a testament to the enduring taste for landscape photography in the modern period. Moreover, this was a landscape photography that sought to produce not simply tourist views and mementoes but intricate images loaded with symbolic meaning. If commerce would eventually overwhelm this sentiment it did not completely obliterate the desire. Nevertheless Valentine, and Wilson too, were working within an ideological frame that privileged a romantic sense of the landscape tradition. Meanwhile, a space was opening up for competing or parallel projects within the paradigm of landscape photography, projects that were partly political, potentially environmentalist, and just possibly 'spiritual'.

It might be argued that the tensions inherent in landscape photography, and the potential for a radical 'socially conscious' landscape imagery, began to be realised in the career of Robert Moyes Adam (1885–1967). With Adam the demands for commercial imagery were resisted largely because he was, in a qualified sense, an amateur cameraman. Likewise, the temper to produce standard images with recognisable historical associations was mitigated by Adam's sense of nature and the natural. He was, perhaps, one of the first photographers to consciously document the environment from the point of view of an environmentalist. In this sense, at least, he helped to reshape the conventions of landscape photography in Scotland.

It is significant that Adam was, in the professional sense, not a photographer at all, but made his living as a botanist.[6] Yet he can be recognised as perhaps the most significant photographer of his generation in Scotland, and was certainly one of the most successful. Adam was essentially a landscape photographer who specialised in images of Scotland's mountain wilderness, of the Highlands and Islands, and of the remoter areas of the mainland. He produced, throughout his life, some 15,000 glass-plate negatives, all carefully catalogued and systematised. Moreover, he developed the process of printing to a fine art such that his original prints were technically superior to the illustrative material that was the common currency.[7] Consequently, his work became a feature of publications on the Scottish scene, being reproduced in travel books, histories, poetry books, and throughout the panoply of popular magazines and newspapers. Indeed his archive would eventually become stock material in the holdings of the publishers D. C. Thomson of Dundee, where it accompanied, as illustrative material, their many and diverse titles.[8]

This commercial aspect to his work occurred almost by accident for, in a practical sense, Adam was an amateur and photography was simply his hobby. Indeed, he approached the activity with the single-minded commitment of the enthusiastic hobbyist, but it was never his main income stream. Significantly, in the era of Paul Strand and Henri Cartier-Bresson, of Ansel Adams and Group f.64, of Bill Brandt and 'Picture Post', Scotland's most important photographer was a civil servant employed as an assistant in the Botanical Gardens in Edinburgh.

Despite these contradictions Adam intervened in the project of landscape photography at a number of levels. In some degree he was instrumental in conjuring an emblematic 'landscape of association' that would parallel and overwhelm the fine art tradition. In this respect he inherited and developed the mission of 19th-century landscape photography. More significantly he created a sense of the Scottish landscape that was panoramic in its vision and epic in its scale, scope and range. In doing this he generated a notion of the contemporary landscape as a frontier world, on the edge of urban and urbane society and suffused with the menace and majesty of nature. Simultaneously, however, he visualised the landscape as a democratic panorama opened out to the people and available for access through the emerging popular activities of rambling, hillwalking and climbing. As an adjunct to these themes he touched on issues that were prescient in their profound ecological concerns. In all, he gave expression to an idea of landscape that reflected the social and the psychological needs of people in a contemporary and changing Scotland. Here, then, he gives the lie to his amateur status, for his photographs give access to some of the most important cultural themes of 20th-century Scotland.

At their core Adam's landscapes were panoramic and epic, and in this sense he parallels the aesthetic of his American namesake, Ansel Adams.[9] Formally, he sought out views that emphasised the sweep of the land, pinpointing multiple horizons where broken peaks and steep cliffs created a sense of the unending, near impenetrable, Highland.[10] His *Skye Peaks and Mists, Amid the High Tops of the Cuillins, View from Sgurr Na Banachdich* [FIG.45] is a case in point, for here the peaks and glens assert an awe-inspiring notion of rugged and broken mountaintop. The combined textures of the image, from the scree in the foreground, to the silhouetted mountain backdrop, and on to the billowing mist and cloud, all combine to emphasise a view of the land that transcends the picturesque and even the sublime. It is a panorama of a world at once solid, enduring and near unfathomable. It might be noted in these respects that Adam adopts a viewpoint that is, generally, the opposite of Ansel Adams' positioning. Whereas Ansel Adams would usually look upwards towards the monumental cliffs of the Yosemite Valley as in *Monolith, The Face of the Half Dome, Yosemite Valley, California*, of 1927, Robert Moyes Adam made a virtue of travelling on the high tops and pointing his camera across the peaks. At once then, the Highlands of Scotland become intimidating, endless and curiously intimate.

This notion of journey, however, becomes an important feature of the photographs. In *Mists Over the Cuillins, Sgurr Nan Gillean and the River Sligachan in Flood* we are presented with the vista that we are about to view from the top of Sgurr Na Banachdich. The photograph combines the promise of a more universal view, yet to be realised, with a sense of the effort, physical and mental, involved in reaching this goal. Those few critics who have commented on Robert Moyes Adam's work have noted his insistence on the journey as a component part in taking the photograph.[11] In a rare interview with Jeremy Bruce-Watt, from 1958, Adam notes, 'I used to make a speciality of pictures taken from the summits of hills... Not more than two per cent of all I took are taken from anywhere near a road.'[12] Here is a key feature of his relationship with the land. The land is a kind of challenge where an elemental human relationship with nature might be acted out. In this event the photograph is evidence of triumph, but the panoramic view of multiple horizons

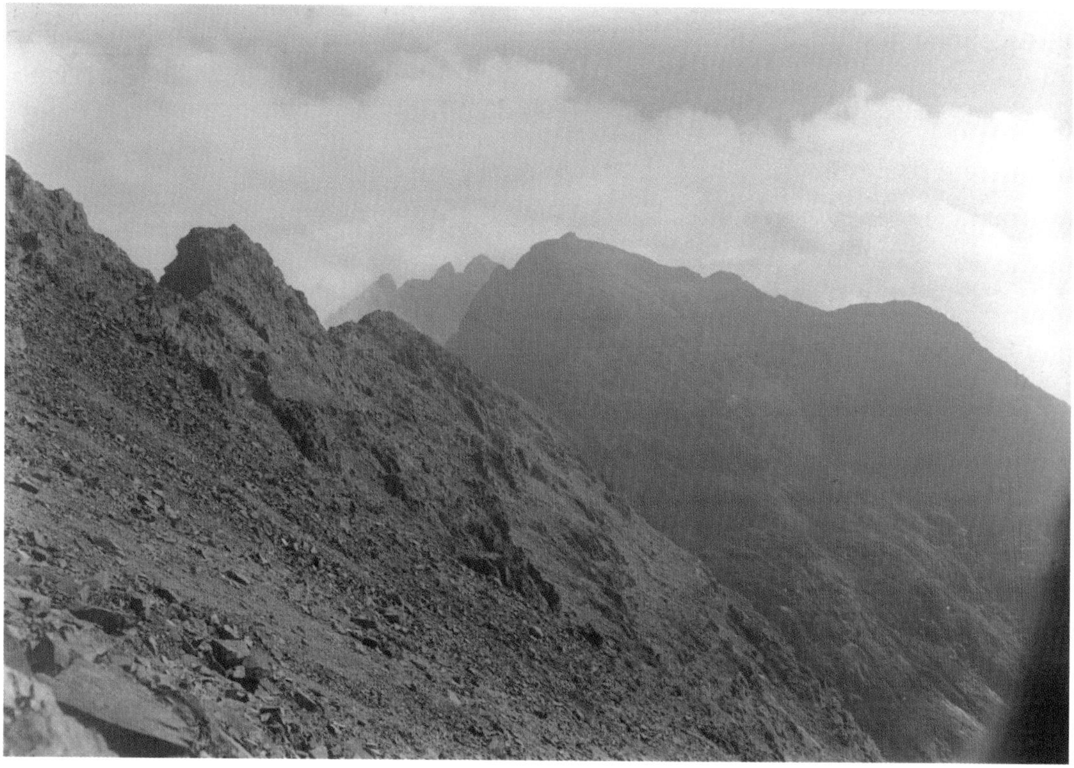

FIG.45
Robert Moyes Adam
Skye Peaks and Mists, Amid the High Tops of the Cuillins, View from Sgurr Na Banachdich
1926

accents the idea of an unending journey, of peaks yet to be scaled. The landscape, then, grows into an unconquerable, limitless presence.

Importantly, the sublime and imposing aspect of these panoramas is often allied to a notion of geographical time. The hills are significant for Adam because they speak of infinite vistas and unimaginable periods of time. Hence the photographs will often emphasise rocks and mountains formed out of glacial shifts and geological faults. *The Cleft of Slochd Mor, Looking Towards Glen Avon, in the Cairngorms* is a case in point. The sweeping glen in the foreground connotes a sense of the ages-old passage of ice through the Scottish Highlands. When this is combined with the photograph of *The Lairig Ghru Pass and the Pools of Dee, in the Cairngorms*, where snow lies between broken rocks and water and this is set off against a backdrop of steeply sloping mountainsides, the idea of an elemental landscape is complete. We are drawn in to a vision of nature as a sustaining force that exists before and beyond human enterprise.

As an adjunct to this geological consciousness it is noteworthy how many of Adam's images are concerned with weather and weather systems. *Sgurr Alasdair, the Highest Point of the Cuillins, Isle of Skye* [FIG.46] is typical in the way the tops are wrapped in cloud and a billowing mist, which falls into the glen. This is not mere sentiment, nor can it be reduced to the level of the crassly romantic; these features are symbolic of a deeper sense of the elemental forces that form, shape and change this landscape through geological time. In this way we are confronted with an epic, nature-oriented vision.

While the panoramic photographs of Robert Moyes Adam are concerned with time and nature understood on this epic scale, it is also true that he

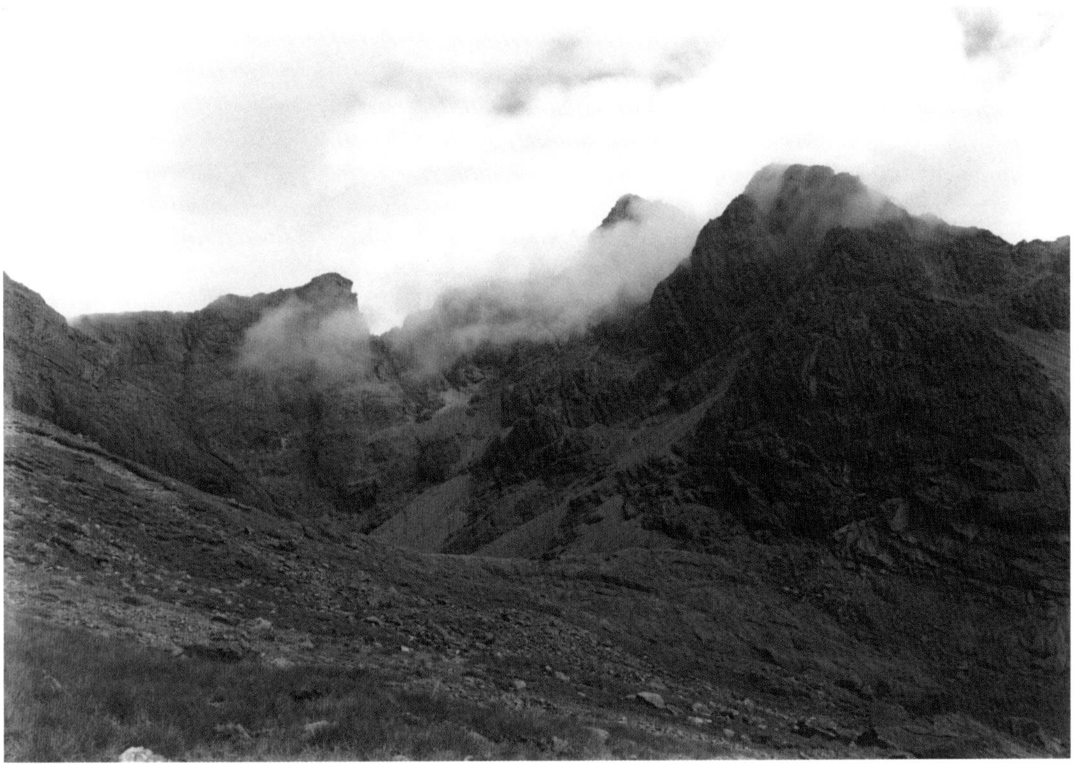

FIG.46
Robert Moyes Adam
Sgurr Alasdair, the Highest Point of the Cuillins, Isle of Skye
1926

produced many images concerned with historical time. It was in this aspect of his work that he ran close to the 'landscape of association', the idea that symbolic sites and places connote a sense of the history of the nation and its people. This, of course, had been a feature of the history of photography in the 19th century, when places like Glencoe and Killiecrankie became the stock images of the studio system, notably in the photographs of Wilson and Valentine. Adam was not immune to this approach, and indeed he was chosen to represent the 'sacred' sites of Scottish history in Alexander Maclehose's enormously popular *Historic Haunts of Scotland*, published in 1936. Adam's view of *Glencoe* has a lineage that goes back to Wilson, but as an image the deep glen and imposing peaks simultaneously parallel his visual meditations on geological time.

Glencoe, however, is a significant site because of its association with the massacre of the Macdonalds by the Campbells in the political turmoil following the first Jacobite uprising of 1689. This massacre, which took place in 1692, was part of the subjugation of the Highlands by William III and remained a mythic memory in Scottish history well into the 20th century. Interestingly Adam also took related images like *Killiecrankie*, the site of the defining moment of the first Jacobite uprising where a small Scottish guerrilla army led by John Graham of Claverhouse, Viscount of Dundee and a supporter of James VII, routed the government troops led by one General Mackay. In fact Dundee was killed in this action and from this point the rebellion declined. Adam's atmospheric photograph focuses, not on the Pass of Killiecrankie, but on a snow-covered patch of land broken by four leafless trees. The symbolism of this image is evident, representing isolated and lifeless form subsumed by the tragedy of a winter frost. To this group of images it is appropriate to add his *Dulsie Bridge*, which shows one of the bridges across the River Findhorn. This particular bridge is usually credited to Field Marshal George Wade and signifies that process where military roads were built in the Highlands, in the period between the 1715 and 1745 rebellions, in order to allow military communications and better control the insurgent Highland clans. Clearly these photographs belong to a tradition of historical association that was a commonplace, indeed a cliché, of Scottish landscape, and are designed to resonate with a sense of tragic history. Adam, then, was also a 'bearer' of the tradition, so that the tension between the 19th-century conventions of landscape photography and the 20th-century reappraisal become manifest in his diverse works.

In this respect it is noteworthy that Adam was also interested in the early history of Scotland and some of his most poignant images relate to this half-remembered time. In *Historic Haunts of Scotland* he reproduced a photograph of a *Pictish Broch, North Sutherland*, a dark-age fortress designed as a place of refuge from marauding Vikings. One of his most interesting photographs is *Cross at Loch Aline* [FIG.47], a composite image uniting an early Celtic Christian cross with a dramatic luminescent sky.[13] These photographs develop the geological history of Scotland into the human history in a manner that unites land and people and time. In this way Adam was compiling and constructing a visual representation of the nation, but one that would continually accent the land as something separate; touched by human history, certainly, but enduring and independent of that history.

For all these ambitions it must be noted that Adam was not particularly interested in industrial Scotland. His photograph of *A Colliery Near Kelty in Fife* is significant for the way he marginalises the industrial architecture of pit-head and chimney stacks, and foregrounds the 'stooks' of the cornfield.[14] His vision was profoundly rural, but even this description underplays the ideational momentum of Adam's landscape photography. In fact Adam was most interested in the idea of a wilderness or 'frontier' landscape. This is partially evidenced in his fascination for the high tops of the Highland ranges, but it was also a feature of his earliest work. Adam's first memorable work with the camera was undertaken in 1905 when he travelled to the Hebrides in order to photograph colonies of kittiwake gulls on the island of Mingulay.[15] The key images emerging from this visit, however, were portraits of the native inhabitants who lived a subsistence lifestyle. Adam produced images of a populace living at the very edge of civilisation and bordering on extinction. In fact there was a significant depopulation of Mingulay in 1908, and the island was abandoned by 1912. Adam's photographs, here, have an anthropological and elegiac quality. His *Calum McPhee, Slopes of Hackla, Mingulay*, from 1905, is a heroic image of survival in confrontation with the elements. Likewise his *Children of Mingulay*, from the same year, is an extraordinary vision of dignity in the face of hardship that notably presages the archetypal imagery of Walker Evans and Dorothea Lange in the 'dustbowl' of American economic depression during the 1930s.

However, the sense of the frontier in Adam's work is both practical and metaphorical. He examines the real frontiers that are the wild and barren hills, places nearly impenetrable and resistant to cultivation. And he explores the condition and character of those individuals who exist on the edge of this frontier, the barely habitable lands where subsistence is always contingent on the whims of nature. In its entirety this vision functions as a metaphor, not for the appropriation of land and landscape, but for the resistance of such to the conceit of human colonisation. It is a frontier vision in the sense of marking out the point at which human hubris is challenged and overwhelmed. In essence he is examining the moment when the contest between humankind and nature reaches stalemate, and his photographs containing the human figure are often heroic images of individuals at that absolute edge.

Yet, paradoxically, throughout the period when Adam was picturing the Scottish scene the land was becoming a social space where a new political dynamic was unfolding. If at one level Adam was visualising a natural world that was somehow inviolable, at another he was instrumental in opening out those forbidden and forbidding places. Through-

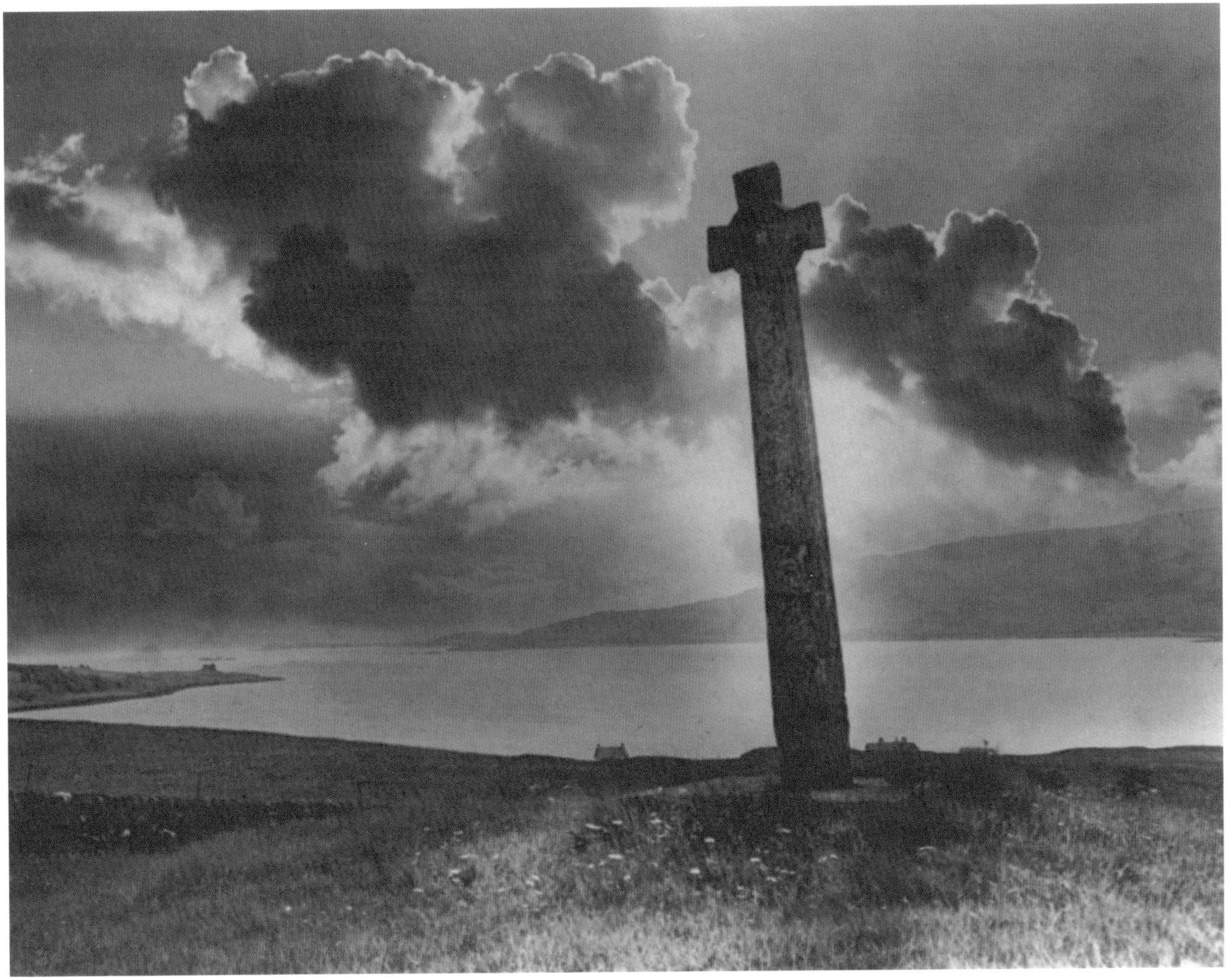

FIG.47
Robert Moyes Adam
Cross at Loch Aline
1919

out the 1930s and beyond, the Scottish hills were to become a terrain for ramblers, hillwalkers and climbers.[16] His photograph of 1920, *Celebrated Climber Harold Raeburn on Salisbury Crags*, documents this type of activity, but in fact the hills were soon to be colonised on weekend visits by the urban working class. One aspect of a newly mobile inner city populace, now accommodated by trains, buses and cars, was the desire to free itself from the towns and cities and factories and shipyards, and to experience the wilds of Scotland. A literature began to surround this phenomenon and interestingly it was Adam's work, particularly in the *Scots Magazine*, which illustrated the new nirvana. In fact the first photograph reproduced in Hugh Quigley's *The Highlands of Scotland* is Adam's *The Climber: Beneath the Cliffs of Cairn Lochan in the Cairngorms*.

There is little doubt that Adam welcomed this development, for he was a major benefactor of the transport timetables, the 'bothy' system and the commercial interest in the hills, but he was also sensitive to one crucial by-product of these changes. It is important to recall that Adam was, by profession, a botanist. His principal employment in the Botanical Gardens was to produce photographic illustrations of flora and fauna. Equally, when travelling in the Highlands he would often take pictures of rare plant species and his attitude to the environment generally was protective. There is, then, in Adam's work an incipient ecological element. A number of points highlight this idea. At least one of Adam's photographs displays signage that requests ramblers to desist from picking or stepping on the indigenous plant life of upland Scotland. Adam would take this image precisely because it was, for him, a heartfelt plea, a signal of the fragile ecology and a testament to the need for conservation in the face of new social pressures on the land. Likewise he offered a confession to Jeremy Bruce-Watt concerning the significance of the image *Winter in Strathspey*, taken in January 1946 [FIG.48]. This photograph, which was 'hard-won' in the sense that like so many of Adam's photographs it required planning and patience, depicted for him an emblematic and highly significant birch tree. Adam regarded this tree as an icon of a mature and meaningful ecological system. Bruce-Watt noted that, 'Adam took a long time to get this picture and is eminently satisfied with the result. The tree, he says sadly, has now been felled. For him there will never be another quite like it.'[17] For Adam every single item in the ecology of the Highlands was precious and irreplaceable, and therefore required protection.

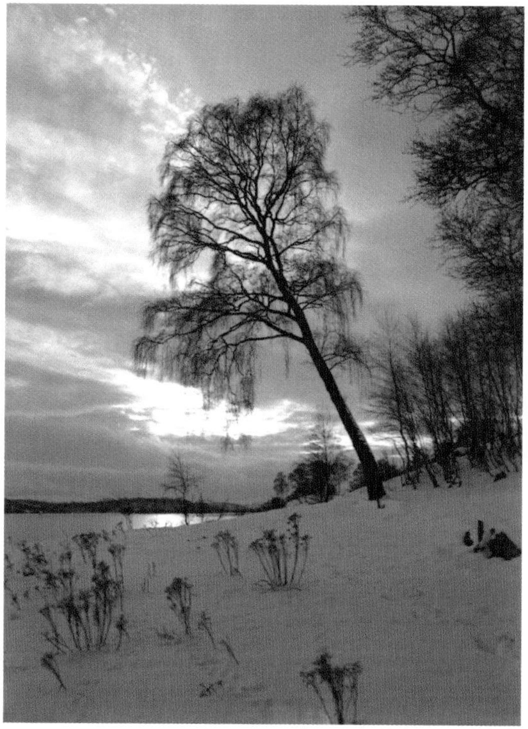

FIG.48
Robert Moyes Adam
Winter in Strathspey
1946

Finally, it is important to note Adam's role in mitigating the impact of hydroelectric stations and quasi-industrial developments in the Highlands. As early as 1929, at the point where hydroelectric developments were first being proposed, Adam began to photograph areas under threat. This was particularly the case in Glen Affric, where the proposed scheme threatened to despoil an area of ancient forest and outstanding natural beauty. An associate of Adam, Mary Noble, has recalled how:

> Two of Adam's black and white photographs were especially satisfying to him as a pioneering conservationist. In 1929 hydroelectric schemes seemed to

> threaten many of Scotland's most beautiful and important landscapes especially in the North. His pictures of the old Caledonian forest in Glen Affric are said to have persuaded the authorities to avoid the despoiling of the whole land.[18]

Adam's images, then, would become instrumental in the re-evaluation of the schemes to develop the Highlands, and stand in defence of ecological and conservation interests.

At root Adam attempted to be the conscience of nature in the modern world. While a fraction of his photographs conform to the conventions of commercial landscape imagery, it can be argued that he subtly radicalised the tradition. For Adam represented the landscape in its elemental form; he visualised and articulated the frontier between civilisation and the untamed spaces; he reflected on the changing nature of the hills as a social space; and he reminded the new travellers, ramblers, tourists and settlers of their ecological duty. This new social and environmental consciousness in landscape photography would become one of its most significant features during the later 20th century.

Aerial panoramas and semi-abstract verticals

Landscape imagery contained the potential for critical interventions that stepped beyond the clichéd commercialism of Wilson, Valentine and the studio system. And it can be argued that Robert Moyes Adam's panoramas of the 'high-tops' helped initiate this more analytical approach. Something of this critical mission has been developed in the extraordinary imagery of Patricia Macdonald (b. 1945), an artist-photographer of the environment whose most usual viewpoint is from the air.[19] Simultaneously, Macdonald's work has been profoundly influenced by American and European traditions of aerial photography.

Aerial photography has been a feature of the medium almost since its inception. In 1858 the French photographer Nadar journeyed by balloon over the city of Paris and recorded its prospect from the air, a vision that must have been as strange as it was novel. Nadar's balloon was a massive affair, complete with gondola carriages and an integrated darkroom. Some 60 years later Alfred G. Buckham (1880–1953) would take his astonishing photograph *Aerial View of Edinburgh* [FIG.49], circa 1920, centred upon the Castle Rock and incorporating a mist surrounding Holyrood and the base of Salisbury Crags, as well as an impressive cumulus cloud formation and an accompanying biplane. Buckham had been an aerial reconnaissance photographer during the First World War, and it was at this time that the mainstream tradition of aerial photography was initiated and developed. In the contemporary period, in Scotland, Gunnie Moberg has taken landscape photographs from the air in order to complete her photobook *Stone* with images that parallel the poems of George Mackay Brown. Also, an interesting variation on 'aerial' photography has been developed by Mark Johnston (b. 1963), who, having graduated from Glasgow School of Art, began to photograph the ancient stone circles of Scotland by improvising a camera attached to a six-metre pole that rotated in a circle and created a montage image of the sites.[20] However, the pre-eminent aerial photographer of recent times has been Patricia Macdonald.

Aerial photography lends a formal fascination to Macdonald's work, for the unaccustomed perspective of the low-flying aircraft produces shapes and patterns in the landscape that approach abstraction. The images, however, most often denote the imprint of human activity on the land, and project, on occasion, a sense of unease. Macdonald's background, in biological science, has made her sensitive to environmental issues, while her visual training and dedicated commitment to the subtleties of the aerial viewpoint have provided for the most nuanced and intriguing of photographic images. Like Robert Moyes Adam, and indeed Fay Godwin, Macdonald is an environmentalist and hillwalker[21] and consequently the dialogue between humankind and nature, development and conservation, growth and decay, establishes one of the principal dynamics of her photographs.

Importantly, Macdonald is sensitive to the symbolic weight of her imagery, and this she has sometimes chosen to parallel with a literary context. In this respect she has divided her work into two broad but overlapping categories: 'prose-structured' photography of the land and 'poem-structured' imagery. In a lecture of 1995 she noted how a proportion of her work was situated in a 'prose-equivalent' tradition,[22]

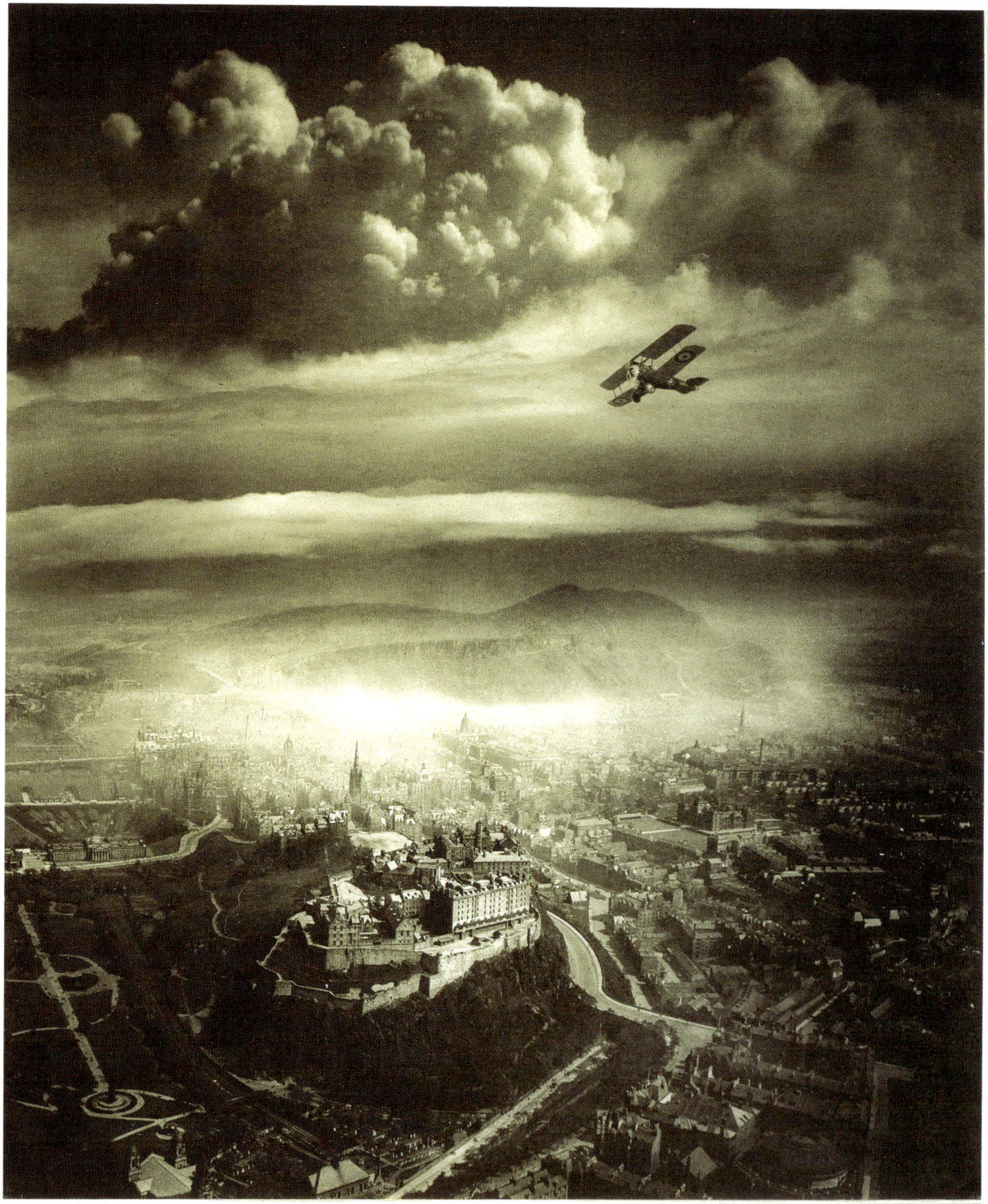

FIG.49
Alfred G. Buckham
Aerial View of Edinburgh
circa 1920

meaning that it tended to be expressive of editorial content and associations leading into environmental, social and philosophical discourse. In this respect she has singled out *Rape Field, East Lothian* [FIG.50], from her project of 1985 titled *Shadow of Heaven*, as a 'prose-equivalent' image. Here, 'the true subject... despite the superficial "beauties" of the "colourful" foreground landscape with its central feature of an intensely yellow field of oil-seed rape, [is] the human domination of the land in the form of modern agribusiness.'[23] And certainly the perspective on Tantallon Castle and the Bass Rock in the Firth of Forth, a subject closely studied by James Valentine's company in the 1880s, is overwhelmed by the uncompromising geometry of the controversial rapefield. This type of engagement has been developed in a number of her photographs, which invoke associations with the processes of erosion, the drainage of moorland for forestry, dying and felled woodlands, the burning of stubble and heather, and every type of interventionist environmental management. The images themselves are profound, strange and beautiful, but the close analysis of their implications opens out current debates on land use, and abuse.[24]

There is a sense in which these photographs are campaigning images, and sometimes this is an intentional component of their purpose, but their challenging abstract form, crafted production and use of metaphor raise them above this station. An even more subtle sense in which the aerial landscape has been integrated into a narrative is found in Macdonald's 'poem-structured' images. She has noted that 'the pictures that now really interest me... are those which are the equivalents not so much of prose and linear narrative, but of poetry.'[25] Here, she has cited the rich abstractions of *Braided River and Ancient Pines, Glen Feshie* and its partner image in the diptych form *Lochan Uaine, Below the Angel's Peak of Carn an t-Sabhail*, both photographs taken in the Cairngorm mountain range during 1988, as important examples of this type. These evocative arrangements of arcs and curves and circles are redolent of organic

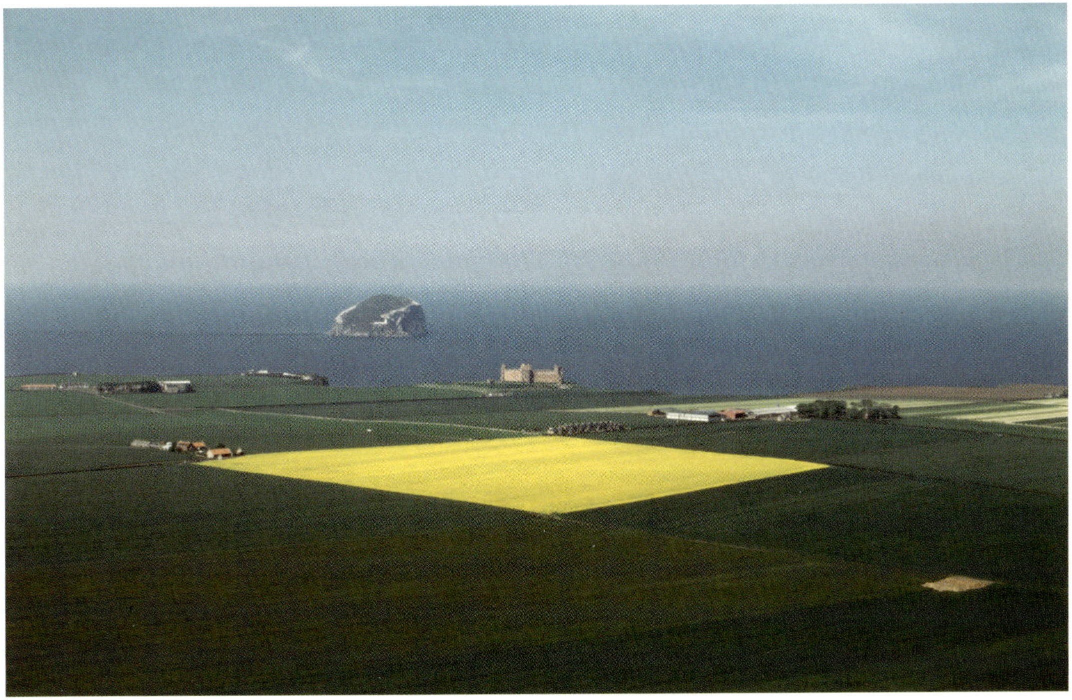

FIG.50
Patricia Macdonald
Rape Field, East Lothian
1985

forms suggestive of the life-force, while recording also ecological change and movement. In this way their intention is to conjure with 'poetic' suggestion. Not, it should be said, in a romantic or lyrical sense, but in the structural sense that they 'relate to the more diffuse, radical, overlapping or network-like patterns of the poem... rather than the linear structures of prose.'[26] This approach was fully developed in Macdonald's large-scale, columnar, 10-part photographic artwork *The Sonnets to Orpheus*, from 1995.

The Sonnets to Orpheus [FIG.51] relates to Rainer Maria Rilke's poem cycle of the same name and the 10 parts of the photographic sequence parallel the journey of Orpheus, the legendary musician and poet, into the underworld, and his return. This is a complex ambition, for Macdonald was selecting aerial views that paralleled and evoked the condition of Rilke's sonnets. In the event she composed an integrated series of images that echoed the structure and the 'feel' of the poem cycle in mood and temper. The photographic sequence opens with the evocative image of a tall ash tree casting a long shadow on the landscape. The cycle of photographs proceeds down through an image of 'a still and inky pool, unconstrained by the maker of fences',[27] the underside of which appears as an area of waste disposal. This last photograph represents the entrance into Hell, and the cycle progresses finally upwards to a view of what appears to be a sky with stars and clouds above a landscape of increasing decontamination. Here is a return from the underworld, and the parallel resolution of an 'ecological parable'. This is, without question, an ingenious and creative use of landscape photography perhaps only made possible through the semi-vertical oblique view of the aerial technique. It is, moreover, an approach that Macdonald has continued to develop in her engagement with the landscape as a place of symbolic narrative.[28]

These, evidently, are examples of the panoramic landscape; images that sweep the horizon and encompass every aspect of the unfolding scene. They are all, also, photographs that embrace specific landmarks, sites, and indeed sights. In this sense they aspire to some degree of universality. Much recent critical theory has accented the idea that this approach is evidence of human hubris, and that it indicates a kind of colonialisation or dominion over the land and the landscape. John Taylor, for example, in his interesting book *A Dream of England: Landscape, Photography and the Tourist's Imagination*, suggests that the landscape photographer's ethos is predatory and exploitative.[29] In essence, shooting and capturing the landscape in a panoramic photograph is an equivalent to claiming, possessing and controlling that space. It is manifestly an error to ascribe this dubious motive to Patricia Macdonald's ecologically-inspired work. Equally Robert Moyes Adam's panoramas and Fay Godwin's photography have countered this nefarious concept. And, importantly, a further category of landscape imagery contests this darkly imperialist intent; the intimate view.

Intimate landscapes

A parallel convention to the panoramic landscape has existed since the technology of the camera allowed for the interrogation of the less commanding spectacle and vista. This was an interest in a kind of intimate view of nature, a close focus on the fecund and dank and mysterious places that were overrun with vegetation and moss. This was, and is, a curious taste, but one that alludes to that secret dimension of nature, the sense of the mystical.

A fascinating early example of this taste was evidenced in the work of John Muir Wood (1805–92).[30] Wood was a professional pianist and music teacher in Edinburgh whose photography, generally, displayed an interest in topographical views, architectural sites and portraits. The most interesting sub-section of his work, however, was the near-view or intimate landscape photographs from the late 1840s and 1850s, which remain remarkable for their prescience. A photograph like *Woodland Study* [FIG.52], for example, appears to harbour no recognised subject. It examines a dense woodland space, the silver bark of some willowy birch trees emerge from a dark coppice, and in the foreground there is a meandering trickle of water flowing through some jagged, lichen-covered rocks. This is, certainly, the study of a shadowy woodland space, but its metier is ambiguous. There is a case for suggesting that Wood was concerned with exploring the potential for the camera to work at the very limits of its

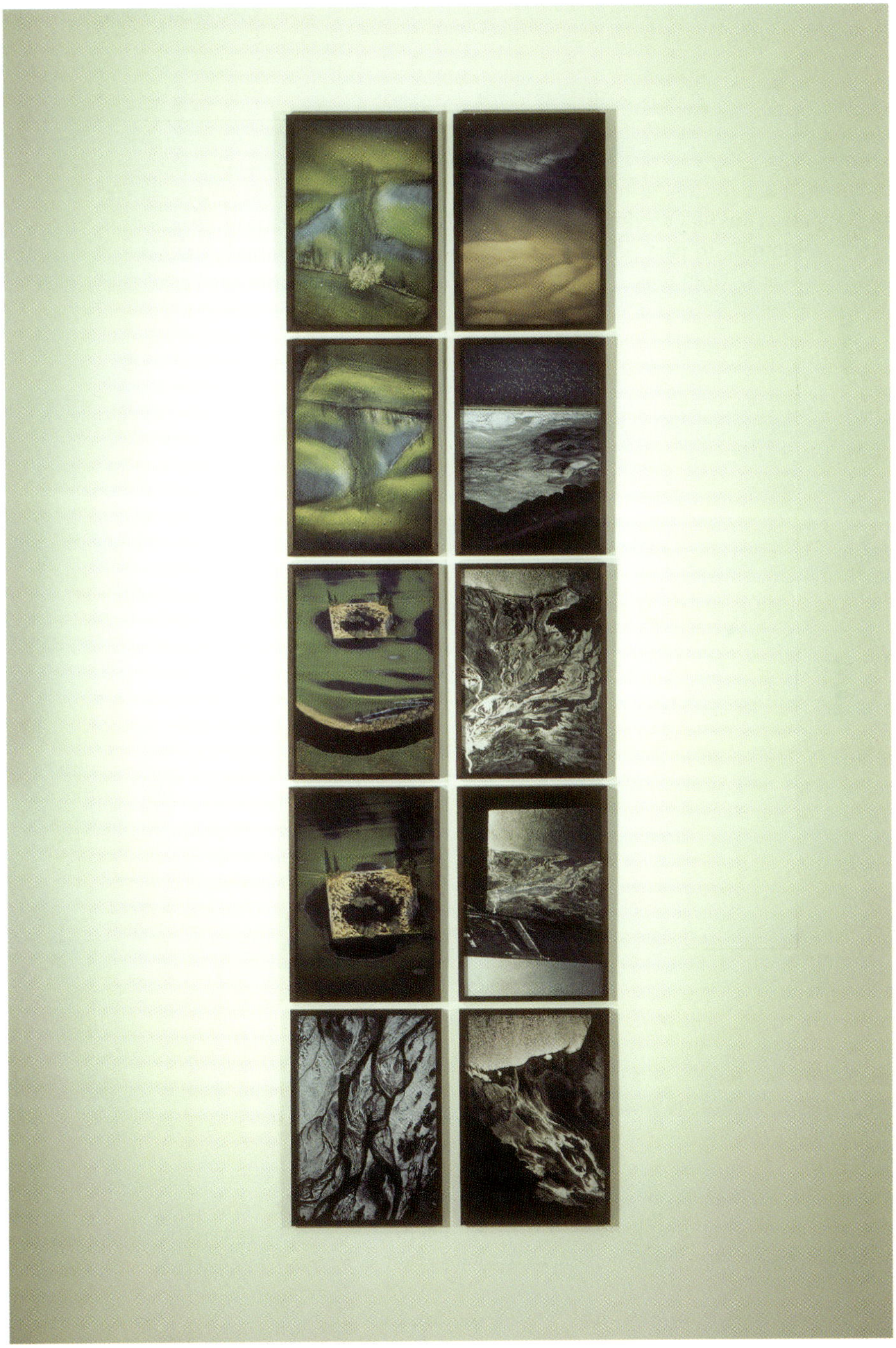

FIG.51
Patricia Macdonald
photographic series
The Sonnets to Orpheus
1995

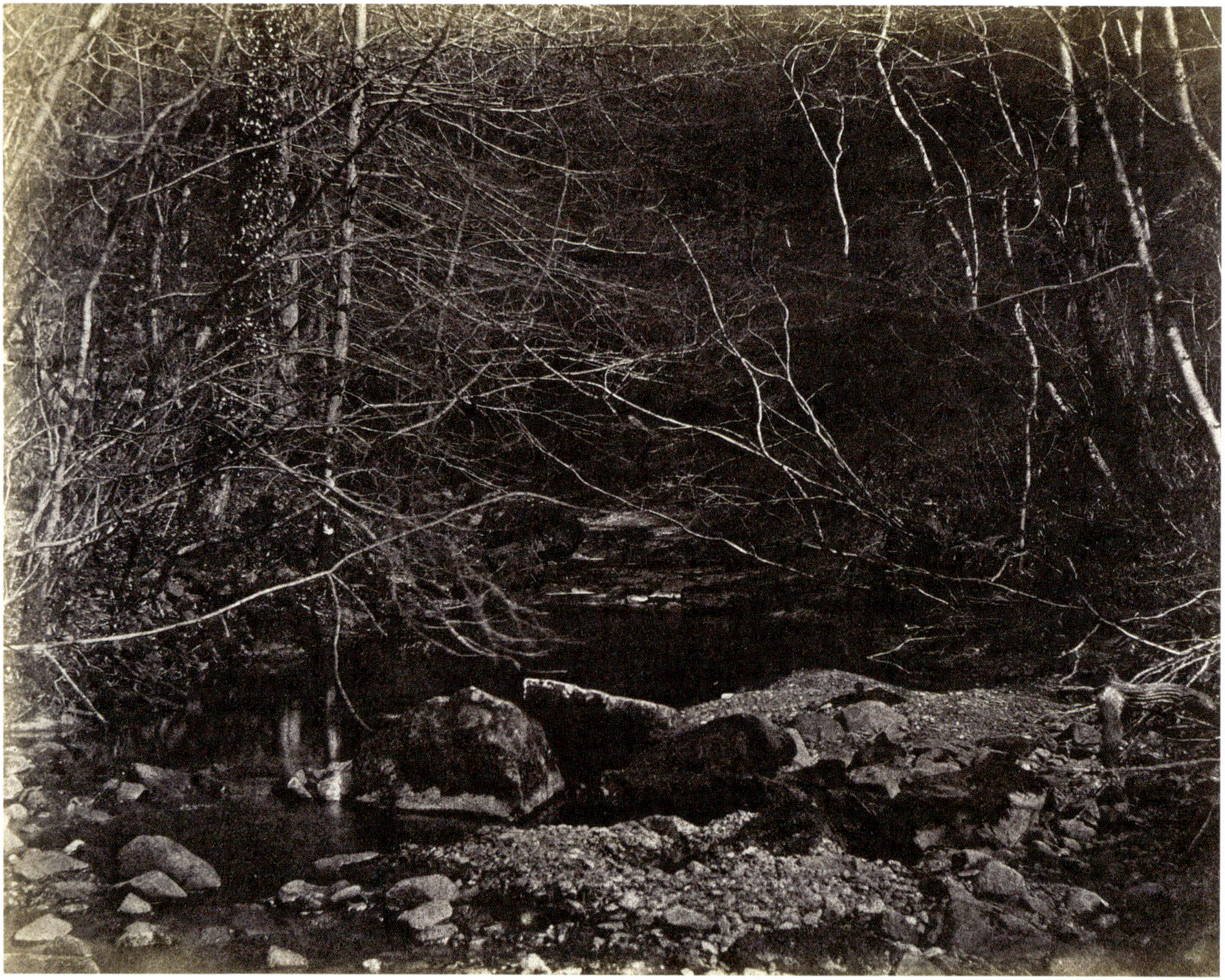

FIG.52
John Muir Wood
Woodland Study
n.d.

technical capacity. In this case the attenuated light source becomes a challenge and the image a kind of experiment. In practical terms this interpretation might be augmented by the contest inherent in the creation of a print from this image. The manipulation of the calotype negative would have involved Wood in tests and trials designed to accommodate the most subtly textured and tonal of photographs. While these are worthy goals it is also true that such challenges were available in all fields of photography. In fact Wood chose to focus on these deep, dark, intimate spaces that were evidence of an ethereal Nature. His concern seems to have been with the mystery of place, and a sense of timelessness. Here, the loaded symbolism of the image appears to be ahistorical and points to a fascination with the untamed and the primeval.

There are sources for this view in art, and in literature. Caspar David Friedrich, that extravagant exponent of the northern romantic tradition, often favoured woodland places heavy with a dark symbolism. Equally, the Pre-Raphaelites indulged a taste for densely packed forest glades and flowered dells. In some ways these are the contrary sites to the open landscape. If the panorama conjures ideas of historical association, ancestral memory and human dominion over the land, then the intimate view will often evoke a sense of the underworld, of darkness and primal forces, and of threat.

This dimension of landscape, then, remains quite exclusive and can be distinguished from the more predictable approaches to the subject. In 1980 Murray Johnston (1949–90) was appointed as Resident Photographer for Northern Arts and was based in the Kielder Forest in Northumberland. Johnston would go on to found the Stills Gallery in Edinburgh in 1982, and became the Head of Photography at Edinburgh College of Art in 1988, the first person to hold such a post in Edinburgh. His residency in the Kielder Forest, however, produced a number of intriguing landscape studies. It is clear that Johnston was captivated by the intricate geometries of earth and tree and shrub, and also by the dappled light in closed and shadowy spaces. In this way he was presenting a distant echo to Wood's intimate landscapes, and acknowledging the primordial power of nature.

A more self-conscious and considered version of this trope is evidenced in the photography of Thomas Joshua Cooper (b. 1946). Cooper is, without doubt, one of the most skilled and interesting photographers of the contemporary period. Born in California, he settled in Scotland in 1982, having been made the first Head of Photography at Glasgow School of Art. His engagement with landscape is both physical and cerebral, for Cooper has developed an aesthetic that is informed by ritual and by craft. Working within a fine art tradition, he journeys into the landscape carrying with him a 19th-century field camera and all the paraphernalia of his vocation, and evidently there is a parallel here with the approach of Robert Moyes Adam. But Cooper searches out particular sites, sites that are 'physical and emotional aspects of place' and are 'emotionally charged in the gestural conditions of their object matter (grass, rocks, leafless-branches, etc.).'[31] He will then, as conditions dictate, take a single negative of the scene. This photograph is the point of a singular and concentrated energy; an image that is the culmination of a journey, a meditation on place and a focused study in technique. Much of the authority of Cooper's work is derived from this uncompromising aesthetic. Images are 'hard-won' and they are then completed with a degree of craft and finish that is exceptional. Moreover, they respect the most demanding codes and conventions of fine art photography, they are subtly tonal black and white images that move towards the darker end of the spectrum and evoke a genuine sense of mystery and wonder.

All of Cooper's photography is, in some sense, intimate, but many of his most absorbing images have been near-view landscapes. Nowhere is this more clearly revealed than in his series of photographs, 'Mythic Stones (Message to E. S. Curtis)', completed between 1983 and 1988. These images, variously and poetically titled *Soot Streaked*, *Leaf Stained*, *Ice Cracked*, *Earth Anchored*, *Shadow Strewn* [FIG.53], *Wind Creased* and *Stream Smoothed*, are esoteric and cryptic studies of woodland and rocky hollows. All of these scenes, evidently, are named after natural processes, whether geographical or weather related, and allude to the land as a symbolic site. The evocative *Wind Creased* is one of the most interesting. This is, to some degree, an abstract work. The landmarks and foliage that made John Muir Wood's *Woodland Study* an identifiable glade are barely recognisable in this image. Rather, the photograph is composed of dark shadow and intense streaks of dappled light. Concentrated viewing discerns the trunks of deciduous forest and the leaves of a graceful arcing canopy, as well as a mass of moss covered stones and foliage on the forest floor. But these revelations are secreted in the shadowed image. Cooper sets out to recover the mystery within the site by forcing the viewer to engage with the photograph in an act of slow meditation and gradual release. This, of course, mirrors his own experience in visualising and capturing the scene, and it completes that sense of journey that is core to his aesthetic.

Something of Cooper's intention is exposed in the subtitle to this series of photographs; they are a 'Message to E. S. Curtis'. Edward Sherrif Curtis has been one of America's most celebrated photographers. His life's work consisted in a romantic documentation of

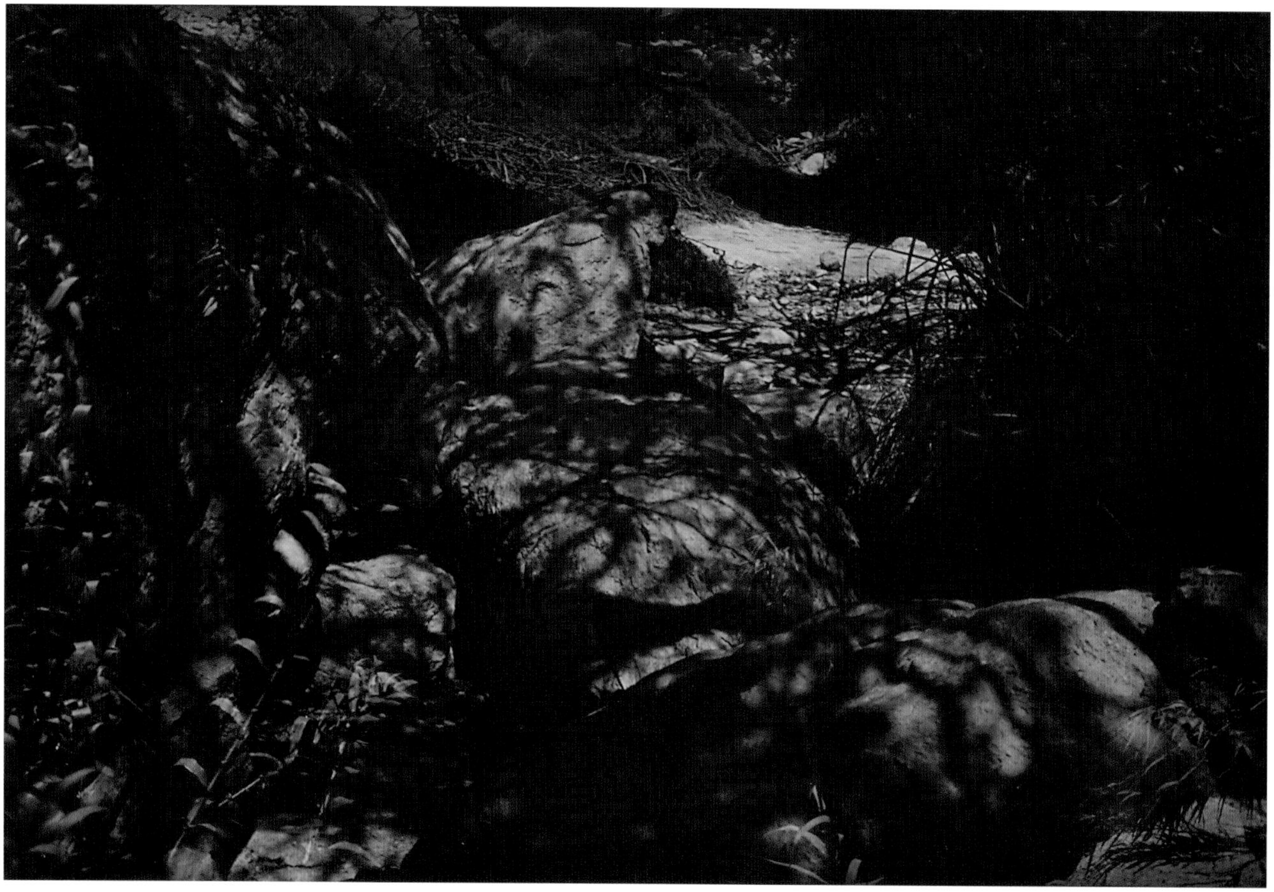

FIG.53
Thomas Joshua Cooper
Shadow Strewn from 'Mythic Stones: Message to E. S. Curtis'
1983–88

the Native American tribes. Beginning the project in 1895, it was finally completed in 1930. During this period Curtis travelled amongst the tribal communities, documenting their customs and rituals and recording their champions in imposing portraits. Curtis's motivation was the production of a multi-volume archive of Native American culture and he succeeded in publishing the first volume of *The Native American Indian* in 1907, with volume 20, the final volume, being published in 1930. It was a venture that left him impoverished and divorced, and with little recognition during his remaining lifetime.

Curtis, however, produced an elegant body of work born of an epic journey and a total commitment to his art. His signature photograph was titled *The Vanishing Race* and depicted a group of figures on horseback moving across a canyon floor and towards a mountainous horizon. This image indicated that core value in Curtis's oeuvre and the implication that is recognised by Cooper. Curtis longed to evidence an intimate connection between humankind and the natural environment and to express the potential for that connection to dissipate in the move towards modernity. Cooper, with his determined journeys into the natural world, sets out to resurrect that atavistic connection and to witness this in his photographs. This is his message to Curtis, recognition and respect, and honour.

Cooper's work extends beyond these images,

however, and much of his output has been presented in photobooks. His *Dreaming the Gokstadt* from 1998 and *Some Rivers, Some Trees, Some Rocks, Some Seas* of 2003 are exemplary artists' books that reveal his range and depth as a photographer of the landscape. In projects like these Cooper has explored and revealed Scotland's river systems, islands and archipelagos, and marginal lands, while further accenting the darker pantheism of select sites and loci. He has also travelled throughout the world selecting places that symbolically connect with his epic mission. In 1990, for example, he began an undertaking to photograph various points of land at the edge of the Atlantic Ocean; this, *The World's Edge – the Atlantic Basin Project*, is a venture allied to his many related schemes such as *The Great River: Rio Grande River Crossings – From the Source to the Sea*, a task completed between 1994 and 2000. In these endeavours Cooper is careful to locate the precise place where the image is taken, often including geographical position and point in time, as well as other associations. Hence his photograph *'Broken Boulder in the Late Afternoon Sun' Remembering Timothy O'Sullivan 'Along the Snake River', Pillar Falls Canyon, Jerome Co. Idaho,* USA, an image produced in 2004 [FIG.54], provides not only a powerful landscape picture but a weathercast, some historical associations, geographical precision, and a related mindscape. It is these features of Cooper's work that lend it a conceptual edge and can relate his photography to the aesthetic of those 'land-artists', like Hamish Fulton and Richard Long, whose documented journey into the landscape is, itself, the artwork.

There is, nevertheless, an implicit rejection of human conceit in Cooper's work, for his images foreground the sense of nature as a sacrosanct place. In this way, at least, he is related to the spiritual atmosphere of Curtis's project and even the discreet ecological mission of Robert Moyes Adam. His ambition, however, is majestic and it is in the desire to document and celebrate the untamed places across the globe that his vision is most pronounced. Of course, in travelling to other lands and encountering different landscapes he is treading in the footsteps of many Scottish photographers, not all of whom have had the imagination or the skill of Cooper.

Other lands

Where the various approaches to Scottish landscape have established a discourse that might memorialise, mythologise, commercialise or indeed politicise the land, the views that Scottish photographers have taken of other countries have, most generally, been categorised as imperialist and colonialist. Kathleen Stewart Howe, writing on Sergeant James McDonald's photographs of Jerusalem and the Sinai Peninsula taken in 1864 and 1868, has suggested that 'photographs made in the course of official or quasi-official government surveys inscribe a set of colonial assumptions in the images produced.'[32] More generally, Derrick Price has written:

> Photography grew up in the age of Empire and became an important adjunct of imperialism for it returned to the Western spectator images of native peoples which frequently confirmed prevailing views of them as primitive, bizarre, barbaric, or simply picturesque.

He adds that the 'coloniser's gaze', expressed through photography, 'has been used as a way of consuming the world in a manner that gives us power over it.'[33]

These are powerful analyses of the myriad landscape photographs of foreign territories, and powerful indictments of many photographers. Certainly there is a case that photography was used as one way of visualising 'the other', and that it also served in the appropriation and exploitation of empire. But photography was also a means for understanding and reviewing the world and world cultures, and photographers were not, exclusively, malevolent instruments of Western repression.

One of the first Scottish photographers to recognise the potential of photography to create a visual encyclopaedia of the wide world was, as might be imagined, George Washington Wilson. Wilson's business rapidly moved beyond the Highland landscape and on to catalogue most every site of note in the British Isles. Wilson himself first journeyed south to photograph London and the south coast of England in 1860, picturing emblematic sites like Stonehenge on the way. Subsequent views, chiefly of English cathedrals, would become a significant part of his stock. Indeed these photographs of English cathedrals were highly praised by *Photographic Notes*, who reported that 'On the whole it is a noble collection, and many of the views go far

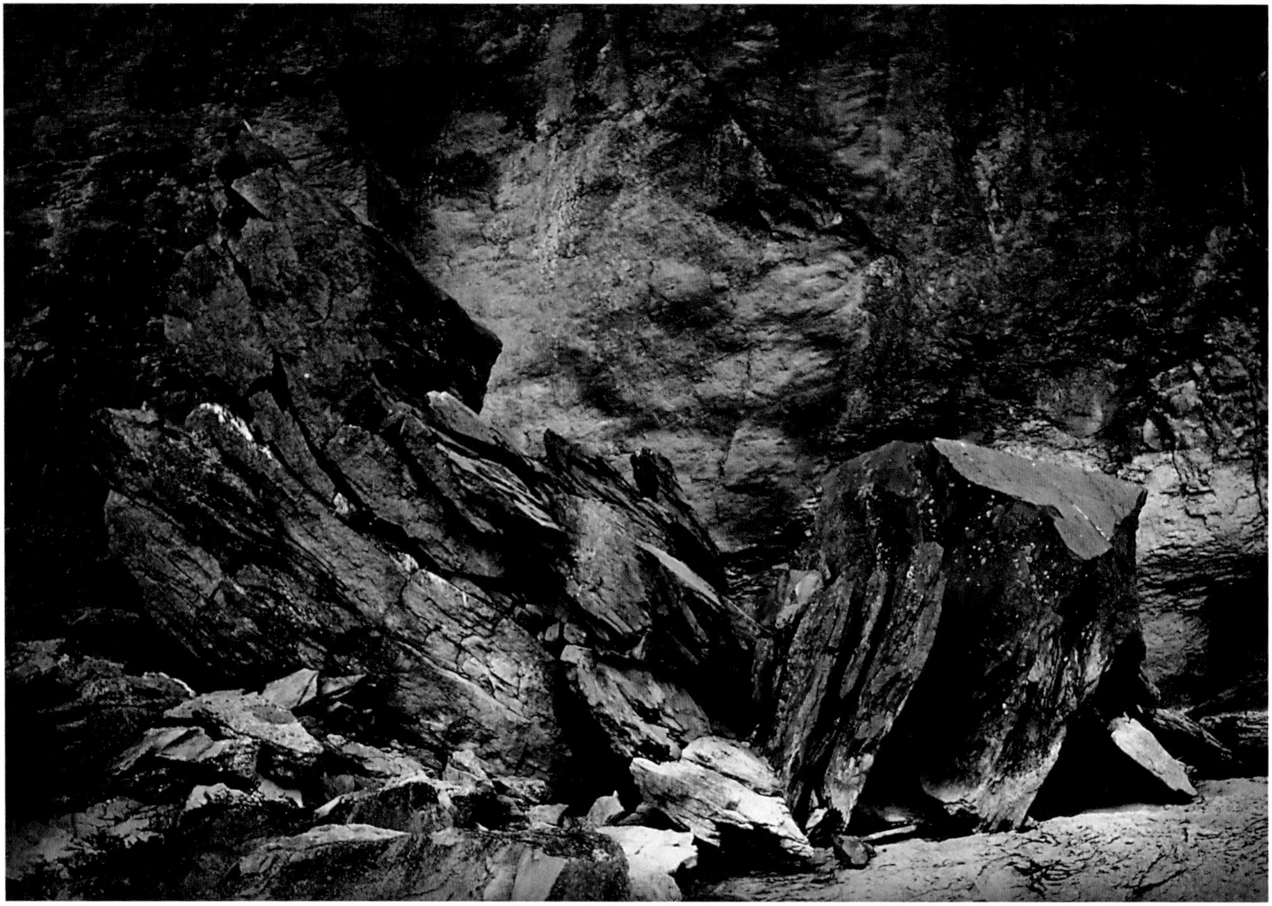

FIG.54
Thomas Joshua Cooper
'Broken Boulder in the Late Afternoon Sun'
Remembering Timothy O'Sullivan 'Along the Snake River',
Pillar Falls Canyon, Jerome Co. Idaho, USA
2004

beyond anything that we have yet seen in photography.'[34] As the business expanded, in the middle years of the 1870s, Wilson began to employ a staff of fellow photographers who would, eventually, be given assignments to produce viewbooks of sites and landscapes from throughout the world. Notable amongst these were the late 19th-century catalogues of *Landscape, Architectural and Figure Photographs in Gibraltar, South of Spain and Morocco*, most likely taken by Wilson's son Charles Wilson, and the *Photographs of Life and Scenery in South Africa*, probably taken by Wilson's erstwhile caption-writer, Frederick Hardy.[35]

Wilson's company was, as always, exploiting and developing the burgeoning tourist industry, and so, in his own way, was one of the most colourful of expatriate Scottish photographers, Robert Macpherson (1811–72). Robert Macpherson, it is suggested, was distantly related to James Macpherson, the esteemed 'translator' of the Ossian saga, and was, like his kinsman, a 'character'. Having initially trained in medicine he came to settle in Rome, circa 1840, where he supplemented his attempts to exist as a painter with a little trading in artworks. Famously, he identified Michelangelo's *Entombment of Christ* and later sold this, with dubious legality, to the National Gallery in London. Ever the caricature Scot, he bestrode the streets of Rome in kilt and regalia, and eventually turned to photography in 1851. In this he proved himself more than adept, and produced some of the finest topographic views of the ruined classical city.[36] Macpherson was, in some degree, a competitor to the Alinari studio, and his large prints of Roman sites and topography remain models of technical achievement. The *Façade Temple of Antoninus and Faustina (San Lorenzo in Miranda) Roman Forum* [FIG.55], photographed circa 1860, is testament to his skill. A finely detailed study of these classical ruins, it adopts a high viewpoint in order to fully survey the sweep of the rooftops and the complexity of the site. The longer exposure time, in which Macpherson specialised, allowed for a close study of each building and the fullest discovery of both streets and temple.

It might be suggested that Macpherson's detailed photographs allow the viewer to vicariously access the locale, and therefore to experience the Roman Forum and the classical world. In part, this was precisely the intent of landscape photography from these 'other lands'. Macpherson offered, through his photographs, a contemporary equivalent to the Grand Tour; one, moreover, that was available, at a small cost, to the new middle classes located in the suburbs of the modern industrial cities. This substitute 'tour' presented the ever ambitious and socially dynamic middle class with an encounter that paralleled the leisured education of the young aristocratic nobleman. It existed as an ersatz version of patrician privilege, and was accessed as a correspondent of that desired status.

The Grand Tour, of course, was chiefly fixed upon the classical world, notably Rome, Florence and the environs of Naples. But it also might include a trip to the cradle of the Christian world; Jerusalem, Palestine and the biblical lands. Amongst the most prescient of photographic travellers to the area was the Reverend Alexander Keith. Alexander Keith was an esteemed figure in the Church of Scotland who was a friend of Thomas Chalmers. In 1843 he became a member of the secessionist Free Church of Scotland and was, naturally, a subject for Hill and Adamson's portrait studies of the dissenting ministers. However, Keith seems to have been familiar with Talbot's experiments from as early as 1839, and Kathleen Stewart Howe records that:

> Even before any official announcements or descriptions of a photographic process... the Reverend Alexander Keith attempted to use Englishman William Henry Fox Talbot's paper process in Jerusalem. Keith's unsuccessful attempt in April 1839 must stand as the earliest photographic project in the region.[37]

Keith's motivation, as Howe notes, was not simply to document the landscape, but somehow to prove the veracity of the biblical story by visualising and realising noted biblical sites. In 1844 he returned to Syria with his son George Skene Keith, a surgeon and amateur photographer, who succeeded in taking daguerreotype studies of the relevant and revered places. These were used as the basis for illustrations in the 1848 edition of Alexander Keith's *Evidence of the Truth of the Christian Religion Derived from Prophecy*; a riposte to David Hume's scepticism and a book first published in 1823 but subject to innumerable reprints thereafter.

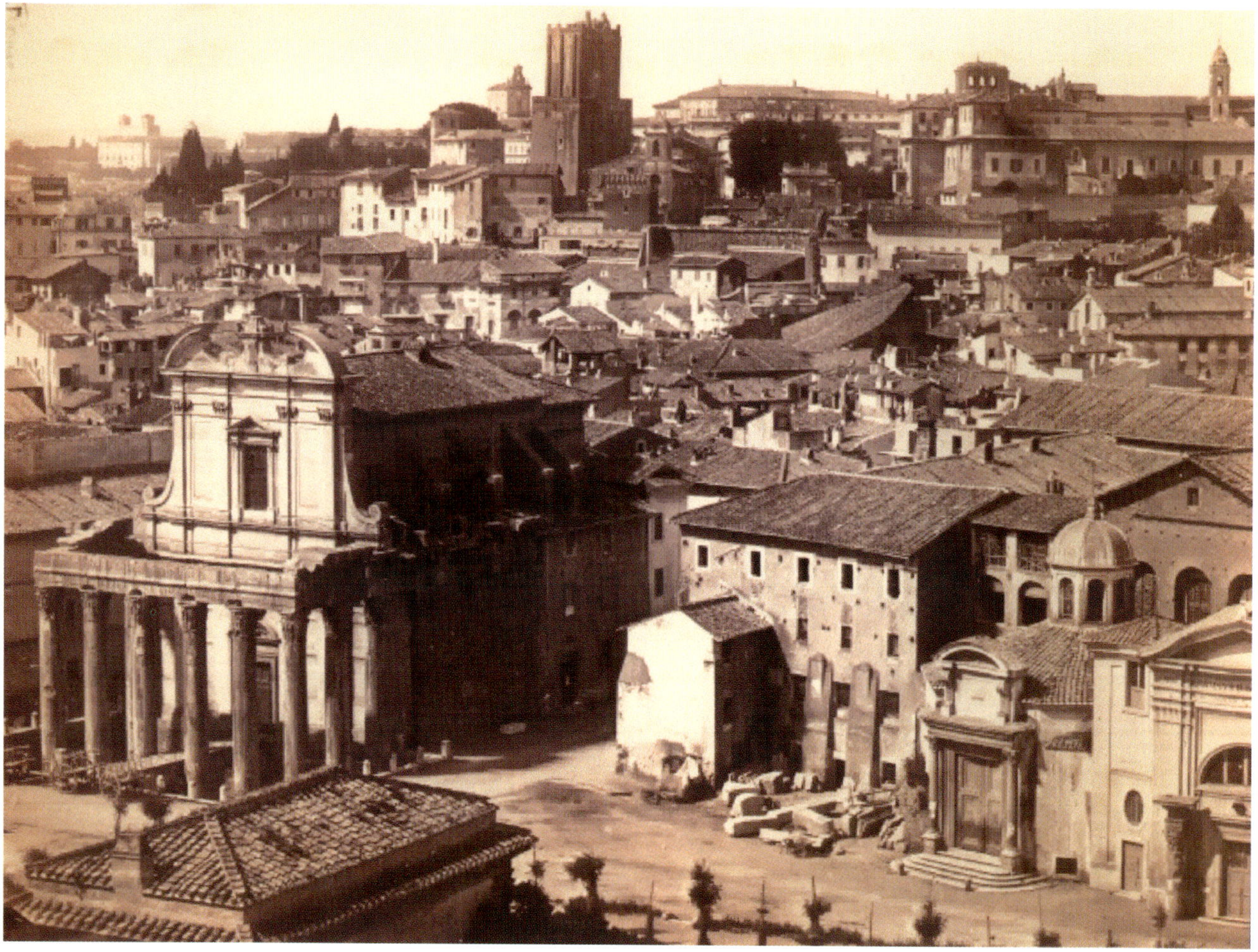

FIG.55
Robert Macpherson
The Façade Temple of Antoninus and Faustina (San Lorenzo in Miranda) Roman Forum
circa 1868–69

The Keiths were not unique in this type of enterprise however, and another reverend gentleman, James Graham (1806–69), whose family estate was titled Fereneze, travelled in Italy during the 1850s, notably photographing Pompeii, and moved on into Jerusalem. It is no surprise that the camera should be used as a tool in the advocacy of a Christian position. The depiction of a 'real' biblical site, previously only available as narrative scripture, lent a form of authenticity and authority to the word, especially at a point in time when the photograph was revered as a kind of 'truth'. Yet a more practical use for the camera was found in the area of the Sinai, and in the city of Jerusalem, by the Scottish soldier Sergeant James McDonald.

James McDonald was enlisted in the Royal Engineers and was trained as a surveyor and photographer. During the 1860s he was required to photograph sites in the Sinai that might benefit in the search for a secure and clean water supply for the city of Jerusalem. This photographic survey would be included as part of the multi-volume report *Ordnance Survey of Jerusalem*, published in 1864. Later, in 1868, McDonald would be ordered to undertake a further photographic survey of the Sinai Peninsula itself, recording the barren desert landscape in a panoramic style [FIG.56]. McDonald was a soldier and a surveyor, and not a self-conscious 'photographer' – in this sense his work is difficult to situate within a landscape tradition. Nevertheless Kathleen Stewart Howe has, powerfully, suggested that his photographs in particular 'encode possession'. She argues that:

> Whether in the stance taken by expedition members at the holy places in Jerusalem, in the sequential penetration of the Sinai, or in the integration of map, photograph and elevation in the three-dimensional model and its dissemination as a stereoscopic photograph... the photographs are graphic articulations of a physical possession.[38]

Herein McDonald becomes an instrument in the process of British colonial expansion, and the camera a tool in imperial conquest. Consequently, the propensity for the photograph to 'capture' a landscape ceases to be aesthetic or even metaphorical, and becomes literal.

Certainly this is one of the ways in which con-

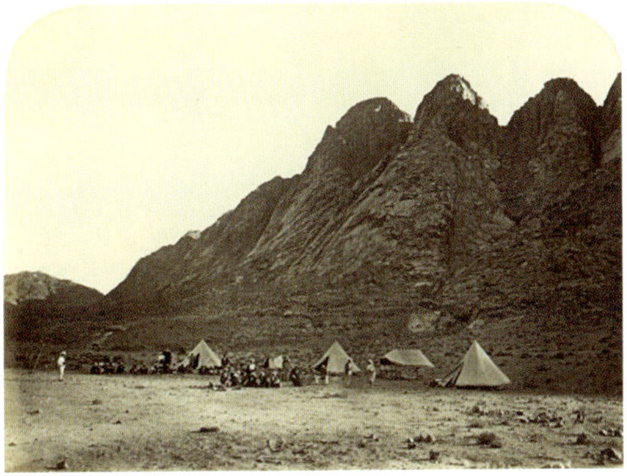

FIG.56
James McDonald
Camp in Wady Ed-Deir from Ordnance Survey of the Peninsula of Sinai
1868–69

temporary photographic theory has conceptualised the camera's role in travellers' hands and in foreign lands. In this respect the category of landscape, as utilised within Britain's imperial possessions, is particularly interesting. Naturally the sub-continent of India, a British interest since at least the late 18th century, was much photographed. Dr John Murray (1809–98), by vocation a surgeon and a colonial administrator in India from the 1840s, photographed the key sites around the Mughal city of Agra following the Sepoy rebellion of 1857; an uprising against British rule that is now generally regarded as the first struggle for Indian independence. Given the fact that Murray was based in Agra it is unsurprising that he photographed the Taj Mahal. His image, *The Taj Mahal, from the East, with Ruins in the Foreground* [FIG.57], from circa 1857, a 'paper negative',[39] is an extraordinary spectral and evocative photograph of this majestic palace. What remains significant is that this is really an homage to Indian civilisation and culture, and, even at this period of intense political agitation, remains marginal to the 'colonialist' vision.[40]

This might equally be said of Frederick Bremner's (1863–1941) *River Crossing, River Jhelum, Kashmir*, photographed circa 1900. Bremner was a colonialist, without doubt, staying in India for some 40 years after leaving his native north-east Scotland in 1882. He was, moreover, intrigued by the caste system in India and studied native life as a kind of colonial tourist, but at the intersection of anthropology, sociology and the pseudo-science of racial typology. Nevertheless, when

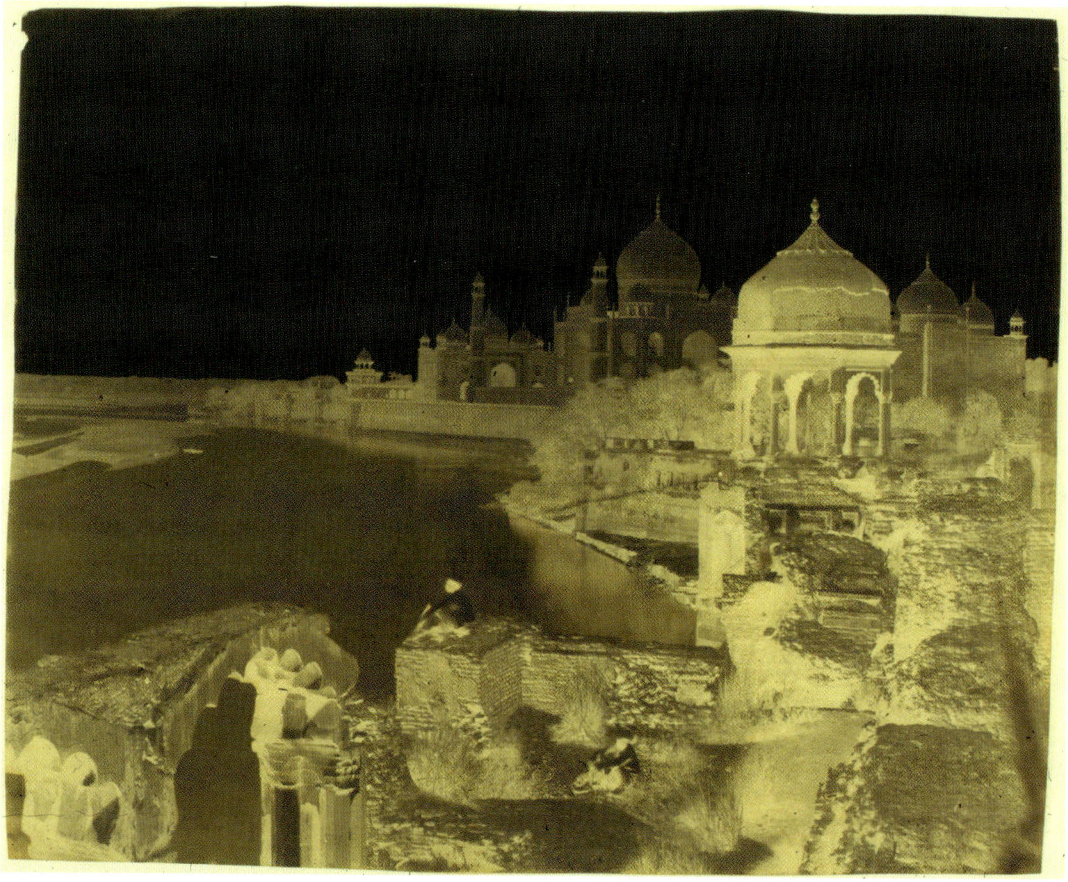

FIG.57
John Murray
The Taj Mahal, from the East, with Ruins in the Foreground, a 'waxed paper negative'
circa 1857

journeying in Kashmir he recognised the extraordinary ingenuity and beauty of the Kashmiri people and landscape in his photograph of a rope bridge across the Jhelum valley.[41] Equally, his *View of the Jhelum River* [FIG.58], is a profoundly aestheticised view of different lives and cultures.

It would be a mistake to overstate the benign influence of photographers working in the colonies. Fundamentally they viewed foreign lands through the lens of racial stereotype and a western European conviction in the supremacy of the colonialising powers. But, alongside the images that derogated the native cultures and typecast the conventions and traditions of native peoples, there existed photographs that marvelled at the initiative and resourcefulness of humanity while gazing in wonder at human creativity.

This is, perhaps, more in evidence in those 'other landscapes' that were not directly under the flag of Empire. In Egypt, Charles Piazzi Smyth (1819–1900), the Astronomer Royal for Scotland and an enthusiastic amateur photographer, produced his remarkable view of *The Great Pyramid of Giza* in 1865 [FIG.59]. Smyth was then engaged in a survey of the pyramids borne of a desire to resist the mooted introduction of the metric system of measurement into Britain. Smyth, alongside Sir John Herschel, supported the imperial standard measure of the inch and argued that this was based upon the biblical measure of the cubit. This, he

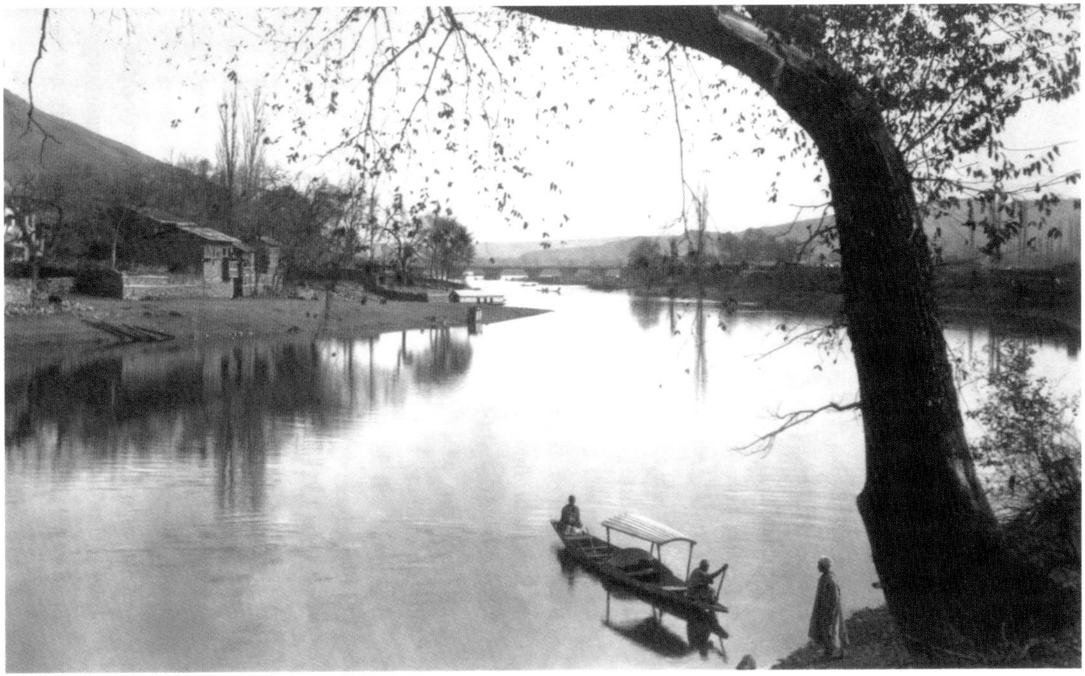

FIG.58
Frederick Bremner
View of the Jhelum River, Kashmir
circa 1900

suggested, was the fundamental mathematical measure of the pyramids and his survey set out to authenticate this dubious claim. His photograph of the largest of the three pyramids at Giza incorporates the remarkable head of the Sphinx and exists, at least in part, to record the power and splendour of the edifice as a human achievement. Likewise, James Robertson (circa 1813–88) and his brother by marriage, Felix Beato (1825–circa 1908), worked in partnership in the city of Istanbul from the 1850s. Their image of *The Sultan Ahmet Mosque (The Blue Mosque)*, from 1855 [FIG.60], besides highlighting the central dome of the mosque also drew attention to the unique characteristic of the six minarets incorporated in the architecture. This is surely a photograph of a remarkably beautiful building and a spiritual place. The potential for it to be categorised, as Price has claimed, as an example of the 'primitive, bizarre, barbaric, or simply picturesque' may yet be challenged as a cruelly reductivist view.

Of course photographs of foreign lands would always enfold the potential for a voyeuristic response on the part of the viewer. No one, perhaps, was more aware of this than John Thomson (1837–1921), and most especially in his views of China. Thomson was 24 years old when he moved to the British colonial possession of Singapore in the Far East. There, he joined his brother in a business that prepared optical instruments for the merchant fleets. He was, however, already a proficient amateur photographer, and he had a genuine passion for travel and geographical

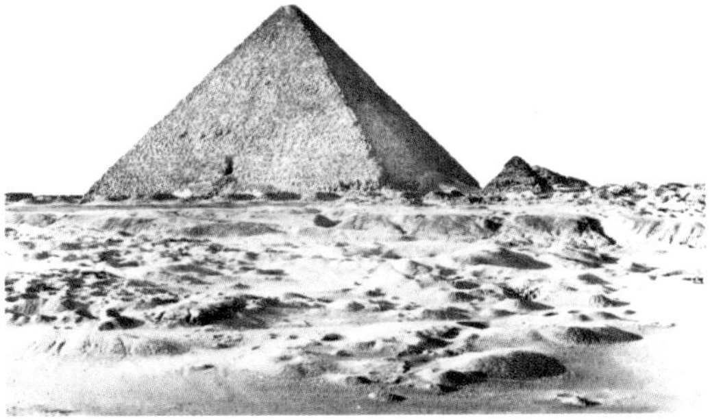

FIG.59
Charles Piazzi Smyth
The Great Pyramid of Giza
1865

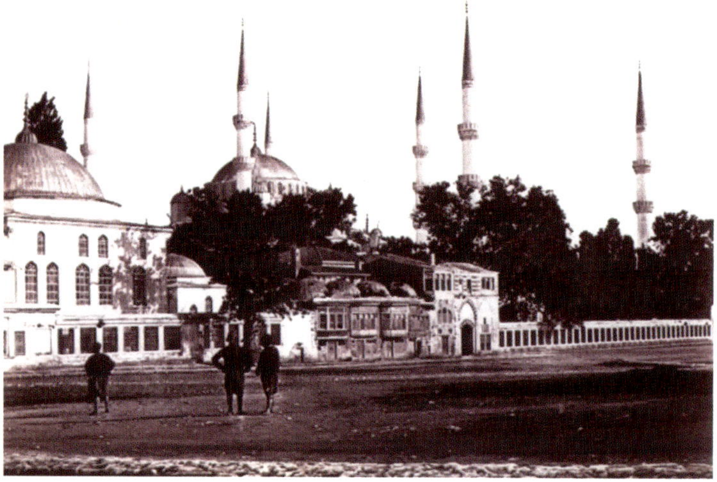

FIG.60
James Robertson and Felix Beato
The Sultan Ahmet Mosque (The Blue Mosque)
1855

FIG.61
John Thomson
Yang-Fu Rapid
1871

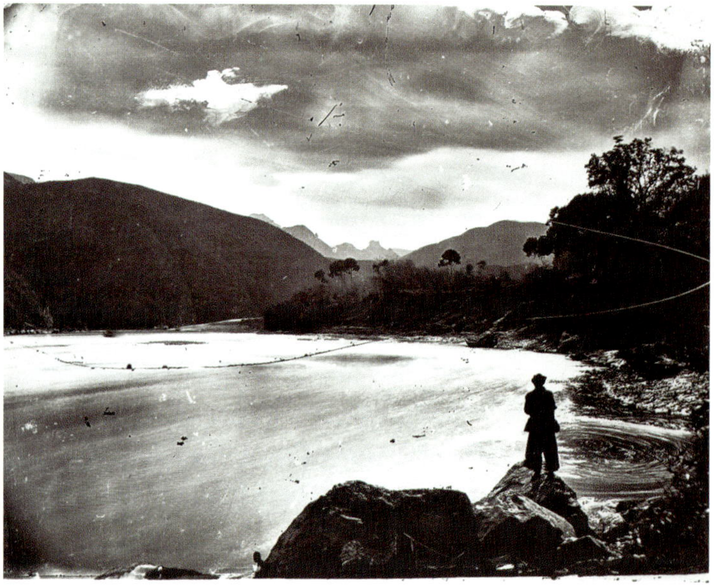

exploration. During a journey to Cambodia, in 1865–6, he photographed the royal family and the ancient sites of the country. Following a return to Britain in 1867 Thomson moved, once again, to the Far East, this time establishing studios in Hong Kong. In 1870 and again in 1872 he travelled in the provinces of China, then barely known to the Western imagination, and he produced a number of landmark photographs from this journey. Thomson was drawn to the documentary image, and his studies of subjects like *Street Gamblers*, and the terrifying *Punishment in China*, remain astonishing insights into the nature of Chinese life and society in this period. His landscape photographs are monumental and were completed as he travelled along the main river arteries in the country. An example like *Yang-Fu Rapid* [FIG.61], from 1871, transports the romantic vision of the panoramic landscape into the heart of the Orient. Thomson was also visionary in promoting his work through early examples of the photobook; his first publication was *Foochow and the River Min*, published in 1873, and later publications included *Illustrations of China and its People*, from 1874.

Thomson was a pure example of the 19th-century Scottish photographer abroad; part imperial adventurer, part voyeur, a photographer with a colonialist mindset, and a traveller who stood in wonder at the variety and spectacle of the wide world. The world he viewed was markedly different, and this would have made it doubly interesting to his audience in the West. But where Thomson journeyed east in his search for business and a notable subject others would journey west, to the new world and the land of pioneers.

Of most note in this respect is William Notman (1826–91). Notman, a Paisley-born businessman, emigrated to Canada in 1856, by all accounts just one step ahead of the law. Whereas his original business, and the root of his legal problems, had been in the cloth trade, Notman developed his interest in photography after having escaped to Montreal. There, he established an industry that was, in many respects, the mirror of Wilson's in Aberdeen. Notman was prolific in producing staged studio portraits, views of the developing city, memorial photographs of official dignitaries and functions, images of the expanding railways, and, of course, landscape pictures. In fact the landscapes that Notman and his company tended to produce were not of the wilderness areas but of those lands that were in the process of being opened to transport. His *Mount Stephen and East End Tunnel, Kicking Horse Valley, British Columbia* [FIG.62], taken in 1884, has all the appearance of an impenetrable mountain scene, but the mountain itself is named after George Stephen, who was the first president of the Canadian Pacific Railway company. In fact it was the railway company that created the tunnel through the mountain, and it is this achievement that is celebrated in Notman's image. Typically Notman's photographs record and mythologise a 'pioneer' landscape and sensibility; notating the progress of immigrants and industry as they tame and control the land. And, equally as noteworthy, it was another Scottish emigrant, Alexander Henderson (1831–1913), who would become the principal figure in the Canadian Pacific Railway Photographic Department, a position that afforded ample scope for images of outback territories and monumental landscapes so reminiscent of the Scottish Highlands.

These were other lands, in the sense of being foreign landscapes that were traversed by Scottish photographers, often, it must be said, carrying with them the tropes of their native tradition. But it is also the case that photographers, particularly in the contemporary period, began to view landscape differently.

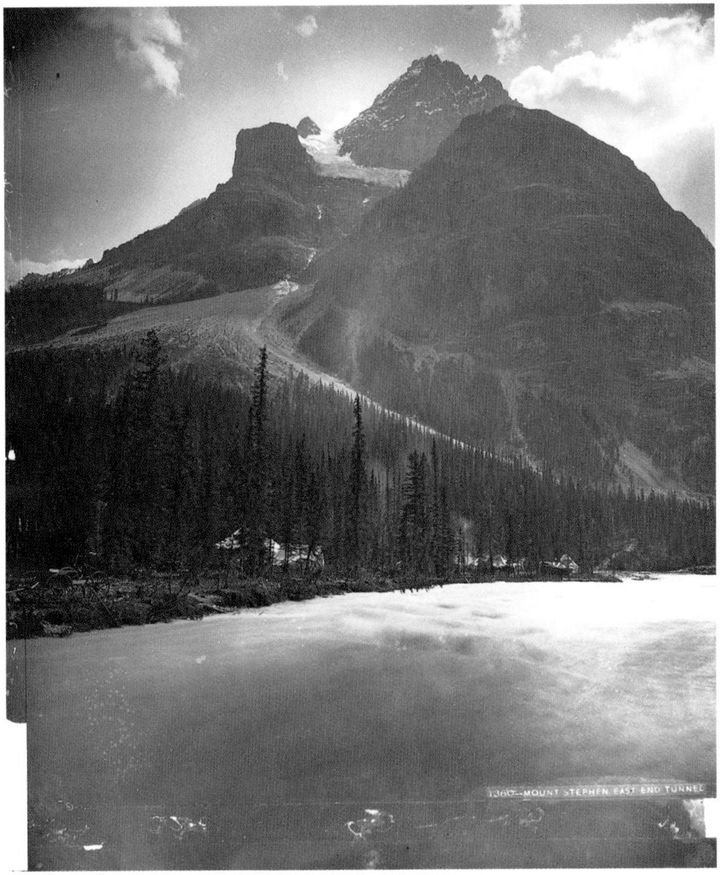

FIG.62
William Notman
Mount Stephen and East End Tunnel, Kicking Horse Valley, British Columbia
1884

Different landscapes

In the period after the Second World War something of the formalist dynamic in photography began to emerge within the field of landscape photographs. That is, landscape images were less denotative of place, and increasingly a meditation on 'look' and atmosphere and style. This coincided with the increased sense that photography was a unique art with a discreet set of aesthetic parameters; in fact the period of fashionable and celebrity photographers who would re-orientate the fundamental nature of the activity during the 1960s. In part this had been foreshadowed in the work of Bill Brandt, who, it might be argued, moved from documentary photographer to aesthete in the post-war period. Brandt had, on his many forays into Scotland while working for *Picture Post*, taken some extraordinary images of the Highland landscape. Extraordinary, for they so comprehensively spoke to the archetypal view; precipitous mountains, misty glens, even the clichéd sentiment of the long-haired, long-horned, Highland cattle. But the formalism that Brandt helped encourage during the post-war period established a taste for a stylised landscape often devoid of association, memory and myth.

Raymond Moore (1920–87), the English-born photographer and teacher, was certainly influenced by the conceptual dimension of this new approach to landscape. Having trained as a painter, and rejecting this for photography, Moore would travel to the

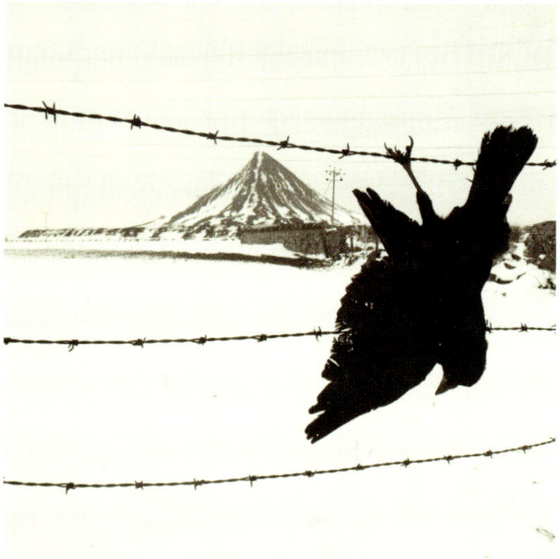

FIG.63
Peter Cattrell
Shot Crow, Lothians
n.d.

United States during the late 1960s, where he came under the influence of Minor White. Something of White's approach to landscape is evident in his many images taken in Scotland. Moore's eye was drawn to aspects of the mundane and the commonplace that were pictured in an abstract, almost surreal, manner. His photograph titled *Dumfriesshire*, from 1985, is a poignant example of this different kind of landscape. The image depicts the junction of a back-road in winter-time. Besides the barren tree and sparse hedgerow a telegraph pole creates a strong vertical dynamic, while the roadside is scattered with signposts. In the foreground there is a concrete litter bin, and scraps of litter can be seen among the roots

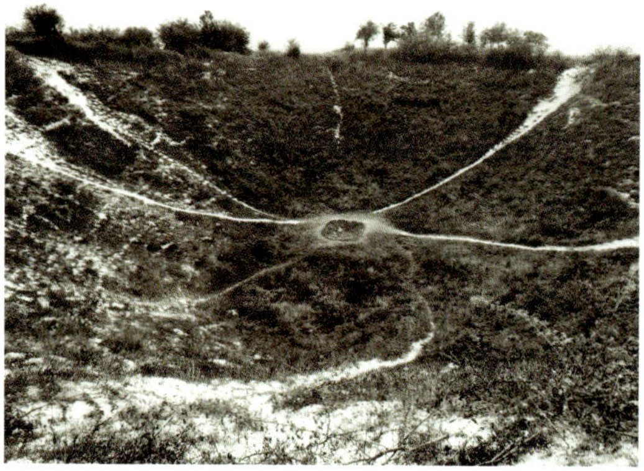

FIG.64
Peter Cattrell
Lochnagar Crater, La Boisselle, Somme
2000

of the hedgerow. The whole image is suffused by a melancholy fog, and, emerging in the background, there are the just-visible lights of a vehicle – a bus or lorry. This is a strange and fascinating image, hardly a landscape in the traditional sense, but a kind of elegiac scenario. It is markedly ordinary and in some sense without interest, but Moore has created a vision of this back-road in the border county of Dumfries that is evocative and haunting.

In creating this kind of landscape Moore had moved the tradition away from the 'site' and the 'vista'. This image was neither an historically significant location, nor a scenic wonder. Quite the reverse, it was landscape seemingly without interest, yet a landscape remarkably intense in its emotional impact, for in many ways this is a landscape governed by its strangeness. This quality would become a feature of a significant minority of post-war landscape photographs. And it might be suggested that something of this quality would emerge in the work of Peter Cattrell (b. 1959). Certainly Cattrell's early work, like the photograph *Shot Crow, Lothians* [FIG.63], demonstrates an acute sense of the ordinary landscape made unfamiliar by a combination of surprising elements. Here, a snow-scene landscape features a peaked hill, in fact an artificial mound of mine-working waste. In the foreground there are three strands of a barbed wire fence, and from the topmost strand hangs a dead crow. This macabre symbol is, of course, an example of the gamekeeper's craft, but the picture as a whole enfolds the everyday and the extraordinary. In doing so it reprises that strangeness evidenced in Moore's work.

Cattrell, however, sustains other interests in his landscape photographs. He was, at an early point in his career, the dedicated printing technician for Fay Godwin and something of her environmentalism is recalled in his landscapes. Moreover, Cattrell will often elide his landscape images with a discreet personal content. His many images of the trenches and battlefields of the First World War, the ongoing project titled *Terrain: Landscapes of the Great War*, are created partly as a memorial to his kin who died at these sites. Hence his photograph *Lochnagar Crater, La Boisselle, Somme* [FIG.64], taken in the year 2000, shows the remarkable and still extant hollow left by a mammoth explosion from the catastrophic battle of 1916. These are works that speak not only to the strangeness of some landscape scenes, but, once again, to the concern with humankind's extraordinary arrogance in relation to the natural world. This approach has also been a constituent part of the most contemporary of landscape practice, notably in the work of Dalziel & Scullion.

Dalziel & Scullion, who are Matthew Dalziel (b. 1957) and Louise Scullion (b. 1966), have worked together as multimedia artists since 1993. Their work encompasses the practices of still photography, film, video, installation and ambient sound. Fundamentally, the many projects they have engaged reflect upon the interrelationship between humankind and nature, and they have been instrumental in encouraging an ecological consciousness within a contemporary, neo-conceptual, art practice. In the project titled 'Storm', first exhibited in 2003, the artists collaborated with the academic ecologist Hugh Ingram to identify key sites throughout Scotland that signified primary biological and ecological processes. These they photographed and presented in light-box format complemented by ambient sound and a spoken commentary on the geological import of these landscapes [FIG.65]. An earlier project, 'Aura A' from 2002, presented digital photographic prints that combine and juxtapose 19th-century photographic images of environmental destruction with contemporary scenes, a direct commentary on the propensity of human progress to develop at the expense of the natural environment. In fact Dalziel & Scullion's imaginative displays meditate upon this core idea of sacrifice; they are, in part, presenting a threnody on the defeat of nature.

Landscape

These are different landscapes, but perhaps not so different. The threads of this landscape tradition have woven their way through a fairly consistent pattern within Scottish photography. Evidently, the early history of landscape photography is one of aesthetic appropriation from the fine art tradition, and commercial exploitation in the work of the major studios. Photographic images of landscape, particularly in the 19th century, tended to mirror the aesthetic canons first established in the art of painting, and so the photographer and his camera journeyed in the landscape as an eye that witnessed and popularised the idea of the land as metaphor. The metaphor might connote the notion of a sacred place, an historically significant site, a panorama of the nation, or indeed, in the case of 'travel' photography, a potential or actual imperial acquisition. Fundamentally, however, the coalescence of this metaphor signified history and identity. Hence the land bore the imprimatur of the 'people', and this was given a mythic expression in the visual culture.

If this can be viewed as the paradigm of landscape photography in 19th-century Scotland then it can be seen to conform to the dominant economic conditions of the period, a developing and expanding capitalism, and to the pressing ideological forms of the landscape ideal, an atavistic romanticism. Meanwhile, photographs like John Muir Wood's highly symbolic 'intimate' landscapes conjure with a pagan mysticism, and Dr John Murray's views of Indian temples project a more benign vision. Such examples do point to tensions within the landscape tradition, wherein the convention of an atavistic sentiment and imperialist ambition was constantly set against competing programmes that were partly spiritual, partly humanist.

The key moment within this process may prove to be Robert Moyes Adam's 'environmentalist' intervention, though it is important not to overstate Adam's credentials as an ecological evangelist. There is little evidence that he self-consciously sought a messianic role in the creation of an ecology movement, at least in the contemporary sense of that concept. He was, however, sympathetic to nature and an instinctive conservationist. In this respect his photographs prioritised a vision of wilderness at once inviolable and yet subtly endangered. And, for all his near-invisibility within the historical literature, he established a set of values that became ever more important as the 20th century progressed.

In the period after the Second World War, landscape photography from Scotland has increasingly explored the radical potential of Adam's legacy. This history describes a subtle and nuanced response to the threat to existing ecosystems as represented in

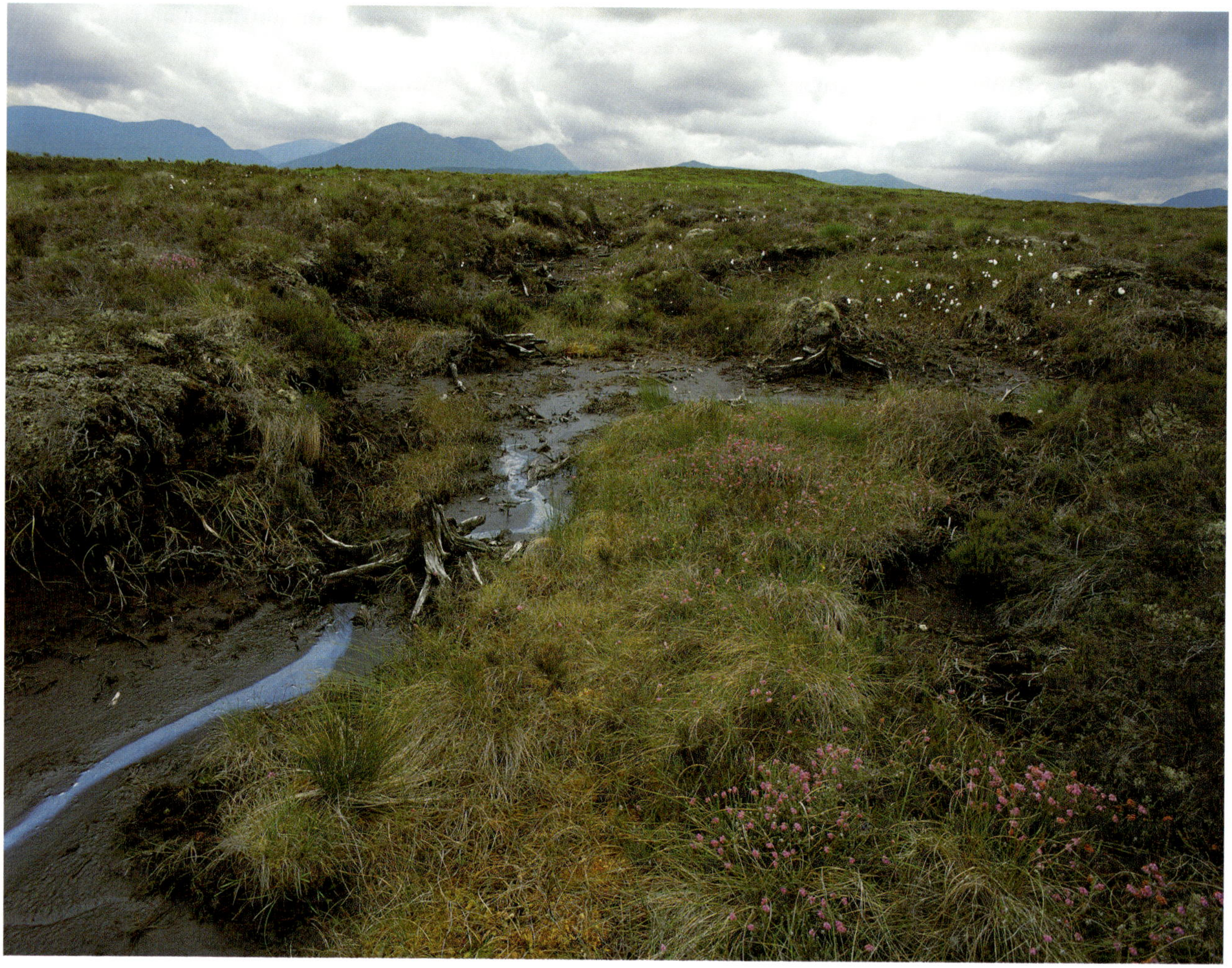

FIG.65
Dalziel and Scullion
Peat Bog from the project 'Storm'
2003

landscape images. Broadly, photographers have travelled one, or more, of three possible pathways. Images have emerged that focus on the mystical and intimate, perhaps transcendent, qualities of the natural world; a landscape still largely devoid of human intervention and, in that sense, primordial. Here the foremost example is the work of Thomas Joshua Cooper, an artist whose sense of the 'journey' is presaged in Robert Moyes Adam's project, and who has created one of the most significant bodies of photographic landscape in the contemporary period. At the other end of the scale there exist those landscape photographs that seek out the points of contact between the human and the natural in order to expose the 'stain' of intervention; these variously 'political' forms look to sensitise the viewer to issues of erosion and destruction occasioned by human action. Within this broad spectrum it is possible to locate the very different imagries of Patricia Macdonald and Dalziel and Scullion, as well as aspects of Peter Cattrell's work. Finally, there exists a 'landscape of form' that explores the interaction of humankind and nature as a necessary, though not always harmonious, partnership. Within this frame the land maintains an integrity that is yet vulnerable to corrosive pressures. Most obviously this approach has been evidenced in Raymond Moore's strange landscapes, but it is possible to see aspects of this aesthetic in most of the above.

The catalogue of contemporary landscape photographers who have adopted a more critical practice is, of course, broader and more diverse than those noted. But this must be balanced against the massive weight of commercial photographers who continue to produce images of 'romantic' Scotland. In truth the spirit of Wilson and Valentine lives on in the myriad depictions of castles, lochs, bens and glens that are the stock of the studio photographer. What is interesting, however, is the way this paradigm has been outflanked by more ambitious photographers. Landscape photographs, in this radical form, now view the land not only as an 'historic' space, that is to say a space embodying the suspect conceits of racial memory and national mythologies, but explore the land as a 'political' space. Within this frame the land is a place where social classes struggle, be it in the battle over ownership or simply concerning access. Here, also, the land assumes a role as the battleground wherein corporate ethics can be challenged. A landscape can represent the arena in which issues of commercial use, resource management and ecological sustainability might be opened out. Finally landscape photography itself may confront the greatest of all conceits, the notion of humankind's dominion over the earth and all therein. For a photography that privileges the 'otherness', the permanence and the primacy of nature serves to subordinate the destructive ego of humankind. In part, it seems, this has been the mission of the most advanced landscape photography from Scotland.

CHAPTER FOUR

Documentary

Documentary photography is a contested area, perhaps the most contested area in the history and theory of photography. The aspiration of photographers to recover reality, to comment upon the conditions of the poor, to examine the social world, to explode cultural norms, to 'document' the variety of life itself has, in recent years, become the subject of an unforgiving and rigorous critical analysis. This analysis focuses upon the means in which documentary photography has, historically and in every practical circumstance, engaged a 'discourse' that is ideologically and conceptually 'loaded'. That is to say, the documentary photographer, whatever his or her claims to realism and empiricism, has consistently viewed the world through the lens of personal and political value. More tellingly, in the post-modern environment, the documentary photographer is classified as an atom within a broader sphere of socio-cultural relations, and hence his or her photographs are locked into a normative system. In this case the documentary photograph becomes a 'sign' or 'index', corresponding to and symbolically expressing a universe of customs and practices that remain politically circumscribed. And so the documentary photograph may be challenged and 'unpacked' in order to reveal its implicit assumptions, those categories of belief that are the witness to an overarching power-matrix and dogma.

Of course, it was not always so. In the 19th century the photograph might be assumed to document the real world in an unmediated and 'scientific' fashion. The camera would simply record what it saw, and this record was viewed as an empirical truth. Moreover, if some ideological component was expressed, then it was the latent humanism of the documentary photographer, a desire to reflect upon, and so to ameliorate, the conditions of the poor. For, if portraiture presented the public face of the aristocracy and the middle classes, and landscape offered a meditation upon the history and memory of the nation, then documentary became the voice of the silenced. In the documentary photograph the living conditions of the urban masses were revealed, the working world of the labouring class was scrutinised, the nature of rural poverty and hardship was exposed, and the majestic, progressive, rapid social change of the modern world was publicised. In all this it was the world of the everyday and ordinary that was documented, and remarkably this world was shown to be exceptional and sometimes incredible.

Within this frame the documentary photographer might give voice to the power and agency of the mass of humanity, but equally the perceived voyeurism of the documentary photographer might project that mass as spectacle, or victim. In consequence the documentary movement has a mixed history. Beginning in the 1860s with a mission to witness the lives of the urban poor in order to facilitate municipal programmes for social improvement, the documentary photograph was a weapon in the armoury of paternalistic social reformers. In the first decades of the 20th century, and following from the radical agendas of Jacob Riis and Lewis Hine in the United States, documentary photographers mainly presented a political manifesto concentrating on the unrealised power of the working classes. Equally, the desperate poverty of rural communities was reported, in fact often aestheticised, again as a response to those politicised champions of the documentary movement who had worked under the auspices of the Farm Security Administration in the United States during the 1930s. In the period after the Second World War the epic, committed photo-essays of inter-war years were challenged by a more subjective notion of the documentary wherein the position of the photographer, in correspondence with the role of the subject, became a contingent element in the complex meanings of the photograph. And consequently the very category of 'documentary' became an arena for dispute and challenge.

All of these developments have been present within the Scottish context, but still the idea of the photograph as document has a special place within Scottish visual culture. In many ways this approach corresponds to that aspect of the Scottish Enlightenment that privileged a 'common sense' philosophy, the notion that the world existed as practical fact and could be recovered through empirical study. Equally, the implied reformist agendas of the documentary style paralleled the compulsion for social reform and charitable acts that lay within the Presbyterian consciousness. Likewise, there exists within the documentary aesthetic a humanist and progressive impulse that echoes the democratic, and democratising, sensibility of Scottish political and cultural life. For these reasons documentary photography has been prevalent within Scotland, and, it might be said, has been the dominant form within Scotland's photography; for all that Hill and Adamson photographed the worthies of the Free Church, they were also driven to recognise the fisherfolk of Newhaven, and everywhere it was the people of Scotland who emerged from the darkrooms of Scotland's photographers.

The sense of 'documentary photography', however, was an invention of the 1920s. Among the first to construct this concept was the Scottish film-maker John Grierson, a pioneer of the documentary film and an advocate of political reform. Grierson famously described documentary as the 'creative treatment of reality' and produced groundbreaking films on the fishing industry, on coal mining, and perhaps most prominently on the 'Night Mail', which was created for the General Post Office film unit and utilised the commissioned poem of that name by W. H. Auden, with music by Benjamin Britten. All of these were prime examples of documentary that recognised the contribution of workers to the general good and prosperity of the nation. Grierson, of course, was giving a name to a style of image making that was already firmly established, but not yet properly categorised. Before this time the camera was recognised as a mechanism that might record real events in an 'objective' manner, an instrument that recorded reality rather than interpreting the real world 'creatively'.

Yet this notion of the camera as a disinterested witness, an 'eye', is manifestly false. One of the first practical uses to which the camera was put was in the reporting of war, notably in the Crimean War. Roger Fenton's photographs of British actions in the Crimean conflict were specifically designed to assuage public opinion on the home front, and hence offered reassuring images of a sanitised war. Scottish photographers, also, would work in the Crimea, where James Robertson photographed actions at the Siege of Sebastopol in 1855,[1] and by 1857 Robertson would be employed by the British army in India. Meanwhile, Joseph Cundall (1818–75) would photograph soldiers destined to fight in the Crimean War, and produce, in partnership with Robert Howlett, his volume of portraits, *Crimean Braves*.

In fact both Fenton and Robertson seem to have been presaged as war photographers by a Scottish surgeon working in India, one John MacCosh (1805–85). The ethnographer John Falconer has reported that:

> The East India Company surgeon John McCosh [sic] was photographing during the Second Sikh War of 1848–49; in a later campaign, the Second Burmese War of 1852–53, McCosh was again an active photographer and as well as taking landscape, architectural and military scenes, illustrated his own interest in ethnological matters with a series of portraits of Indian, Burmese and African types, several of which are posed in full face and profile in the approved scientific manner.[2]

John Hannavay has offered the more interesting insight that 'MacCosh's pictures are "at war" rather than "of war"', and has remarked that MacCosh's work 'predates Fenton not only in war photography but in trips overseas'.[3]

War photography has been viewed as an archetype of the documentary image, an arena that demands objective report and frank assessment. Fenton, along with Robertson, and including MacCosh, began to map the terrain of this style but was surely compromised by patriotic obligation and personal preconception. However, the most scrupulous and innovative of war photographers in the 19th century was a Scot working in America, Alexander Gardner.

Alexander Gardner would emigrate to the United States in 1856 but he had previously travelled there, with his brother and fellow photographer James Gardner, in 1850. His project was to establish an ideal working community in the nature of Robert Owen's experiment in philanthropic management at New Lanark. This initial plan collapsed and, returning to Scotland in 1851, he became involved in the creation of a radical newspaper and would himself review photographic exhibitions. He is known to have admired the work of the noted American photographer Matthew Brady when this was exhibited at the 'Great Exhibition' in London in 1851, and he would review Roger Fenton's photographs of the Crimea in 1855. On emigrating to the United States Gardner was employed by Brady, quickly aspiring to the management of Brady's Washington studio in 1858. Brady's studio was chiefly known for its facility in the art of portraiture. But, of course, the United States were about to be torn apart by civil war. Brady's company became the favoured studio of the northern, Unionist states, and Alexander Gardner one of their most esteemed war photographers.[4]

The reputation of Brady's studios in the creation of portrait studies meant that the company was used as a dais for solemn portraits of newly commissioned Unionist officers, displayed in all the finery of their new uniforms. Gardner was part of this process and procession, helping take those famed shots of generals and staff. However, when sent into the field with a travelling darkroom he was to create two canonical images of the Civil War, one of which may be among the finest of war photographs. These were *President Lincoln on the Battlefield of Antietam*, 1862, and *Home of a Rebel Sharpshooter*, 1863 [FIG.66]. The posed image of Abraham Lincoln at Antietam Creek, flanked by the self-conscious Major General McClernand and the sullen, suspicious figure of another émigré Scot, Allan Pinkerton, has become an enduring symbol of the President at the battlefield. It is the photograph of the dead Confederate sharpshooter, however, that is a fixture in the annals of war photography. This is a curiously staged image.[5] The dead sniper lies, face to camera, within the protective carapace of his 'home'. This walled fissure between two large rocks is set with an opening that would allow the protected sharpshooter to select and target his quarry. Mortally

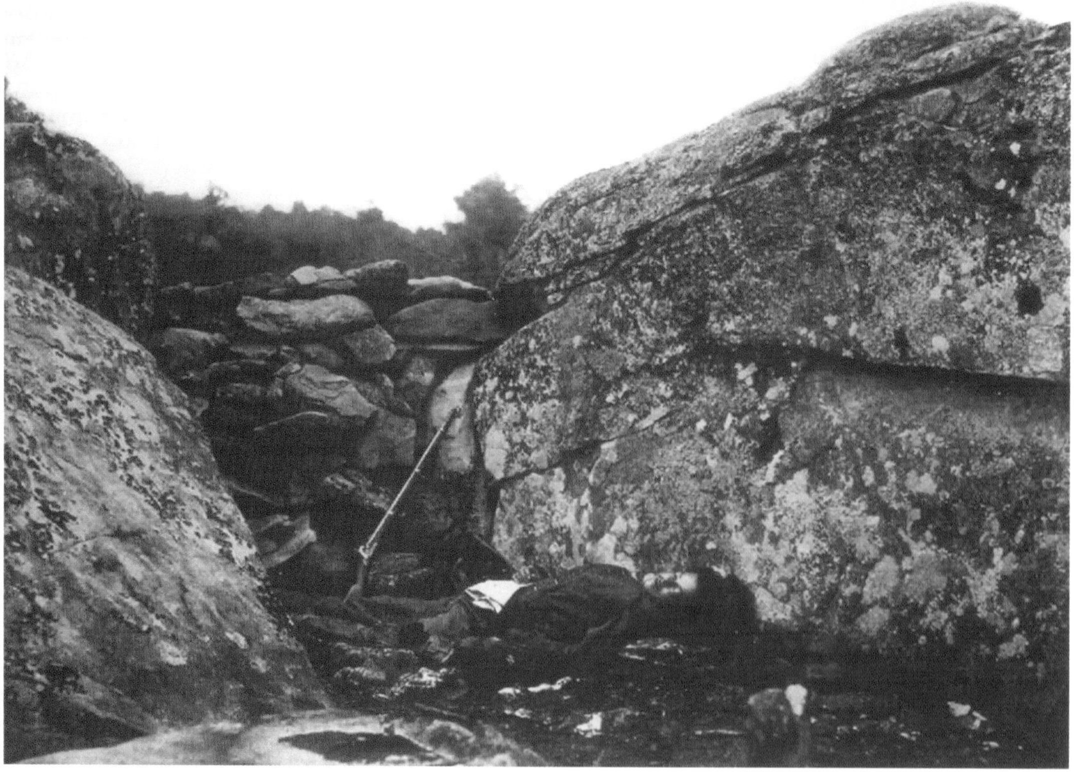

FIG.66
Alexander Gardener
Home of a Rebel Sharpshooter
1863

wounded, and evidently dead, he is posed with his canteen nearby and his rifle carefully propped against the constructed wall of stone. As a composition it is almost too perfect not to have been 'assisted', but Gardner has certainly created a manifesto for war photography; painfully realistic, identifiably of the battlefield, a detailed study of the conditions of warfare, and the embodiment of grim death. Gardner's work is amongst the first potent imagery depicting the terror and ugliness of war, and sets a standard that would become the measure of war photography in the 20th century.[6]

The unremitting torrent of wars in the 20th century was relentlessly photographed, and the camera became a singular weapon of modern warfare. It was, among other things, an instrument for reconnaissance, a tool of propaganda, a mechanism for recording action, and an unrivalled means for the creation and expression of protest. Few Scots have appeared in the record of eminent 20th-century war photographers, but a number were engaged in the First World War of 1914–18 and would create the unparalleled visual record of that momentous conflict. Most of these individuals, working for the British Ministry of Information, were anonymous or were plucked from the ranks to be trained with the camera. One fascinating example, however, is the figure of Mairi Lambert Chisholm (1896–1981).

Mairi Chisholm was a maverick individual. A daughter of the chief of Clan Chisholm, she was an early convert to motor transport and a renowned motorcycle rallyist, even in the first decade of the 20th century. At the outset of the First World War she immediately volunteered her services, working firstly as a despatch rider, then subsequently as an ambulance driver. With her associate, Elsie Knocker, she established a field hospital at Pervyse on the front line near Ypres and immediately adjacent to the battlefield. These extraordinary women became famed as the 'two women of Pervyse'. Astonishingly, in addition to Chisholm's heroic efforts caring for casualties, she was accompanied by a camera, in fact a Vest Pocket Kodak Autographic camera,[7] and there exists some five albums of papers and war photographs featuring Chisholm at the front.[8] A number of these photographs show the moment of bombardment and might be regarded as amongst the first authentic 'action' shots in modern warfare. The incendiary *Chisholm and Knocker Under Fire at Pervyse* [FIG.67] graphically depicts the moment of bombardment and a frantic search for cover. Importantly, these images were not part of the 'official' account, and in many ways these are the frankest expressions of the imminence of modern warfare, made all the more powerful for their naked realism.

Evidently, war, and war photography, was at the extreme of documentary. The core activity of the documentary photographer remained within the orbit of 'ordinary' life. In this context it was the activities in the new and expanding cities that became a focus for the documentary movement. And, within these cities, the world of lived associations; industry, work, home, leisure, play and the multiple, manifest facts of social being.

The city and urban life

The early history of photography in Scotland had, principally, been centred in the genteel capital city of Edinburgh. The key moment of documentary photography, however, occurred within the municipality of Glasgow. At the dawn of photography Glasgow was a city of extraordinary change and expansion. The technology of the camera and the chemistry of the

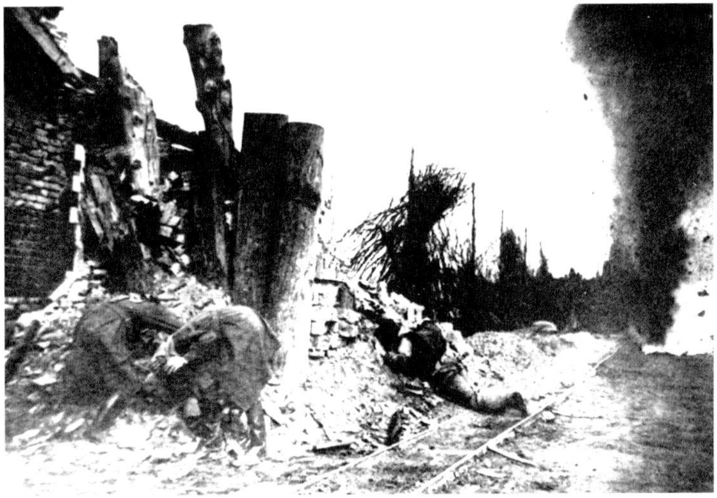

FIG.67
Mairi Chisholm
Chisholm and Knocker Under Fire at Pervyse
1917

photographic print had been parallel developments with the process of industrialisation, the enlargement of empire and the triumph of capitalism, and the city of Glasgow had been a hub of this change. By the 1850s Glasgow was already a central trading port with a mercantile class whose wealth had been founded on the tobacco trade, and then upon the industry of weaving. As the nature of commerce changed this was augmented by a powerful chemical industry, an unrivalled shipbuilding and engineering base, and a manufacturing industry that was both widespread and matchless. In truth Glasgow was 'the second city of Empire', and if London was the administrative centre of the British Empire then Glasgow was the thudding mechanical heart.

Of course, all this industrial development was accompanied by transformation in the city itself. T. C. Smout reports that Glasgow's population trebled between 1755 and 1831, and that in the next three decades it trebled once again.[9] This kind of exponential growth was occasioned by the opportunity for work and sustenance presented in the city, but it inevitably led to overcrowding, social problems and distress. By the middle of the 19th century Glasgow's inner city streets and hidden closes had become a byword for social congestion, crime, disease and poverty. Municipal authorities, government and church committees, philanthropic bodies and every kind of charitable organisation began to produce reports and demand changes that would ameliorate the social conditions of the poor, and allow for a greater control of the city's underclass. The most famous of these was Edwin Chadwick's *Sanitary Conditions of the Labouring Population of Great Britain*, a Poor Law Commission Report from 1842 that singled out the desperate poverty of Glasgow's inner city. By 1866 the municipal council had established the Glasgow Improvement Trust with the authority to redevelop the worst of the city's slums, notably those old closes around the High Street. And by 1868 the city fathers had commissioned Thomas Annan to make a photographic record of the 'old closes and streets' that were now condemned.

Annan's catalogue of these thoroughfares, wynds and closes has now become an archetype of documentary photography, recognised as one of the earliest and most celebrated of 'photo-essays'. Yet it can hardly have been conceived as such during its creation. Annan was requested to evidence the conditions of the urban slums, with a view to verifying the changes inaugurated by the Improvement Trust. Consequently, single albumen prints were provided after the first stage of the project was complete in 1871. Subsequently, 31 albumen prints were bound as a customised portfolio, with a published edition containing 40 carbon prints appearing from Robert Nelson and Son after 1877. The larger editions of these photographs, *The Old Closes and Streets of Glasgow*, with additional photogravure images taken either by John Annan or by James Craig Annan, appeared in 1900.[10] The trajectory of this distribution moves from a need to demonstrate the product of Annan's efforts to his commissioners in 1871, to an already aestheticised and nostalgic vision of 'Old Glasgow' in 1900. At no point was this a 'documentary' project in the sense of identifying the causes and nature of poverty, nor even a self-conscious proselytising for social change. Thomas Annan was recording social life, certainly, but he was recording this world as the fulfilment of a duty, a practical, commercial sponsorship.

Yet Annan would certainly have been sympathetic to the qualified aims of social progress and public health. Thomas Annan (1829–87) arrived in Glasgow, from Fife, in 1849. He was to continue in his chosen profession of lithographer and engraver until 1855, when he first recognised the opportunity afforded by commercial photography. By 1857 he had his own studio in Glasgow's principal thoroughfare, Sauchiehall Street, and in 1859 he had created his own photographic printing works. Annan's company, then, was a West Coast counterpart to Washington Wilson in Aberdeen and Valentine in Dundee. Like these illustrious figures he produced a number of worthy portraits, notably his image of the Scots missionary David Livingstone taken in 1864, and was awarded medals and honours for his landscape works. His specialist activity, however, was in photographing artworks, and it was Thomas Annan whom David Octavius Hill called upon to create the photographic reproductions of his epic canvas *The Signing of the Deed of Demission*. This link through Hill to the Free Church is significant, for

Annan was a religious man, an advocate of abstention from alcohol, and something of a socially conscious reformer. His drive to reform was fundamentally shaped by his religious commitment and so the desires of Glasgow's Improvement Trust – sanitary housing, a disease-free environment, a policed inner city, a morally constructed community – were allied to Annan's views. In other words, Annan's 'documentary' photographs were 'political' only in the qualified sense that they propagated a paternalistic form of social engineering.

Something of this ideology is evident in the actual photographs. Set with the task of photographing in dilapidated streets, and in dark, dank and dangerous alleyways, Annan chose the wet collodian process as the most advantageous technique. Of course this also required time and effort in preparing the plates, on site, and in setting up his composition. In the event he created remarkably redolent images, most particularly of the 'old closes'. These warrens of human life are described in infinite detail; steeply sided and closely gathered tenements, doors, windows and stairwells set at every angle, all gathered upon a bedrock of fractured cobbles and flagstones running with water. *Close No. 37, High Street* [FIG.68], from 1868, is a case in point. This photograph explores the closed and claustrophobic character of the tenement architecture, especially in the back passageways. The buildings are ramshackle and decaying, the living conditions rudimentary and demeaning. Yet the view contains elements of the picturesque. Annan, typically, has been careful to note the washing-lines and freshly laundered clothing. He has ensured that a primitive street lamp is located near the centre of his photograph. And he has arranged groups of figures at the front, mid-point and background of his composition. These individuals were surely compliant models, obviously so for they would have been required to stand still for the period of exposure and one child, in the front left of the picture, has clearly moved. The scene, then, is one of human fortitude and endurance in conditions of decay. Annan was highlighting the notion that these were the 'deserving poor', individuals who were put upon by circumstance but who would respond to the provision of a healthy and socially constructive environment. In this respect he was mirroring the ideology of those agencies who were commissioning his project, while simultaneously constructing an aesthetic of urban poverty.

This aesthetic of urban poverty can not, strictly speaking, be proclaimed a 'documentary' programme for its roots lay in the notion of the picturesque. In fact this became something of a paradigm in 19th-century urban photography. Julie Lawson has written on the work of the Edinburgh photographer William Donaldson Clark (1816–73), noting that:

> Clark's depiction of the city and its monuments often conform, as might be expected, to established ideas of pictorial composition. His *Whitehorse Close*, for example, is a fairly conventional view of a traditionally 'picturesque' motif.[11]

Whitehorse Close, a scenic passageway in Edinburgh's 'Old Town', and possibly the original site of the stables belonging to Holyrood Palace, was a common subject for academic painters. Later, in 1905, and again in 1954, it would be lovingly photographed in a 'pictorial' style by the American photographer turned British national, Alvin Langdon Coburn. Clark's signature works, however, were topographical views of Edinburgh's 'New Town' architecture, notably his singular view of *The National Gallery and the Royal Institution (Royal Scottish Academy)* [FIG.69], taken in 1858. In parallel to these images of modern Edinburgh, Clark would journey into the late-medieval 'Old Town', chiefly the area around the Cowgate. Here, he photographed the subterranean streets and wynds, occasionally juxtaposing these against the architecture of the new 'classical' Edinburgh above, as in *The Cowgate Arch of George IV Bridge* [FIG.70], from circa 1860.

In the final third of the 19th century Edinburgh's 'Old Town' was, like the 'Old Closes' of Glasgow, a subject for municipal concern. Consequently, while Thomas Annan was reflecting upon the living conditions of the inner-city poor in Glasgow at least one Edinburgh-based photographer was being commissioned to document the condemned medieval slums of the capital city's 'Old Town'. This was Archibald Burns (active 1858–89). Thomas Annan, of course, was commissioned by the Glasgow Improvement Trust as early as 1868, whereas Burns was sponsored by the Edinburgh Improvement Trust in 1871. Hence

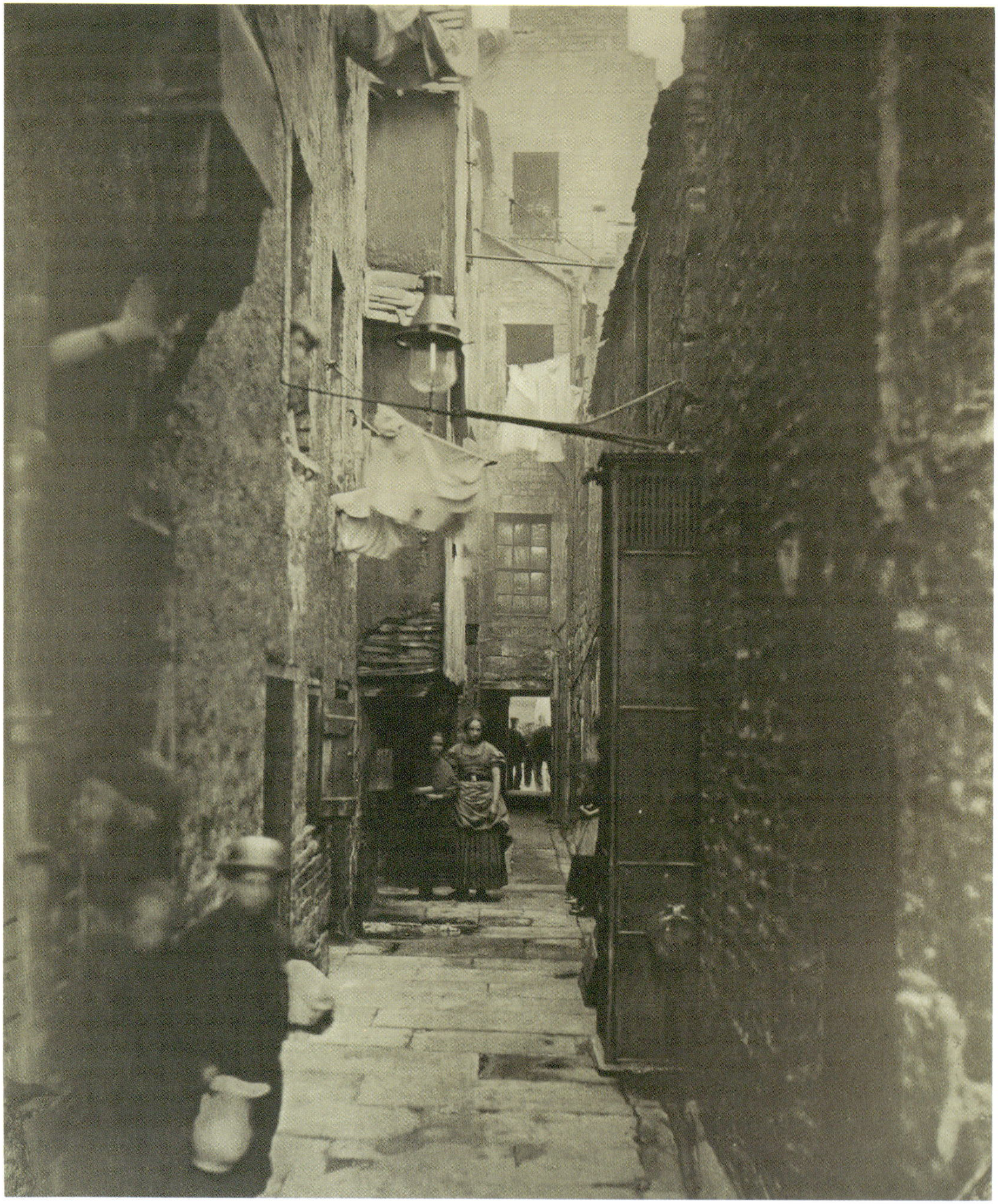

FIG.68
Thomas Annan
Close No 37, High Street
1868

the twist of fate that allows for Annan's canonical place in the history of documentary photography and Burns' relative obscurity. However, there is a fascinating connection between Annan and Burns, and one that links them to that great pioneer of photography, David Octavius Hill. Hill's studio was, famously, Rock House, situated at the bottom of Calton Hill at the eastern end of Edinburgh's Princes Street. Hill, evidently, had connections with Thomas Annan and his company, who photographed his painting of the dissident Free Church ministers. Moreover, Hill's widow would bequeath his negative plates to Annan, and it was through the connection of James Craig Annan and Alfred Stieglitz that these would become celebrated in the journal *Camera Work*. Thomas Annan, a committed admirer of Hill, would occupy part of the Rock House studio for a brief period between 1870 and 1871.[12] At this same time Archibald Burns is registered as occupying part of this building, and in fact the building was registered as a photographic studio from Hill and Adamson's occupancy in 1843 until the 20th century. Burns would have had some knowledge of Annan's work, though not, perhaps, his urban photography. In any case Burns was to create some extraordinary images of Edinburgh's decaying back streets that correspond with Annan's project.

Archibald Burns' photographs, most particularly *The Horse Wynd, Edinburgh* and *The Cowgate, Edinburgh* [FIG.71], both from 1871, should be framed within the context of the picturesque. Indeed his most famous photographic publication, *Picturesque Bits from Old Edinburgh*, proclaims this aesthetic in its title.[13] Burns, then, was clearly interested in the scenic aspects of urban decay, and this quality is replete in his views of imposing gables, derelict buildings and dilapidated shops. The tumbledown nature of these scenes has been curiously accented by the absence of any human presence, for these streets have already been abandoned in preparation for demolition. The vision, then, is that of a ghost town and the urban environment is presented as a ruin. Naturally this initiates a feeling of melancholy and an overwhelming desultory air. In this respect, at least, these works are to be separated from Annan's views of Glasgow.

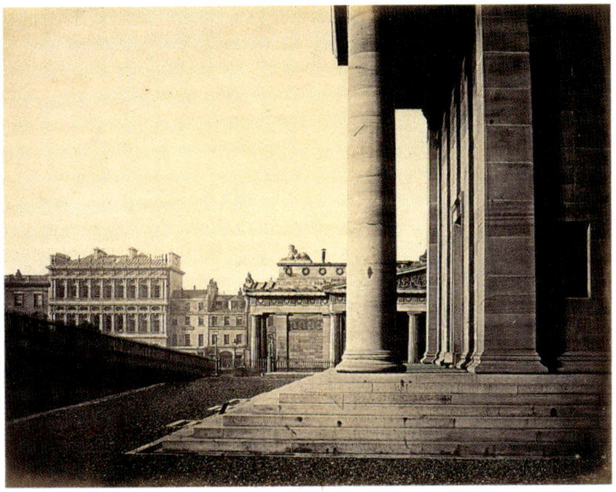

FIG.69
William Donaldson Clark
The National Gallery and the Royal Institution (Royal Scottish Academy)
1858

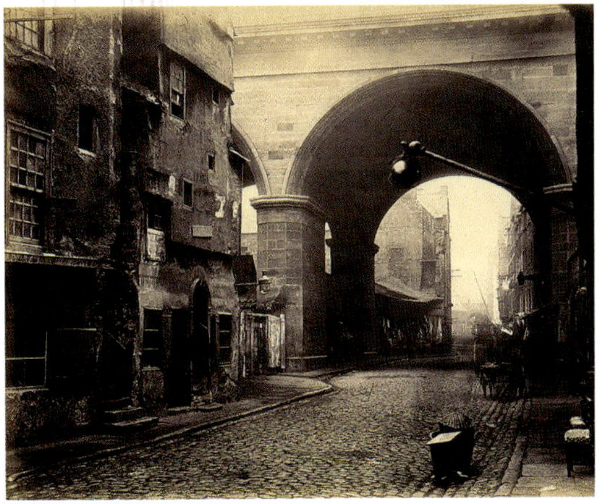

FIG.70
William Donaldson Clark
The Cowgate Arch of George IV Bridge
circa 1860

Annan's was a social world, figures were posed and composed, but it was, nevertheless, representative of human interaction with the environment. Burns' Edinburgh is deserted. Given this, it is evident that Annan comes closer to a modern sense of the 'documentary' image. His Glasgow is a world of activity and negotiation, a place where people can be seen to live and work and create.

If the urban photographs of Thomas Annan and Archibald Burns represent moderately divergent enterprises at the nebulous pole of a 'documentary' spectrum, then the claim of prescience in the construction of a radical documentary photography may well be cited with another Scottish protagonist, John Thomson. In 1872 Thomson was to return from

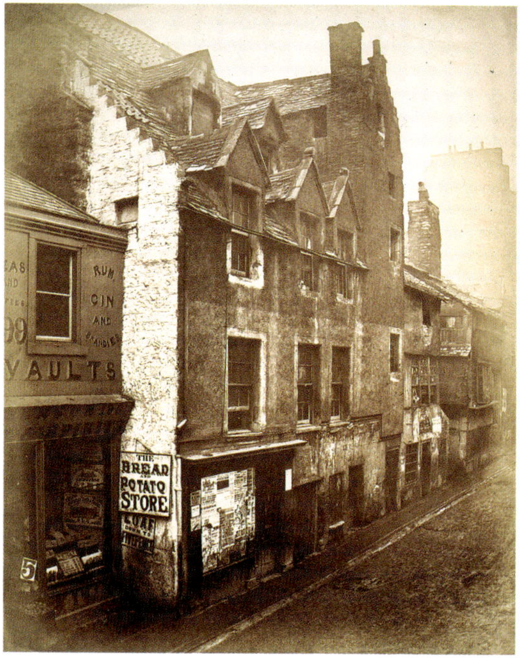

FIG.71
Archibald Burns
The Cowgate, Edinburgh
1871

his various journeys in the Far East as an established photographer and already a champion of The Royal Geographic Society, where his photographs were treasured as documentary accounts of foreign parts. Such was his reputation, not only for his landscape images but also for his candid street scenes, that he was approached by the journalist Adolphe Smith to help create a documentary account of London street life. Smith was recognised as a radical journalist and his ambition to document the nomads of the London streets was part of a reformist agenda that had its roots in Victorian philanthropy and social concern.[14] In 1876 Smith approached Thomson to illustrate his articles, which were published, initially, as monthly serials titled *Street Life in London*. Thomson would create some 36 photographs between 1876 and 1877, and these would eventually be published in book form, using woodburytype reproductions, in 1878. This book, *Street Life in London*, with a text by Adolphe Smith, can be identified as a pivotal moment in the history of documentary photography.

In *Street Life in London* Smith's ambition was to record the lives of itinerant street dwellers and outdoor tradespeople. In this event Thomson was to take images of costermongers, fish-sellers, locksmiths, flower-women, and also 'Nomades' or travelling people complete with their Vardo. The purpose of the project was, partly, to accent the enterprise of these individuals such that they might be classified as 'deserving poor' and so respected despite their situation. An image like *'Hookey Alf' of Whitechapel*, for example, shows a crippled man who is yet making himself available for work. The point at which Thomson moves towards a radical documentary image, however, is with his most reproduced of photographs, *The Crawler* [FIG.72]. Whereas many of Thomson's documentary photographs were posed and staged, this image remains blunt and uncompromising. It depicts an aged, destitute woman collapsed in a doorway; a provocatively off-centre photograph. Around her are a few objects of use, a pot and a teacup, and in her arms an infant child. This child, her charge, seems to have been left with her while the mother works at some other labour. The 'crawler', as Smith makes clear in his text, is simply too fatigued to undertake any other kind of work. This, then, represented the sink of despair and poverty, and this woman sits at the lowest point in the social scale. It is possible to accuse Thomson of voyeurism and a kind of exploitation in taking this photograph, but it remains rooted in the cultural values of Victorian reformism. It was these values that were to expand into 20th-century documentary photography, and in many ways Thomson's *The Crawler* looks forward to the socially engaged photography of the 1930s.

Thomas Annan first produced his views of urban squalor in 1868, and John Thomson's photographs of the urban poor were completed in 1877, but nearly a century would elapse before this documentary component in photography from Scotland was given further expression. In fact, there is a lacuna in Scottish documentary photography from the late 19th century until the early years of the 1960s, and there appears to be no Robert Moyes Adam-type figure to fill that gap. This is not to say that documentary was altogether absent. The increasing use of photography within the field of journalism and the newspaper industry relied upon a sense of the photograph as report and record, though this was never 'photo-journalism', and the publishing industry was dedicated to the use of photographs as illustrative material. The sense of a self-conscious 'documentary' convention was, however, rare. This is all the more surprising given the fever for documentary images in the early years of the 20th century. In America, Lewis Hine established a manifesto for the documentary image, and was followed by his protégé Paul Strand as well as the canon of celebrated documentary photographers from Dorothea Lange through Walker Evans and on to W. Eugene Smith. In Europe, documentary was the favoured style of the Soviet bloc countries, while the photographic cooperative Magnum was founded in 1947, with Robert Capa, David Seymour (Chim) and Henri Cartier-Bresson privileging a humanistic photo-journalism. In Scotland, local photographers were distanced from these momentous developments, and the tradition of documentary photography was carried by outside photographers moving to the country in search of a subject.

Given the propensity for boom and slump within the Scottish economy there existed a rich harvest for documentary image-makers, most especially within Scotland's urban and industrial cities. Moreover, the radicalism of the inter-war years occasioned a significant interest in the life and culture of the working class. This was manifest in a fascinating exercise in social anthropology, or rather sociology, the influential study titled 'Mass-Observation'. Established in 1937, the Mass-Observation unit was created in order to 'discover' the lived world of the working class. Initiated by the young dilettante and adventurer Tom Harrison, along with the communist poet Charles Madge, Mass-Observation set out to document the life and activities of ordinary people in their everyday environment. In this event they collaborated with groups of volunteers who were assigned to observe and note the behaviour of individuals in their communities, at work and during leisure times. The signature study of 1937–40, titled 'Worktown', was based in Bolton in the north-west of England, and set the pattern for their dissection of working-class life. Besides the observational histories, the Mass-Observation unit also contained the expertise of the film-maker Humphrey Jennings and the photographer Humphrey Spender. Jennings was an established documentary film-maker working, from 1934, with the General Post Office film unit; this, of course, made him a colleague and associate of John Grierson. Spender was a recognised documentary photographer who would become a prolific contributor to the ground-breaking journal *Picture Post*, alongside luminaries like Bill Brandt and Bert Hardy. 'Mass-Observation', for all its methodological eccentricity and public-school radicalism, established a pattern for the documentary study of working-class communities in the late 1930s, and Jennings, Brandt and Hardy, among others, would come to photograph in the cities of Scotland.

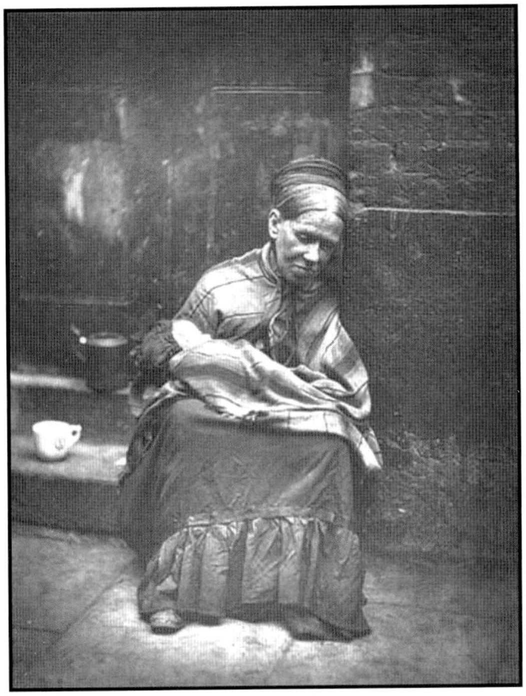

FIG.72
John Thomson
The Crawler
circa 1877

Once again, it was the industrial city of Glasgow that became the focus for these documentary studies of the 1930s and 1940s. In the period after the First World War Glasgow became recognised as a pre-eminently working-class city. Its denizens were engaged in industrial production, and with these industries came political organisation and radical activism. Glasgow, logically, was the city base for the revolutionary movement of 'Red Clydeside' in 1919, and a centre for the establishment of Labour Party politics in the general election of 1922. The Labour Party, then, was wholly committed to a government-sponsored welfare programme, and Glasgow was sorely in need of welfare throughout the inter-war years. Naturally, the economic slump of the late 1920s and 1930s bit deepest into the living conditions of Glasgow's industrial workers, and this became manifest in desperate poverty, serious social problems and hopeless housing conditions. The areas most exposed to this distress were those where unskilled workers and immigrants lived closest to the line of abject poverty. In Glasgow this dubious distinction was held by the neighbourhood of the Gorbals, just to the south and east of the city centre. The Gorbals was, in the 1930s, a densely populated urban slum that housed not only the unskilled and unemployed working class, but also Irish and other immigrants and a high proportion of Jewish refugees from Europe. Moreover, it gained a national reputation for violence and gang warfare in the period after 1935. This was occasioned by the publication of the book *No Mean City: A Story of the Glasgow Slums*, by Alexander McArthur and H. Kingsley Long. McArthur's story of razor-gangs and poverty, set in the Gorbals, was edited by Long, a London-based journalist, and came to represent the face of urban squalor in Scotland's largest city. This was a representation that held a considerable appeal to politically inspired documentary photographers.

Documentary photography, in Britain, was given momentum by the establishment of journals that sought to review and reveal the life of the country in photo-essays and through photo-journalism; chief amongst these was *Picture Post*. *Picture Post* was established in 1938 and its mixture of compelling documentary images, campaigning journalism and upbeat stories made it an instant and popular success. Under the editorship of Tom Hopkinson it grew to become a proselytising, though still populist, journal circumspectly promoting social change through socially conscious photo-essays. In 1939 Humphrey Spender (1910–2005) was sent to Glasgow, where he recorded the political and social life of the city, including the more positive aspects of working-class life. Nearly a decade later, in 1947, the veteran war photographer Bert Hardy (1913–95) was sent to document life in the Gorbals.[15] Hardy's essay for *Picture Post*, which appeared in January 1948, was fascinating for the way it engaged with the streets of the community, and the individuals within their cramped tenement flats. In fact Hardy established a convention for images that recorded the dilapidated streets in conjunction with children playing. His *The Gorbals, Glasgow* [FIG.73], 1948, for example, presents a street scene that is characteristically bare and unadorned, but nevertheless fills the frame with two young boys about to cross the road. These children look straight into the camera lens, and are far from hopeless cases. In fact they represent a form of confidence, enterprise and resilience despite their surroundings. This was not always the case in Hardy's images of the Gorbals, which could show evidence of heartbreaking despair, but this would become a familiar trope of documentary images relating to the urban poor; endurance in the face of adversity and children as the representatives of hope.

A similar theme was developed by another visitor to Scotland who would embrace the radical potential of the documentary image. Wolfgang Suschitzky, the Austrian émigré who had fled his native country in

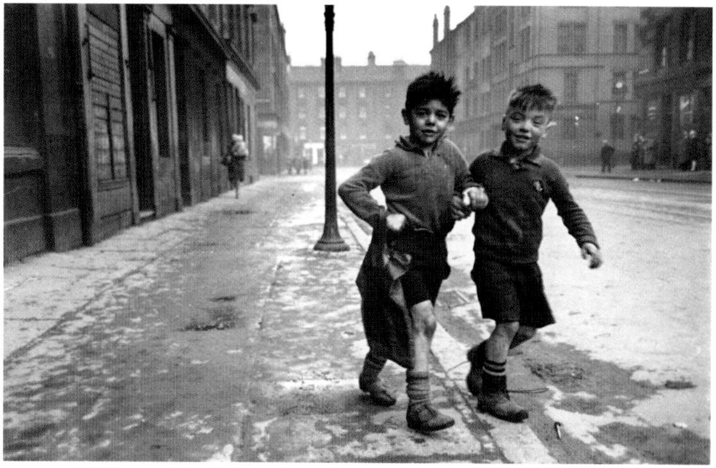

FIG.73
Bert Hardy
The Gorbals, Glasgow
1948

1934, would photograph in both Glasgow and the city of Dundee. Suschitzky, who was both of Jewish origin and socialist commitments, had every reason to leave Austria in the 1930s, and arrived in London in time to see a flowering of his favoured documentary style.[16] Employed, in part, by the Ministry of Information, he photographed children in Scotland's cities as a component of a government-sponsored project to control aberrant youth. Suschitzky, however, presented an extraordinarily vivid and lively picture of young people. His *Washing Strung Between Tenements, Dundee* [FIG.74], from 1948, remains a stunning symbol of working-class fortitude and the energy of the urban poor. A low perspective accentuates the clean laundry, hung like triumphant banners, while the two young girls in the foreground, leaning on dustbins, signal a vibrant resistance to social inequality.

In fact the overriding mood of these documentary images from the 1930s and 1940s is one of defiance and optimism. Certainly the aura of 'no mean city' feeds through the scenes and episodes, but the sense of these photographs is one of potential and confidence. In part this was dictated by editorial policy, and the demands of commissioning agencies like the Ministry of Information, but the politics of these photographers also leant towards notions that the working class held the key to the future. As post-war austerity developed into economic prosperity this future would begin to be realised and it was, once again, documentary photographers working in the Gorbals who would record these changes.

Glasgow's perennial health and housing problems were beginning to be addressed with The Housing Act (Scotland) of 1954. From this period the close, tenement-based communities of Glasgow were gradually re-housed in high-rise, modernist flats. In 1958 a plan by the architect Basil Spence, already famous for his design for Coventry Cathedral and his pavilions for the Festival of Britain in 1951, proposed the demolition of the Gorbals' tenements and their replacement by high-rise blocks. Consequently, nearly a century after Thomas Annan photographed Glasgow's inner city slums at the point of their demolition and re-development, documentary photographers began to record the streets of the Gorbals as they were fundamentally transformed. The most important figures in this ambitious documentary programme were the photographers Oscar Marzaroli (1933–88) and Joseph McKenzie (b. 1929).

Oscar Marzaroli was of Italian birth but his parents moved to Scotland in 1935, part of that wave of immigration that would provide Scotland with a welcome cultural, and culinary, pluralism. Marzaroli, however, developed as a photographer, after a short period at Glasgow School of Art, spending an apprenticeship as a photo-journalist in Europe and in London before returning to Glasgow in 1959. For the next 30 years Marzaroli, in conjunction with a liveli-

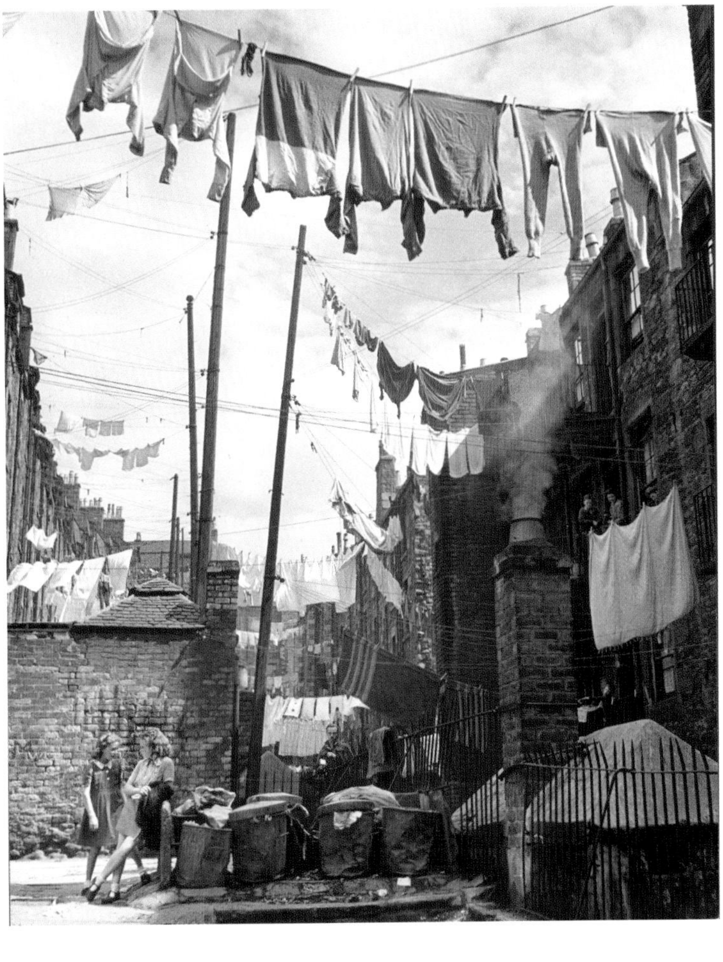

FIG.74
Wolfgang Suschitzky
Washing Strung Between Tenements, Dundee
1948

hood made as a film-maker, would photograph the changing streets of Glasgow and the lives of the city's people. His photography was a hymn to the everyday world; offering praise to working people, street life, children at play, public parades, fun-fairs and festivals, markets and shops, communions and weddings. All of this was captured in a documentary style, informal, sometimes utilising the distance employed in Cartier-Bresson's 'decisive moment', but more often with the full participation of his subjects. This was most pronounced in his photographs of children at play. The young look directly into the camera lens, more with curiosity than self-consciousness, such that Marzaroli offers up the most honest and convincing story of childhood in urban Glasgow.

In the early 1960s Marzaroli was able to photograph the fundamental changes being made to the area of the Gorbals. His *The Old and New Gorbals* [FIG.75], from 1964, juxtaposed the old and condemned tenement blocks of a Gorbals street against the background of a modern high-rise block under construction. Typically, the old street is occupied by children playing while the cranes in the background create their new world. There is a shade of nostalgia here, but little rancour. Marzaroli was a photographer gripped by the patterns of social change, yet passionate about the resilience of individuals and the processes of adaptation to environment that characterise human life. It is for this reason that children were a favoured subject. In their patterns of play and their fluid social interaction, children consistently adapt to new situations and create other worlds. A significant group of Marzaroli's street images consist of children on swings, girls skipping, boys climbing, infants drawing on walls and, naturally, boys playing football. These are the representatives of the everyday world of the child, but they symbolically denote the power of human fortitude. They are an emblem of creativity in the midst of poverty and so signal resilience. In this event it is difficult to view Marzaroli's ideological position

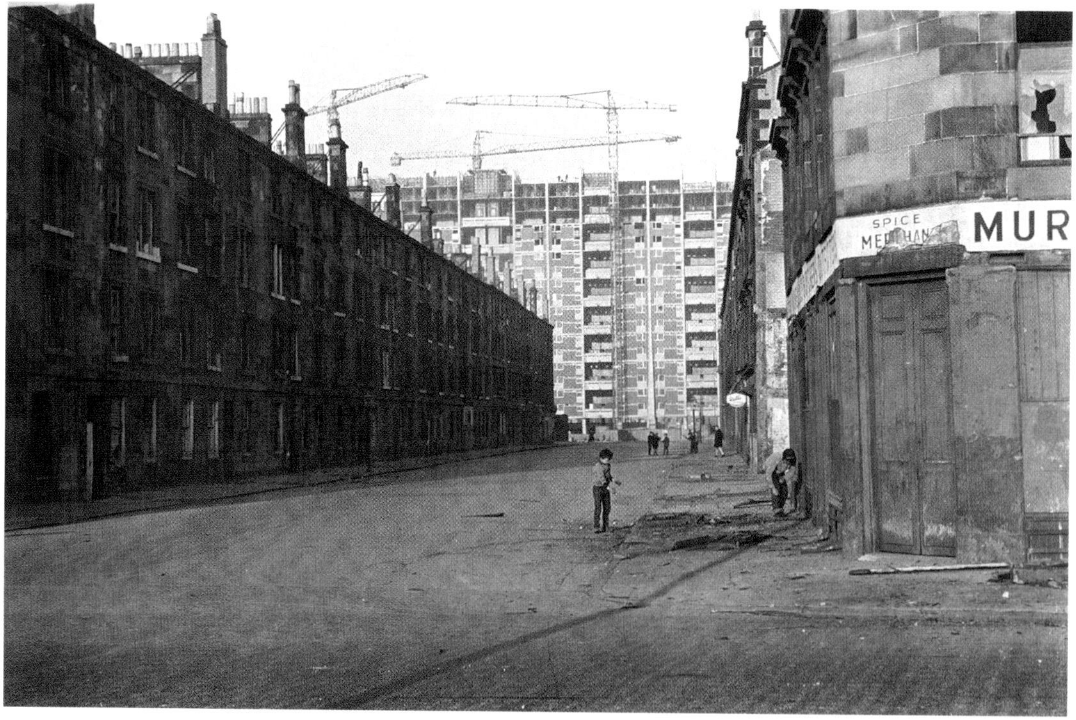

FIG.75
Oscar Marzaroli
The Old and New Gorbals
1964

as paternalist, in the manner of Thomas Annan, or even as a socially concerned reformism, in the style of the documentary radicals from the 1930s. Rather, Marzaroli presented a documentary form that offered a non-judgemental reportage, which nevertheless viewed its subject with respect and something approaching awe.

Marzaroli's view of childhood had been, partly, informed by the work of a painter, Joan Eardley. Eardley and Marzaroli were friends and he was aware that she would photograph in the area around Port Glasgow. Her photographs were often of the graffiti drawn on the tenement walls, and of the local children themselves. In some ways Eardley 're-discovered' childhood in the late 1950s, moving it away from the mawkish connotations of Victorian sentiment and into a realist frame. Marzaroli was sensitive to this idea, as was Joseph McKenzie.

Joseph McKenzie had trained as a photographer at the London School of Printing from 1952 until 1954. Previously he had served in the Royal Air Force and had been involved with air reconnaissance. As a young man in London's Hoxton area, McKenzie had photographed street markets as a hobby, and had joined the local camera club in Bethnal Green. Following his period at the London School of Printing he worked as a lecturer in photography, and was employed in this position by Duncan of Jordanstone College of Art in Dundee, in 1964. It was at this time that he took a group of students through to Glasgow to review an exhibition of paintings by Joan Eardley.[17] Eardley's studies of Glasgow children chimed with McKenzie's early interest in street life, and subsequently he would travel from Dundee to Glasgow's Gorbals to photograph the world of the changing streets. This project, 'Gorbals Children', ran in parallel to Marzaroli's photography and would become McKenzie's signature work.[18]

McKenzie's view of the Gorbals tends to focus on the comic interaction of children. There are a number

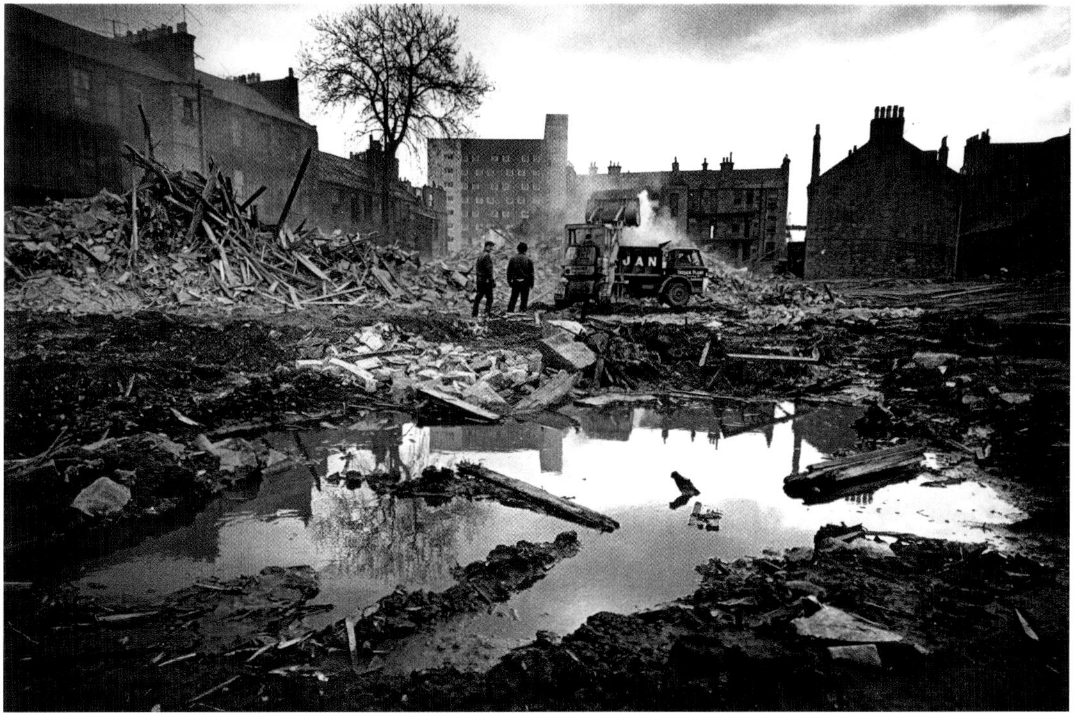

FIG.76
Joseph McKenzie
from 'Hawkhill: Death of a Living Community'
1972

of more contextual images, but the most potent works are closely-cropped studies of young children engaging with the camera. Very often, as in *Beatle Girl*, and again in *Two Boys*, both from 1964–65, there is a deliberate sense of playful clowning. Here, the subjects are allowed to pose for the camera, and the notion of uncompromising documentary reportage is usurped. Nevertheless, McKenzie's work has consistently maintained a documentary edge. He has completed a number of projects throughout Scotland that have looked at social change and the ordering of the everyday world. Following his studies in the Gorbals of 1964–65, McKenzie undertook assignments including: 'Dunfermline and its People', sponsored by the Carnegie Trust in 1968; the controversial 'Hibernian Images' focusing on the Troubles in Northern Ireland and completed during 1967–69;[19] and also various endeavours recording industry, oil-production and Highland life.

McKenzie's most consistent subject, however, has been his adopted city of Dundee. From 1964 until 1987, he photographed this most neglected of cities in all its guises [FIG.76]. This subject has progressed through various themes and projects, 'Dundee: City in Transition', 'Men and Locomotives', 'Women of Dundee', 'The Building of the Tay Road Bridge' and the epic 'Hawkhill: Death of a Living Community'. Invariably it has been the people in these communities who have been most closely observed; children in the backstreets, workmen on demolition sites, women in factories. Everywhere these individuals are shown as part of a thriving community, impoverished certainly, but rich in personality and a sense of self.

Both Marzaroli and McKenzie emerged at a point in 20th-century history where a number of social changes began to converge. Post-war austerity was giving way to an economic boom, and so the faces and the nature of Scotland's cities began to change. The working class were 'discovered', not only as a potent political force but as a richly diverse cultural group with a valuable store of customs and traditions and rituals. Moreover, the hierarchies of class and privilege were beginning to erode, such that opportunity was afforded to a wider cross-section of individuals. There is a sense in which these were years of expectation and hope, and both Marzaroli and McKenzie represented this prospect. Interestingly, neither seemed particularly aware of the photographic tradition they were employing – the documentary themes of Annan, Spender and Hardy – nor of the corresponding explosion of 'Young Meteors' of documentary photography emerging in London during the late 1950s, including Don McCullin and David Bailey.[20] What Marzaroli and McKenzie articulated was intuitive and spontaneous, a sympathetic reaction to manifest social change and the people most closely touched by that change.

Industry

The story of Scotland's people was intimately connected to the changes in Scotland's cities, but it was also bound to the world of work. During the 19th century in particular, the workforce shifted from the countryside into the cities as the nature of production changed from an agrarian base to a substantial industrial economy. Scotland became the motor of the British industrial revolution, and the engine room of empire. Much of the coal, the steel, the ships and the component machine parts of industrial expansion were mined, made and manufactured in Scotland's central belt; that hub of heavy industrial landscape that spread outwards from the Forth and Clyde valleys. It was the camera that documented this expansion and industry, and the camera that celebrated this achievement. A correlate of scientific and technical engineering, the camera was comfortable with the industrial world, and perhaps the only creative tool capable of generating an aesthetic compatible with the subject of industry. Certainly, the photograph was, early in its history, the preferred medium for recording industrial triumph.

It was Thomas Annan who first documented historic feats of industrial engineering. The redevelopment of Glasgow that he was to record in 1868 was predicated upon the creation of a safe and sanitary water supply. In 1855 the British government sanctioned the construction of a pipeline from Loch Katrine, in the Trossachs, to the heart of the city. The building of a dam, aqueducts and distribution pipes, as well as sophisticated water-works and water storage facilities, was recognised as a miracle of Victorian engineering and enterprise. Queen Victoria would open the new waterway in 1859, but Annan had already produced his *Views from the Line of the Loch Katrine Water Works*.[21] These photographs were a kind of reportage, documenting the complicated aquatic engineering and most particularly the vast pipeline as it swept through the countryside to the north of the city. His *Syphon Pipes in the Endrick Valley* is typical in the way it juxtaposes the metal water pipes with the natural landscape.[22] This sense of the new industrial reality imposing itself upon the natural world would become characteristic of many documentary images, but this was not generally presented as a negative feature. Rather this industry was viewed as evidence of a regenerated and increasingly democratic economy.

There was, in fact, a single and incontrovertible emblem of this brave new world and one that was rightly celebrated in photographic studies; the Forth Bridge. As the nation industrialised, and the need for a fast and efficient communications network became ever more insistent, the railway spread northwards. The east-coast line, through Edinburgh and on to Dundee and Aberdeen, was an economic necessity, but was thwarted by two mighty natural features, the rivers Forth and Tay. The River Tay was bridged by a railway line in 1877, but the disaster of December 1879 created a public anxiety concerning the capability for successfully spanning these natural features.[23] Thomas Bouch, the designer of the first Tay Bridge, had been involved in a proposal to span the even more challenging River Forth. Following the tragic failure of the Tay Bridge he was replaced by Benjamin Baker, who employed the ingenious William Arrol as his contractor, with John Fowler as a consulting engineer. Together, and with an international workforce, they created an epic cantilevered bridge that remains today a wonder of the industrial age, and the finest work of art in Scotland.

The Forth Bridge was opened to international acclaim, official fanfare and public marvel in 1890. Baker had cleverly overcome any sense of unease regarding the stability of the structure by generating a public discourse on the nature and strength of his cantilevered design. In part, he completed this advocacy by employing a photographer, Evelyn Carey (1858–1932), to record every step in the conception and construction of the bridge. Carey was, in fact, an assistant engineer on the project who developed his skills as a photographer on site. Naturally, he held the distinct advantage of understanding, in intimate detail, the nature of the design and the intricacies of the project. Moreover, he had access to all the areas of construction and the co-operation of the workforce. But Carey's photographs are remarkable documents, deeply sensitive to the subject, technically sophisticated, and presented through an industrial aesthetic that was both innovative and unique.

A perfect example of Carey's extraordinary viewpoint is presented in his *Soundings around Sites of Deep Piers off Inchgarvie* [FIG.77] from an early period in the construction, June 1884. Carey was observing the wooden platform on which surveyors stood to measure the submerged rock base near the island of Inchgarvie in the River Forth. Working in a flat calm and with little 'context', other than the ghostly becalmed sailing ship in the background, the men appear to float on a surreal raft. He would create a similarly obtuse vision as he recorded the 'caissons', the sunken metal and concrete foundations on which the towers of the bridge would stand. Here, as in *Caisson of Inchgarvie, Northeast, Main Pier, Looking West*, from 1884, he showed the arc of the vast circular caisson, filled with stabilising rocks, and surmounted by a group of engineers. There was an abstract quality to these works, and throughout Carey echoed the industrial construction of the bridge with a series of viewpoints that would accent grid and rivet, armature and frame. Above all, he seemed to focus on the geometry of the bridge as design, construct and assembly. In doing this he fully conformed to Baker's strategy of placing stress on its strength and stability.[24]

Evelyn Carey attempted to document every aspect of the bridge's construction, including work taking place underwater in the pressurised caverns being excavated for the caissons. Here he was advised by William Dobson Valentine, and, as might be expected, the companies of both Valentine and Wilson were everywhere photographing the progress of the main structure. In truth the company photographers must have been tripping over each other in their enthusiasm for the finest viewpoint, for many of the photographs

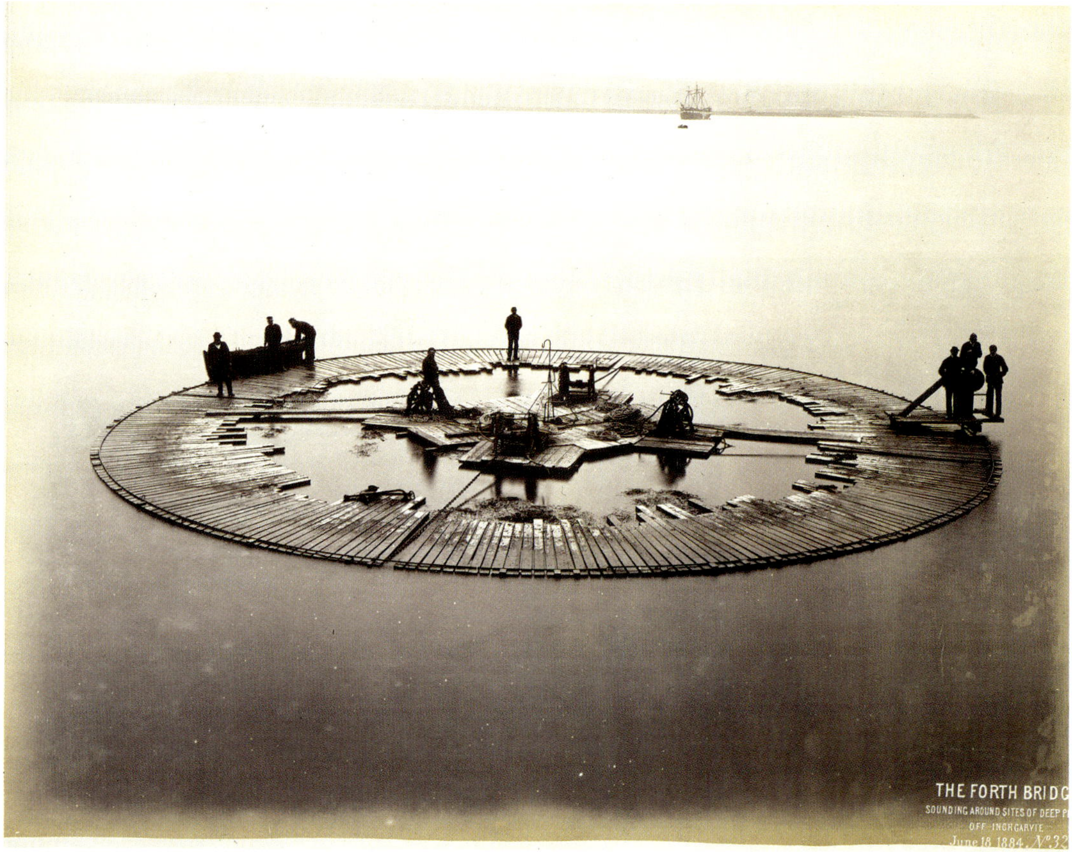

FIG.77
Evelyn Carey
Soundings around Sites of Deep Piers off Inchgarvie
1884

record the same view and at the same point in the construction. The wonder of the design and assembly is a common feature of these studies. Valentine's *Forth Bridge, Main Pier* [FIG.78], from 15 August 1888, shows the complicated armature of the cantilever topped by cranes and surrounded by floating workshops and storage yards. Wilson's *Forth Bridge from the South* [FIG.79], taken in the same year, foregrounds the stone pillars supporting the main railway line, with the spectacle of the three half-formed cantilevered sections in dramatic perspective towards the northern shore.

Photographs like these became commonplace as the bridge developed from a skeletal armature to a completed industrial masterpiece. In the century after its construction it would become a symbol for Victorian engineering and creative ingenuity. Often, the crossing arms of the frame would be viewed with the same reverential awe as the arches of a medieval cathedral, and indeed this became a familiar metaphor when discussing the inspirational qualities of the bridge. It was also a reference point for further photographs and photographers. A favourite view, here, was the projection along the railway line from inside the framework of the supporting iron girders. This was particularly impressive in stereoscopic form, and this approach was favoured by commercial photographers throughout the globe. The image *A Vista through the Forth Bridge, Scotland* [FIG.80], for example, was created in 1903 by 'H. C. White and Co., Chicago, New York, London'. Designed for use with the 'Perfec' Stereograph, the title is given on the back of the card in six different languages, including Russian.

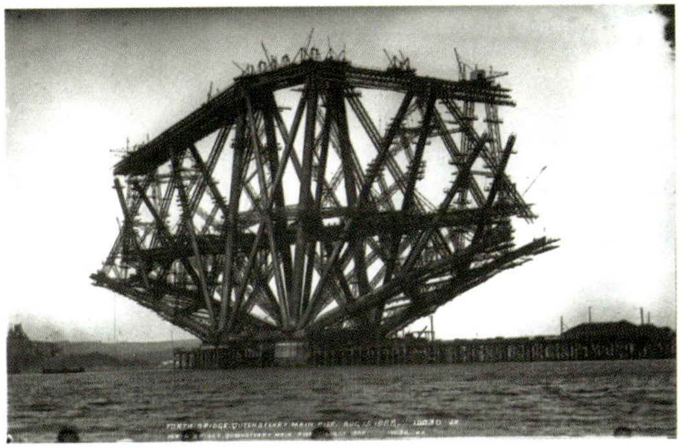

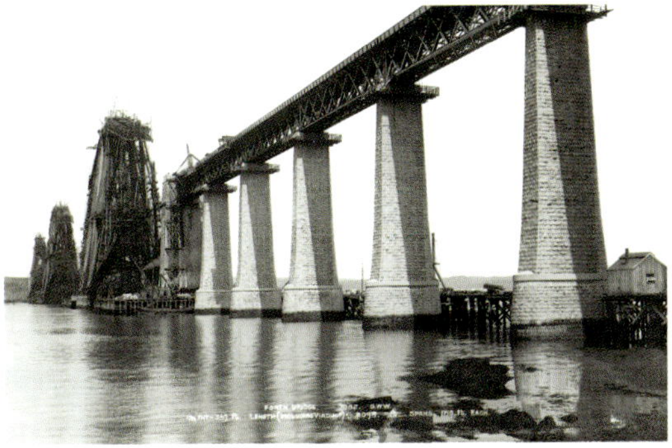

Left:
FIG.78
James Valentine
Forth Bridge, Main Pier
1888

Right:
FIG.79
George Washington Wilson
Forth Bridge from the South
1888

The inventive technical nature of the stereoscopic image, and viewer, was a correlate to that spirit of innovation and design that produced the bridge itself.[25] In 1988, as the bridge approached its centenary year, a further experimental technique would be deployed to photograph the bridge. Stephen Lawson's *The Forth Bridges, Photographed from South Queensferry on Thursday 29th September 1988* [FIG.81] is a time-lapse study of the Forth Bridge and its modern sib the Forth Road Bridge. In this respect it is interesting to consider how many images of the bridge were informed by time. The photographers of the 1880s, Carey and Valentine and Washington Wilson amongst others, tended to focus on the construction as it advanced in time and space. Likewise the many views of the bridge that looked through the gallery of the railway track spoke to the notion of a train in progress. Stephen Lawson, who initially trained as a sculptor in Edinburgh during the early 1960s, developed an interest in photography that would foreground issues of time and moment in the photographic image. In this event he manufactured rigs for his cameras that would allow him to image a selected scene through time. The camera, either driven by a motor or manipulated by hand, would take a photograph at given intervals throughout a period of minutes, hours, days

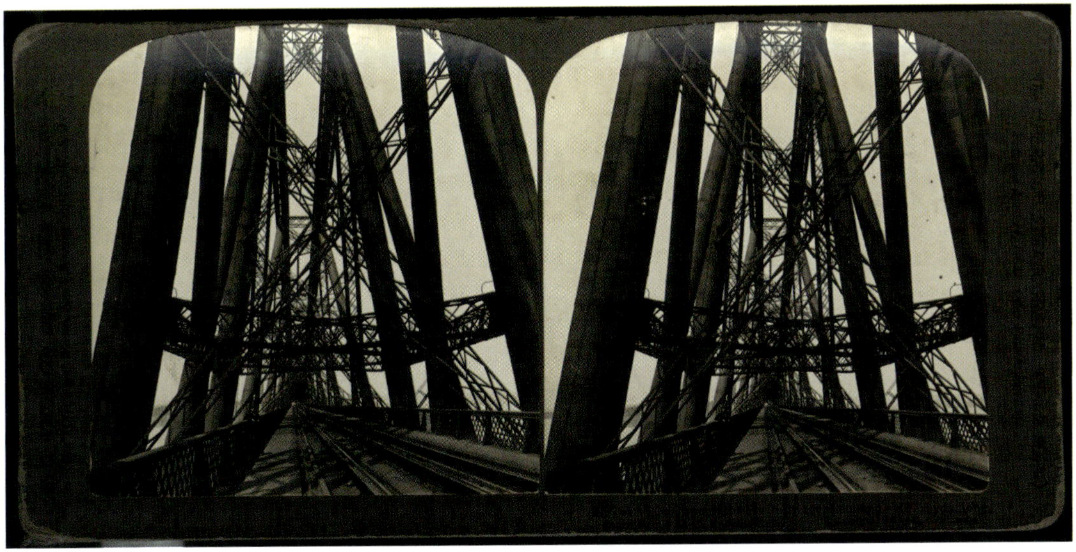

FIG.80
H.C. White and Co., New York, Chicago, London
A Vista through the Forth Bridge, Scotland
1903

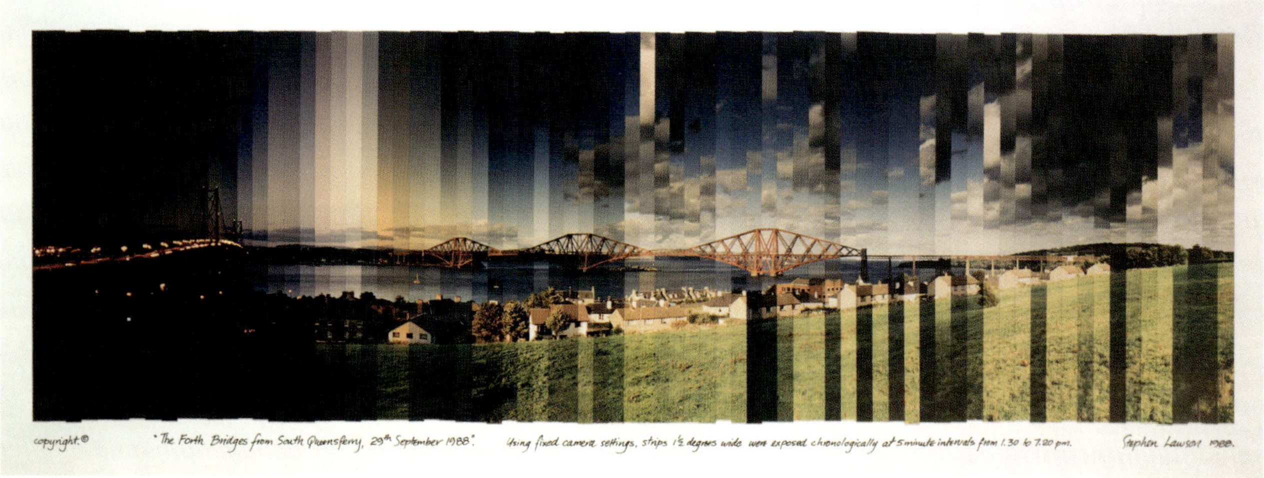

Top:
FIG.81
Stephen Lawson
The Forth Bridges, Photographed from South Queensferry on Thursday 29th September 1988

Below:
FIG.82
Charles Piazzi Smyth
Second Mate of the Yacht 'Titania' Observing Radiation Thermometers on Mount Guajara, published in *Teneriffe* 1858

or months. These images would then form a single or collaged panorama. The subtitle of his *The Forth Bridges...* image gives an account of the method employed in the creation of this particular work; it reads 'Using fixed camera settings, strips one and a half degrees wide were exposed chronologically every fifth minute across the afternoon from 1:30pm until 7:30pm'. The completed photograph, used to commemorate the centenary of the Forth Bridge in 1990, presents a panorama of the scene looking north to the Fife coast. It shows the shoreline of South Queensferry in the early afternoon, all sunshine and cloudburst, and sweeps around westwards to the Forth Road

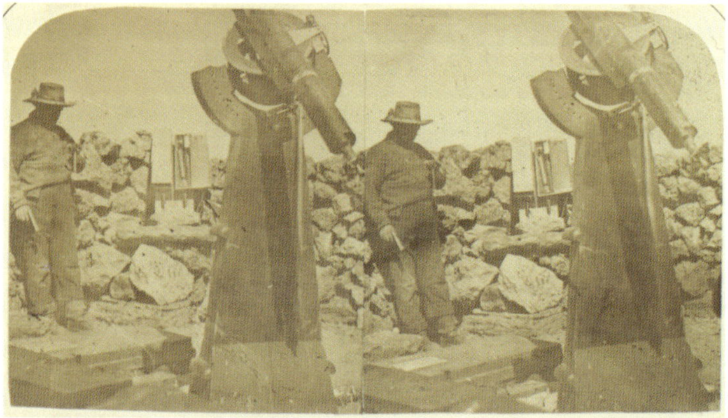

Bridge illuminated at nightfall. This inventive notation of the subject through time and space, a kind of fluid memorial, parallels the invention and creativity of the original makers. It connotes the camera as science and art, just as the construction of the bridge itself melds the expertise of the designer and engineer with the creativity of the inventor.

The abundant photographs of the Forth Bridge were one manifest celebration of Scotland's industrial prowess, but these types of images flowed through the history of Scotland's photography. Charles Piazzi Smyth, the Astronomer Royal for Scotland and the eccentric photographer of the Pyramids at Giza, marked the construction of Sheepshank's Telescope on the island of Tenerife with a number of stereoscopic photographs taken in 1856. These would include *Second Mate of the Yacht 'Titania' Observing Radiation Thermometers on Mount Guajara* [FIG.82], and were published as *Teneriffe, an Astronomer's Experiment: or, Specialities of a Residence above the Clouds*, in 1858. The Annan studio, besides photographing the triumph of the Loch Katrine waterworks, also documented the industrial might of Glasgow's shipbuilding industry. John Annan (1862–1947), the son of Thomas and elder brother of James Craig, was largely responsible for the 'Glasgow Harbour' series taken during the 1890s; a series that would include the extraordinarily abstract *Graving Dock, Glasgow* [FIG.83] from 1898. John Annan,

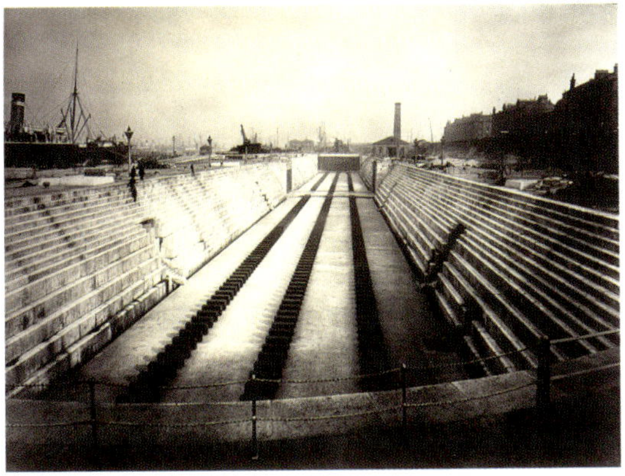

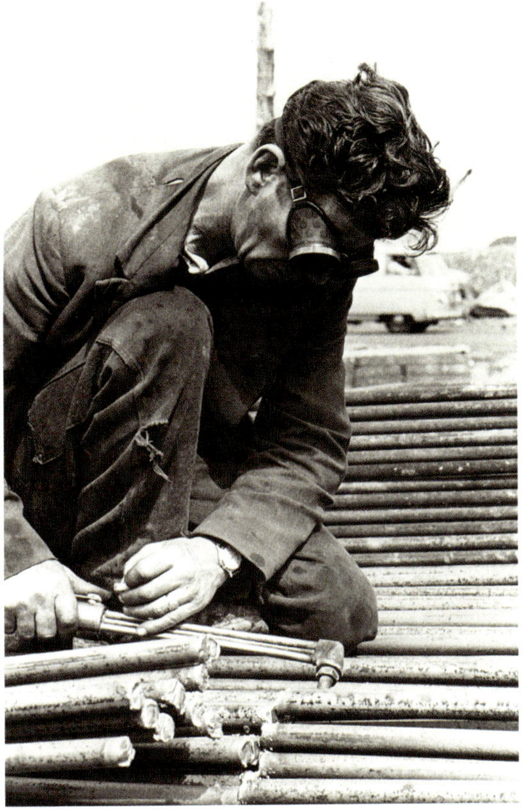

Left:
FIG.83
John Annan
Graving Dock, Glasgow
1898

Right:
FIG.84
Oscar Marzaroli
Ravenscraig
1962

besides completing his father's studies of Glasgow's old streets and closes in the period circa 1900, would also photograph industrial constructions like Glasgow's Central Station roof, which, all iron girders and fretwork grids, was viewed as yet another cathedral of the industrial age.

Nor were the workers themselves lost to this celebration of iron and industry, though they had to wait until later in the 20th century before they became the focus of the documentary photograph rather than an incidental, picturesque note. Certainly, Evelyn Carey would photograph both engineers and labourers on site at the building of the Forth Bridge. These attendant figures gave a sense of scale and the reality of labour, though more often it was the eminent architects, designers and engineers who were portrayed. By the middle of the 20th century, however, Oscar Marzaroli was presenting a heroic and romantic vision of the working man. This is most evident in his *Ravenscraig* [FIG.84], from 1962, where the steelworker is allowed to occupy the whole of the frame and is represented in the epic manner of W. Eugene Smith's *Steelworker with Goggles*, taken in 1955. This sense of the archetypal industrial worker was allowed something of a swansong in Colin Cavers' (b. 1957) documentary study of coal miners at Scotland's last deep-shaft coal mine, Longannet Colliery in Fife. This project, *Black Diamonds: Longannet Coal Mine*, was completed in 2000, just two years before the mine flooded and signalled the end of the entire industry in Scotland. Cavers' photographs showed the physical nature of underground labour in cramped and dangerous conditions. His *Engineer Building Coal-shearer Machinery for Coal-face Work, Section* B-78, *Castlebridge, Longannet Complex* 2000 [FIG.85] illustrates the nature of this hidden work and demonstrates the photographer's need for meticulous documentation.

The city, and the interrelated industrial world, was fundamental to the documentary style. They existed as clear evidence of the modern, of modernity, and of all its associated characters. But the city, along with the new industries and mammoth industrial structures, existed in a subtle dialectic with pre-industrial forms. The city grew as the village contracted; industry spread as the countryside diminished, populations shifted and rural lives changed in perceptible ways. Documentary photographs of these changes were sparse, and often tinged with nostalgia and the ethos

FIG.85
Colin Cavers
Engineer Building Coal-shearer Machinery for Coal-face Work, Section B-78, Castlebridge, Longannet Complex 2000
commissioned by Fife Council Museums West

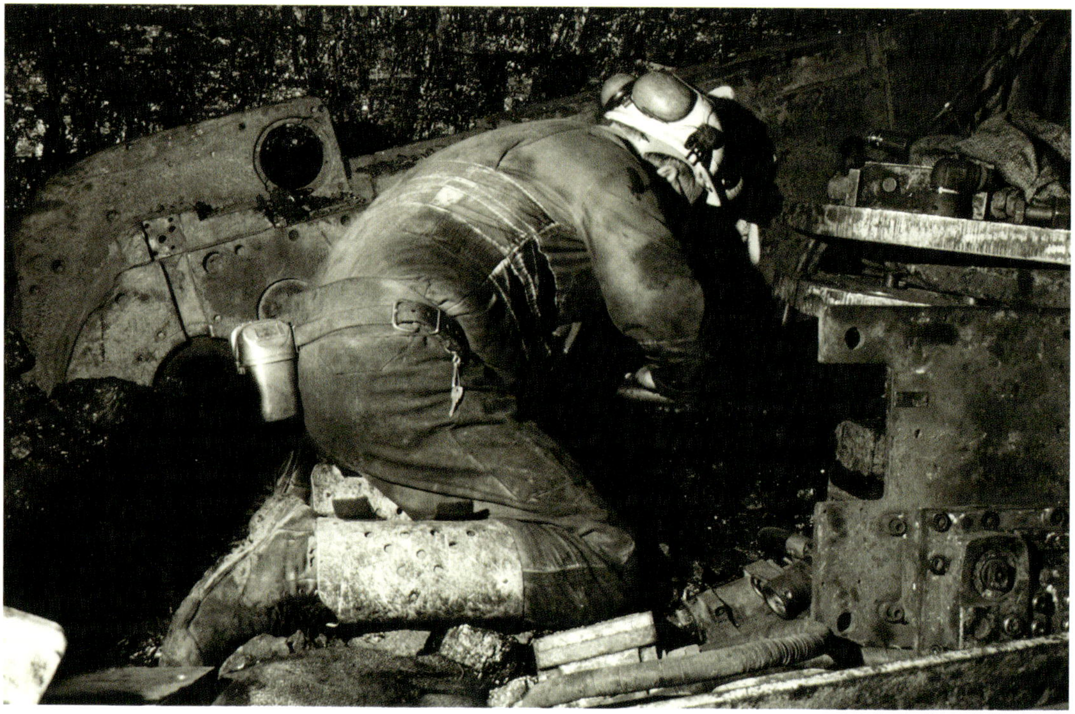

of the picturesque, but they were sometimes immanent and real, a record of understated transformation.

Rural and Highland documentary

Hill and Adamson were quick to identify rural life as a worthy subject for the photograph. Besides their prestigious portraits of eminent Scots and visitors to Scotland, they photographed the fisherfolk of Newhaven, near Edinburgh. These works represented, in some sense, a primitive form of 'documentary', though tempered by the tendency to name the subjects. Early in their career they had created the remarkable *North Street, Fishergate, St Andrews; Baiting the Lines* [FIG.86].[26] This street scene, taken from the high vantage point of an adjacent stairwell, shows a large group of fisher-women, seated outdoors in the sunlight, baiting fishing lines for their menfolk. The photograph displays the traditional dress of the fisher-women and the typical architecture of their cottages, as well as giving the sense of a living and vibrant community. However, within the small town of St Andrews, at this time, the fishing community was becoming regarded as something of an embarrassment. A byword for 'primitive' living and unsanitary housing, the world of the fishing community was at odds with the 'civilising' ambitions of the local town council. Hill and Adamson may well have been aware of this debate, but their focus was not political. In fact they have framed this photograph within the conventions of the genre tradition. This was Hill the painter at work, centring the lilting swagger of the basket-carrying woman in the foreground, presenting a dazzling view of rural harmony, grouping his figures in a ramshackle rustic synchrony. For all the aesthetics of this composition it remains, nevertheless, a record of time and place and the living world of the rural poor.

For a more authentic vision of rural life, because less self-consciously aesthetic, it is useful to turn to the photography of James C. Cox (1849–1901). Cox was an amateur photographer, being in his public life

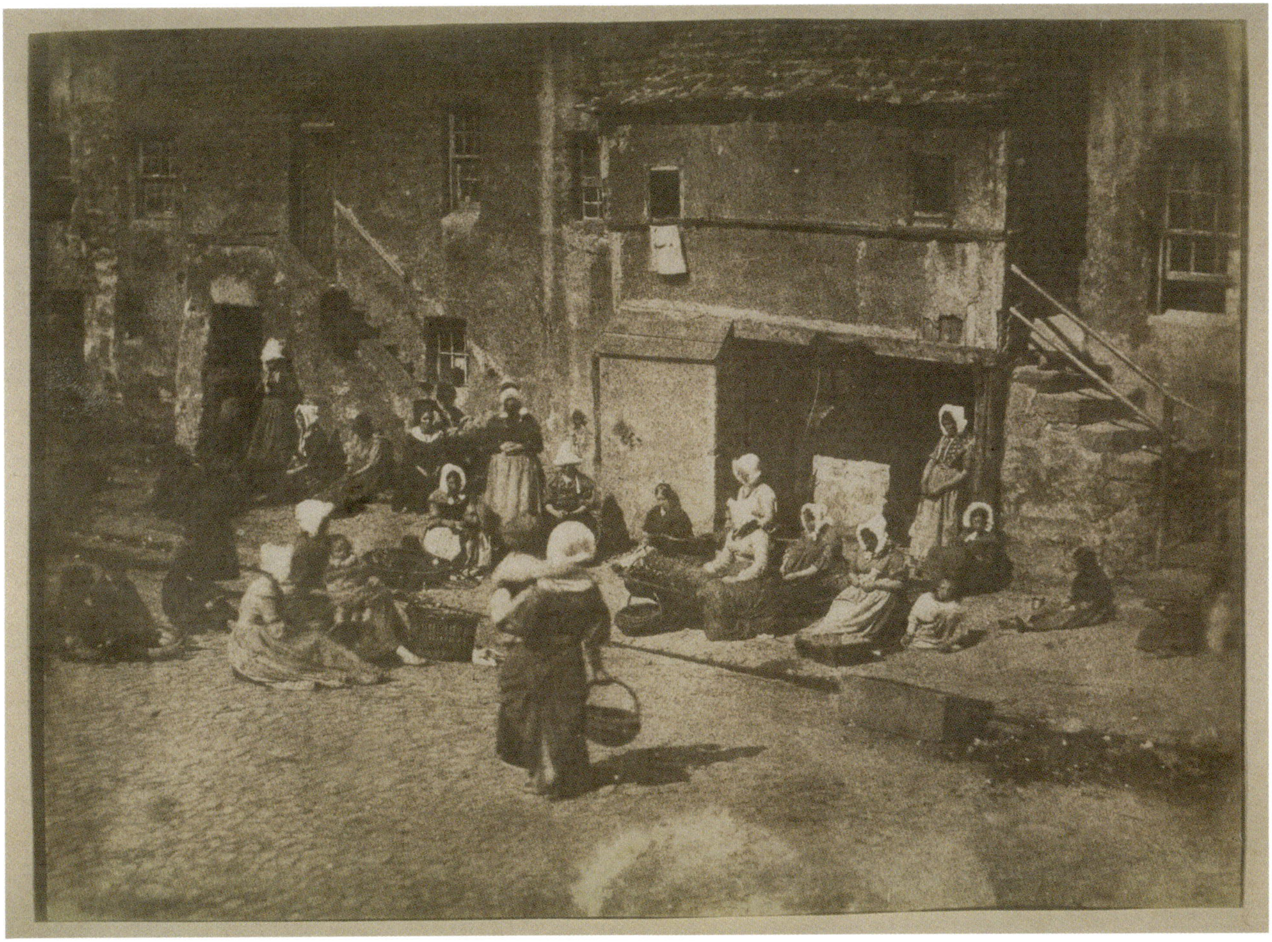

FIG.86
Hill and Adamson
North Street, Fishergate, St Andrews; Baiting the Lines
1843–46

the heir to a magnate in Dundee's world-famous jute manufacturing industry. Moreover, he was instrumental in organising Dundee's first photographic society, The Dundee and East of Scotland Photographic Society, which was formed in March 1880 with Cox himself as the first president. It is recorded that the inaugural trip of the newly-formed society was to the aristocratic Bowes-Lyons residence of Glamis Castle just 12 miles to the north of Dundee, but Cox himself is best remembered for his study of the fishing village of Auchmithie, near Arbroath in the county of Angus. In the 19th century this was one of the east coast's most active fishing harbours, specialising in the catching of haddock, which would be smoked and sold as the famous 'Arbroath Smokie'. It was also, however, a community that lived close to the poverty line, in a subsistence economy that was subject to seasonal slump and extremes of poverty. Certainly this is the evidence of Cox's most famous photograph *At Auchmithie* [FIG.87], taken in 1881, where three young children are arranged on the sea-cliff and are open to the closest scrutiny. Their ragged clothes, dishevelled looks and suspicious stares speak of a group consumed by poverty and resistant to the

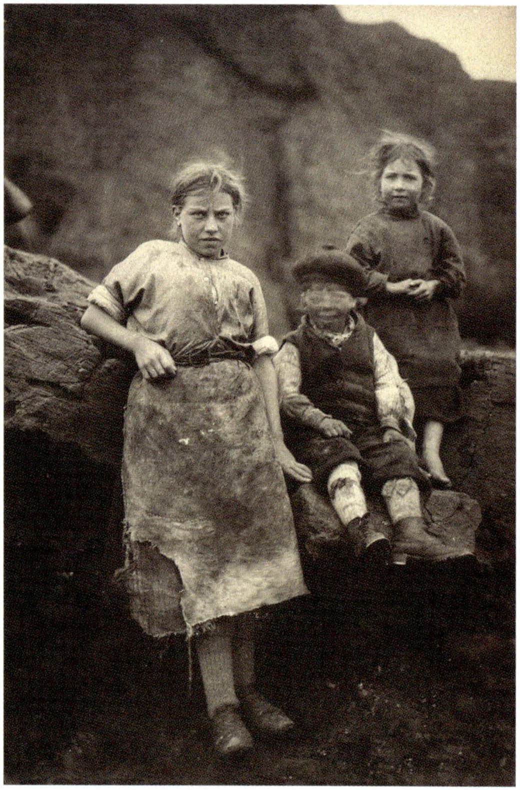

FIG.87
James Cox
At Auchmithie
1881

flattering lens of the camera. In consequence, the young boy in the centre of the group has been distracted by some passing event, for he has clearly moved during the exposure of the plate, his face now an unfocused blur. Cox has produced a remarkably uncompromising document with this photograph. The children are neither mawkishly sentimental nor prosaically picturesque. Rather, they are closely interrogated, revealed in all their ragged glory and presented as fact. In this sense Cox was approaching a kind of documentary realism, a form that was rare even by the 1880s and certainly unknown in the amateur camera clubs and salons of the east coast.

Fisherfolk were a common focus for photographers and painters alike throughout the 19th century. This was occasioned by the fashion for genre subjects and by the related demand for comforting images that countered the mechanical march of modernity. Fishing and rural communities represented stability at a period of rapid social change, they spoke to a notion of 'organic' life during a time of the increased mechanisation of society, and they signalled a sense of community in an epoch where the alienated life of the city was becoming a norm. In effect these images were a kind of consolation. Cox's work at Auchmithie is interesting for, generally, it resisted this trope. Equally, a number of photographs of Highland life defied this presentation of the poor as a kind of solace.

The history of Scotland's Highlands and Islands was, of course, a familiar concern of the landscape photograph. Herein, sites and sights associated with clan skirmishing and Jacobite rebellions were a common subject matter. The more recent history of the Highlands, however, was the subtle context for many of the photographic projects undertaken in the 19th and 20th centuries. This recent history covered the period of shifting and declining population, and the vexed legacy of the Clearances.

This last remains a contested area within documented history, though not within the cultural imagination of the nation. The Highland Clearances commonly connote the forcible removal of native populations from the Highlands of Scotland. This process is generally assumed to have taken place throughout the 19th and early 20th centuries, though its origins are in the land reforms of the period circa 1760. Here, the capitalist revolution in farming and land management practices resulted in clan chiefs and other landowners evicting local inhabitants from marginal crofts and reallocating the land for sheep and deer. These crofts were, of course, ancestral lands and the native populations did not go willingly. Stories of factors and agents ruthlessly engaged in a war of attrition with crofting families, and of the heartless avarice of clan chiefs, remain a constant of the Highland narrative. The process itself is generally regarded as marking the end of the clan system in all but a ceremonial form, most especially as the native Gaels migrated from the land to the city and would subsequently emigrate to the New World.

In some part the Clearances are presented as the wrecking of a lived Gaelic culture, though the traditions and ceremonies of the Gael remain vital in song and story and poem. Nevertheless the presentation of Highland life, most especially in the Scottish visual culture, has borne the stigmata of a people betrayed. This is most clearly the case in Scottish painting, where Highland life has often been represented as marginal and tragic, but it is also a subtext, or context, for photographic projects in the Highlands.[27]

As so often it was George Washington Wilson who first tapped this seam of images, though more by accident than design. In the 1880s the Wilson Company, perhaps using materials from George Washington Wilson himself, created a series of hand-coloured lantern slides from images of the Highlands and Islands. This novel use of photography, where the images are printed on to glass plates and coloured by artists, subsequently to be sequenced as a 'magic lantern' lecture show, was a highly marketable commodity in the 1880s. The actual works, a travelogue of photographs starting in the town of Oban and journeying through the Isles to Skye and Lewis and on to the wild periphery of St Kilda, depicted both the scenic splendour of the Western Isles and the living conditions of the local peoples.[28] Martin Padget has commented on Wilson's project:

> By the 1880s, however, when Scottish photographer George Washington Wilson travelled to the Highlands and islands, crofters throughout the region were in the midst of resisting the continued enclosure of former common lands and the conversion of no longer profitable sheep farms into sporting estates. In creating his lantern slide narrative, The Road to the Isles, Wilson had to negotiate the contemporary unruliness of crofters, acknowledge their often desperate poverty, and realise that distress and discontent were an unavoidable facet of the Highlands and islands landscape.[29]

Padget is right to accent this discreet dimension of Wilson's travelogue, for this was precisely the period of the 'Crofters' War'; an uncharacteristic uprising of the Gaelic people which took the form of riots and 'land raids', most notably on the isles of Skye and Lewis. The crofters' grievances stemmed from the period following the Clearances, and were partially addressed in the Crofters' Holdings Act of 1886 and the subsequent establishment of a Crofters' Commission.

Wilson's photographs, besides the archetypal romantic landscapes, included such works as *Corn Grinding* [FIG.88] and *The 'Cas Chrom'* (Crooked Spade).

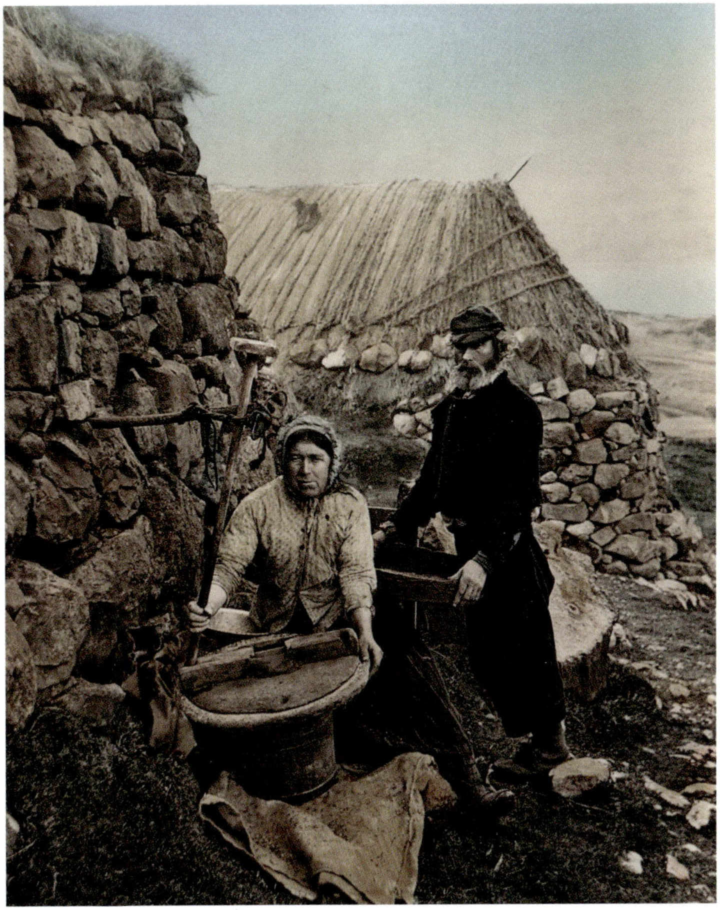

FIG.88
George Washington Wilson
Corn Grinding
circa 1880

These were genuine documentary photographs, recording the particularities of lifestyle and the desperate social conditions of the local people. Importantly, each slide was accompanied by lecture notes so that the travelogue might be delivered, remotely, in various halls and residences. The notes for *Corn Grinding* recall:

> This is an old custom still existing in Skye... Although an old law so far back as the thirteenth century provided 'That no man shall presume to grind his own corn'... and more recently the laird could oblige his tenants to make use of the more expeditious methods of grinding, and empowered his miller 'to search out and break any querns he can find', as machines that defraud him of the toll. The quantity of oats raised by a crofter in a good

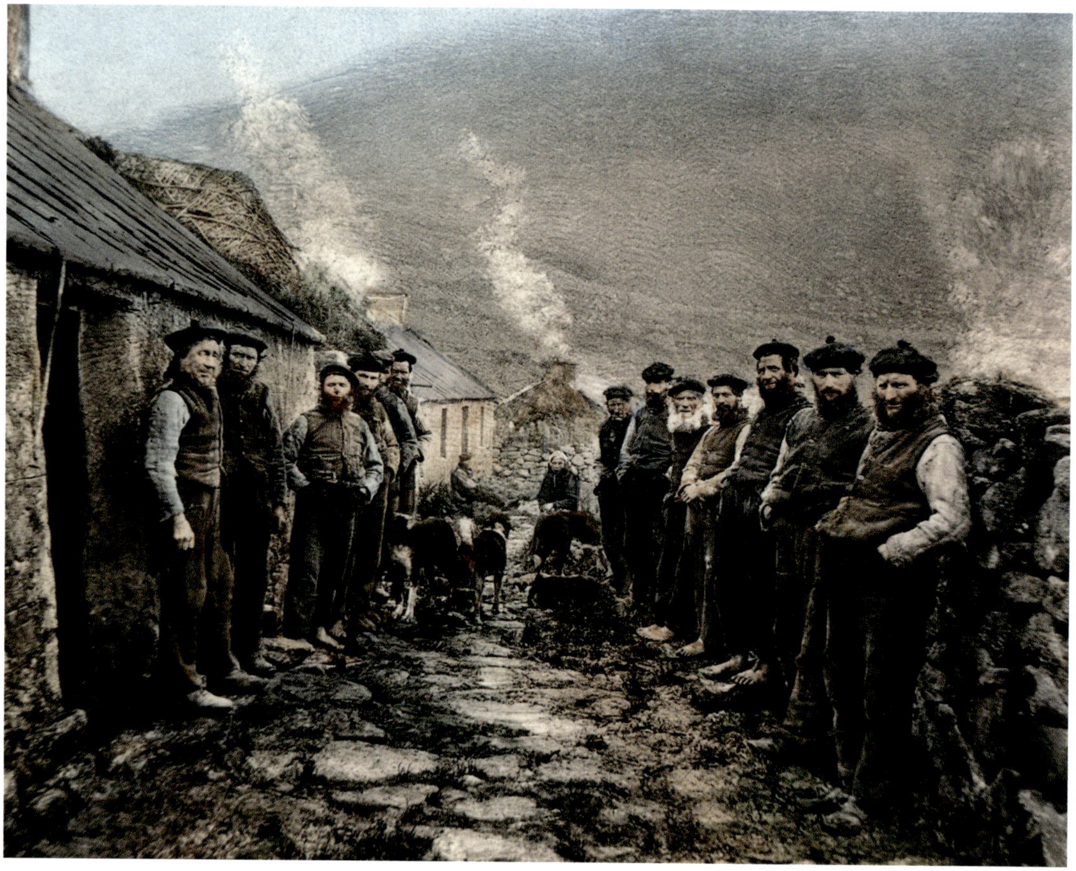

FIG.89
George Washington Wilson
St Kilda's Parliament
circa 1880

> season is not large, and not infrequently, as the result of an unfavourable season, or the ravages of deer, it is too insignificant to take to the mill. In such a case the 'clach-cuaich' is brought into requisition.[30]

The writer here was sensitive to the tensions within these communities; the resentment of the laird's power, the unconscionable demands on the crofters, the intrusion of the new economy that was deer-stalking and the subtle resistance of individual crofters. All of this was given a discreet expression in Wilson's photograph, where the 'clach-cuaich' is worked behind the cottage wall and the determined crofters, man and wife, secure some semblance of a future.

Similar frictions were revealed in *The 'Cas Chrom'*, where the notes recall that 'a Highlander will tell you that the crooked spade is a certain indication of poverty.'[31] This photograph, of crofters quite literally scraping a living from the shallow soil, remains an epitome of peasant labour. In fact many of these photographs create a singular, documentary register of life in the Highlands and Islands. They subtly recall the clearance of Highland communities, they invoke the introduction of sheep and deer to the lands, they signal the crofters' gradual shift to even more marginal land on the seashores at the fringes of island life and they connote avenues of resistance and insurgency amongst organised local peoples.

Perhaps the most evocative photograph in the entire collection, however, was the astonishing record of *St Kilda's Parliament* [FIG.89]. Here, at the very margins of civilised life, Wilson has given testimony to the ingenuity and the resilience of the community. The lecture notes tell how:

> Beyond the reach of the laws that govern this realm they make their own laws. The solitary minister on the Island may advise in certain matters, and certainly has a limited influence, but it is their Parliament that fixes matters beyond appeal, and no stranger dare take part in its deliberations. The Parliament meets daily, discusses the weather and state of the sea, &c, &c, in a few Gaelic phrases; and by a majority the order of the day is fixed, and no single individual takes it upon himself to arrange his own business until after they unitedly decide what is best.[32]

And evidently this communal democracy was presented as a civic good and, subtly, as an alternative to the oppressive power of laird and chief and the ravages of the mainland economic system.

Although Wilson seems prescient in his allusions to the Clearances and the long history of discontent that they engendered, their presence had been subtly evoked in the photography of Horatio Ross. Ross, an early vice-president of The Photographic Society of Scotland, a landed aristocrat and a champion sportsman, produced a number of images that celebrated the activities of hunting, shooting and fishing; precisely those leisure pursuits that would flourish in the Highlands following the Clearances and the establishment of sporting estates. In this respect the compositionally eccentric *Craigdarcourt* [FIG.90], from circa 1850, is notable in that it shows a Highland scene complete with the upper torso of a female figure aiming a shotgun at the half-glimpsed horns of a stag. Though clearly a fiction this photograph is interesting because it records the new conditions of Highland life, a world closed to native peoples and privatised for the leisure pursuits of the rich. Ross, of course, was party to this process and like Wilson some 30 years later photographed these scenes largely in innocence of their latent political implications.

This was not always the case, for the world of the Scottish Gael was often viewed as a repository of 'authentic' living and a subtle denunciation of dehumanised, or alienated, modernity. This was certainly the discourse in respect of Paul Strand's work in Uist and Benbecula during the 1950s, but Strand was not unique or even prescient in this kind of project. During the 1890s the Edinburgh-based amateur photographer Alexander Hutchison (1840–1924) followed George Washington Wilson – and it must be said the increasing flotilla of tourist excursions – to St Kilda. There he photographed the native community in all its 'primitive' glory. Hutchison's images were part of a sensibility that looked in wonder at this remnant of a forgotten world; an organic community complete with its customs and mores and an independent, collective parliament.

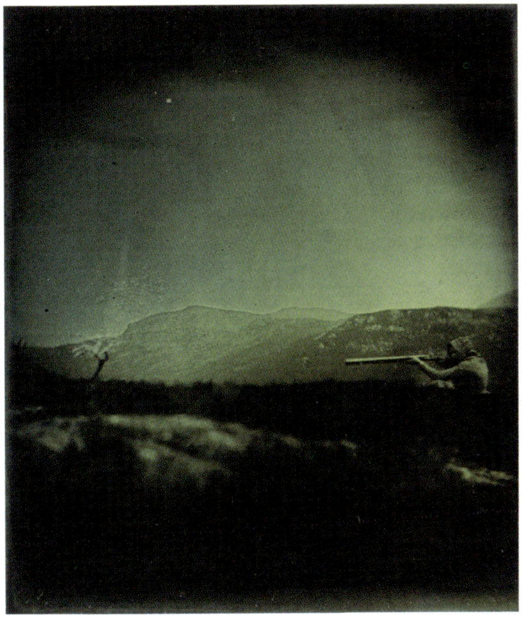

FIG.90
Horatio Ross
Craigdarcourt
circa 1850

The majority of Hutchison's photographs have been lost, but others followed, at least as far as the Hebrides, to photograph indigenous Gaelic communities. Amongst Robert Moyes Adam's first works were images of native peoples on Mingulay taken in 1905. Adam, whose principal interest remained in botanical specimens and panoramic landscapes, could not resist the allure of these authentic communities and would take documentary images of peat cutting on Harris, sheep dipping on Barra, and the lifestyles and peoples of the Gàidhealtachd. His photograph of *Children of Mingulay* [FIG.91], 1905, is remarkable for its objective assessment of these hard lives. The children, barefoot and awkward in front of the camera

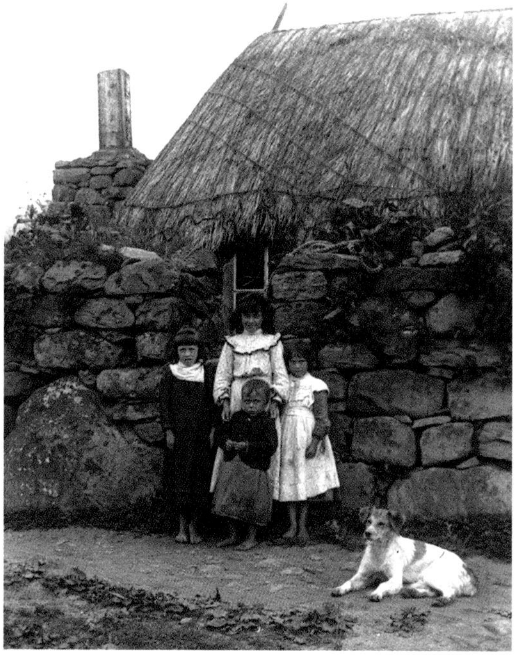

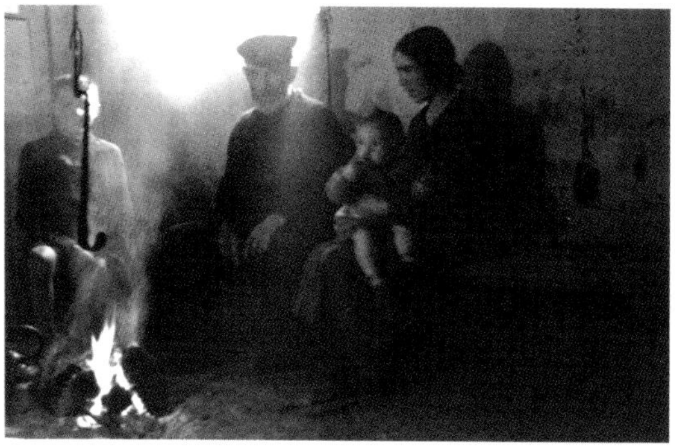

Left:
FIG.91
Robert Moyes Adam
Children of Mingulay
1905

Right:
FIG.92
Werner Kissling
Interior (Black House), South Uist
1934

lens, are portrayed against the backdrop of a 'blackhouse'. This traditional dwelling, of local stone and thatch anchored against the brutal winds, was common to the Hebrides. It was heated by a central, open fire that was ventilated by a simple hole in the roof. Naturally the downdraft held the smoke in the building and hence the 'blackhouse'. In Adam's photograph of 1905 the traditional building has been augmented with a chimney stack, but even this innovation could not help sustain the marginal lives of the Mingulay people. The island was abandoned by its population in 1912, some 18 years before the residents of St Kilda would accept the same fate.

Robert Moyes Adam's photographs of these communities were significant, but as documentary images they were secondary to his principal concern. More recently Michael Russell has uncovered the extraordinary archive of Werner Kissling (1895–1988).[33] Kissling, a German-born diplomat with an abiding interest in ethnography, travelled to the isle of Eriskay in circa 1932. According to Russell this was with the express aim of recording the 'blackhouses', but Kissling's relationship with the Hebridean islands would continue for a further quarter of a century and would overlap with Paul Strand's visit to South Uist. In fact Kissling was photographing in the Uists during 1953 and many of his images, focusing on the vernacular architecture and on the craft skills of the populace, offer a parallel vision of the community. At his best Kissling's documentary works are intimate and sympathetic, clearly engaging with the community as an advocate and supporter. His *Interior (Black House), South Uist* [FIG.92], from 1934, is an almost mystical evocation of the domestic interior, while his *Rope-Making, Lochboisdale, South Uist*, 1936, achieves the remarkable feat of being both a commonplace scene and an epic study of island life.

The sense that photography in the Highlands was exclusively a matter of visitors, arriving in the outback with some interest in ethnology or romantic primitivism, is surely suspect. The photographic studio would become ubiquitous during the late 19th century and every town, of any size, would be the focus of a photographer's lens. One example is the isle of Orkney, where Tom Kent (1863–1936) was a native photographer who documented the life of his community from the late 1880s and throughout the early decades of the 20th century. Kent had, early in his life, taken the emigrant's trail and had found himself apprenticed to a photographic studio in Chicago. When he returned to Orkney he established himself as a community photographer, with interests in documentary, public events and landscape.[34] A photograph of 1922 shows the

Kirkwall City Pipe Band as it marches past the studio of 'J. W. Sinclair, Photographer and Photographic Dealer', while Kent's photograph of *Peace Celebrations, Broad Street, Kirkwall* [FIG.93], taken during July 1919 – shortly after the scuttling of the German fleet in Scapa Flow – provides a document of the community gathered in commemoration and celebration.

Tom Kent was but one example of the numerous commercial photographers resident in towns throughout the Highlands who reflected the everyday life of local communities. However, the Highlands and Islands have remained, in the contemporary period, a focus for more self-consciously 'documentary' projects. The Suffolk-born photographer Gus Wylie (b. 1935) travelled to the Uists, partly as an acolyte of Paul Strand, but by his own testimony under 'a direct influence of the social documentation of the Farm Security Administration in America in the 1930s.'[35] Wylie was resident in the Hebridean islands throughout 1974 and 1975 and created a catalogue of remarkable photographs recording the very heart of island life. One of the most evocative of these, *Gaelic Bibles, Sleat, Skye* [FIG.94], is a powerful study of that core accord in the life of these communities; language and the church, while yet other photographs explore the poles of landscape and culture, lifestyle and environment.

There is a case for suggesting that post-war photographers have pursued Highland and Gaelic subjects largely as a corollary to political and cultural developments. The long political process of Scottish devolution was seriously mooted in the first devolution referendum of 1979, and realised in the vote of 1997. This process has been accompanied by debates on nationhood and national identity, and on the role of Scotland within a multicultural, globalised, world system. It can be contested that these debates have occasioned a re-evaluation of the entire social organism that is Scotland. Importantly, the place of the Gael and the role of the Highlands in this new Scotland has become a matter of moment. Herein, the marginal nature of the Highland economy, coupled with the threat to the indigenous culture, has been viewed as the most pressing concern. Moreover, within this debate it is often the fragile condition of the Gaelic language that has taken precedence. Documentary photographers have responded with close analyses of the complex variety, and the particular patterns, of Highland life. Amongst the most noteworthy of these photographers are John Charity (b. 1946), Glyn Satterley (b. 1947) and Chick Chalmers (1948–98).

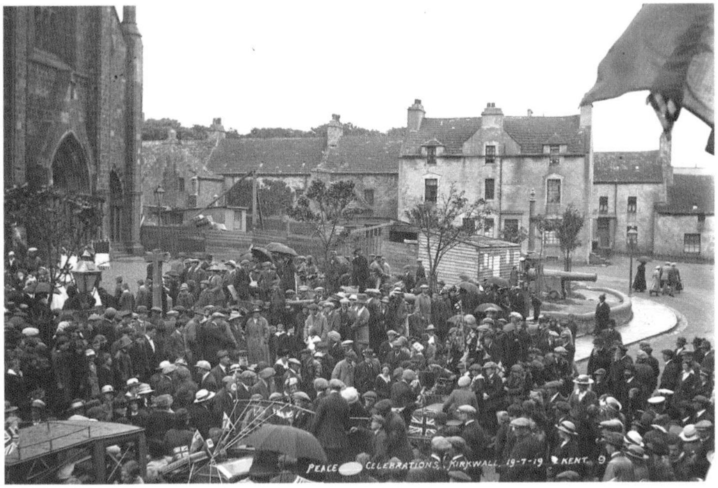

FIG.93
Tom Kent
Peace Celebrations, Broad Street, Kirkwall
1919

John Charity's documentary project in the Highland district of Ross and Cromarty, begun in 1986 and completed in 1988, was a commission from the local council. Charity, who lectured in documentary photography in Wales throughout the 1970s, moved to Wester Ross in 1981. His images, chiefly of the farming community and the processes of sheep farming, were welcomed as a record of local life and the Highland economy. The best-known work from this series, *Rùsgadh aig an fhaing, Loch a' Bhraoin, Ros an Iar (During the Clipping at Loch a'Bhraoin)* [FIG.95], was reviewed by the photographer in a manner that revealed both his working method and his eye for the 'decisive moment'; indicating the shepherd's son, in the clipping pen, attaching some sheep's wool to his chin as a comedy beard.[36] Here is documentary at play, but equally an intimate narrative of rural and Highland life.

The refined prints of Glyn Satterley have also concentrated on Scotland's Highland communities, with a special interest in the hunting, shooting and fishing estates of Caithness and Sutherland. Satterley committed himself to photographing this area after

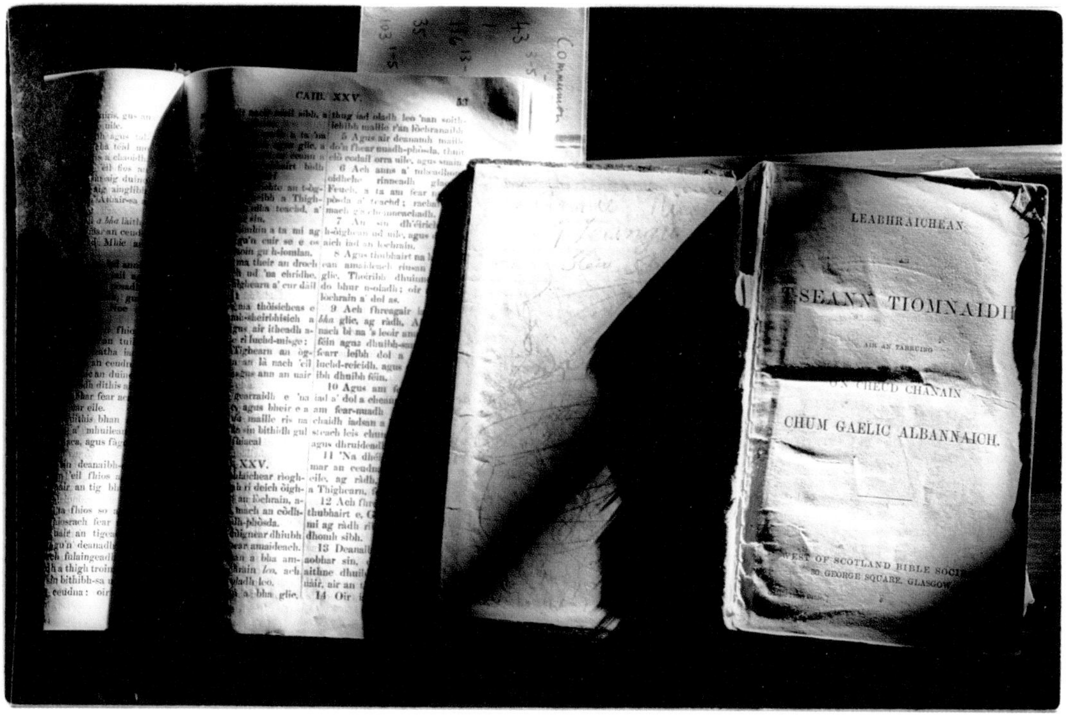

FIG.94
Gus Wylie
Gaelic Bibles, Sleat, Skye
circa 1974

locating himself in the north of Scotland in 1982. His two key projects, 'Life in Caithness and Sutherland' and 'Life on Highland Sporting Estates', document the rural economy and present a sympathetic account of a world that Horatio Ross would recognise; the leisure pursuits of Highland tourists. A photograph like *Stalking Party, Ben Armine* returns, iconographically and emotionally, to 19th-century archetypes, while an image like *Oyster Farm, Mull* [FIG.96] presents an epic vision of everyday labour under a majestic sky.

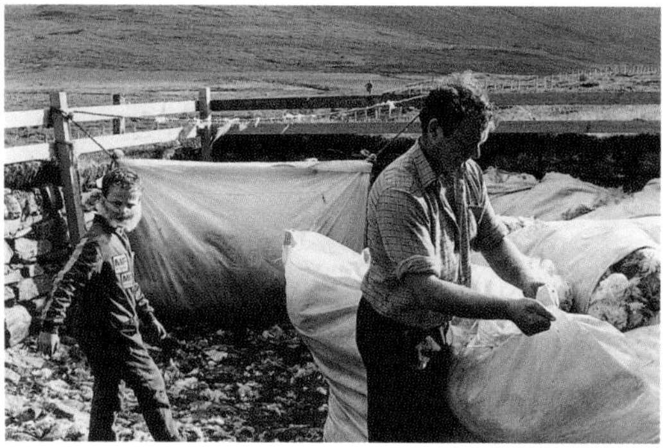

FIG.95
John Charity
Rùsgadh aig an fhaing, Loch a' Bhraoin, Ros an Iar (During the Clipping at Loch a' Bhraoin)
circa 1987

In the previous decade Chick Chalmers, who was Edinburgh-born though trained in London, looked to the north and the archipelago of the Orkney Islands for his signature project. During the mid 1970s, and particularly circa 1977, he created a catalogue of Orkney pictures that rivalled Tom Kent's of half a century before. His pictures of boat building, farming, craft skills and local festivals were meticulous observations of island life, and were fully presented in the photo-book *Life in the Orkney Islands*, published in 1979. One of the most redolent, *Fisherman's Co-operative, Stromness, Orkney* [FIG.97], is a picture of crabs being cooked in a fish-shed. The intense chiaroscuro of the photograph, the dramatic flash of the steaming cauldron and the paraphernalia of the crab box and assorted basins all set a scene wherein the working figure is presented in a near-religious atmosphere.

These projects are all notable studies of an

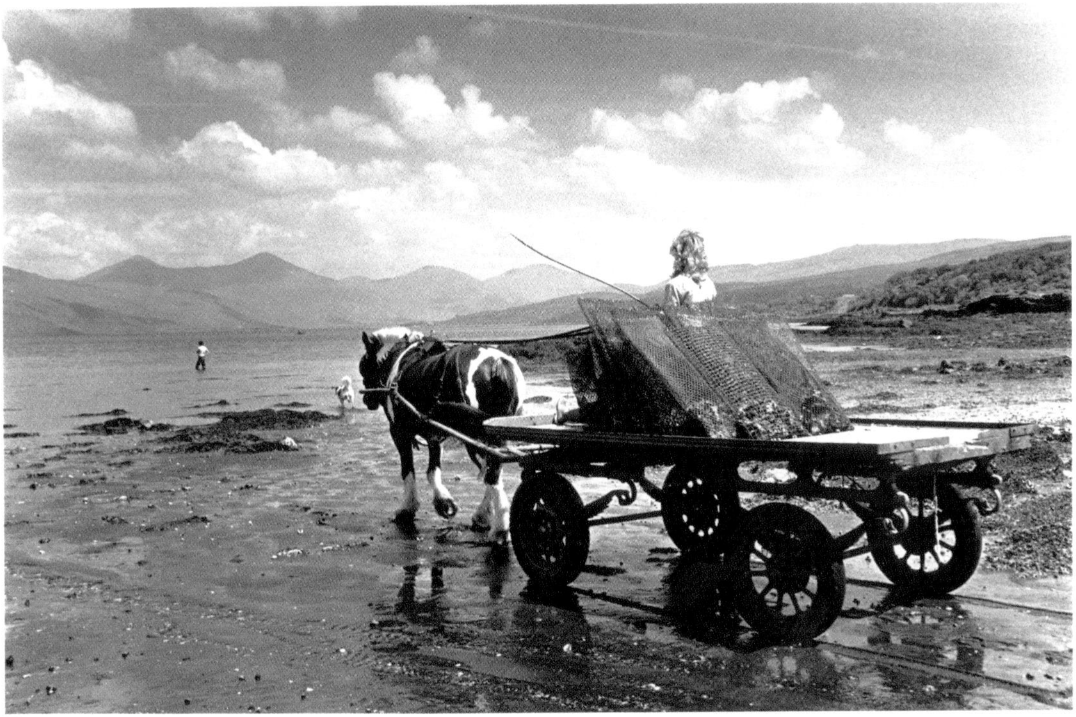

FIG.96
Glyn Satterley
Oyster Farm, Mull
n.d.

exceptional landscape and an extraordinary way of life. Moreover, they embody, in different ways, a unique story. Photographs of the Highlands and Islands of Scotland speak of a people whose history is circumscribed by Clearance, emigration, hardship, revolt and uncommon resilience. Simultaneously they record a rich culture, lived on the far margins of metropolitan life, but redolent of human values. This, of course, was their fundamental appeal, for these images represented a residual organic community in a period of challenging, mechanistic co-existence.

Documenting difference

The documentation of the Highlands and Islands, and indeed the rural corners of Scotland, was, fundamentally, a record of a geographical homeland. Certainly these places were peripheral to the intensely-populated and industrially-developed central belt, but they were recognisably Scotland. However, documentary photographers, both historic and contemporary, have engaged in a practice that visualised the world outside of this homeland. Indeed, some of the finest examples of the genre consist in works by Scots travelling the compass and giving testimony to the cultures and mores of all the world. In some part these were voyeuristic excursions, glimpses of 'difference' that excited the dulled imaginations of a populace already familiar with the high-street photograph. But often, and certainly in the contemporary period, these might be socially conscious and politicised views of an ideologically fractured, artificially 'globalised' culture.

Historic examples of documenting different cultures have been many and varied. John Thomson's travels in China, and before that in Siam, were celebrated with images of exotic landscapes and imperious local dignitaries. But Thomson was photographing street life in China even before his famed illustrations for Adolphe Smith's report on London's poor. His record of these interventions on the Chinese streets remains instructive:

In some places there were many who had never set eyes

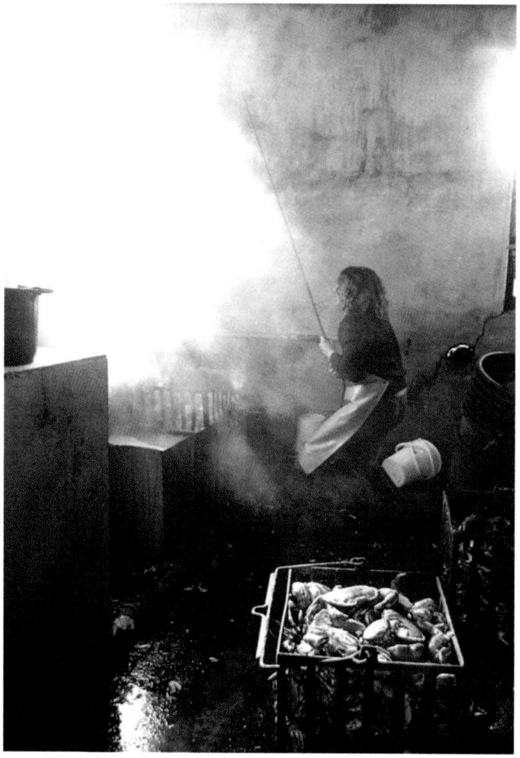

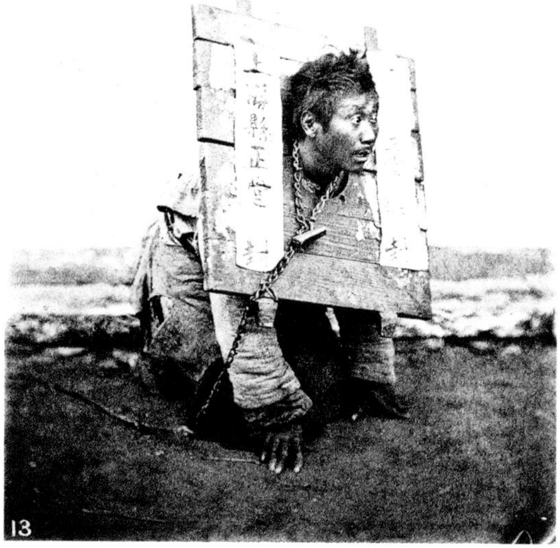

Left:
FIG.97
Chick Chalmers
Fisherman's Co-operative, Stromness, Orkney
1978

Right:
FIG.98
John Thomson
Punishment in China
circa 1870

> upon a pale-faced stranger; and the literati, or educated classes, had fostered a notion amongst such as these, that, while evil spirits of every kind were carefully to be shunned, none ought to be so strictly avoided as the 'Fan Qui' or 'Foreign Devil', who assumed human shape, and appeared solely for the furtherance of his own interests, often owing the success of his undertakings to an ocular power, which enabled him to discover the hidden treasures of heaven and earth. I therefore frequently enjoyed the reputation of being a dangerous geomancer, and my camera was held to be a dark mysterious instrument, which, combined with my naturally, or supernaturally, intensified eyesight gave me power to see through rocks and mountains, to pierce the souls of the natives, and to produce miraculous pictures by some black art, which at the same time bereft the individual depicted of so much of the principle of life as to render his death a certainty within a very short period of years.[37]

Thomson's melodramatic account of his adventures repeats all the clichés of the photographer abroad and amongst a 'barbarian' culture, and he goes on to recount how 'superstitious influences, such as I have described, rendered me a frequent object of mistrust, and led to me being stoned and roughly handled on more occasions than one.'[38] Leaving aside the proposition that the local peoples might legitimately have been protesting against his outrageous prose style, Thomson was clearly at pains to assert the ways in which he suffered for his art. One particularly perceptive phrase, however, shows a sensitivity to the documentary photographer's problematic role, for he 'appeared solely for the furtherance of his own interests'. Thomson gathered images of the most extreme and bizarre kind not in order to document a different culture, but to exploit an 'outlandish' society. His photographs of *Punishment in China* [FIG.98] and *Indecent Exposure: a Chinese Woman Unwraps her Feet before a Man*, both circa 1870, were, and are, an extraordinary intrusion into indigenous culture. Moreover, whatever the power of these images, and they are immensely powerful, their lack of cultural sensitivity borders upon the pornographic.

Thomson was a particularly prominent example of the 19th-century photographer abroad, bringing back to the home marketplace sensational samples of the bizarre and the beautiful. An equally interesting example of 19th-century documentary was revealed in the practice of William Carrick (1827–78). Carrick was born in Edinburgh but opened his studio in Russia, specifically St Petersburg, in 1859. His introduction to Russia came through his father's business, for Carrick senior was in the timber trade and the infant William accompanied his parents to their new home in Kronstadt when he was in his first year.[39] He was not lost to the influence of Scotland, however, for after a period as a student of painting in the St Petersburg Academy of Arts, he returned to Scotland in 1857 and trained with the Edinburgh-based commercial photographer James Good Tunny (1820–87). There he made a friendship with one John MacGregor (d. 1872) who would become his business partner in the St Petersburg studio. Carrick's business was essentially in portrait studies, and while there was a fair market for this kind of practice it was, naturally, attenuated. This led Carrick, with his partner MacGregor, to experiment with a kind of documentary portraiture. He would select street people, chiefly itinerant traders and vendors, and photograph them in his studios. These were semi-formal portraits of an urban working class. Their distinctive outfits and the paraphernalia of their various trades made them both distinguished and idiosyncratic, and these 'Russian Types' became a signature motif in Carrick's output. The dramatic *Nightwatchman, St Petersburg* [FIG.99], from the 1860s, is typical in its selection of an individual made unique by the uniform of his office and rendered remarkable by the eccentric, if entirely practical, headgear that protects him from the Russian winters.

However, William Carrick's 'Russian Types' were not simply chosen for their astonishing dress-sense. There is little doubt that a political vector informed Carrick's practice. He was known to have been on the fringes of anarchist circles in Russia,[40] and his choice of urban workers and street-sellers was surely allied to a leftist sympathy. Beyond the portraits of urban workers, Carrick made two important journeys along the River Volga and into the province of Simbirsk, in 1871 and again in 1875. Here he photographed the Russian peasantry, a serf class who had been given a partial liberation through Tsar Alexander II's Emancipation Manifesto of 1861. This was but one footstep on the road to revolution, but Carrick seems to have been interested in this peasant class for its dramatic and militant potential. Indeed it might be suggested that his choice of subjects presaged the symbolism of the hammer and the sickle.

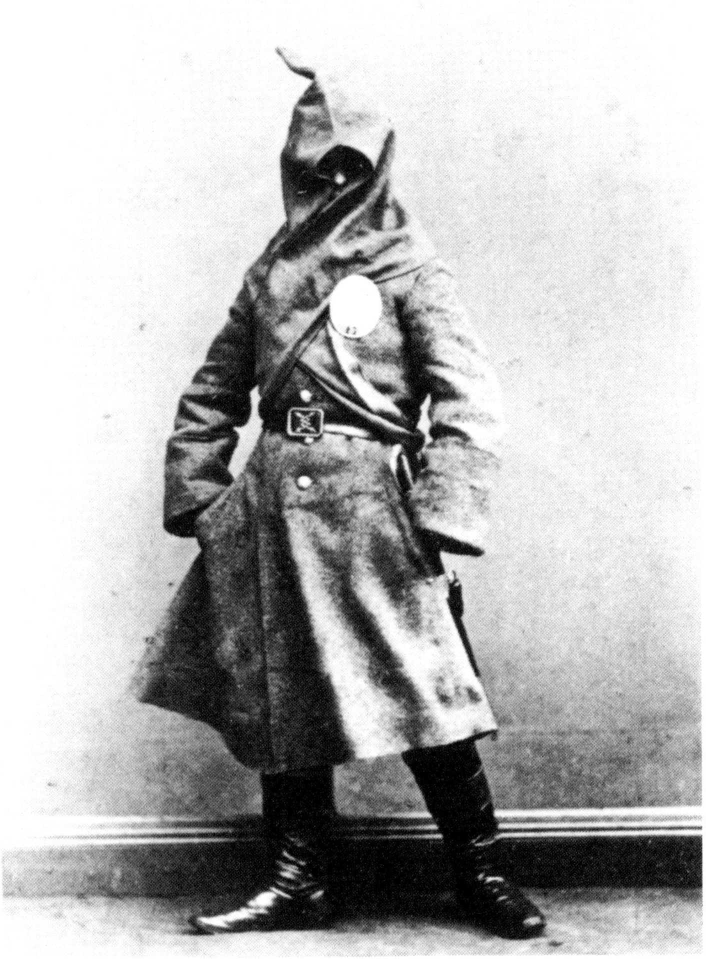

FIG.99
William Carrick
Nightwatchman, St Petersburg
1860

The crypto-politics of William Carrick's studio would become a manifest feature of much documentary photography in the 20th century, and certainly in terms of the study of domestic inequalities. In the contemporary period Scottish photographers have become sensitive to the ways in which the world economy threatens the distinctive patterns of life in various marginal communities and homogenises local cultures.

During 1988 Ruth Stirling (b. 1957) began a project with the Igloolik community in the north of Canada. This ancient Inuit community has remained committed to its traditional culture, and has stood guard to the Inuit way of life, though Europeans began to visit as early as 1800. Notably, in the late 1860s, the community was a stopping point for those Europeans searching for survivors of the lost Franklin expedition of the 1850s. Later, in 1930, it became a focus for Christian missionary work, with prominent Catholic and Anglican missions to the territory. The corruption of Inuit culture, generally, has been a subject of study for government agencies, sociologists and anthropologists for decades and it is to the credit of the Igloolik peoples that they have resisted intrusion.

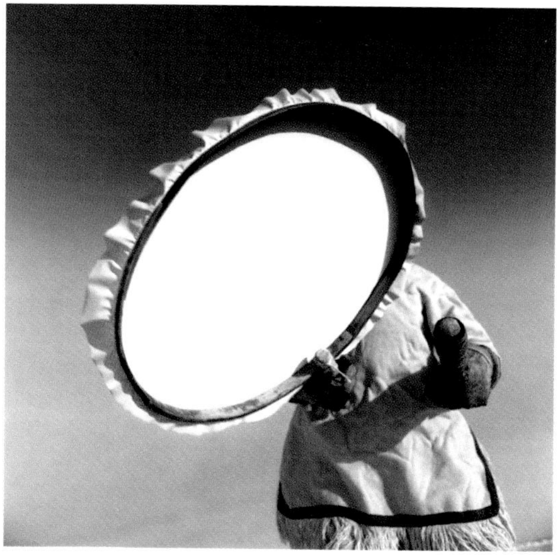

FIG.100
Ruth Stirling
Noah Pivatuk
1988

Ruth Stirling was commissioned by the Canadian Science Council to work as an artist-in-residence with the community for a period of six months. This commission followed some important experiments when she held residences at the Marine Biological Station on Cumbrae, in the west of Scotland, and at the Gatty Marine Laboratory in St Andrews. Here she began to explore the problematic relationship between art and science, particularly in relation to the photographic image, and the means through which text might be deployed as a constitutive component of a complex pictorial nexus. In her project with the Igloolik community these concerns crystallised in an exhibition that combined image, text and sound. She has commented on this approach:

> In my own work, the use of images, with either text or sound, came about quite naturally as a direct response to some of the situations I found myself in. The tapes of the people of Igloolik, used in the exhibition 'Towards the Night, the Light' were crucial to the body of work as a deliberate contribution of Inuit thought. The Inuit wanted Europeans to understand about their own indigenous culture... it is important to work from the position of Listening and Respect.[41]

The multimedia dimension of this practice is significant, but the visual works hold a power and intrigue that is compelling. Her study of the shaman *Noah Pivatuk* [FIG.100], 1988, is remarkable for the low viewpoint, and the mysterious way that the animal-skin drum veils his face. Equally, the untitled combine print of Inuit figure with graffito of painted rifles speaks to the elements of continuity and change within this culture.

Ruth Stirling's photography, while committed to some aspects of the documentary genre, nevertheless remains keyed to issues in contemporary art practice. A more characteristic documentary style can be evidenced in the work of the Glasgow-born photojournalist Jeremy Sutton-Hibbert (b. 1969). From the early part of his career Sutton-Hibbert has focused on issue-led subjects, and his celebrated signature work was a record of the lives and lifestyles of the 'Calderari' Romanies resident in the Sintesti village in Romania [FIG.101]. This project, begun in 1990 shortly after the fall of the Nicolae Ceasescu regime, was a kind of 'participant observation' study and would continue, intermittently, until 1997. Sutton-Hibbert engaged with the community and reflected its everyday life and work practices, its festivals and its celebrations. Through a continued and ever more intimate engagement with the group he looked to create a sympathetic portrait of the community and one that would subvert the commonly-held Romanian view of the Roma population; that they were an outlaw criminal class. His portraits of the community offer a startling and informal view of a group who cling to an authentic culture while, paradoxically, longing for the trappings of change. Moreover, his monochrome photographs of the village and its people display an uncommon trust between the photographer and his subjects. Revisiting the project in 2004, Sutton-Hibbert recognised a community that had undergone a fundamental transformation as the economy of Western capitalism seeped through the former Communist enclave, and his colour images of the Roma in this epilogue to the original venture reflect this development. He has commented on this event:

> My translator warned me I'd find changes, the camp would be unrecognisable to me. My friends remained, but new families had moved into the rapidly growing camp. Hammering metal work had been replaced by scrap metal dealing, earning the Roma by their terms a lot of money. They'd built ten room houses, furnished with leather sofas, BMWs sat gleaming outside. The Roma had purchased the trappings of the West they so desired, but I found that it hadn't brought them the happiness they'd hoped for.[42]

In some degree Sutton-Hibbert offers an archetype for the practising photo-journalist; selecting important topics that reflect current concerns and exploring them in detailed studies and expositions. Consequently his subsequent projects have included work for Greenpeace, photo-articles on the whaling industry and on prostitution, as well as more commercial assignments.

Perhaps the most provocative and challenging of these types of documentary projects, however, has been initiated by Owen Logan (b. 1963). From the early part of his career Logan has been interested in the nature of documentary photography and in its role in exploring difference, or rather, in exploring the complexity of connections. Something of this concern is evidenced in his early work on the Sikh community in Britain, an undertaking begun in 1983. The photograph *Scottish Sikh Girls in London* [FIG.102] offers a fascinating discourse on the complicated nature of identity. These young Sikh girls share a common domestic space. Their costume is mixed, being partly from the Sikh tradition but also showing the tartan check favoured in their chosen, Scottish homeland. Finally, they are resident in London. The photography, then, focuses on the intricacies of identity; an immigrant community in Scotland; one that maintains an original tradition and faith yet adapts to the host culture; and a group who negotiate the double dislocation of a further move to the south. Logan has shown a stimulating sensitivity to the nuances of this displacement, and a sense of the political import of these conditions.

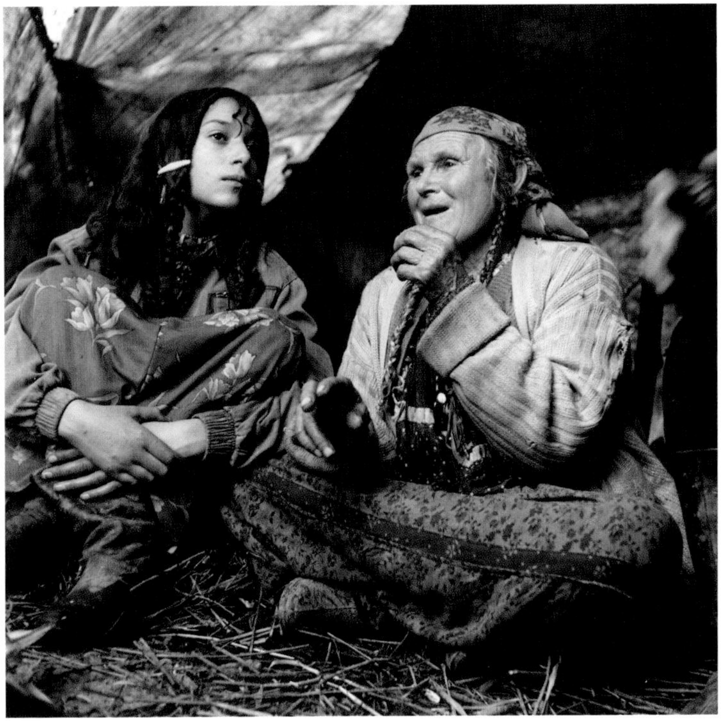

FIG.101
Jeremy Sutton-Hibbert
Talia Mihai and her Granddaughter Garoafa, Kalderariroma Camp of Sintesti, Romania
1994

In fact the development of Logan's work is witness to an ever-intensified engagement with the politics of documentary photography. He has noted that:

> The problem with the traditional documentary agenda, for me, is the notion that reality can somehow speak for itself instead of being 'spoken' for by the photographer or 'spoken over' by the viewer. I'm interested in a kind of representation that is engaged with social realities in a more mobile way, that is to say, one which relies on not being able to pin down certain kinds of pictures as simply versions of the world to be agreed or disagreed with on the basis of a perceived authenticity.[43]

Consequently, early projects like the study of the Sikh community, the assignments covering life in Morocco

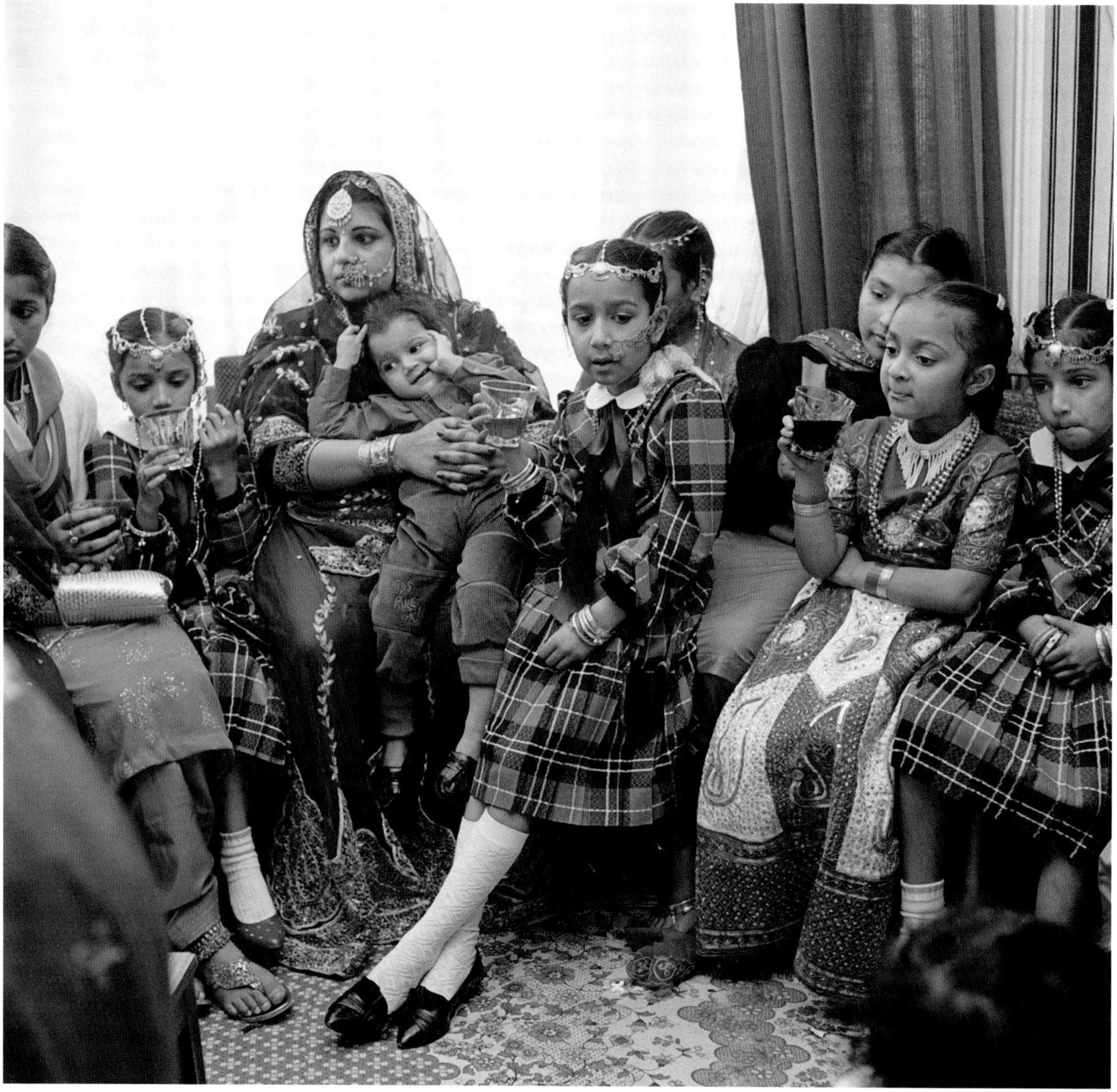

FIG.102
Owen Logan
Scottish Sikh Girls in London
1983

undertaken between 1983 and 1989, and the highly personal examination of the Scottish–Italian affiliation,[44] have seen Logan move to a sophisticated documentary realism that incorporates the subjectivity of the photographer, the integration of the subject in front of the lens and the consciousness of the institutional and political network within which the image is visualised. His documentary, then, moves beyond the 'empty... formalism sustained and forged in the marketplace', which 'was concerned with putting the autonomous author back into [documentary] photography at the expense of [an] active sense of social realism,'[45] and so moves to a radical and contingent documentary practice.

Aspects of this practice are realised in Logan's recent documentary study of Nigeria; an analysis that intersects the political economy of the state, the ethnic and religious tensions within the nation, and the role of Nigeria's oil in the geo-politics of the world economy. This continuing programme, which has developed into a study of the oil economy and the nature of globalisation, has also seen the expansion of Logan's documentary technique into digital manipulation. In this event a number of the images in his published and exhibited projects, 'A Home of Signs and Wonders' of 1997 and 'Masquerade: Nigeria Hits Michael Jackson' from 2000–04, undercut the sense of an authentic documentary 'truth' reflected, innocently, in the eye of the camera. He has commented on this prospect:

> I think digital techniques might encourage a broader social and political responsiveness, a re-engagement with the contexts of representation sidelined in the rush to build a canon of great photographers. I don't see my use of digital techniques as a contradiction of social realism, or even of documentary. As a documentary photographer I work the same way as I have always done. However, I'm now able to work on more than one level and translate different sorts of things into images.[46]

Logan's photographs, in this respect, present a re-evaluation of the documentary method through the conscious acceptance of the photographer's role in constructing the scene, and by accepting the right of the subject to negotiate and re-interpret that event.

In Logan's project 'Masquerade', for example, he has offered an extended series of images which use a 'Michael Jackson' persona, in fact one of the many 'lookalikes' who mimic the singer's style, in order to construct scenarios that both satirise Nigeria's political elites and present a subtle metaphor on Nigeria's post-colonial condition. In these photographs, a number of which are ingenious digital composites, the conventions of documentary are stretched in order to explore the underlying circumstances of Nigeria's political and economic culture. Hence:

> Most of my work has addressed the complex articulation of power and resistance in the post-colonial state. The Masquerade project in particular, is addressed to the indigenous and western elites in Nigeria... The work I've done in Nigeria has actually been very much concerned with how the false conception of a consensual audience hinders communication. It has instead been concerned with metaphor and allegory as an area of 'linguistic' consensus that can sometimes be used to open up arguments.[47]

And so the documentary photographer becomes protagonist and agitator, rather than a reflecting eye. Consequently, with this manifesto, didactic but also nuanced and open-ended, the latent humanism of the documentary tradition might be empowered and radicalised.

Documentary

Despite Logan's spirited intervention the mores of documentary photography generally remain within conventional boundaries. Historically these have been officially sanctioned records of 'social ills' and civic celebrations of public works projects. Alternatively the documentary photographer has often seen an aspect of the picturesque in rural, and especially Highland, life; a notion of the picturesque that will sometimes confuse poverty with authenticity and squalor with an organic, natural existence. Where the politicised documentary photographer has moved, independently, to record the world of the dispossessed, it has generally been as a privileged tourist. The documentary photographer might visit these other worlds, sympathise and indeed empathise with the plight of the poor, take the film, then retire to the sealed room of gallery exhibitions. It would be unfair to categorise all documentary photographers in this way, but the documentary of 'difference', the project that emotes on the despair of others or sensationalises the cultures of 'aliens', remains open to accusations of a predatory and acquisitive exploitation of the unfamiliar. Yet the best of documentary, humanist and radical, still has the power to challenge, and offend, and surprise.

This history, in a way, ignores the most potent form of the documentary image; the newspaper photograph. This unselfconscious, commercial, work-a-day form of reportage carries within it a world of meaningful discourse, for the archives of Scotland's newspapers are replete with the modern history of the nation. While commercial photo-journalists like Tom Kent in Orkney and George Cowie (1902–82) in St Andrews[48] might record the everyday life of local communities, at the general level newspaper photographers tell the nation's story. Notably, Stewart Attwood and Ian Rutherford have been award-winning photo-journalists working on Scotland's major broadsheet newspapers. And, impressively, Harry Benson (b. 1929) has worked internationally, photographing all the major events of the post-war period, from Churchill in his late years, to the Watts Riots in Los Angeles, to Robert Kennedy's assassination and Richard Nixon's resignation, and on to the Clintons during the period of the Democratic presidency. These are samples from a documentary history untold, largely because it has been viewed as temporary and 'disposable', yet it remains vital and polemical.

The history of documentary photography from Scotland, then, is richly layered and replete with instances of the most outstanding images. In some degree it remains the most characteristic of Scottish genres; empirical, political, socially aware, intellectually provocative and visually stimulating. Above all, it carries a humanitarian ethic, and this core value makes this form so manifest a feature of Scotland's culture. For all that, it was not the documentary style that provoked the renaissance in Scottish photography during the 1980s, rather it was those photographers who worked at the intersection of fine art practice.

CHAPTER FIVE

Photography and Art

Documentary photography may be the most characteristic form of Scottish photography, or at least the form that corresponds with the intellectual and the political culture of the country, but it is not the most representative. In her seminal book *On Photography*, the author Susan Sontag makes a singular reference to a Scottish photographer, and it is to David Octavius Hill. Reflecting on photography's universal constituency she notes that 'The plain photographs from the 1870s of abandoned children admitted to a London institution called Doctor Barnardo's Home (taken as 'records') are as moving as David Octavius Hill's complex portraits of Scottish notables of the 1840s (taken as 'art').'[1] Hill and Adamson's works of the 1840s were, undoubtedly, rehearsals of a fine art aesthetic and they could not have been otherwise; Hill's authority was based upon his role as an eminent painter and academician, and the acceptance of the 'mechanical' means of photography was predicated upon Hill's alchemical magic. In this event the problematic nature of photography's role as fine art was less acute in Scotland than in other countries, notably in England and France. In Scotland the debates concerning the relationship of a photograph to a painting were circumscribed and marginal, for the camera was celebrated both as an instrument of 'truth' and as a tool of the creative imagination.

The evidence of Hill and Adamson's illustrious career is testimony to this idea, but it was also writ large in the early history of photography from Scotland. An amateur photographer like John Forbes White (1831–1904), working in Aberdeen, saw no conflict between fine art and the new medium of photography. White was an established businessman who controlled the family flour-mill in Aberdeen. He was also, in the Victorian style, a broker of culture and the arts and would be instrumental in introducing Dutch genre painting to the Scottish scene during the 1860s. As an associate of George Washington Wilson and a confidant of the painter George Reid, who would later become president of the Royal Scottish Academy, White was familiar with both the new technology of the camera and the mores of fine art practice. During the middle years of the 1850s he was in thrall to the camera and photographed landscapes in and around Aberdeen with all the aplomb of a naturalist landscape painter. His photograph of *St Machar Cathedral* [FIG.103], taken in 1856 and viewed from across the River Don, has all the attributes of those Hague School landscapes he would later import into the galleries and private collections of Scottish connoisseurs. A reflective study, framed by tall trees and the twin spires of the cathedral's towers, it embodies a pictorial aesthetic replete with the compositional and tonal artistry of the fashionable painter.

John Forbes White, like many amateurs of the period, would drift away from photography. In White's case this was occasioned around 1860, when he began to satisfy his creative urges by collecting and brokering contemporary Dutch art in Scotland. At this same time another intriguing amateur, Clementina Hawarden (1822–65), was producing some of the most astonishing art-photographs of the period.

Born Clementina Elphinstone Fleeming, in Dunbartonshire, she would become Viscountess Hawarden through marriage and subsequently move to her husband's family estate in County Tipperary, Ireland. Hawarden began to photograph in Ireland, probably in 1858, and developed this interest after the family moved to London in 1859. There, in South Kensington, she established a private studio, where

FIG.103
John Forbes White
St Machar Cathedral
1856

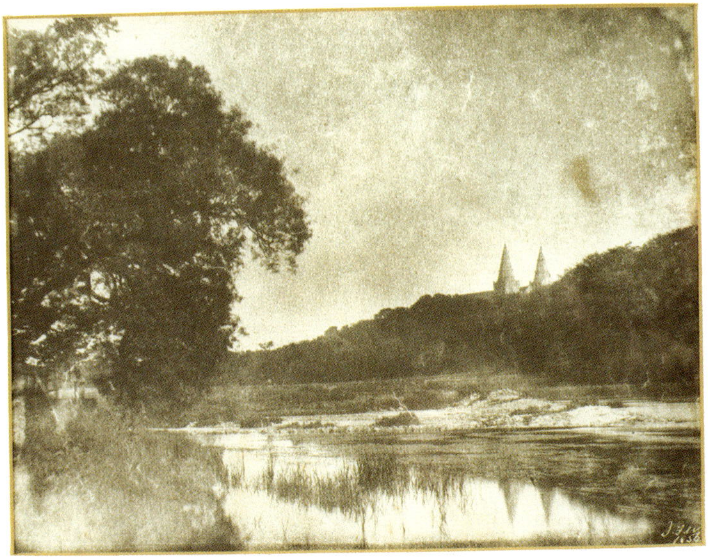

she created imaginative tableaux using her daughters as her principal models. These images, 'Photographic Studies' as they were styled when exhibited at the Photographic Society of London in 1863, remain fascinating and mesmeric visions of the interior life of a Victorian woman. Clearly influenced by Pre-Raphaelite fantasy, and by the aestheticism being explored by James Whistler during this time,[2] they are profoundly evocative apparitions of women in empty, dream-like interiors.

Typically Hawarden's photographs show a single female figure, dressed in a voluminous skirt, and set against a window, mirror or desk. The atmosphere is at once romantically desolate and subtly charged. A mood of isolation and frustration is overlain with an erotic innuendo that hints at an unspoken arousal and desire. Often the photographs will feature two women in liaison. These may be dressed in some theatrical costume, and sometimes dressed as men, but they are presented as if in the final throes of a tragic drama. The sentiments, it might be said, are characteristically Victorian, for they speak of loss and unfulfilled promise, but they remain poignant and intriguing. Hawarden's women are beautiful and frustrated; they are thwarted, obstructed and enclosed. Constantly, they search at windows and in mirrors, looking for that 'other', that 'outside' where the world begins. Interestingly, one of these universally untitled images shows a young woman in a room with an older man [FIG.104]. The woman, her white dress bathed in light, sits at a desk while the gentleman stares out of the window. There is a real tension here; the woman looks downwards at something in her hands, while the man, standing with his back to this scene, stares out into the public space. It is tempting to view these tableaux as a staging of sexual anxiety or a kind of embryonic gender politics; women locked in the domestic sphere and men, ever aspirant, moving towards the public arena.

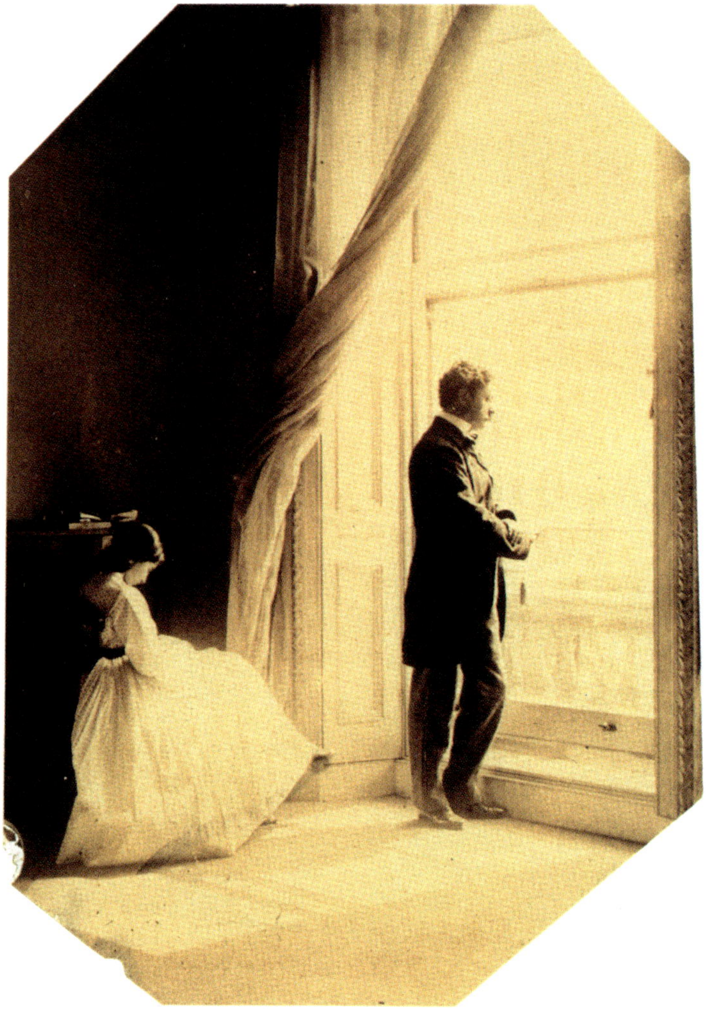

FIG.104
Clementina Hawarden
Untitled
circa 1860

While there is no hard evidence supporting this kind of reading,[3] Hawarden was surely in thrall to the contemporary tropes of her class and gender. More particularly she appeared focused on the artistic debates encouraged by a nascent avant-garde; an avant-garde that celebrated the aspirations of the emerging 'new freewoman' while still presenting womankind as vulnerable and prone to emotional collapse. Hawarden has offered a vision of woman, middle-class woman, oppressively protected within a domestic environment and thwarted in creative ambition. This, of course, was her own fate, for despite the two exhibitions in which she presented her work, her archive was lost for generations.[4] Nevertheless, Hawarden's imagery is bursting with the pictorial values of contemporary art practice and its subtle tonality combined with its evocative use of light re-asserts the notion that the photograph was embedded in fine art aesthetics.

These works are sample examples of the intersection of photography and art in the early history of photography from Scotland, though it is true that most all the early history is run through with 'artistic' photographs. This is evidenced in portraits by Hill and Adamson, landscapes by Washington Wilson, and even some 'documentary' by individuals like Thomas Annan. In the modern period the problematic of 'art photography' has been complicated by the insistence on a 'straight' or unique photographic aesthetic, that powerful ideology promoted by Paul Strand and others which claims the camera as a determining instrument of aesthetic value. In the contemporary period this idea has been, partially, discharged by a commitment to conceptual and constructive photography. That is, the realignment of photographic practice such that artists use photographs as a component in a multimedia discourse with the world. Interestingly, this has brought the dialogue between photography and art full circle in a way that provokes fascinating parallels between the experiments of 19th-century photographers and the adventures of contemporary practitioners. A clear example of this realignment can be seen in the parallel works of the 19th-century art-photographer Oscar Rejlander and the modern-day photographer Calum Colvin.

Oscar Rejlander, who would provide the obituary for Clementina Hawarden in the *British Journal of Photography* in 1865, was one of the most esteemed art-photographers of the 19th century. Born in Sweden, he settled in Britain in the 1840s. Having claimed some training as a painter, he took to photography in 1853 and was chiefly resident in London. From the middle years of the 1850s his work was regularly exhibited in photographic salons throughout Europe and he was a medal winner in the most prestigious international exhibitions. Rejlander, while asserting the independence of the photographer's techniques, was unembarrassed by the interdependence of photography and fine art. His images, ranging across the genres from portraiture to landscape, were uncompromisingly pictorial. Moreover his signature works, figurative subject pictures, were freighted with the high-minded moralising narratives of Victorian painting. This was singularly evidenced in his most famous photograph, *The Two Ways of Life*.

The Two Ways of Life was completed in 1857, and its composition, content and chronicle represent a landmark in the history of photography. The image asserted the potential for photography to contest the arena of the moral subject picture favoured by Victorian taste. Rejlander presented a central, robed and sagacious ancient, demonstrating to his two youthful charges the pathways available for their future. To the right-hand side the road to virtue; hard work, scholarly and religious dedication, family values. To the left-hand side the symbols of a dissolute and wicked life; womanising, gambling, idleness. Controversially the photograph shows a number of naked women, including a magnificently veiled symbol of 'repentance' in the foreground.

Technically *The Two Ways of Life* is remarkable because it was created as a 'composite' photograph. Rejlander was concerned to create a photographic allegory that would exist on a similar scale to an academic painting. In this event he constructed the image from some 30 negatives that were 'combined' in the studio. The technical achievement, however, was soon swamped by the controversy concerning the depiction of nude women. The camera, because of its much lauded veracity, was deemed to have created a vision of naked women that was simply too real. Whereas the fine arts might universalise and so idealise the 'nude', these were images of nakedness. Sensitivity to this condition was most acute in Scotland. The photograph was, naturally, exhibited at a number of Salons throughout the country. Presented to the Photographic Society of Scotland in 1858, it was deemed unexhibitable. Not only might the work teasingly reveal the path of iniquity to the universally virtuous populace, but the sight of so much naked female flesh would surely inflame the dormant libidos of righteous northern manhood. In Scotland the work was eventually exhibited, but with a curtain drawn across the left-hand side of the photograph; a curiously literal, not to say delusional, interpretation of a thing out of sight and out of mind.[5]

Rejlander's *The Two Ways of Life*, nevertheless, grew into acceptance, largely through royal patronage. Queen Victoria is known to have acquired a print as a gift for her consort, Prince Albert, who was an early collector of photography. The issue of 'art-photography' would rumble through the late 19th century, with Rejlander proposed as a champion of the form. And, nearly 150 years later, Calum Colvin would return to this photograph and allegory as a pivotal moment in the construction of a photographic aesthetic.

Calum Colvin's 'Two Ways of Life' is a suite of seven intensely coloured, constructed photographs completed in 1991. Collectively these form a meditation on Rejlander's seminal photograph, but travel some distance from their source. Centred upon a core work titled *The Two Ways of Life* [FIG.105], the associate images describe a surreal journey in the capricious world and are sequentially titled *The Empty Universe*, *Siren*, *His Hand in Mine*, *Crying in the Chapel*, *Bacchus* and *The Great Plenipotentiary*. The iconography of Colvin's constructed photograph is fascinating for it reveals the way in which he, as a contemporary photographer, appropriates the painterly tradition and overlays these references with quotations from popular culture. Moreover he repeats the idea of a passage in the manner implied in Rejlander's allegory.

The central photograph in Colvin's suite, *The Two Ways of Life*, is a complex and ironic metaphor that references, first, Raphael's *St John the Baptist in the Wilderness*. Appropriating Raphael's figure, and giving him the central role in the constructed and painted composition, he becomes an equivalent for Rejlander's sage. To the right and left of this figure, amid an array of items from popular culture, there are collaged photographs of the young and the older Elvis Presley. Elvis, 'the King', represents a kind of secular messianic figure whose life embodied both the paths of righteousness and dissolution. This symbolic 'Elvis' will resurface throughout the suite of images, as both a warning and a guide. The accompanying photographs, however, trace the journey of a young naïf, in the form of a kilted action-man doll, as he travels into an unpredictable future.

It is worth discussing these images for they help develop this important intersection of photography and fine art. The first photograph in the suite, *The Empty Universe*, projects the hero into his voyage. Boarding a toy boat, complete with a sail on which some verse from Robert Burns' more exotic poetry is printed, the hero departs. His first test is in the form of a *Siren*, in fact a visual quote from Tintoretto's *Susannah and the Elders*, who attempts to waylay the virtuous traveller. Of course, she succeeds and the third image, *His Hand in Mine*, shows a shipwreck and a dark seascape witnessed by a brooding Elvis. Following from the revelation of *The Two Ways of Life* our hero finds redemption while *Crying in the Chapel*, and, challenged again by *Bacchus* – this time a quote from Michelangelo's sculpture of *Bacchus* – sails on into *The Great Plenipotentiary*, again a 'sampling' from Burns' verse,[6] and into a golden sunrise.

Colvin's imaginative and witty constructions present a narrative that is both ambiguous and contingent. He replies to Rejlander's influential masterwork with an equally complex artwork. In doing so he playfully subverts the overt moralism of Rejlander's design, creates a dialogue between Rejlander's sense of a stable and ordered intellectual universe and the relativism of the contemporary period, champions a sense of the ordinary in cultural projects, and, once again, opens out the dialogue between photography and fine art. Rejlander was fully conscious of this dialogue, though sensitive to those voices that claimed photography as a mechanistic medium for reporting facts. While these voices were strident in the middle and later part of the 19th century, they were to be muted by the advent of a controversial photographic aesthetic that looked to accent the idea of an intimate complicity between the world of photography and the rarefied atmosphere of fine art, the dawn of Pictorialism.

Pictorialism

By the 1890s the debate on photography and art had become firmly focused upon the issue of Pictorialism. This debate had been initiated as early as the 1860s, and it is the case that Rejlander's 'combination' prints and Julia Margaret Cameron's 'artistic' portraits and Pre-Raphaelite compositions had established a vogue for photographs that emulated the 'look' of paintings. The key moment, however, was in 1867 when the English photographer Henry Peach Robinson pub-

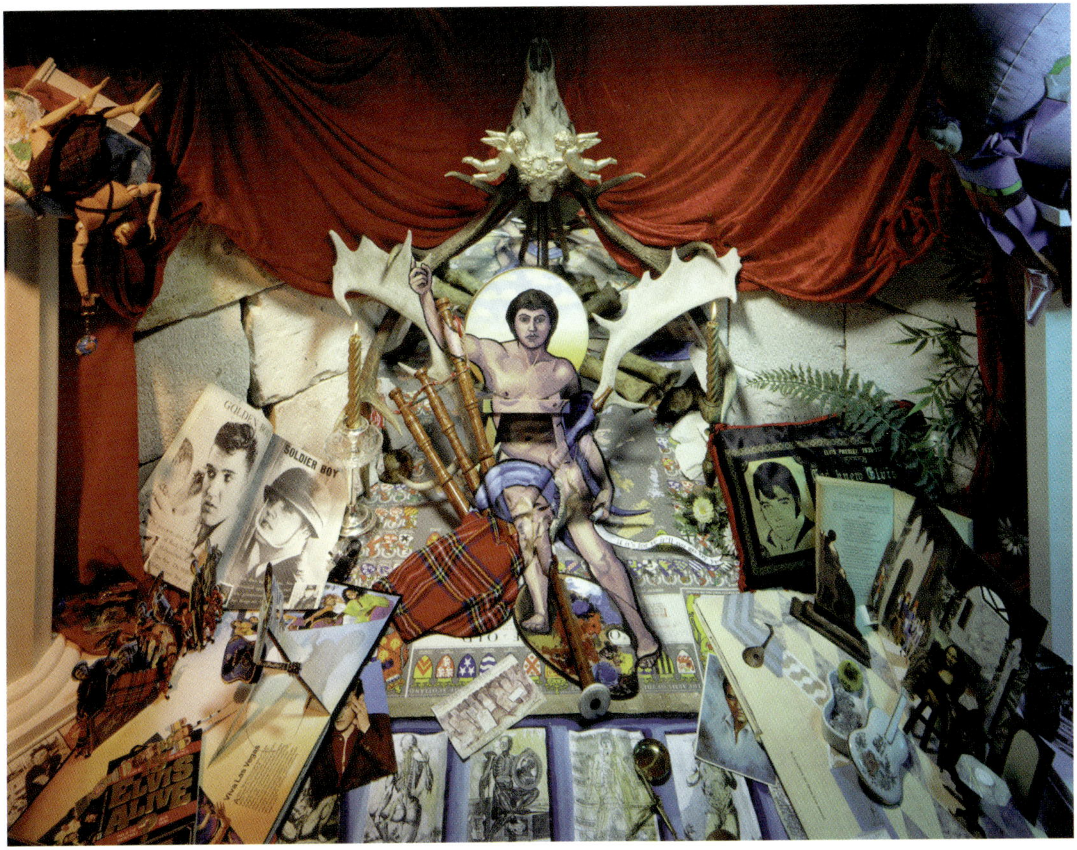

FIG.105
Calum Colvin
The Two Ways of Life
from the suite 'Two Ways of Life'
1991

lished his discourse on photographic aesthetics titled *Pictorial Effect in Photography*. This book articulated Robinson's view, realised in his own practice, that the photographer should deploy every method at his or her disposal in order to create a fully realised artistic vision. In Robinson's case this generally meant the use of combination printing to construct subject pictures that mirrored the narratives of Victorian painting. In this ambition he was certainly indebted to Rejlander, but Robinson's prints were recognised as constructed images that appeared to undermine the authenticity of the photograph, and of photography.

As early as 1860, when Robinson had lectured on his techniques at the Photographic Society of Scotland, there was considerable disquiet at this upstart art, but the debate intensified following the insurgency of Peter Henry Emerson. Emerson was a highly influential English photographer who looked to reject the artificial constructions of Robinson and his circle, and to insist upon a 'naturalistic' photography. This concept was fully articulated in 1889 when he published his counterblast to Robinson's theory in his book *Naturalistic Photography for Students of Art*. Emerson argued for a sense of realism in photography; a realism that was based upon his notion of visual perception as determined by the biology of the human eye. In extending this idea Emerson insisted that the photographic print should not be manipulated or in any way enhanced.

Emerson's position, however, was made more difficult by advances in photographic and printing technologies in this period.[7] The development of a Pictorialist effect was encouraged by the introduction of the Gum Bichromate print in the 1890s. This technique allowed for the printing of a photograph in such a way that it accented tone and softened detail, in effect creating an impressionistic photographic image. Something of this pictorial effect had already been realised in the process known as Photogravure, an innovation of 1879, and would be developed in alternate processes such as the Oil Pigment Print, extant from the 1890s, and the Gum Platinum Print, from circa 1900. Effectively photographers were beginning to counter what had been the holy grail of the photographic process, a sharply focused and intensely 'real' image, and were searching for a method compatible with fine art. While the debate on photography and art would rumble through the period, a few of Scotland's most interesting photographers were committed to the Pictorialist vision, most notable of all, James Craig Annan.

James Craig Annan was, of course, heir to a photographic dynasty. The second son of Thomas Annan and brother to John Annan, he is recorded as a student of the work of Hill and Adamson while still an infant.[8] After becoming a member of the family business at age 14, he studied some chemistry in Glasgow and would accompany his father to Austria in 1883. There, the 19-year-old Craig Annan would be introduced to the process of photogravure by its inventor, Karl Klic. This technique, closely allied to the methods of etching, offered a photomechanical process that produced soft tonal images akin to a drawing in charcoal. It was particularly useful in photographing paintings, one of the principal ventures in the Annan business, and would become a prized technique in the creation of Pictorialist photographs.

Craig Annan's career placed him at the very centre of artistic circles and the Pictorialist moment. His closest friends within the febrile community of Glasgow's avant-garde of the 1890s included the etchers William Strang and D. Y. Cameron. He was, from the early 1890s, a recognised international photographer, exhibiting in Europe and America, and recorded in the most prestigious photographic journals of the period. During 1895 he opened a dialogue with Alfred Stieglitz that would continue until Craig Annan's death, and he would reproduce his own works in Stieglitz's *Camera Work*, as well as providing photogravures of Hill and Adamson's finest images for that landmark journal. When, in 1892, Henry Peach Robinson left the Photographic Society of Great Britain in order to found the Linked Ring, Craig Annan allied himself to the secessionist group and became a full member in 1894. In this role he became an associate of those photographers closest to the idea that photography was a fine art, and that its forms might emulate the aesthetic of painting.

Meanwhile Craig Annan's own photography was becoming established and radicalised in both form and content, and it was through his associations with recognised artists. In 1892 he travelled with D. Y. Cameron to Holland, where he complemented Cameron's etchings of fishing communities and peasants with photographic studies like *The Beach at Zandvoort* and *The Road through the Sand Dunes*. Again, in 1894, he and Cameron were journeying from Genoa to Venice in an expedition that would, famously, see them compete in picture-making; most especially in their twin images of Franciscan monks walking in the streets and the parallel pictures of *Venice from the Lido*. In 1896 Craig Annan would publish his photogravures of this trip as a folio of 11 images titled *Venice and Lombardy*. Finally, in 1913, Craig Annan would travel with William Strang to Spain, where each would produce evocative images in and around Granada.

Evidently it was with artists, and with like-minded pictorial photographers, that Craig Annan was most comfortable. However, William Buchanan has been careful to note that 'In the taking of exposures [Craig] Annan is modern, but in the making of prints he is not.'[9] Craig Annan's photographs, in particular those taken in Italy, tend to be near-spontaneous images of figures in motion. In this event his work was allied to a 'realist' or 'natural' aesthetic, one that was initiated by his use of a hand-held camera. In this approach Craig Annan signalled something of the modernism that would characterise much 20th-century photography. Interestingly, in respect of this, Craig Annan was cited in a very early 'Plea for Straight Photography' as part of a talk given to the Scottish Photo-Pictorial Circle in 1912 and subsequently produced as an article for the journal *Photo-Era*. Here, the author Dan Dunlop, himself a photographer, proclaimed:

> It is more, however, in portrait-photography that we find the straight print excelling itself. Take the work of Craig-Annan [sic]... In Craig-Annan we have *the* portrait-photographer of the world. There is an honesty and straight-forwardness in all his portrait-work that is admirable, and yet behind that we have the genius of the man stamped in every picture.[10]

Dunlop was objecting to the trend for 'very-much-faked productions'[11] that were viewed as the commonplace output of art-photographers, but he was arguing for a 'straight' photography that would be 'perfectly delightful in its spontaneous handling'[12] and would therefore qualify as art. This approach was certainly evidenced in some of Craig Annan's work but in the creation of photogravure images he had the opportunity to manipulate the plate and here he was an archetypal Pictorialist.

In fact Craig Annan would clearly manipulate the image in one of his most famous of portraits, *The Etching Printer – William Strang Esq.* ARA [FIG.21], from 1902. Buchanan has noted that '[Craig] Annan worked this plate aggressively, fading out both background and foreground to allow concentration on the real subject which is the artist in the heat of work.'[13] Moreover, in some of his most distinguished works Craig Annan would develop this pictorial style to produce singularly epic images; none more so than *The Dark Mountains* of circa 1890 and *Stirling Castle*, taken in 1906.

The Dark Mountains [FIG.106] is an early work by Craig Annan, yet remains one of his most redolent and mysterious prints. It was worked as a photogravure and exhibited internationally, including in the salon of the Linked Ring in 1895. The photograph itself was taken atop Ben Vorlich, an imposing and perilous mountain in the Trossachs to the north of Glasgow. Craig Annan has photographed a group of four figures, dressed in heavy woollen coats and with gloves and hats. The group drifts away from the camera, their backs to the recording lens, and, following an irregular pathway, create a ragged file of walkers along the precipitous ridge of the dark mountain. They move in a landscape, patched with snow and scree, towards a horizon of mountain peaks through which there appears an aurora of sunset. The spectacular glow of the sunset has surely been worked into the gravure, but it signals a romantic and symbolist intent in Craig Annan's photograph. This is an image that speaks, enigmatically, of life's journey and the perils and pitfalls of that treacherous road. Small wonder, then, that it became a masterwork of the Pictorial movement; bought by Stieglitz and reproduced in *Camera Work* in October 1904, it evidenced the soft focus and suffused mood of a dedicated art-photography.

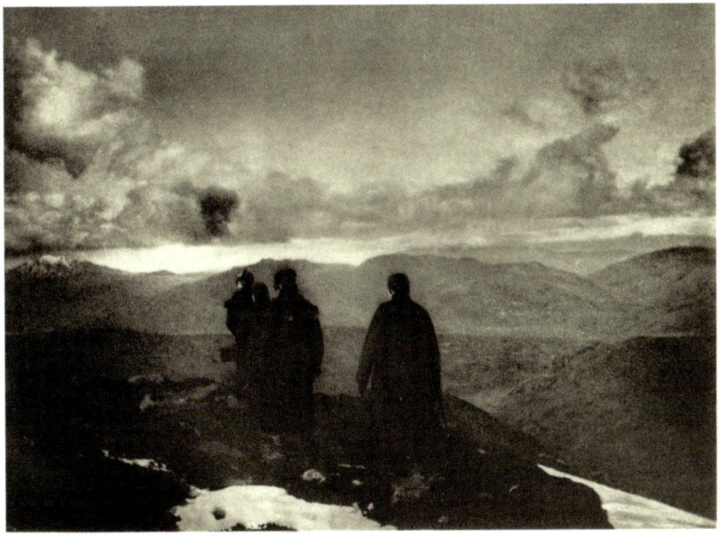

FIG.106
James Craig Annan
The Dark Mountains
circa 1890

The sense of a symbolist intent in Craig Annan's photography should not be surprising for though he was closest to etchers like Strang and Cameron, and a confidant of the Scottish Impressionists, he was also the individual who photographed Charles Rennie Mackintosh and his circle. In the 1890s Mackintosh, along with Margaret and Frances Macdonald and Herbert MacNair, was producing intense and inscrutable watercolours that looked to evoke the occult landscape of the human psyche. Craig Annan was never drawn to this extreme, but *The Dark Mountains* certainly plays with a metaphysical and symbolist dynamic. This may also be the case with his photogravure of *Stirling Castle* [FIG.107].

The subject of Stirling Castle would appear to be one of the most clichéd notions in 'the landscape of association'; an imposing 12th-century battlement, set high on a rock above the valley of the River Forth, it has been witness to some of the most momentous episodes in Scottish history. Craig Annan's photo-

FIG.107
James Craig Annan
Stirling Castle
1906

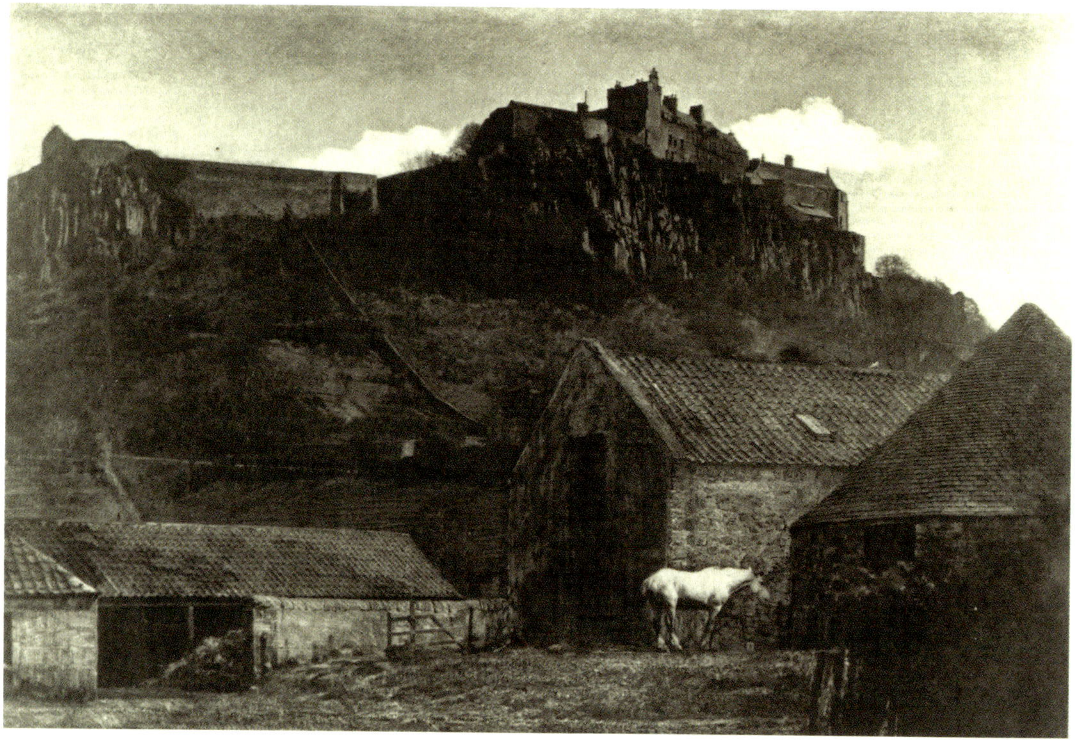

graph, probably taken while in the company of William Strang and with an instantaneous camera, looks up to the castle walls guarding the enclosed palace and chapel. In the gravure the castle is dark and daunting, but Craig Annan has photographed the scene from a farmyard in the shadow of the historic edifice. Among the farm buildings a white horse appears, moving lazily through the yard. This juxtaposition is extraordinary. Craig Annan has countered the notion of historic time with a perception of everyday life. In fact, he has presented a multi-layered dialectic, high and low, the majestic and the ordinary, the exceptional and the commonplace. All of this projects a contest between a sense of epic, official history and the social world of daily life. Craig Annan's viewpoint, within the farmyard, suggests a symbolic identification with the democratic consciousness of the modern world. And, whatever the veracity of this interpretation, the photogravure is certainly an evocative and complicated picture of a seemingly conventional subject.

Craig Annan's photogravures remain among the most beautiful and compelling images in the history of photography from Scotland. In period, the debate over their status as 'art' or 'photography' exposed the confusion concerning the unfolding discourse surrounding this convoluted concept. When Peter Henry Emerson objected to the artifice of Henry Peach Robinson in the 1880s, he was protesting against any manipulation in the printing of the image. But Emerson's own prints, however 'realist', were composed within the frame of a fine art aesthetic; his images of Norfolk looked like monochromatic paintings no matter how 'untouched' the print remained. Equally, when Dan Dunlop proposed Craig Annan as a master of 'straight' photography it was because he directed his camera on the scene without overt manipulation. Dunlop, a pictorial photographer himself, was objecting to the 'retouching' and physical manipulation of the Gum Bichromate printmakers whose photographs became muddily impressionistic 'paintings'. Even Stieglitz, who would later champion the 'straight' photography of the American modernists, saw in Craig Annan a poet of the camera whose work excelled at the level of the aesthetic. In consequence of this Craig Annan helped establish a Pictorialism which, while projecting a notion of photography as a legitimate art, remained loyal to the integrity and authenticity of the available technologies. Moreover, his Pictorial style would radiate through the salons of photography in Scotland.

When writing in the *Special Summer Number of 'The Studio'*, 1905, an edition titled *Art in Photography*, the critic Clive Holland noted that 'The work of Mr. Craig Annan... has for years past not only been a feature of most of the large Exhibitions, but also has served to show how great a degree of excellence in pure portraiture can be attained through the medium of the camera and – artistic perception.'[14] He went on to champion the work of another less well-known Pictorial photographer, Alexander Allan:

> The work of Mr. Alexander Allan, who is such a tower of strength in that regard to the Scots Salon and other Northern Exhibitions, is well known. Its main characteristics place it in almost the same school as that of Frederick Hollyer and Craig Annan, a fine example being his 'Mary', hung in the Scots Salon of last year. Mr. Allan has not, however, confined himself to this class of work, but has produced from time to time landscapes of distinct individuality and charm.[15]

Alexander Allan (n.d.), who often worked with his brother as 'Allan Brothers',[16] had his work illustrated by an extraordinary photogravure titled *Winter* [FIG.108]. This image owes much to the example of Craig Annan and depicts a solitary figure in a snow-filled landscape. The dark figure, wrapped in a heavy cape-coat and hat, trudges away from the camera past a ramshackle fence and a snow-capped country cottage. Holland notes that 'In the picture reproduced herein some idea of the sentiment and controlling influence which pervades much of the work in this genre of Mr. Allan and his brother will be apparent',[17] but it remains clear that Allan is invoking the nuanced symbolism of Craig Annan. Moreover, his gravure

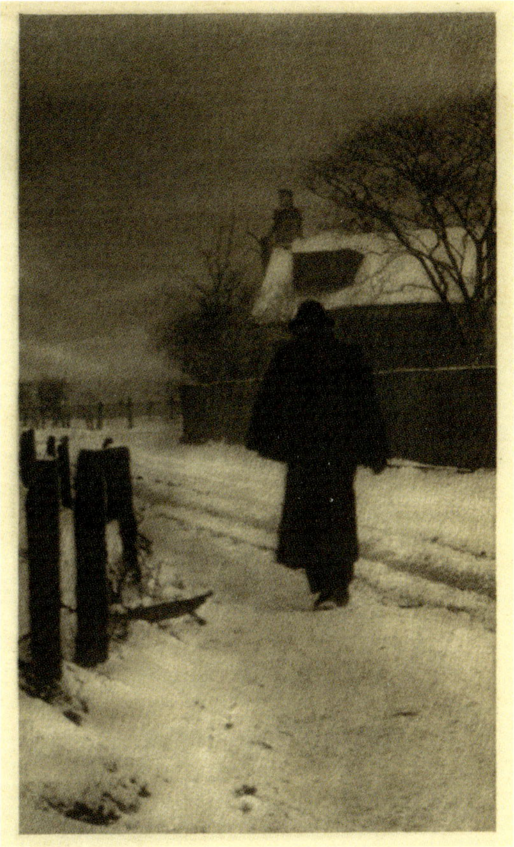

FIG.108
Alexander Allan
Winter
circa 1904

maintained the pictorial quality championed by Craig Annan, with all its sense of shade, tone and gradation.

The year of this publication on *Art in Photography*, 1905, was also the year in which that other giant of Pictorial photography would first visit Scotland. The precocious American Alvin Langdon Coburn (1882–1966) came to photograph Edinburgh in search of the ghost of Robert Louis Stevenson. Coburn was a young talent – initially resident in Boston, he had his first professional exhibition aged 15 – and after travelling to London in 1899 he would exhibit with the Royal Photographic Society in 1900.[18] By 1905 he was an established transatlantic photographer, and an associate of some of the most significant intellectual figures of the age. His project in Edinburgh was undertaken in homage to Stevenson and, in particular, in relation to Stevenson's affectionate memoir of his native city *Edinburgh: Picturesque Notes*, first published in 1878.[19] Coburn knew Stevenson's work intimately, and certainly revered his quirky, charming, tender and melancholic description of his native city. He was later to reflect:

> I never met Stevenson in the flesh. It is one of my great regrets that I came just a little too late to make his portrait, but I have all his books and have read them many times, so that I seem to know him better than some of my older friends. Through his Edinburgh and in his Edinburgh I seem to know him best of all.[20]

And it was in Stevenson's Edinburgh, in 1905, that Coburn would take some of the most enthralling images of his career.

FIG.109
Alvin Langdon Coburn
Weir's Close
1905

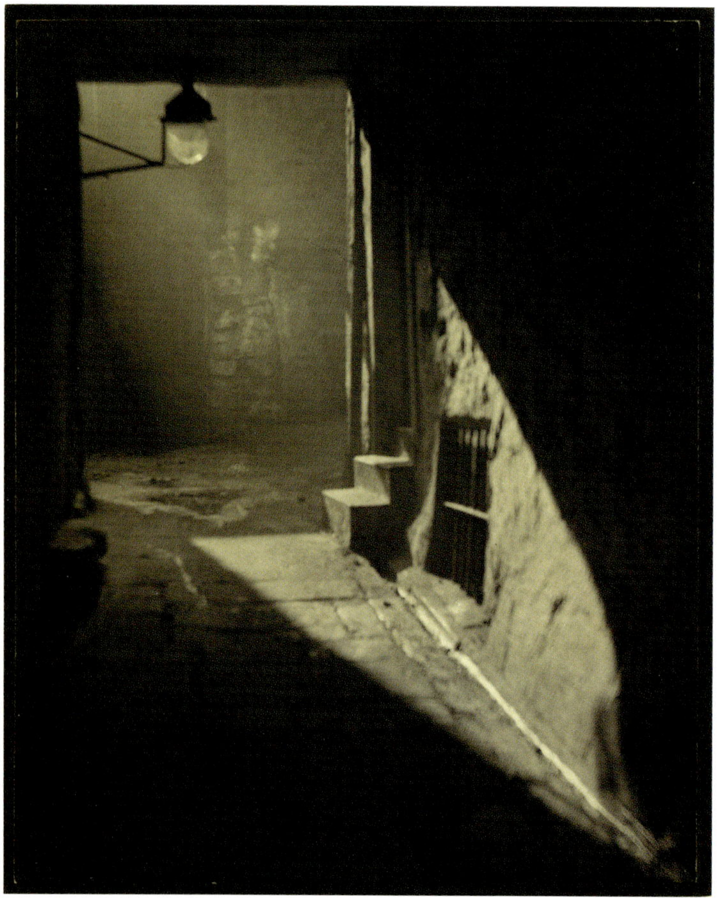

Stevenson had described Edinburgh as 'a dream in masonry and living rock'[21] and Coburn followed his mentor into this dreamscape with scrupulous care. Like Stevenson he favoured the 'Old Town', photographing the medieval 'tall lands' or tenements and the dark 'closes' and passageways between these precipitous buildings. He also moved through to the historic centre and on to the photographer's grail that is Greyfriars Churchyard, before a summary excursion into the 'New Town' and its environs. Stevenson had noted that 'the whole city leads a double existence'[22] and Coburn reflected this in the contrast between the rigid symmetry of the neo-classical 'New Town' and the 'disordered heart'[23] that was the medieval quarter perched on Castle Rock. It was in this cavernous 'Old Town' that Coburn took some of his most astonishing photographs. *Weir's Close* [FIG.109], canonised by Stieglitz as one of Coburn's finest works,[24] is typical of the sense of mystery and menace that informed so many of Coburn's symbolist works.

Late in his life Coburn would declare, '*Weir's Close* I fondly believe is one of my most convincing achievements'[25] but in 1905 he was creating this image as a response to Stevenson's tale of occult ritual and fiendish practice. The eponymous 'Major Weir' was an Edinburgh evangelical preacher and demon wizard who had been unmasked and hanged in the 17th century. Stevenson tells the tale with relish and speaks of how Weir's carriage haunted the closes of Edinburgh's 'Old Town'. Coburn's photograph, a dark, softly focused, ambiguous view of an empty passageway, evokes the atmosphere of Stevenson's fable. The few signifying features – a lamp, some steps to a doorway, a basement window barred and blocked – are revealed by a single shaft of light piercing the close. The photograph is typical of Coburn's fascination with the supernatural and its spectral qualities are characteristic of his Pictorialism.

Coburn, however, was not the only esteemed North American Pictorialist who would discover an association with Scotland. Margaret Watkins (1884–1969) was born in Canada, though her mother was Scottish and she would spend the last 40 years of her life in Glasgow.[26] After a faltering start in a variety of posts she attended a summer school organised by the renowned American Pictorialist, Clarence White. White was both a member of the Linked Ring and a founding member of its American equivalent, the Photo-Secession, established in 1902. From 1910 White had organised, and had taught at, a summer school in the art and techniques of photography, and Watkins would begin to attend these events from 1914. Within the orbit of White she developed as one of America's foremost Pictorial photographers and became an important teacher at White's schools. Bonnie Yochelson has remarked of Watkins:

> Her subtle manipulation of value, texture, and form recalls the delicate tonal harmonies of White's own work. More than any other student, Watkins, who taught technique in the school during the 1920s and was secretary of the PPA (Pictorial Photographers of America), carried White's sensibility into the modern era.[27]

In the period circa 1919 Watkins would create some of the finest art photographs in America, and would expand into the creation of some pioneering advertising images. In 1928, however, she moved to Glasgow, ostensibly to care for her mother's sisters, and she never returned to America. Though she subsequently travelled and photographed in France and Germany, and, intriguingly, in revolutionary Russia, her career fell into a decline. Lori Pauli reports that 'she had been elected to the Royal Photographic Society in 1929 and was the first female member of the Glasgow and West of Scotland Camera Club'[28] but the opportunity for a career as a professional art-photographer seems to have been lost when in Scotland.

The key difficulty for Watkins was that she arrived in Scotland at the point where Pictorialism and its values were collapsing. Certainly, she developed her symbolist aesthetic into a modernist frame, and this was clearly evidenced in the geometric abstraction of a photograph like *Blythswood* [FIG.110], taken in Glasgow during 1937, but Pictorialism and modernism were both to be marginalised to the point of near invisibility in Scotland after the First World War. This was a fate shared by Craig Annan and Coburn alike. The former all but gave up his role as a creative photographer in the period after 1919, when he took to dealing in etchings through the family business. Likewise Coburn set his camera aside in the 1920s after having experimented with an abstract modernism in his 'Vortographs'. Both would live for decades after this time, but their respective contributions to photography were complete. In effect neither of these individuals could adapt their symbolist and Pictorialist aesthetics to the nature of modernity. Moreover, the ethos of 'straight' photography, now being propagated by Stieglitz and his dazzling acolyte Paul Strand, held no intrigue for these photographic sorcerers.

Watkins, too, was subject to this fundamental shift in taste, though she found herself in the place where Pictorialism would remain a dominant form, the camera clubs and their annual salons. The Glasgow and West of Scotland Camera Club, where she had broken the gender barrier, was typical of the groups affiliated to The Scottish Photographic Foundation, and here a kind of sentimental Pictorialism would linger as an aesthetic norm. In part this was occasioned by the changing economics surrounding the production of photographs. The notion of the photographer as an independent artist, the support of

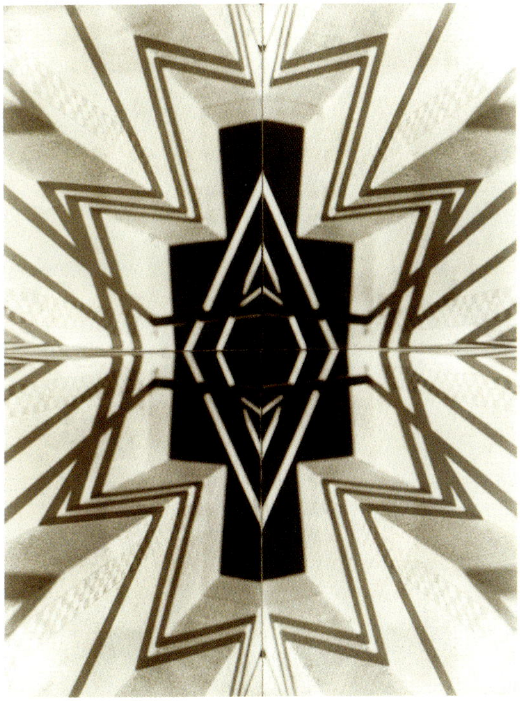

FIG.110
Margaret Watkins
Blythswood
1937

pioneering journals, the opportunity for meaningful exhibition and international esteem all contracted between the two world wars. Photography, at a professional level, belonged in the working studio, with newspapers and in the world of advertising. Photographic-artists like Craig Annan, Coburn and Watkins stood outside this commercially-driven streamline new world and Pictorialism was viewed as a quaint anachronism.

Constructed narratives

The renaissance in art-photography in Scotland can be traced to the 1980s and the emergence of a number of dedicated photographers who worked on the boundaries of fine art and photographic practice. Of course, in this period, the very idea of an artist working in a single medium or style was challenged and the opportunities for a new photography were abundant. This was assisted by more innovative and enterprising official institutions. The art colleges began to recognise photography as a serious discipline to be taught within the syllabus, the official funding bodies began to sponsor photographic projects, museums presented prestigious exhibitions of photographic works and smaller, independently organised galleries offered opportunities for creative photography. In effect photographers in Scotland were liberated from commercially orientated workloads, and the opportunity for a vibrant photographic culture was realised.

One of the clearest signals of this renaissance was the exhibition 'Constructive Narratives' held at the independent Stills Gallery in Edinburgh during 1986. Here two emerging photographers, Calum Colvin and Ron O'Donnell (b. 1952), exhibited their intensely coloured, exuberant and kaleidoscopic constructed photographs. Colvin had trained in sculpture at Dundee College of Art, though he had taken a subsidiary study in photography under the tutelage of Joseph McKenzie. O'Donnell had studied photography at Napier Polytechnic and had worked in photographic laboratories. Independently, they had begun to experiment with constructed images and these were brought together in this landmark exhibition of 1986.

Calum Colvin's art college degree show had consisted of built environments, decorated with the detritus of abandoned schoolrooms, over-painted with scenarios from a remembered childhood and subsequently preserved as a photograph. In this way he fulfilled the aims of a 'sculptural' practice, but realised this in photographic work. On moving to graduate studies in photography at the Royal College of Art in London in 1983, he developed this idea, employing ever more elaborate constructions and visually erudite scenes. Increasingly Colvin began to work in colour, usually the intensely vibrant colour of advertising images, and to deploy references to the fine art culture. An early example, like *Heroes I* [FIG.111] from 1986, samples the male nude from Jean-Auguste-Dominique Ingres' *Oedipus and the Sphinx*, 1808, and reworks the image in a stage set of old armchairs, bric-a-brac, magazine covers, fast-food packaging and *Superman* wall-hangings. Here, Colvin began to conflate high art and popular culture. More importantly, he introduced an eclectic mix of genres, layering references to the commonplace and the everyday with associative ideas that quoted the academies, and combining this with an ironic, not to say comic, explosion of connections.

For all the vigour and élan of Colvin's work, these remain profound and subtle images. Throughout the 1980s he developed and extended these photographic constructions, re-interpreting valued artefacts like Hieroymus Bosch's *The Garden of Earthly Delights* and revered subjects like *The Temptation of St Anthony*. Increasingly his work was presented in series that reflected upon allegory and myth. Apart from the esteemed 'Two Ways of Life' he also explored 'The Seven Deadly Sins and the Four Last Things', 1993, based on Bosch's rondo in the Prado museum, and 'Ossian: Fragments of Ancient Poetry', 2002, sourced in the mythic narrative of James Macpherson's epic 18th-century poetic 'translations'. From 1989 Colvin has experimented with computer-manipulated photographs, introducing his complex iconography of figures, objects and scenery into the databank of a computer and organising these characters into surreal scenarios. In the earliest of these manipulated images, *Jacob's Ladder* [FIG.112], of 1989, he incorporated the ubiquitous kilted 'action man' figure, placing him on a ladder reaching towards enlightenment and against a landscape of peaked mountains and scenic loch. He embroidered the scenario with references to Robert Moyes Adam's photography, discarded household ornaments and episodes from the ever-popular Scottish cartoon series, *Oor Wullie*. In all his photography he has presented a comic-epic study of personal and cultural identity within the frame of an unstable and relativist modernity.

His Ossian project of 2002 distilled these colliding themes into a meditation on James Macpherson's invention of Ossian; the 'Celtic bard' and 'northern Homer' conjured in his 'translated' epic poem of 1760.[29] This exhibition consisted of a variety of complex images associated with the core themes in Macpherson's work but took, as a central motif, the etching that was used as the frontispiece for the Highland Society of London's *Poems of Ossian*, published in 1807. This etched head, sometimes ascribed to the Scottish neoclassical painter Alexander Runciman, has been reworked by Colvin as the bard 'Blind Ossian'. In this guise the portrait exists as a spectral presence haunting a ruined landscape in the central group of nine images that sits at the heart of Colvin's 'Ossian'.

This is a core image that is remarkable for its profound melancholy. Remarkable, for Colvin is often viewed as an artist who has embraced the comic. Historically, his images have appeared joyous, infinitely decorated with a kitsch symbolism and replete with a ribald humour. In fact, there has consistently been a dark core to Colvin's photography. His photography has, almost unfailingly, described landscapes in decay, a world littered in ambiguity and a humanity sated by doubt and uncertainty. The cycle of images at the heart of this Ossian project is, perhaps, the starkest testimony of this vision.

Formally, these nine photographs of the 'Blind Ossian' cycle are a significant development in the artist's oeuvre. While depicting an architecture in ruins, the broken and fragmented temple of the Romantic landscape, they are pre-eminently concerned with light. Each image is shaped, and re-defined, by the lighting. In some darkness pervades, details within the ruins are obscured and lost. In others the light opens out hidden areas, flooding a detail and focusing on a minute incident. In yet others the light is filtered, a darkened blue or an umber. These subtle tonal gradations enhance the mood of despond that creeps through these spaces. Overall there is a sense that the ruined landscape has a temporal or historical presence. Each shift in lighting unveils a different moment in time and reveals the gradual, insidious disintegration of the scene. There is, throughout, a sinister and menacing feel to these images, a sense of inevitable decay and melancholy regret.

Closer examination releases those spectral presences that help show the tragic sentiment at the heart of these photographs. In each the ghost of 'Ossian' is present. In more than half of the nine works the head of the blind bard is clearly seen; a totemic, omniscient figure brooding in the ruined

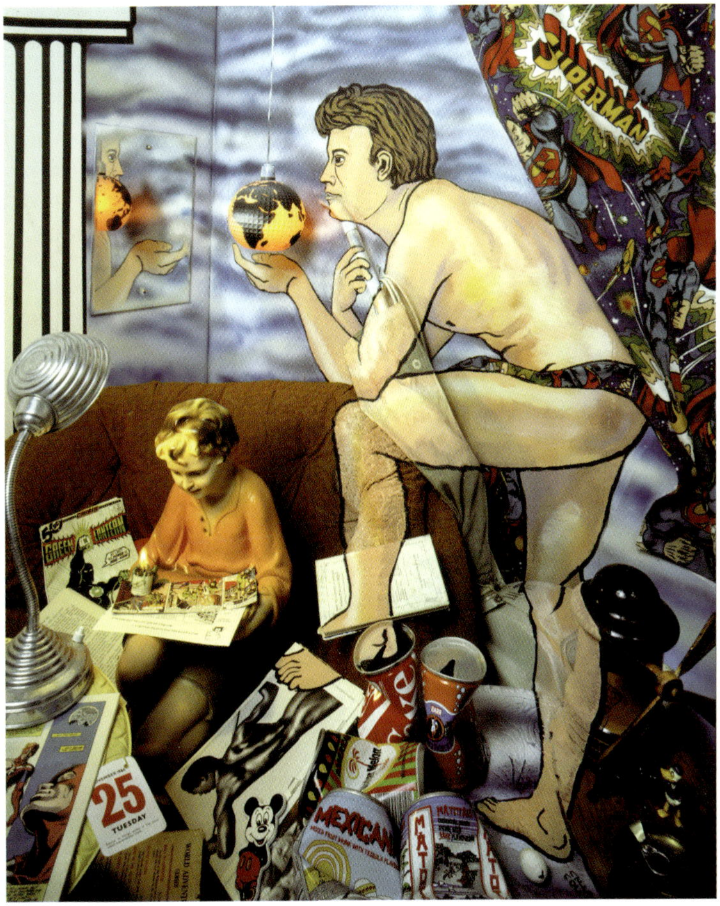

FIG.111
Calum Colvin
Heroes I
1986

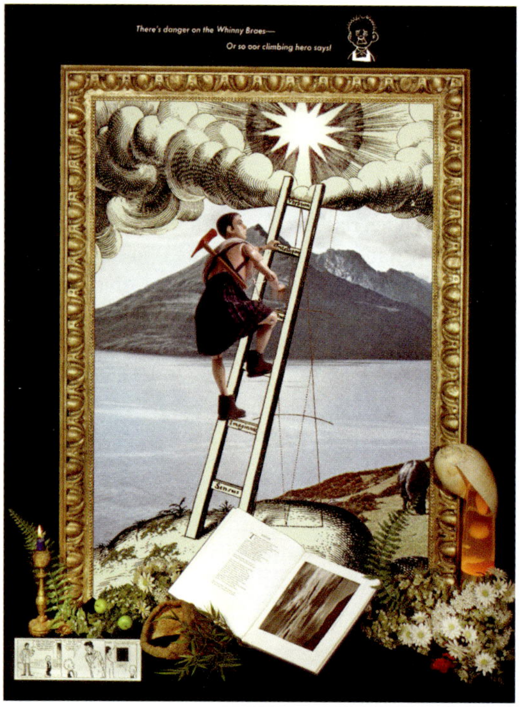

FIG.112
Calum Colvin
Jacob's Ladder
1989

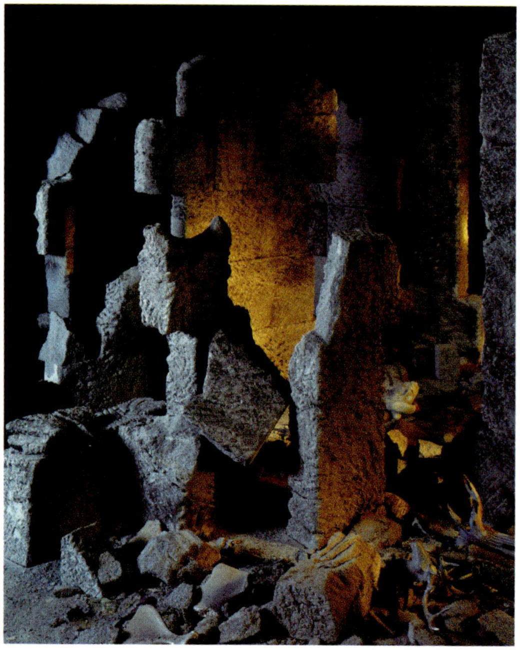

FIG.113
Calum Colvin
Blind Ossian IX
2002

landscape. In *Blind Ossian* I, for example, the flowing hair and beard of the bard falls into a pattern of loops and curls. This pattern becomes mapped on the broken stone of the temple architecture, a fractured tracery recalling the interlace of Celtic design. In the debris a few iconic images are just visible. In the bottom left of these photographs there sits the partly scorched image of an aboriginal head, a tattooed Maori. The rhythmical facial tattoos mirror the Celtic tracery in Ossian. More subtly, this juxtaposition recalls that fatal conceit in Macpherson's creation myth of the Scottish people, the suggestion that the Scots were not an Irish tribe but a native and indigenous Celtic people who colonised Ireland.[30] Colvin introduces the Maori, in part, as a comic leitmotif representing the fallibility of history and the problem, even the absurdity, of those narratives that search for essences, particularly racial essences. To the right of the nine images in the cycle there is a more straightforward symbolism. Among the broken stones there sits the head and antlers of a porcelain stag. The stag appears as an emblem that references the Clearances of the Highlands. Hence the decapitated stag is omnipresent in this series as a memory of these events, a counterpoint perhaps to Edwin Landseer's triumphalist *Monarch of the Glen*.

For all this the atmosphere of the 'Blind Ossian' cycle is deeper and darker than the sum of its parts. Throughout the cycle there is a measured disintegration. By the ninth and final image, *Blind Ossian* IX [FIG.113], reference to Ossian has faded, the 'Maori' doppelganger has been seared, and the ruined landscape has collapsed further. Colvin's tragic world has become a nightmare landscape, an apocalyptic vision of destruction and devastation. Here again the references are layered. At some level Colvin is reflecting on the sense of loss and regret that exists at the core of Macpherson's project. He is reprising the Romantic idea that a world can be vanished yet remain known as a shadow of itself, the romance of the 'ruin'. Equally he is reproducing the kind of devastated landscape that has become a recognisable feature of our contemporary world, the bombed and battle-scarred landscapes of newsreel footage. Yet his mind is constantly alive to even more obtuse associations and relationships, and these are manifest throughout the various accompanying images in the 'Ossian' project; in all the project is a triumph of the postmodern imagination as represented in contemporary art-photography.

Calum Colvin is a fascinating photographer because he reflects upon the nature of photography itself, challenging its value as 'truth' or 'document' and its purpose as 'art'. Simultaneously he questions the nature of contemporary culture in his allegorical works, through a discrete consideration of ethics, morality and the conventions of social life. Finally, he confronts the puzzle of the 'self', of personal, and political, and social 'identity' in the contemporary world. These are far-reaching, searching ambitions but they are also, increasingly, the territory of contemporary photographic practice.

Something of this approach is also evidenced in the photography of Ron O'Donnell. O'Donnell has maintained a fascination with popular culture and the visual kaleidoscope of everyday life, from an early period when he photographed vibrant street scenes, advert-strewn commercial premises and litter-shrouded derelict buildings. These documentary images of Edinburgh life in the 1970s were fashioned into pulsating constructed photographs in the 1980s. Increasingly O'Donnell began to create scenarios, usually within derelict factories and abandoned buildings, which reflected the cultural conundrums of a developing and devolving Scottish culture. These scenes were often composed from objects and apparatus found within the sites, though this was augmented by junk-shop paraphernalia and applied decoration. Here, O'Donnell would introduce painted elements and, often, sculpted cardboard and paper constructions. This last is most clearly demonstrated in his *Adam and Eve*, a constructed image from 1989 that offers a tightly composed scenario wherein a collaged Eve presents a similarly assembled Adam with a paper apple; all under a Tree of Knowledge composed of cardboard leaves.

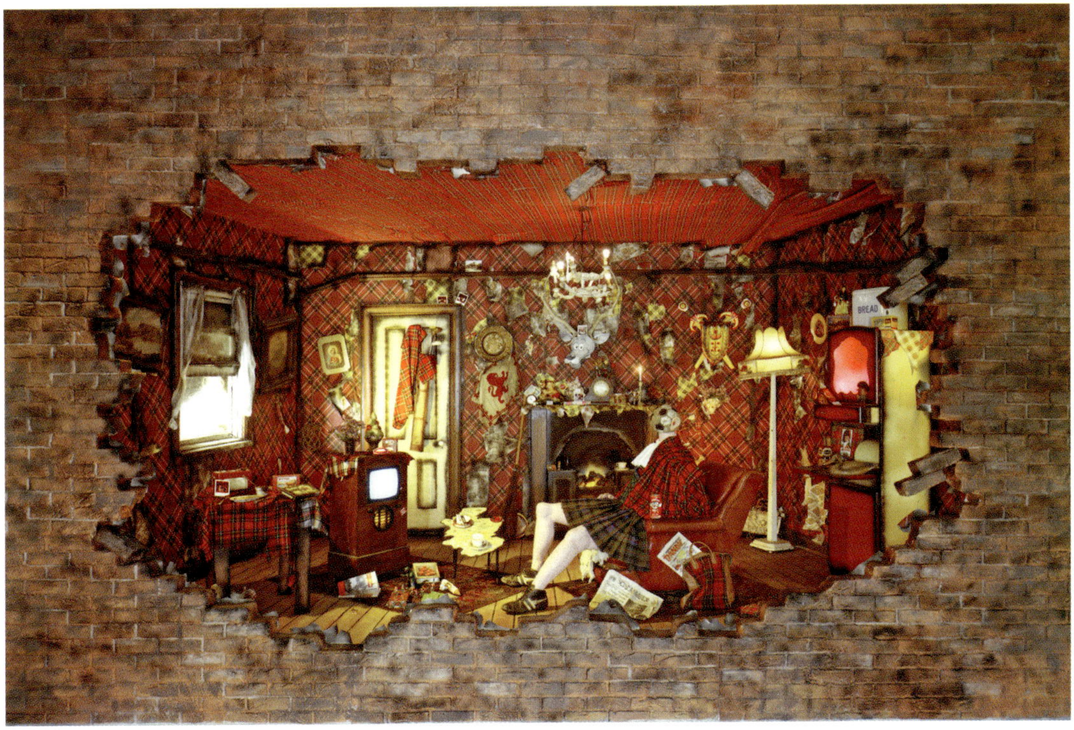

FIG.114
Ron O'Donnell
The Scotsman
1987

The venture into a biblical subject, and a central theme in classical art, remains unusual in O'Donnell's work for, in contrast to Calum Colvin, he is not overly concerned with fine art precedents. In fact an abiding and subversive humour is the key note in O'Donnell's photography. His *Adam and Eve* are headless characters whose principal focus is their naked genitalia, and they are offered, by a passing angel, a packet of condoms; a particularly apposite metaphor for the realisation of Original Sin. Equally, in his dissident image of *The Scotsman* [FIG.114] from 1987, O'Donnell constructs a tartan-bedecked sitting-room, complete with kitsch ornaments and memorabilia, and settled by a shop-fitter's mannequin in a kilt and plaid who gazes at a television set. Ironically the head of this tartan monster has been fashioned from a football, and so the nation's obsessive-compulsive psychosis is presented as parody. Indeed O'Donnell's fascination with the nature of a distinctively Scottish culture has been an axis for his most recognised photographs.

However, during 1998 O'Donnell was able to travel to Mexico, where he extended his interest in expressions of popular culture into a study of Mexico's 'Day of the Dead' festival. The series of photographic constructions that emerged from this trip are among his most distinctive works. Working alongside Mexico's foremost papiermâché sculptors, the Linares Brothers, he deployed paper skeletons within his elaborate constructed scenes and presented a darkly comic celebration of mortality. These photographs represent both masquerade and *vanitas*. The skeletons are resurrected for their day of festivity and indulge in every kind of human conceit. They cavort in dance and display, parade and pageant, feast and fête. And, of course, they return underground. One of the most interesting images concerns this return. *No Articles Beyond this Point* [FIG.115], from 2000, shows a skeleton at the mouth of a cavern, about to return to the world of the dead. The skeleton is viewing its most treasured objects, items that are proscribed in the afterlife. The objects are photographs, and O'Donnell is re-enacting that core identification between the photograph and the memory, the memory and the memorial. In this series, a *danse macabre*, O'Donnell completes the social dimension of his art, for he reflects on human folly and vanity in a comic realisation of life's absurdity.

Within the orbit of Colvin and O'Donnell's constructed narratives the use of colour has a gravitational pull. In both photographers the colour is intense and strident, often emulating the saturated colour of advertising images. In part this is a self-conscious notation of the artifice involved in their respective approaches to the photograph. Equally, it is a means whereby styles of popular culture can be referenced, and the preciousness of the fine art photographic print may be subverted. In historical terms it is worth noting the Scottish sources for this approach and technique. As early as 1850 the St Andrews-based photographer John Adamson had produced a photograph, *Tableaux* (FIG.116). This 'constructed narrative' consisted of an assemblage of stuffed birds and model soldiers, including a kilted Highlander, all presented on a table and engaged in a mock battle; in some sense an early Colvin or O'Donnell. Likewise it should be noted that the earliest experiments in colour imaging was fomented by a Scot. James Clerk Maxwell (1831–79) was a physicist with a fascination for the nature of colour. Early interests in colour refraction in prisms and crystals developed into experiments in the reception of colour in the eye. This led to the creation of a photograph, using three coloured filters subsequently projected simultaneously, and so producing a colour mix [FIG.141]. This image, produced in 1861 and appropriately showing a tartan ribbon, may be construed as one of the first colour photographs.

Both Calum Colvin and Ron O'Donnell, then, were tapping into a reservoir of historical associations with their colourful constructed narratives, and their approach would be echoed in related photographers. Andy Wiener (b. 1959) trained and works as a psychiatrist, though he also took a degree in photography from the Royal College of Art in 1987. During his time there he created his first photo-series based on William Hogarth's *The Rake's Progress*. This narrative of decline and fall was photographed in a contemporary setting, with all the characters using a mask, in fact the photographer's portrait, to provoke the sense of an identity in decay. Wiener's subsequent series, 'Love Scenes' [FIG.117], completed in 1989, developed the mask theme, though now using the personas of the popular toy dolls 'Barbie', 'Ken' and 'He-man'.[31] These masked and posed figures, set in a bijou familial environment with an ever-present television set, speak of frustrated desire and forced complicity in suburban domesticity. Further projects, like 'Living Scenes' of 1990 and 'Death Scenes' from 2002, expanded the concern with the trauma of ordinary life into, respectively, constructed and montaged episodes that conjured with psychological aspects of mortality and decline.

Maud Sulter's imagination has also journeyed into this area where fine art practice overlaps with photography. Besides her outstanding portrait studies she has created a number of photographic images using a collage technique. In the series 'Syrcas', completed in 1994, she has freely associated ideas concerning history, race, storytelling and visual culture. The 18 collaged photoworks in the series are based on a self-penned narrative. This concerns the story of Monique, an émigré who travels from Cameroon to Germany in the 1920s and, finding a home in a circus, marries a German of African descent. In the trauma of pre-war European history the family is subject to extremes of dislocation and violence.[32] This trauma, where history and ethnicity collide, is the focus of Sulter's photographic series. Working in the form of collage, a method that allows her to provoke an association with the idea of a scrapbook, she has composed images that appropriate German landscapes and fine art paintings and has overlaid these with tribal masks and related artefacts. The photograph titled *Helas L'Heroine* [FIG.118], for example, has taken an image from the Swiss neo-classical painter Angelica Kauffmann. This painting, *Portrait of Catherine Skawronska*, 1789, is held by the German National Museum in Nuremberg, and shows the young aristocratic woman with the helmet of a warrior. In Sulter's remodelling of the work the sitter's face is overlain with an African mask, and so the notions of ethnic identity, the assumptions of social class and the presuppositions of gender are all challenged. In a series of increasingly complex collaged photographs Sulter has also occupied images by the classic German photographer of social

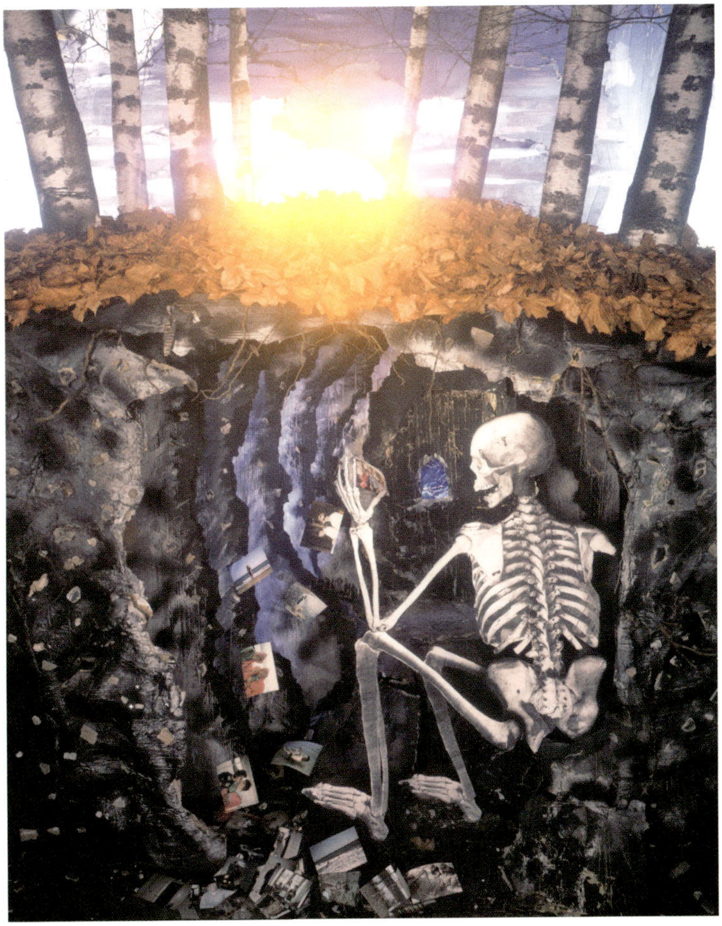

FIG.115
Ron O'Donnell
No Articles Beyond this Point
2000

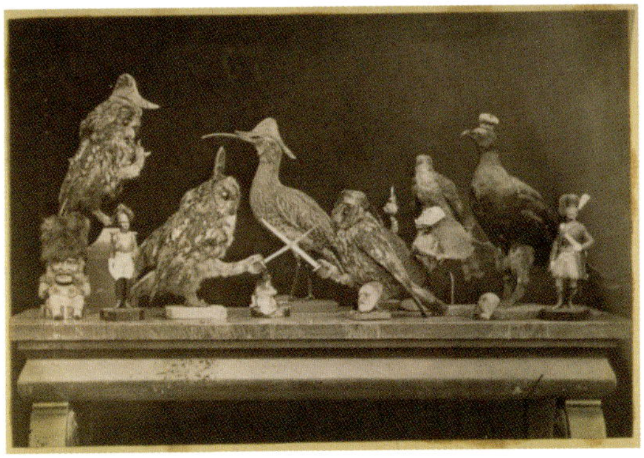

FIG.116
John Adamson
Tableaux
circa 1850

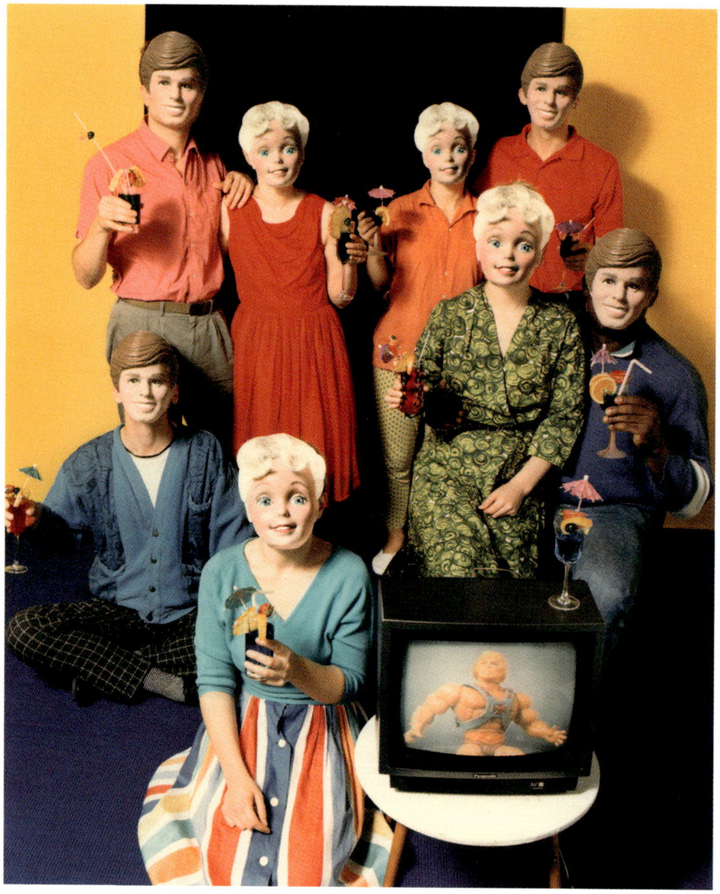

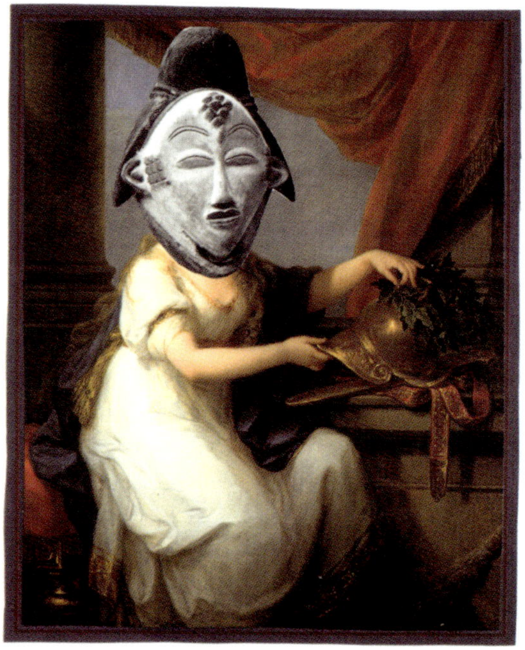

Left:
FIG.117
Andy Wiener
Love Scenes 7, Separation
1988–89

Right:
FIG.118
Maud Sulter
Helas L'Heroine
1994

and ethnic 'types', August Sander, and has sampled photographic images of Alexander Dumas and George Sand. With this work, Sulter has created a layered and provocative visual world, and one that consistently tests the assumptions of its audience.

The politics of Maud Sulter's photography is important, but it is notable that she has chosen a collage approach to the images. In some sense the works of Colvin, O'Donnell, Wiener and Sulter all rest upon the established methods of modernist practice. These are photographs that have appropriated and developed the technologies of painting, constructed environments, montage and collage. In this way they stretch the sense of the photograph; they undermine that privileged notion of the 'straight' photograph by opening out the medium to fine art practice. An even deeper challenge to the convention of the realist photograph has been presented within the fine art model, the 'abstract' photograph.

Abstraction in photography

The debates surrounding photography and art have, historically, settled upon the essential nature of the medium. Because the camera was a mechanism for reproducing an external reality, an 'authentic' photograph was viewed as an image that properly mirrored the world. Resistance to 'manipulation' and Pictorialism was based upon the artifice employed in the varieties of technique. The canonisation of 'straight' photography consequently became viewed as a triumph for the integrity of the form. In the contemporary period this kind of essentialism has been marginalised, not to say humbled. Photographers and artists have been enthusiastic to utilise every kind of medium and crossover technique in order to produce the most vital of visual cultures. Perhaps the most subversive of photographic styles, in that it so completely sabotages the 'authentic' and 'straight' photograph, has been the fine art photographic print that projects the 'look' of abstract painting. These images can be amongst the most fascinating of photographs, and they have been legion in recent photography from Scotland.

The most interesting work in this style has been that of David Williams. Williams is an extraordinarily versatile photographer who has produced suites of prints with widely differing moods and atmospheres. From an early interest in documentary, he progressed to a project themed on the closed world of St Margaret's Girls' School in Edinburgh. These works, produced as a photo-book titled *Pictures from No Man's Land*, offered a subtle and sensitive account of the neverland that is childhood and the moment of passage into the adult world. These intriguing documentary projects, however, were a prelude to the oblique abstract photographs that would mark his unique talent. The first signal of this new direction was the suite titled 'Is: Ecstasies I–XXII', completed during 1988. In these dark, intimate, unsettling images Williams created a kind of meditation on form and texture, light and shadow. Working in the bounded spaces of a derelict factory building, he searched out those recesses and surfaces that would provide for an enigmatic, mysterious image. The photograph *Is: Ecstasies XXI* [FIG.119], for example, shows two niches in a textured wall, one large and rectangular and containing an asymmetrical circular form and the other a small dark square. This description, however, fails to realise the intense ambiguity of the photograph. It is at once associative of cubist form and constructivist abstraction, and simultaneously a profound threnody expressed as visual sentiment and mood.

The parallel with music is significant here for David Williams, in a former life a musician of some note, has consistently invoked musical analogies in his photography. In 1995 he produced a monumental five-part work, *Source*, which became a centrepiece of the 'Light from the Darkroom' exhibition held at the Scottish National Gallery in that year. *Source* [FIG.120] remains an extraordinary photograph, and has been described by the photographer:

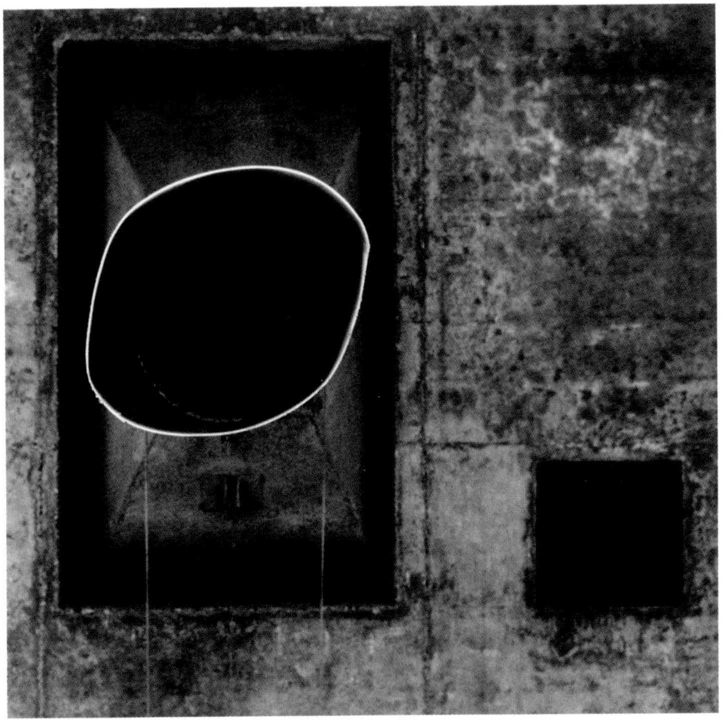

FIG.119
David Williams
Is: Ecstasies XXI
1988

> ... it consists of five, three-foot square panels, unframed and sitting proud of the wall a few inches – hovering as it were. They're printed in deep blue, actually moving to black in the central area; so that when the five are in sequence the blue vibrates.[33]

The image photographed is, in fact, a vibrating string; a metaphor for the plucked or reverberating string on a musical instrument. What is described, then, is a note or a sound, and the photograph may be seen as an equivalent for music. Of course, the 'zip' of white light in the centre of the panel has correlates in painting. Williams, himself, has cited Rothko and also minimalism,[34] while it may also be appropriate to recognise the association with Barnett Newman. The deep blue-black of the photograph has parallels in Newman's colour-fields but this is, unequivocally, a photograph; less concerned with surface and texture than with ambience and mood.

The impression of musical temper in these projects is of fundamental importance. If 'Is: Ecstasies I–XXII' may be sensed as a dark, melancholic, modernist piece,

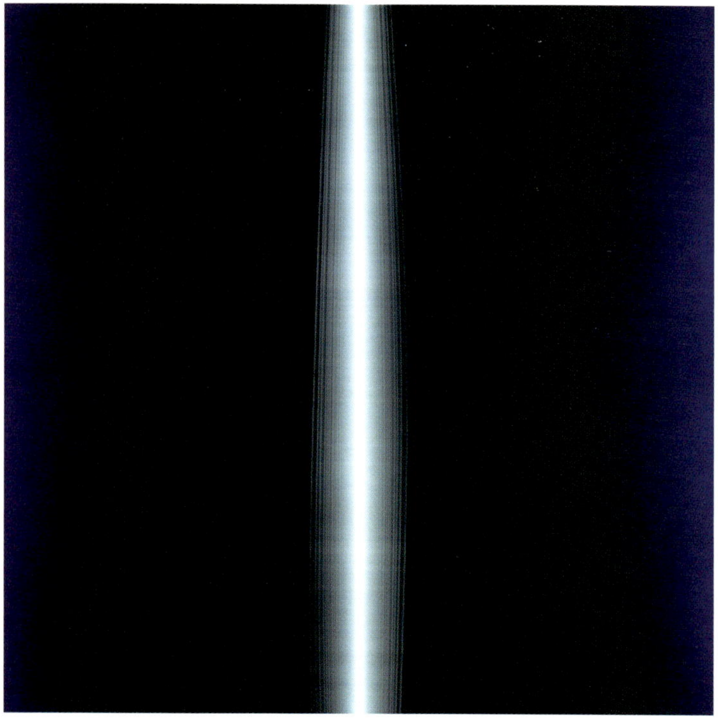

FIG.120
David Williams
Source
1995

then *Source* is surely a revelatory and uplifting blues. More recently Williams has, as it were, returned to melody with the exquisite and beautiful suite of 15 colour prints, 'Stillness and Occurrence', 1995–2000. The 'subject' of these works is less obtuse, being seascapes photographed from a beach near Edinburgh. Williams has, however, searched out the particular moment; that point where the flat azure sea melds with the pale sky to produce a tonal harmony on the theme of blue. In some works the sand of the beach is included and in others, *Stillness and Occurrence #4* [FIG.121] for example, spectral figures are seen wading in the sea. The closing image, a deep midnight blue field of colour, presents a night-time finale to this softly focused dreamscape. The musical parallel may be Debussy or even Satie, for this is the languorous world of impressionism in form and in content.

David Williams has been remarkably prescient and courageous in producing these abstract photographs, but it is clear that these are far from formalist conceits. Rather, they are subtly evocative liaisons with mood and atmosphere that demonstrate the photograph's ability to challenge the authority of painting. In developing this idea Williams has helped encourage a school of photographic image-making that has fully realised the potential of this approach.

After completing prize-winning documentary work and important portraiture, including studies of the writer Alasdair Gray in 1993 and the poet Kathleen Jamie in 1994, Iain Stewart (b. 1967) began to experiment with a form of romantic abstract landscape photography in 1995. Having trained with Murray Johnston and then with David Williams at Edinburgh College of Art he was attuned to the poignancy of landscape. Like these mentors his approach to the subject was shaped by the formal properties of painting such that a picture of the sea's horizon, like *Wake* of 2000 [FIG.122], offers comparison with the late work of Mark Rothko. Stewart has sourced much of his imagery in the north of Scotland and so the intense, cold, clear light radiates through his photography. Moreover, the landscapes, often indeed 'weatherscapes', can be epic and connote the majestic gesture of the romantic tradition.

This interest in northern light has become a leitmotif in the photography of Garry Fabian Miller (b. 1957). Fabian Miller travelled north from his native Bristol while still a teenager, to live and work in the Shetland Isles. In an itinerant career, spent mostly in rural parts of England, he has often returned to northern Scotland and most recently to the isle of Tiree in the Hebrides. The nature of light is the determining factor in Fabian Miller's work, for following more conventional camera and lens-based ventures he has moved to 'cameraless photography'. Here he has experimented with unconventional prismatic conductors and light-sensitive materials in the manner of those pioneer scientist-photographers who first shaped the medium. This technique has been fully exploited in his imaginative undertaking in Tiree, an approach that came to fruition in the collection 'Exposure' of 2005.[35] Ian Warrell has described Fabian Miller's method:

> Unlike conventional, camera-based photography, each print in the Exposure series is a unique object, created by

FIG.121
David Williams
Stillness and Occurrence #4
1995–2000

FIG.122
Ian Stewart
Wake
2000

> projecting light through a coloured vessel filled with water and onto the light sensitive paper that Fabian Miller has favoured since his earliest work in the later 1970s. In the case of these newest images, the path of light has been interrupted and purposefully shaped by a variety of cardboard stencils, used to block the light, except where it has been cut or pierced, permitting it in those areas to pass beyond and sensitise the photographic paper. Stated bluntly, Fabian Miller has devised a means of manipulating light as effectively as paint to make marks.[36]

The body of work realised on Tiree consists of these exposures, usually lasting one hour and sometimes 12 hours, which are subsequently printed in the studio and created as abstract images embodying light, colour, time and change. The work *Exposure (10 Hours of Light) June (4)* 2005 [FIG.123] describes a broken circle of filtered red light against a black background that connotes the idea of eclipse. Throughout the series Fabian Miller has produced abstract images, 'photographs', which connect with the most fundamental attributes of the medium.

This sense of an abstract photography is one that develops and extends the parameters of an historically located art-photography. In the contemporary period there has been clear evidence of a current flowing in the opposite direction; rather than photographers searching to incorporate the values of fine art in their practice, artists have moved to employ the camera as a tool in their armoury of technologies. This has most particularly been the case with neo-conceptual projects and multimedia artists. In effect there has emerged, in Scotland and elsewhere, a movement for artists using photography.

Artists using photography

In a number of ways contemporary artists who work with the camera have set out to fracture the craft-based conventions of photographic practice and history, and to employ the camera as a disinterested marker of a creative process. In part this flowed from the use of the photograph in documenting conceptual, environmental and performance works. These radical strategies, designed to undermine the commodification of the artwork and challenge the museum culture, reach back to the interventions of Marcel Duchamp but have become established custom from the 1970s. Allied to this process the semiotic analysis opened out by Roland Barthes, coupled with the post-structuralist theory of Michel Foucault and the postmodern projections of Jean-François Lyotard and others, have reasoned the photograph as a complicated indexical record. That is, the photograph offers an open-ended coagulation of signs and symbols negotiated through culture, custom, social codes and individual interpretation. In this event the photograph was less a treasured artefact, an 'object', and more an image available to a kind of cultural navigation. Artists have welcomed the ambiguity of this association as a radical intervention in the creative process. Hence the camera has been deployed as an instrument of verification and record wherein the uncertainty of the sign is axiomatic.

In this event artists using photography have, generally, privileged 'snapshot' styles, photographic pastiche and parody, banal and ironic configurations, repetition and serial images, and a kind of anti-composition.[37] Within the Scottish context many conceptual and neo-conceptual artists have employed photography at some level in their practice, including luminaries like Douglas Gordon, Christine Borland and Nathan Coley. Artist-photographers have tended to develop projects wherein the contemporary interest in the cultural negotiation and indexicality of the photograph becomes a concomitant element in the construction of the work. Catriona Grant (b. 1964), in her recent project 'The Examination Room', 2003, created a photographic installation that discerned the tension between institutional and private spaces. Here, she staged scenarios in an abandoned hospital complex. Within this cold institutional space she placed a naked woman, seemingly prepared for medical examination and abandoned to the will of an unseen, official 'other'. The figure often appears as a spectre, created through Grant's long-exposure times, and so occupies the examination rooms in an ambiguous and ethereal manner. Clearly, as in *Untitled* [FIG.124], this is presented as a correlate to the process of the negation of the self within these kinds of institutional and bureaucratic procedures. However, it is also a concept that corresponds with the sense that any 'reading' of the series remains contingent and provisional.

This interest in the relationship between the individual and official institutions has long been a subject for Jane Brettle (n.d.). Brettle has been an important figure in the development of Scottish photography, establishing the education programme at the independent Stills Gallery during the 1980s and helping to direct the work of the Portfolio Gallery in the 1980s and 1990s. She has also lectured in photography at Edinburgh College of Art, and continues to produce significant photographic projects as well as installations and site-specific works. Brettle's principal concern has been gender orientated; she has focused on the correlation between women's bodies and institutional spaces, notably museums and galleries. An early suite of images titled 'Locate: Public Bodies–Private States', completed in 1993, used installation, text and photographs to explore the condition of public and private spaces and the means by which individuals were 'shaped' by institutional structures. 'Restoration', from 2002, produced a number of photographic images that juxtaposed real women with the representation of 'the female' in the work of the neoclassical sculptor Antonio Canova. Here Brettle photographed some of Canova's most esteemed works, situated in galleries and buildings throughout

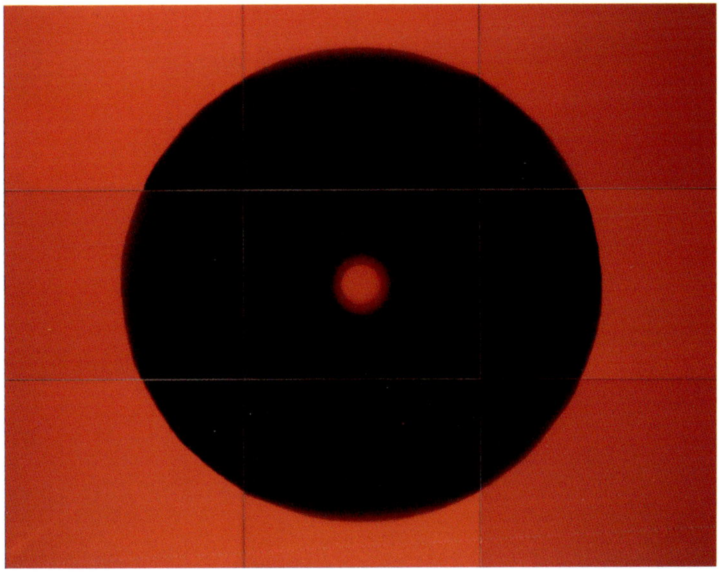

FIG.123
Garry Fabian Miller
Exposure (10 Hours of Light) June (4) 2005

Europe, and contrasted these idealisations with contemporary women; most notable perhaps was the diptych *Fahima, Katy, Clare, Newcastle 1999; The Three Graces: Le Grazie, Antonio Canova, 1815–17, National Gallery of Scotland, Edinburgh 1999* [FIG.125]. Satish Padiyar has reflected upon the careful manipulation in these works, and especially upon the quality of 'finish' or surface in the photographs, a surface that echoes the *ultima mano* in Canova's sculpture and creates a tension between the real woman and the portrayal:

> The dual form of these diptychs suggests a series of culturally profound oppositions; those between reality and phantasy, object and representation, life and death. But, by diverting the viewer into a contemplation of the surface of her subjects, their skin, Brettle alerts us to another series of oppositions; inside and outside, structure and surface, 'me' and 'not-me', self and world; the notion of the skin holds these more intimate categories in suspense.[38]

More recently, with the project 'Airside' of 2002, Brettle has photographed eminent women within their place of work. Conceptually she has been concerned to simultaneously remove these women from their official roles by portraying them in ordinary dress, while assigning them their rank and status in the title of the work, hence *Sumita Sinha,*

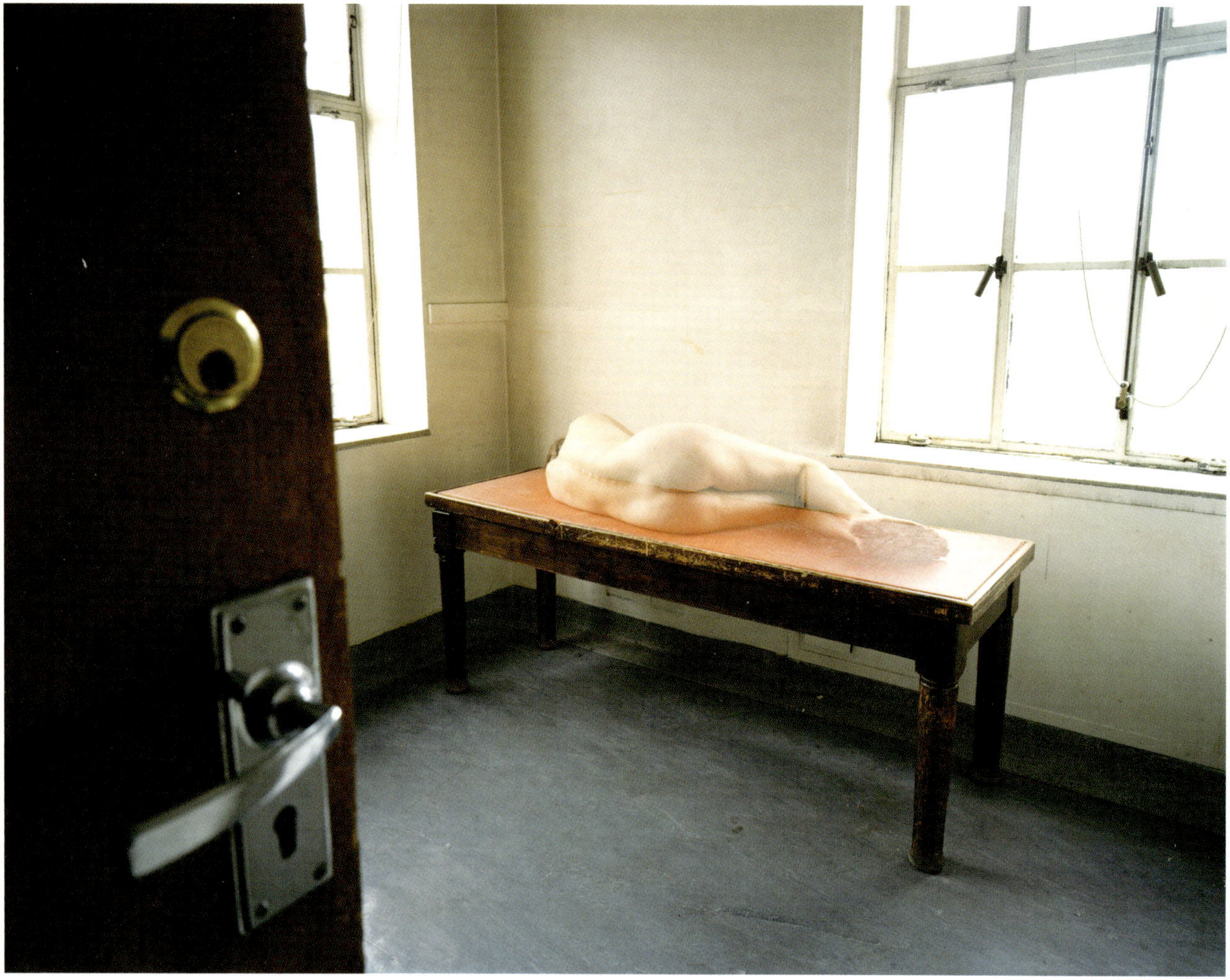

FIG.124
Catriona Grant
Untitled from 'The Examinatiom Room'
2003

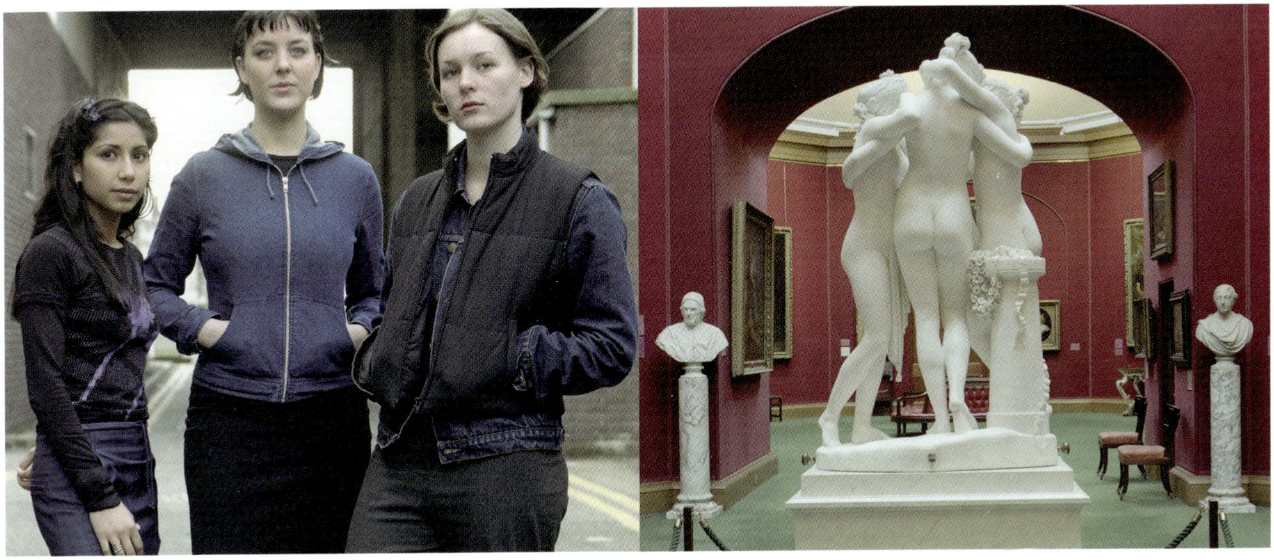

FIG.125
Jane Brettle
Fahima, Katy, Clare, Newcastle 1999; The Three Graces: Le Grazie, Antonio Canova, 1815–17, National Gallery of Scotland, Edinburgh 1999

Architect, Director: Eco= Logic Design and Research Consultancy Chair: Architects for Change: the Equality Unit of RIBA, from 2002. This strategy functions both as an exposure of, and a challenge to, those processes of typecasting that operate within official organisations and establishment practice.

Evidently, Jane Brettle's recent work has staged portraits and created juxtapositions wherein the individual and the institution are projected as part of a critical dialectic. Equally, in 'The Examination Room' Catriona Grant has utilised staged scenarios, and this has been a feature of her work from the early 1990s. These types of events can fall within the territory of performance art, and it is characteristic of artists using photography that the photograph often becomes the medium for the realisation of an event. Wendy McMurdo, who initially trained as a painter but took to digital photography after a period at the Pratt Institute in New York, has been developing this type of approach in her subtle digital manipulations. From her earliest project, 'In a Shaded Place – the Digital and the Uncanny' of 1995, through to 'The Science Museum' in 2000, McMurdo has produced extraordinary images that focus on the dislocated psychic experience of children and childhood. Claire Docherty has remarked that:

> McMurdo's method involves... the processes of selection, erasure and framing, to produce works of evidence. The photographs are taken over a short space of time, but it is her careful digital manipulation of the image that results in the remarkable presence and luminosity of the subjects. Through her interrogation of the constituent parts of the scene, the experience of being a child is revealed.[39]

In this difficult area McMurdo's projects have consistently examined the self-possessed, intuitive, supernatural world of the child, and the description of these photographs as 'uncanny' is wholly merited.

During 1998 McMurdo was commissioned to make images of young musicians at St Mary's Music School in Edinburgh. In these works she photographed the children as they played their respective instruments. She then digitally removed the instruments from the photographs. What remained was a series of extraordinary studies in concentration, even rapture. The intriguing photograph *Solo Violinist* [FIG.126], 1998, exemplifies this process. The young girl is pictured in the moment of the rendition. She is completely focused on her playing, and is transposed. As the violin is digitally removed the image turns to gesture; in fact a kind of delicate, exquisite dance. The tilt of the head, the fall of the weight onto the left leg, the meticulous positioning of the hands, all create a

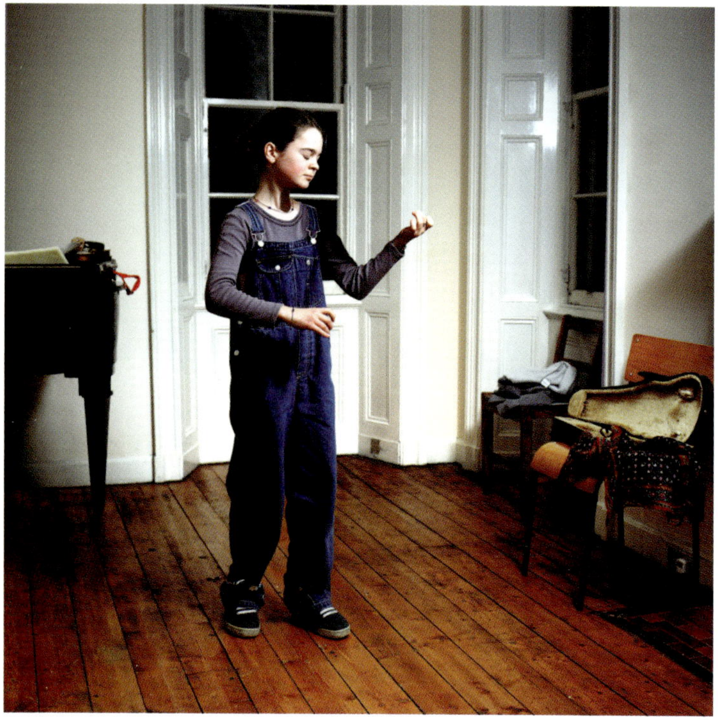

FIG.126
Wendy McMurdo
Solo Violinist
1998

mysterious and elegant ballet. It is this sense of elusive displacement and disposition that McMurdo consistently has revealed. As a feature of childhood it contains that element of the provisional, the intangible, that marks off this universal yet unique moment. Consequently, McMurdo's simultaneously illustrative but enigmatic photographs disclose this supernatural neverland as form, movement and indication.

These types of quasi-conceptual projects may be usefully contrasted with the neo-dada interventions of David Shrigley (b. 1968). Having graduated from the Environmental Arts programme at Glasgow School of Art in 1991, Shrigley has remained in the city and, in his seditious 'guerrilla' anti-art, works across a range of media. He is perhaps best known for his capricious books and drawings, as well as his comically provocative sculpture. Shrigley's academic training in the nostrums of 'public art' became the focus for his subversive interventions in public spaces, episodes that he commonly photographed before they were 'disappeared'. In an interview with Neil Mulholland he has commented that:

> As with my other work, I probably haven't really ever set out to do anything in particular with my photographs, the point that I'm at right now has just sort of happened. As you noted, my earlier photographs were just documents of things that needed to be documented, it was only comparatively recently that I started to think about my photographs as having the possibility to be something other than that. I take a lot of photographs without having anything in mind. Sometimes I draw on them, sometimes they appear interesting on their own or when juxtaposed with another image.[40]

The comically provocative *Leisure Centre* [FIG.127], from 1992, is an example of his earlier photographic records or 'documents'. In a cleared site, among Glasgow's tenements, he has placed a small white box. The box is emblazoned with the logo 'Leisure Centre', an absurdist gesture typical of Shrigley's jester-situationist sensibility.

More recently, Shrigley has produced photographs that, while still challenging the genre, have come closer to a conventional photographic aesthetic. His *A Photograph*, of 2004, shows a ruined classical site in Athens, much in the style of 19th-century travel photography, but presented as a kind of formal snapshot and reverentially labelled 'A Photograph'. Shrigley is, evidently, rehearsing the manner of the fine art photographic print while subtly mocking the conceit of the form. This image is in fact part of a series, including *A Place* and *A Swan*, which continues to touch the hem of a conventional photographic aesthetic.

Shrigley is, evidently, at the extreme of a 'history of photography', but as an artist self-consciously using photography he conforms to the spectrum of genres and styles that construct the catalogue. It is right to view this as a complex matrix. Besides the more established artist-photographers like Brettle, Grant and McMurdo, and the unconventional neo-dadaists like Shrigley, there is a whole range of individuals who use the camera to extend the palette of artistic possibilities. This would include those figures who shone in the 'New Scottish Photography' exhibition of 1990, individuals like Ronnie Scott Simpson (b. 1964), who has pushed his colour photographs into a 'pop' graphic style; and also Roger Palmer (b. 1946) and Vaughan Judge (b. 1956), who both have taught photography at Glasgow School of Art and who have separately explored aspects of conceptual, text-orientated photography and experimental abstraction.

Vaughan Judge, in particular, has been responsible for encouraging a radical programme of photographic art from students at Glasgow School of Art. In addition to this, his practice has developed into one of the more fascinating neo-conceptual forms of the contemporary period. Judge is constantly challenging the nature of the photographic image; working into the surface of the negative, exploring the potential of the print-making technologies and experimenting with photographic process. His staged scenarios, like the recent 'Ritual Space' project from 2006, examine aspects of myth and belief, sacrament and ceremony, within the context of postmodern culture. These large, intensely coloured, formally constructed tableaux mix elements of Christian ritual and pagan myth in a complex narrative of shifting meaning. The core theme, a 'temptation' rite, is manifest in the remarkable *Temptation of Mary III* [FIG.128], 2006, a disturbingly awkward image, at once informal and subtly threatening.

This kind of neo-conceptual practice has grown to something approaching dominance within the arena of contemporary photography. In congruence with developments in the art world generally, it has sought to challenge and undermine established canons while presenting images that confront and contest viewers' expectations. Interestingly, the very subversion that is manifest in these images has become something of a requirement in the construction of photographic images within the world of advertising.

Advertising art

David Shrigley has commented upon the ways in which his subversive artworks, and especially his photographs, have been created as a response to the world of advertising images:

> The ironic thing is that on a subconscious level I think that I made these works in response to advertising. Certainly in response to signage in general which advertising forms a part. I'm pretty ambivalent about the world of advertising. I think it's boring. It only exists to sell things.[41]

Shrigley's training within the Environmental Art department in Glasgow would have familiarised him with the early 1990s 'Billboard Projects' by Alan Dunn, Douglas Gordon and others. This type of art, situated in public spaces and using the convention of the advertising billboard to project esoteric text-works, disrupted the expectations of the public by proposing an obscure or cryptic message within the frame of the commercial hoarding. These posters used the ritual of advertising stimulus and consumer response to provoke dissonance and aesthetic disruption. This approach may be one root of Shrigley's interventions, but it remains fascinating that the photograph as advert bears an omnipresence, indeed an omniscience, in the social world, and that the advertising photograph has increasingly taken on board the disruptive sensibility of these neo-conceptual forms.

In the period after the 1960s the commercial photographer as artist has become a kind of norm, and Scotland has produced some of the most fascinating figures in this category. Albert Watson (b. 1942) studied graphic design at Dundee School of Art,

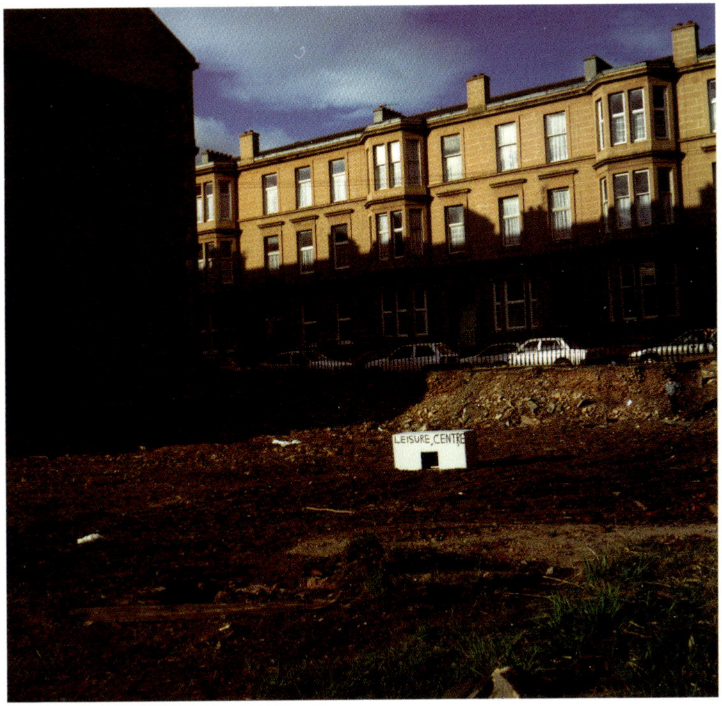

FIG.127
David Shrigley
Leisure Centre
1992

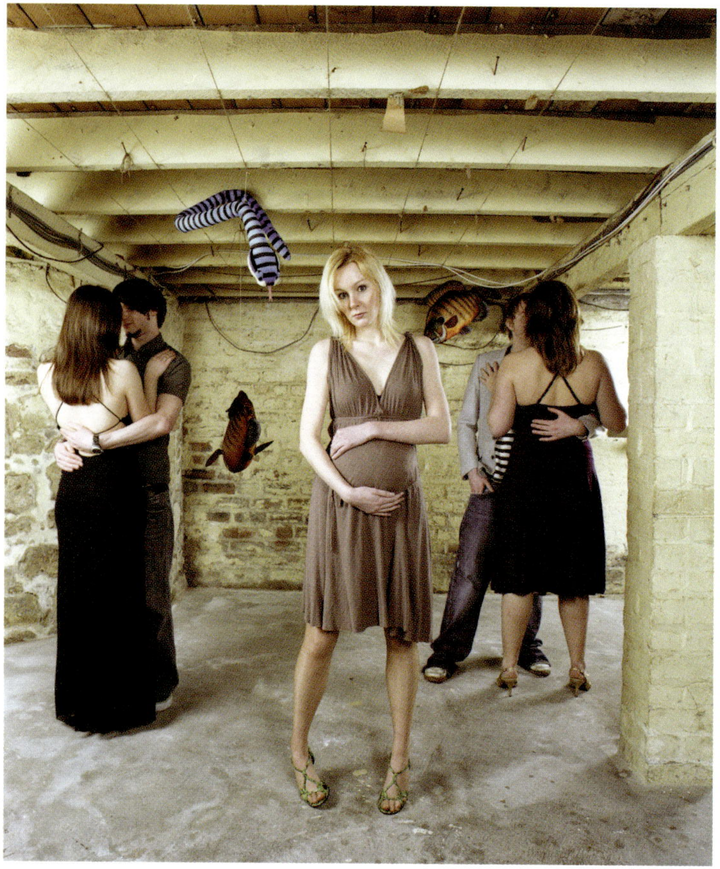

FIG.128
Vaughan Judge
Temptation of Mary III
2006

where he came into contact with the documentary photographer Joseph McKenzie. He subsequently studied at the Royal College of Art in London, before travelling to the United States and opening a studio in New York in 1974. Watson would become one of the most successful fashion and commercial photographers, and a noted celebrity portraitist; his photograph of *Mick Jagger, Los Angeles, 14 June 1992* [FIG.129], with the eminent rocker portrayed as a jaguar, is a masterpiece of punning, ironical agit-pop. Working for magazines like *Vogue*, *Rolling Stone* and *Newsweek*, his photographs remain a familiar part of the visual landscape, while his most noted monographic publication, *Cyclops*,[42] 1995, presents an overview of his diverse career. It is interesting that Watson has frequently returned to Scotland to photograph landscape and standing-stones in the Orkneys; a homage to tradition from within the vainglorious maelstrom of celebrity culture.

Like Watson, the Edinburgh-trained Graham MacIndoe (b. 1963) would move to New York after a period at the Royal College of Art, and would work within a quasi-documentary format before moving into commercial work and portraiture. His client list is witness to a career trajectory that signals commercial success, and he has photographed luminaries like Phillipe Starck and Jeff Koons. Simultaneously, he has completed some intriguing colour images, cityscapes and night-scenes, urban 'types' and isolated figures, that open out a more complex fine art aesthetic.

In Britain the most celebrated commercial photographer of recent years has been the Glasgow-born John Rankin Waddell (b. 1966). Officially styled as 'Rankin', he helped found the iconoclastic fashion magazine *Dazed and Confused* in 1991, and has become something of an *enfant terrible* of the contemporary advertising and celebrity scene. His portfolio of projects is as wide ranging as might be expected in this infinite marketplace, ranging from advertising shoots portraits, motor cars and every upper-end commercial product. His interesting project 'One Dress' presented various models and popular idols all posing in the same dress. The diptych of the Mexican supermodel Liliana Dominguez, *One Dress: Liliana Dominguez* [FIG.130], 2005, poses and reverses the model against a northern landscape painting. The entire series, consisting of some 60 personalities, is a febrile study in narcissism and decoration; the perfect essence of this effervescent, aspirational industry.

These arch, quirky, ironic, commercial exploits have become the common photographic currency of the contemporary world. Their relationship to art, however, is tangential. Stylish and modish, they are designed to create immediate impact and the frisson of desire born of hedonism. Yet for all the kaleidoscopic jamboree and commercial fantasy of the form, the professionalism of these photographers is remarkable. And this professionalism lies in the dedication to the print. In fact it is in the quality of the print, the sense of the photograph as an object, that

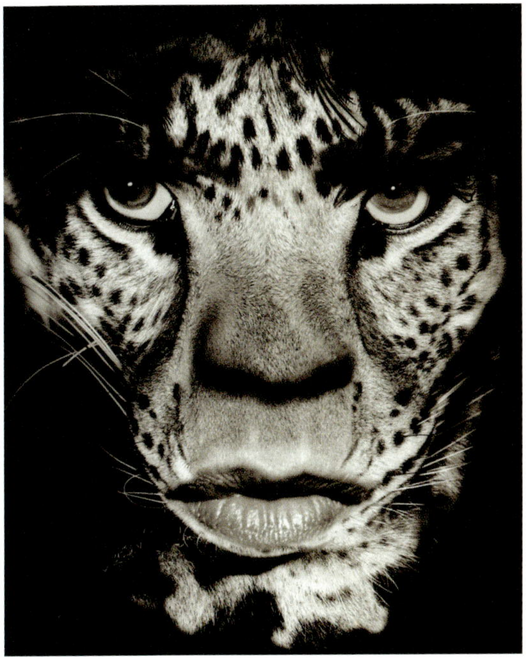

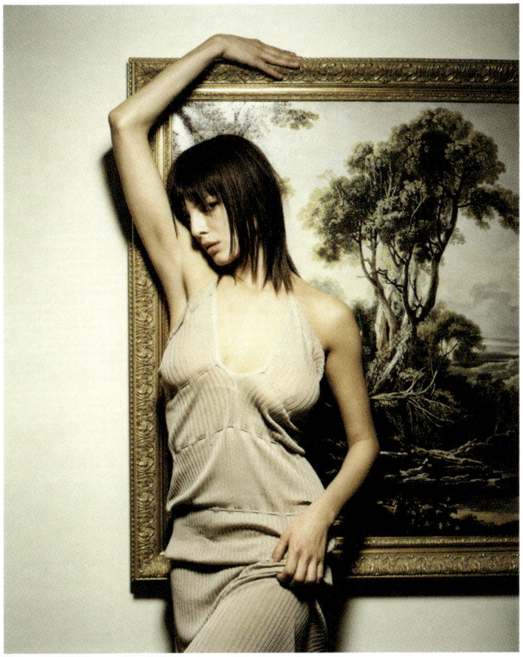

Left:
FIG.129
Albert Watson
Mick Jagger, Los Angeles, 14 June 1992

Right:
FIG.130
Rankin
One Dress; Liliana Dominguez
2005

issues of art and photography may be recovered. In this context it is those photographers that remain committed to the fine art print that complete the circle and recall the ambitions of those esteemed 19th-century pioneers.

The photograph as object

Given that so much contemporary art has been styled as a radical negation of the formal conventions of the artwork, it is surprising that the fine art photographic print still maintains a credibility and force. The element of craft and technical expertise can seem retrogressive in an atmosphere of fevered conceptualism and self-conscious avant-garde dissonance. Certainly the photograph has been subject to this radicalisation with the 'snapshot', the vernacular photograph, the serial study, the neutral or 'deadpan' form, the confessional abject image, the conceptual photograph all finding favour within the contemporary art world. Indeed, all of these forms have now been captured by the institutions, the galleries and the academies, so that in some sense they construct the new establishment. Within this frame those photographers who remain fascinated by the metier appear both conventional and contradictory. Conventional, in that they recognise a history which remains unresolved and open to development, and contradictory, in that they oppose the measured intellectual strategies of the conceptual in favour of a subtly subversive concern with form and content.

Within the Scottish context it has been this latter category of photographer, intrigued by the finite study, the crafted image, the pristine print, that has occupied the foreground of photographic studies. This is not to say that this prevailing approach has been purely formal. In every case there has existed a blend of the formal with a set of intellectual concerns that presents a complete aesthetic. This aesthetic tends to reject the relativism and reflexivity of the postmodern in favour of a kind of contemporary modernism. With this circumstance the initiatives of a number of contemporary practitioners approaching the photograph as object becomes of the highest significance.

The issue of the fine art print has been a feature of the work of Pradip Malde (b. 1957) for a number of years. Malde, born in Tanzania, trained at Glasgow School of Art, and currently working in the United States, has explored historic printing processes, most especially in collaboration with Mike Ware. Ware is a noted chemist who has long been fascinated with the modification and modernisation of 19th-century photographic printing methods. His classic work was on the Cyanotype, a technology first developed by Sir John Herschel in the 1840s and refined by Ware in the 1990s. With Pradip Malde he explored the potential for a new method of creating photographic prints using platinum. This method was originally developed by William Willis in 1873, and, whereas the Cyanotype produced a print suffused with rich blue tone, the Platino-Palladiotype Process created prints with a spectrum of tone through silver, grey and umber.[43] The newly developed platinum process, safer and more stable, has been employed by Malde in a number of situations. He has been commissioned by the Imogen Cunningham Trust to make contemporary platinum prints from the esteemed photographer's original negatives,[44] and has employed the technology in his own practice.

FIG.131
Pradip Malde
Love: 'Bathroom Window, Duckspool' 1989

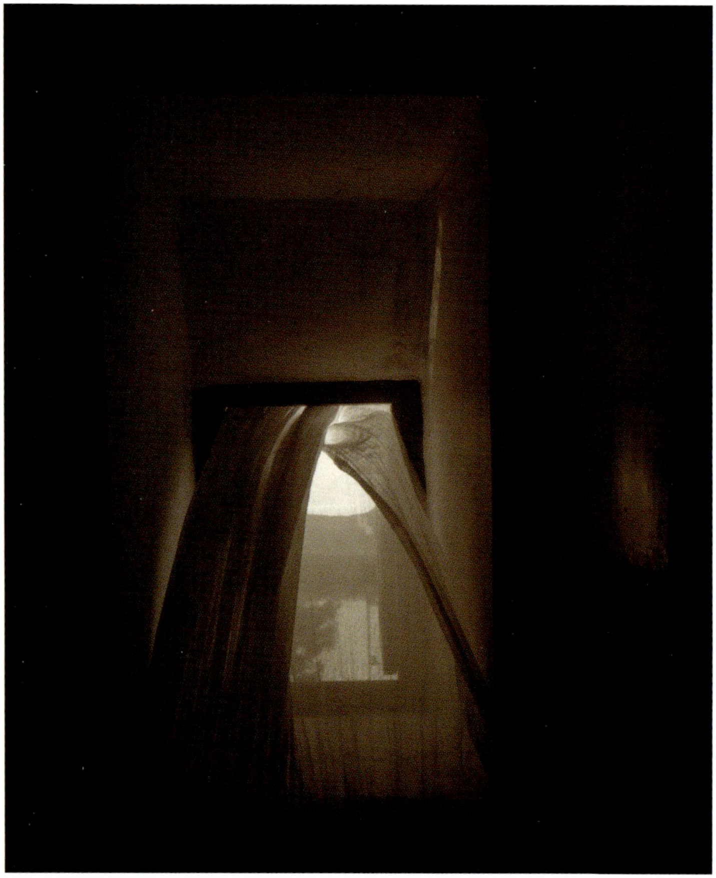

Pradip Malde's meticulous photographs have set a marker for the efficacy of the fine art print. Poignant and mysterious, they conjure with the everyday in a manner that releases the extraordinary potency of the commonplace object. An early work like *Love: 'Bathroom Window, Duckspool'* 1989 [FIG.131] offers a dark, interior space and a blown curtain against a window frame. The open window presents a passage into the softly focused light of the outside world, while the interior space tenders an outline of walls and ceiling in silver and grey. The blown curtain, a frozen moment from a chance billowing of gossamer fabric, connotes notions of transience and passing; a discrete metaphor for mortality and a life bounded, as the title tells, by love. There is a link here to the sentiments and practices engaged by eminent Pictorialists at the end of the 19th century. Like these individuals there is a concern with the virtue of the object and a poetic symbolism at the heart of the design. Even in his more contemporary work, for example *Expiration II* [FIG.132], completed in 2003, Malde has invoked these associations. This image, the crown of a doll's head and a foreshortened face all in the lower quartile of a portrait format photograph, is completed with an exhaled breath that drifts into the central and uppermost spaces of the picture. This unnerving 'still-life' construction, with 'breath' composed from fibre, reprises those themes of transience and the fine thread that binds individuals to life itself, which has become a leitmotif in Malde's haunting photographs.

There is something of this poignancy and tonal 'finish' also in the photographs of Calum Angus MacKay (b. 1964). Much of MacKay's work is related to his island background and is an evocation of his experience within the fishing communities of the Western Isles. However, his oeuvre is far from a documentary approach and he has tended to explore the

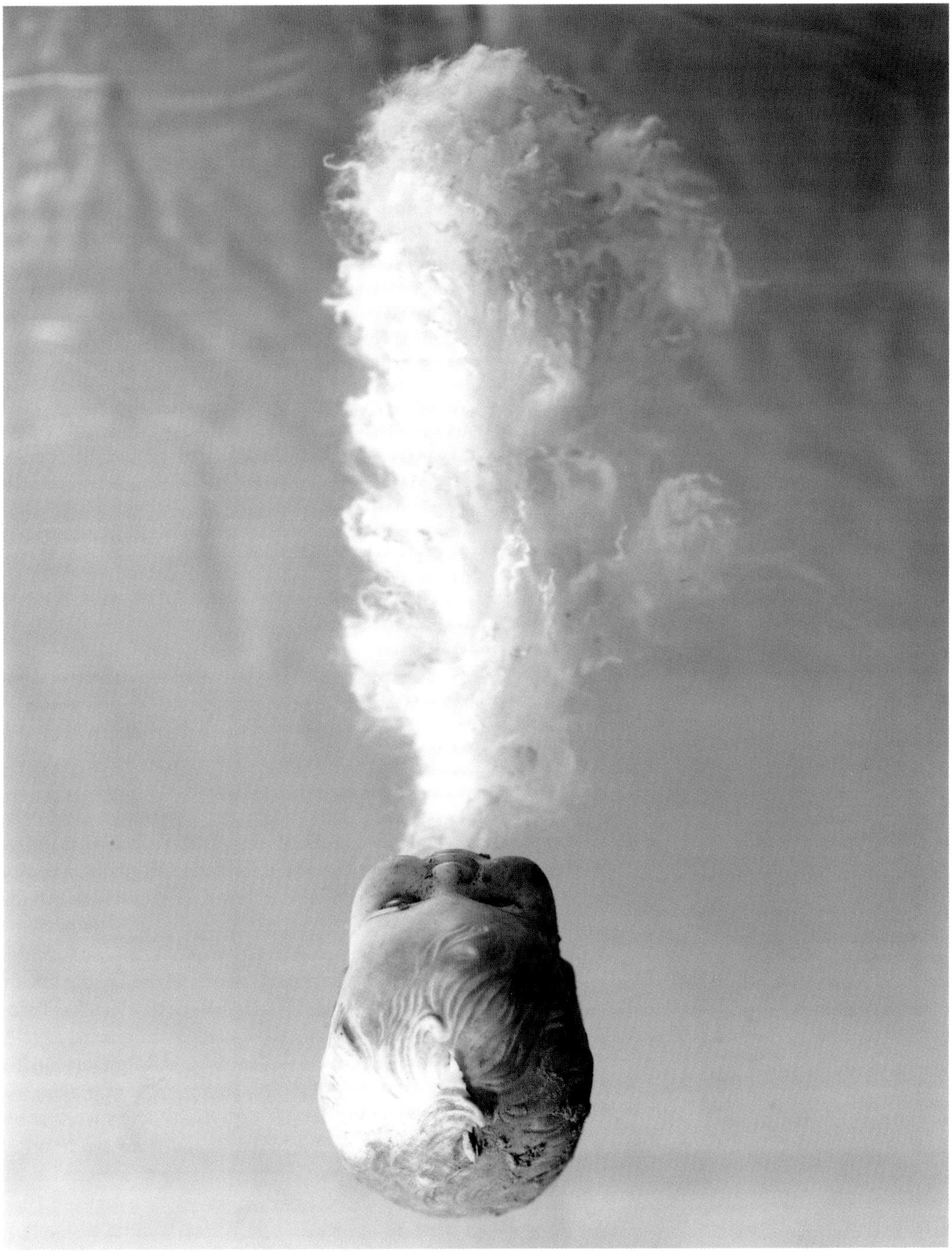

FIG.132
Pradip Malde
Expiration II
2003

visceral aspects of island life in a dark, formalist style. His early project 'By Fin By Wing By Hoof', from 1991, isolated objects and animal parts and re-presented these fragments as an abstract, elemental index of a primeval world. With the project 'Isolate', produced in 1993, MacKay extended this approach. He photographed the corpse of a skate nailed to a board, a frozen mass of dead birds lain out on a table, the carcass of a lamb shrouded in lead. Peter Ride has commented that 'MacKay's work has been described as "brooding", as having a mesmeric morbidity. He likes to photograph dead things and his photographs are dark to the extreme. Light creeps into his images to give a subdued sense of his subjects, not to illuminate them.'[45] This is certainly the menacing pulse of these photographs, for MacKay's work is ominous and portentous. Even his picture of that most ceremonial of Scottish symbols, *Cluarain (Thistles)* [FIG.133], from 1993, presents a claustrophobic and sinister sense of foreboding; a dark mass of spine and piercing needle.

MacKay's work, for all its shadowy necromancy, favours the cultured look of the crafted object and carries the symbolic weight of the Pictorial vision. Within the contemporary scene in Scotland, this aesthetic has been most profoundly expressed in the work of Robin Gillanders. Gillanders' role as a teacher of photography is not only predicated on his renown as a portraitist, but upon his concern for the integrity and veracity of the print as object. This dedication to craft, combined with his unerring vision, led to a long collaboration with Scotland's pre-eminent conceptual artist, Ian Hamilton Finlay. Finlay bequeathed Gillanders with the task of celebrating and documenting his finest artwork, the garden of 'Little Sparta' in Lanarkshire. 'Little Sparta' is a unique site, a philosophical mediation on the

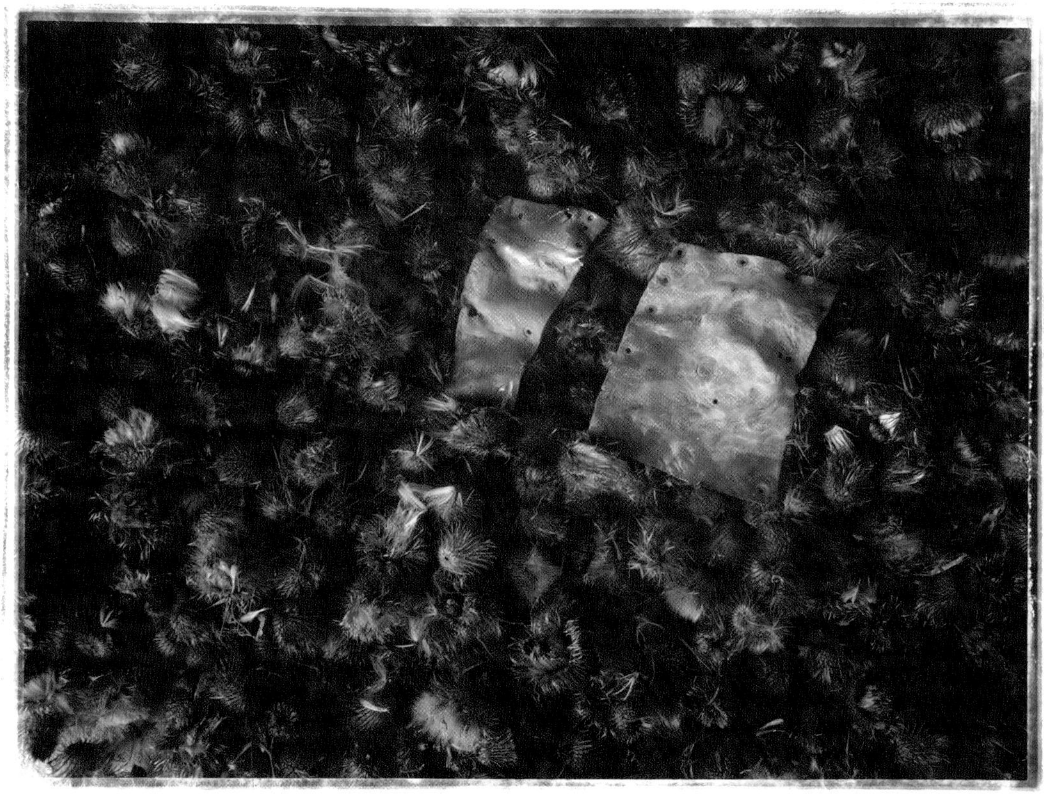

FIG.133
Calum Angus MacKay
Cluarain (Thistles)
1993

polarities of civilisation and barbarism, culture and nature, bliss and terror; it marries the extremes of human life in a poetic mantra replete with idea and symbol. Robin Gillanders was tasked with providing a photographic equivalent for this extraordinary mindscape, and has worked with this mission from the early 1990s.

Gillanders has photographed all the key sites within the garden, and has recorded its growth and development. He has also created finite studies of particular details, notably the construction of the garden walk, 'Huff Lane', a faux rural ramble related to the poetry of the 19th-century nature romantic, John Clare. Gillanders' exquisite photographs of the 'lane' were published by Finlay's Wild Hawthorn Press as a limited edition photo-book in 2000. More recently Gillanders has produced an exhibition and photo-book titled *The Philosopher's Garden*, 2004. This work presents a comparison between Finlay's creations in 'Littla Sparta' and the garden inspired by the French philosopher Jean-Jacques Rousseau at Ermenonville, to the north-east of Paris. Rousseau, of course, privileged Nature before the corrupting and imprisoning bonds of Society and Finlay's work was in dialogue with this conception from its outset. In many ways Gillanders' project was a rich and natural juxtaposition of these ideas – ideas that are expressed as gardens – and his photographs are a visual equivalent to the thought.

It is useful to compare Gillanders' *Fourth Walk* [FIG.134], taken at Ermenonville, with his photograph *Of Flutes & Wild Roses* [FIG.135] from 'Little Sparta'. *Fourth Walk*, like the majority of images taken in Ermenonville, is loosely focused and implies movement. The image shows a garden temple reflected in the mirror-darkness of a lily pond, but the disruption of scale and the reversed reflected projection present a dream-like vision. The combination of elements, water, the dark reflective surface, the dense population of spectral water lilies, suggests an airy immateriality; the photograph is ethereal and abstruse. *Of Flutes & Wild Roses*, a carved stone monument set within a copse in 'Little Sparta', presents its subject in crisp focus with the accompanying foliage only just softening. This is a dark and verdant space; stone meets earth and undergrowth in a complex materiality and solid reckoning. In all its form it implies a stable, still meditation. With these works Gillanders is invoking the conditions implied by the respective gardens; the walk, the studied contemplation, the evaluation of the elements and the elemental force of life itself. Much of this is written into the form that the photographs take, and the form is realised in the nature of the print. In this sense Gillanders presents the perfect expression of the interdependence between form, content and craft, each working to complete an aesthetic totality. And here the complex relationship between the conventions of fine art and the technologies of photography and the photographic print is revealed.

If the debate concerning art and photography is now largely redundant it is because no one, now, would see any contradiction in these terms. In an age where the

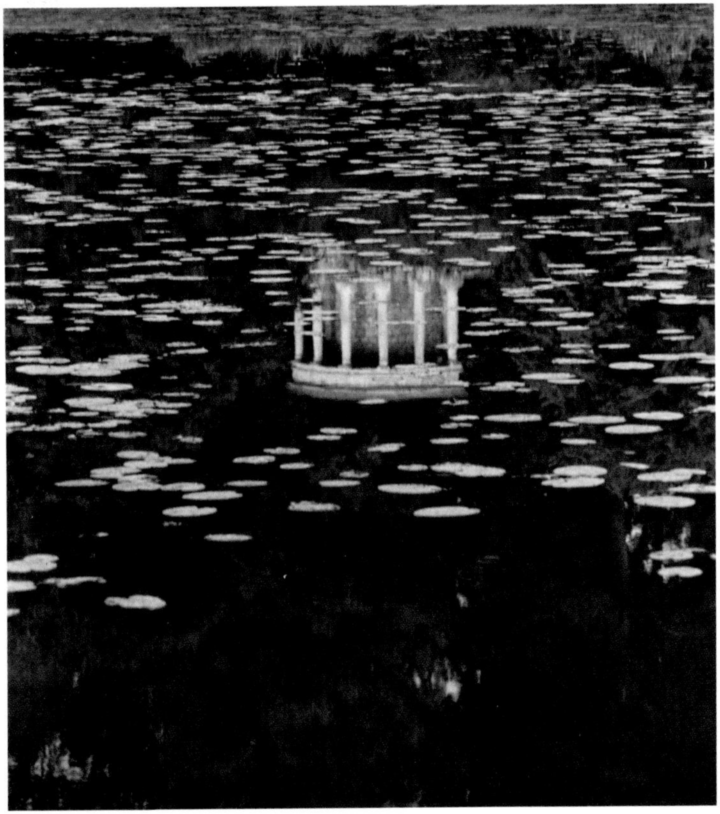

FIG.134
Robin Gillanders
Fourth Walk
2004

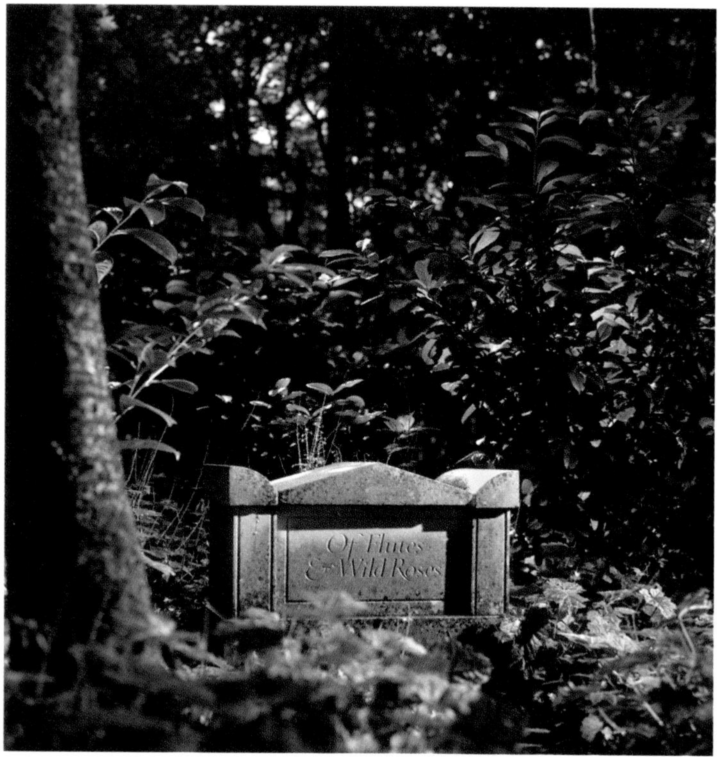

FIG.135
Robin Gillanders
Of Flutes & Wild Roses, 'Little Sparta'
2004

production of works of art takes place across a range of media, the photograph has become one form amongst the multitude of options available for practising artists. Historically, the dualism has been of more significance, but even in that disputed space the incidence of coincidence between art practice and photographic procedure has been more common than exceptional. What is important is the variety of aesthetic forms within the boundaries of art-photography. Given the presumed 'mechanical' nature of the medium the options of art-photography, Pictorialism, construction, abstraction, conceptualist and neo-dada practice, and the aestheticised print have demonstrated the extraordinary flexibility and adaptability of the medium. From Scotland, from Hill and Adamson to Robin Gillanders, the focus has most usually been on the photograph as object. That is, the idea that a photograph is a distilled, charmed, disturbing, intense and ethereal correspondence with the world; a talisman empowered by the ineluctable mystery of the visual.

Conclusion

Memory and memorials

There is an argument that the history of photography from Scotland may be defined in relation to what is not there. While it is fitting to create a taxonomy of those core characteristics that give shape to the arc of a photographic history: a conventional concern with the photographic portrait; a complex landscape tradition bounded by historical associations; a sense of place and an environmental agenda; a humanist documentary programme; and a multi-faceted interest in the relationship between photography and fine art, it is perhaps more revealing to highlight those features that do not appear in the history. In this respect it is notable that a nation so intimately involved in the early history of the medium should decline an engagement with its cultural ascendancy. The intense concern with the science and technology of photography witnessed in the middle decades of the 19th century was not echoed by a commitment to the heroic apotheosis of the photograph in the early part of the 20th century. In fact, during the period when photography became a visual culture in dominance, the defining medium of the modern age, Scotland's photographers withdrew from the scene and declared an interest only in the commercial potential of the form.

This fundamental absence, perhaps, best illuminates the chronicle. In the period after the First World War, when the romantic sentiment of Pictorialism began to wane and a modernist idiom took dominion, photography in Scotland entered its lacuna. The medium, indeed, would triumph in its formalist, modernist and 'straight' styles. In Europe, and especially in the United States, the photograph became the most dynamic and challenging of cultural artefacts. Whereas the traditional canon of individual photographers may, now, be an arena for contest, the intellectual vigour of the divergent, confrontational, contingent and oppositional photographic styles remains significant. The triumph of the uncompromising, committed image, the disruption of the formalist abstraction, the radical experiment of the photomontage, the explicit challenge of the Surrealist vision, the political edge of the neo-realist photograph, all generated a ferment wherein the photograph became the most potent visual form. From Scotland, these dynamics were absent. James Craig Annan withdrew to the business of trading in etchings, his associate in the Linked Ring, Alvin Langdon Coburn, would retire from making photographs after a brief sojourn with abstraction in his 'Vortographs', and Margaret Watkins would be all but lost to the international world of photography after her move to Scotland. It would not be until the 1980s that the spirit of an engaged and momentous photographic practice would re-emerge, and a significant body of committed photographers would engage the global debate. It was at this point that Scotland began to discover its own history as a nation in photographs and photography.

The withdrawal from the contest that was modernism is a noteworthy retreat, but it is not the only absence within the field of photography from Scotland. Soon after the invention of this miraculous medium, in the late 1830s, it would be used for that most predictable of human obsessions; the sometimes humorous, often banal and soulless, always neurotically anatomical description of sex. The virtue of photography's 'realism' made it a prize possession in the hands of pornographers and those commercially-driven entrepreneurs who would feed the market for 'academy' photographs. The subtext of photography's extraordinary growth and expansion was its role in the marketplace for explicit images. These might range from the straightforwardly pornographic to the faux 'artistic', an ersatz mirroring of fine art's nude studies. But not in Scotland. There appears to be no equivalent for the nude study within Scottish photography, neither in its earliest forms, nor in its later manifestations. This is remarkable, for one of the defining characteristics of international Pictorialism, and later modernism, was its fascination with the nude. Certainly, the pages of Stieglitz's *Camera Work* were festooned with tasteful, symbolic nudes by Alice Boughton, Annie Brigman, Robert Demachy, Clarence White and, of course, Edward Steichen. In Scotland there was simply no corresponding subject, and even in the contemporary scene this has remained a marginal theme.

Reasons for this characteristic may not be too difficult to comprehend. There is no sustained and developed tradition of the nude within Scottish art generally, where this subject is the exception rather than the rule. Moreover, the early history of photography from Scotland was championed by clergymen, scientists and academics. These were establishment figures to a man, and intimately bound to the mores and conventions of Victorian rectitude; and hence the comic debacle concerning Rejlander's *Two Ways of Life*. In truth it is difficult to imagine a fascination with the nude, pornographic or otherwise, within a newly established national photography whose signature motif was the portraiture of principled evangelical ministers calling for a more rigorous interpretation of scripture.

One further absence is of note. The inter-war period, during the 20th century, was not only a time for adventurous formal experiment within the medium, but was the moment of radical, politically inspired, documentary photography. During this period Walker Evans and Dorothea Lange would produce their uncompromising views of rural poverty in America's 'dustbowl' states, Bill Brandt would undertake his searing analysis of social class in Britain, Robert Capa would visualise the nightmare civil war in Spain and the seeds of the Magnum photographic agency would be spilled. In Scotland there was little sense of these momentous changes. Rather, the modest amount of radical documentary study evidenced in the country during the inter-war years and beyond was produced by those visiting from other traditions; Werner Kissling, Wolfgang Suschitzky, Humphrey Spender, Bert Hardy, Paul Strand, Lida Moser. Consequently, the lacuna in Scottish photography did not only exempt a modernist canon, but reduced the documentary project at a time when it was most vital amongst the international community of photographers.

Evidently, the history of photography within Scotland is fractured and complicated by strange omissions. A diagnosis for this affliction is important. In part, the reduction of photographic practice to straightforward commercial enterprise was economic. Whereas the early pioneers were gentleman amateurs, hobbyists perhaps, whose main occupations lay in the professions, the idea of sustaining a career as a dedicated photographer in Scotland was impractical. Certainly this profession could be maintained where it was approached as an artisan activity, the production of images for immediate consumption in albums, journals, newspapers and illustrated pamphlets, but the sense of a consciously crafted and radical photography was attenuated. In effect there was neither a market for the art photograph nor a network of institutions, like Stieglitz's gallery in New York, that might promote the photograph as object. In this event the repository for crafted photographs became the salons of the camera clubs, a worthy network of groups but not a platform for avant-garde or oppositional experiment.

These economic constraints were not exceptional to Scotland, but they conspired with other factors to create a culture in confinement. The wave-like rhythm of industrial growth followed by recurrent slump affected all aspects of society, and the fine arts were frequently a luxury too easily disposed. Photography, always a handmaiden to painting and sculpture, could be effortlessly exiled to the annex for cultural ephemera. Those few Scottish collectors who sustained an interest in the fine arts through the lean years of economic slump were committed to officially sanctioned forms, chiefly academic painting. Consequently there was neither an institutional support for the medium, nor a cohort of interested collectors who might act as patrons to individual photographers.

Simultaneously, the supporting exhibitions and programmes that had given photography its initial momentum began to dissolve at the turn of the 20th century. When the Glasgow Photographic Association held its international exhibition 'illustrative of the present state of the art', in 1855, it was sponsored by the British Association for the Advancement of Science. As the scientific issues surrounding photographic technology were resolved, towards the end of the 19th century, so the interest of the wider academic community was lost. Of course the mantle was taken up by the Royal Photographic Society, and by the secessionist members of the Linked Ring, but these were confirmation of the marginalisation of the medium rather than evidence of cultural inclusion.

The ramifications of economic conditions, then, were far-reaching and debilitating, but there were even deeper suspicions relating to the authority of the photograph. The debate on photography's relationship to art was never completely resolved in Scotland, at least during the 19th century and throughout much of the 20th century. The fine arts could point to a craft skill and an established academic training as the basis for their cultural authority, but photographers had no equivalent endorsement. Scottish art colleges would not recognise the practice as an independent study until the 1980s and without this authorisation the status of photography remained suspect. Within this context, and especially within a culture where the ethos of the avant-garde was alien, the opportunity for radical photography was curtailed. Moreover the rich tradition of the modernist photobook, the experimental picture-journal and the committed photo-essay never found an outlet within Scotland's small and conservative publishing industry. This type of media was the principal forum through which the most challenging and forward-looking photography was disseminated and its absence in Scotland created a concomitant vacuum in advanced practice.

Hence, while in Europe, in the United States and indeed in England there developed a photographic activism that propelled the medium to the heart of radical culture, in Scotland the form became dissipated and commercialised. Of course the images that were generated through this period may be subject to analysis as 'indexical' accounts of the culture, but the sense of a high modernism, a contingent formalism or a radical avant-gardism was lost, just at the point where these were most significant on the international scene. Equally it is notable that, in the contemporary period, there is little taste for Postmodern, conceptual, or neo-conceptual practice in photography from Scotland. It is not that these styles are excluded from the present-day scene, but the inclination for the banal, the serial photograph, the abject image, the confessional document, the cult of the self, are displaced by more conventional tropes. In some ways, then, the elisions of the past remain present in the here-and-now; as if a memory of those preferences that were first favoured has come to inform the present and the future in Scotland's photography.

Memorials

Photography from Scotland may, perhaps, be defined by these absences but it is surely best defined by what it presents and represents. Within this framework it might be argued that, throughout its history, Scottish photography has been concerned to struggle with a definition of the nation and national identity. The fascination with portraiture was one way in which a sense of the nation's 'great and good' could be recognised. And so those champions of church and political governance, the catalogue of artists and scientists, the formal portraits of the aristocracy and middle classes all combined to mark the protagonists in a national history and drama. The landscape photograph, perhaps more than any other form, would consecrate this narrative. Images of Scotland's treasured places, the epic panorama of the Highland peaks, the monuments of ancient peoples, the sites of historical celebration and lamentation were offered as the locus of a definitive national spirit and character. Moreover, in the form of an environmentalist programme the landscape photograph was, in part, projected as a memory site in need of preservation. However, it was the documentary form that spoke of the lived, the real or democratic, history of Scotland. Here the populace was recognised in all its vitality and enterprise. A collective defined by work, by leisure, by politics, but above all by energy and strength and humour. This was the language of Scottish photographers from Thomas Annan to Oscar Marzaroli, and with visitors to Scotland from Paul Strand to Lida Moser. In this history the fundamental, inclusive character of the nation was complete.

The world of the art photographer overlapped and mirrored these interests. James Craig Annan would approach Stirling Castle not only as a contemplative meditation on form, but as a symbol of a distinctive history. In the contemporary period photographers like Calum Colvin and Ron O'Donnell have explored, with every degree of vigour and wit, the dark corners and forbidding myths of Scotland's story. In parallel, image-makers as diverse as Robin Gillanders and David Shrigley have reflected upon the inexhaustible variety of local culture and common incident. This interest in history, identity and culture is not exclusive. It is evident that photographers from Scotland have been concerned with world events, global inter-connections and cultural inter-dependence. Nevertheless, the sense that the history of photography from Scotland has been a history that attempts to recover memory is insistent. This is evidenced particularly among those photographers who have visited Scotland in order to undertake projects and assignments. Typically these individuals have sought out the most emblematic and totemic aspects of Scotland's chronicle and the marks of Scotland's people. At the very dawn of photography this mission was recorded in the visual projection of Greyfriars churchyard in Edinburgh.

It is notable that Roland Barthes viewed the photograph as an appointment with death. His insistence that 'the melancholy of the Photograph' was contained in its inviolable relationship with a thing that had passed was surely the fulcrum of his startling thesis in *Camera Lucida*. Moreover he was careful to speak of the photograph in relation to the idea of the monument:

> Earlier societies managed so that memory, the substitute for life, was eternal and that at least the thing which spoke Death should itself be immortal: this was the Monument. But by making the (mortal) Photograph into the general and somehow natural witness of 'what has been' modern society has renounced the Monument.[1]

In addition, Barthes' note on the role of memories and monuments here recalls Pierre Nora's epic studies of memory-places, those sites wherein the nature and consanguinity of the group, or nation, is realised. It is fascinating, then, that a recurring imagery in photography from Scotland should be a cemetery. In fact David Octavius Hill, some 140 years before Barthes' insight, chose the monuments and memory-places of Greyfriars cemetery as a suitable theme for his infant art. It is as if Hill had, intuitively, recognised this distinguishing characteristic of the new medium and looked to represent its quintessence in images of memorial stones and monuments.

Greyfriars cemetery, of course, was no ordinary burial ground. Situated to the south of the High Street in Edinburgh, it falls under the shadow of the castle and is on the edge of the Grassmarket. The church itself was reconstituted in 1562, following the dissolution of the older Friary occasioned by the Reformation, but it was not consecrated until 1620. Burials within the cemetery can be traced back to at least this period, and layers of corpses and burial stones serve as a patchwork history of the nation. In fact many of the most distinguished figures in Scotland's story are found within these grounds; George Buchanan, the 16th-century scholar and reformer; William Adam, the 18th-century architect and landscape gardener; Allan Ramsay, the 18th-century vernacular poet and father to the great Scottish portraitist of the same name; and also Walter Scott, the father of the 19th century's most successful novelist, Sir Walter Scott.

Besides these cultural titans there rests a host of eminent clergymen, academics, politicians and aristocrats. The most famous in this latter category is Sir George Mackenzie of Rosehaugh. As the King's Advocate in Scotland to Charles II, he would become infamous as 'Bluidy Mackenzie', the tormenter and oppressor of the Covenanters. In fact the history of the Solemn League and Covenant is intimately tied to Greyfriars churchyard. This proclamation, a claim to maintain a democratic control of church governance through the ascendancy of the presbytery, was signed within the churchyard in 1638. The Covenanters would become embroiled in the decades of revolt and civil war that followed and would meet their end in the 'Killing Time' after the Battle of Bothwell Bridge in 1679. Both Mackenzie and Greyfriars churchyard would once again become central to the story, for over a thousand Covenanting insurgents were imprisoned within the walls of the cemetery and Mackenzie, as the King's Advocate, would be their prosecutor. Most importantly the romance that accrued to the dissident ministers became memorialised in the 'Martyrs Monument', a commemorative stone erected in 1706, dedicated to the Covenanters and situated, with some irony, in the same grounds as their chief persecutor.

Hill and Adamson would photograph the Martyrs Monument, along with a variety of Greyfriars' finest grave markers and mausoleums, during the highpoint of their collaboration in the 1840s. There may well have been a technical logic to the selection of these grounds. The need for quiet places, devoid of human bustle and the general clamour of the city, was essential for the success of a photographic exposure. In fact, long exposure times and the need for complete still were the necessary precursors to the early photographic image, and where better than a cemetery? Moreover, there was a 19th-century fascination with the spectacle and ceremony of death. This would deepen in Victorian Britain, where gravestones and monuments grew ever more elaborate, and where the cemetery became a spectacular exhibition of mortality. Hill would recognise this taste for the sentimental and the morbid, for it was a feature of fine art practice, but he would also recognise the historical associations buried within the cemetery grounds.

Among the many images Hill and Adamson produced within Greyfriars churchyard, chiefly in the period circa 1843, there were a number featuring the Martyrs Monument [FIG.136] and a few recording Mackenzie's tomb. In some sense Hill was establishing a connection between church history, political history, and the drama of government; a combination of images and an association that would be replete with meaning in that year of the Disruption. Besides these heavily symbolic photographs, the partnership also featured the most celebrated and ostentatious of burial monuments, very often in different light conditions and from differing perspectives. And so the McCulloch Monument was viewed against the backdrop of the Tolbooth Church and the city's skyline but was repeated in relation to its companion the Martyrs Monument. Likewise, the Chalmers Monument was aligned with the Jackson Monument in order to view these structures against the looming façade of the castle, but, through a repositioning of the camera, the Chalmers Monument was subsequently viewed with the Paton Monument in order to establish the background of the Heriot's Hospital. In these cases monuments were set against historic buildings in the skyline, and so obliquely related to the still-thriving heartland of the city.

The connection between the living and the dead was further accented in Hill and Adamson's work through the positioning of various friends and relatives in relation to the monuments. Hill had posed a portrait of his associate and fellow academician, the painter David Roberts, set against an ornately carved sepulchre in the churchyard, but he was more usually prone to featuring groups of people in reflective communion with the tombs and crypts. An image of the Dennistoun Monument, for example, features Hill accompanied by his young nieces within the broad stone frame of the edifice. In another work an assembly can be seen paying homage at the Martyrs Monument, and in yet others there are arrangements of figures around the Naismith Monument, the McCulloch Monument and the Mackenzie Tomb. These are individuals engaged in a sacrament with the dead. They discretely acknowledge their own mortality in respect of the mortality of their forebears, and they sit in congruence with their fate. However, they are also in empathy with the place and the celebrated figures therein, and therefore in union with the complicated and conflicting history that this place represented. In this respect Hill and Adamson's images of Greyfriars were a meditation upon the state of the nation. In prophecy of Barthes, who supposed that the photograph would replace the monument as

FIG.136
Hill and Adamson
Martyrs Monument
1843

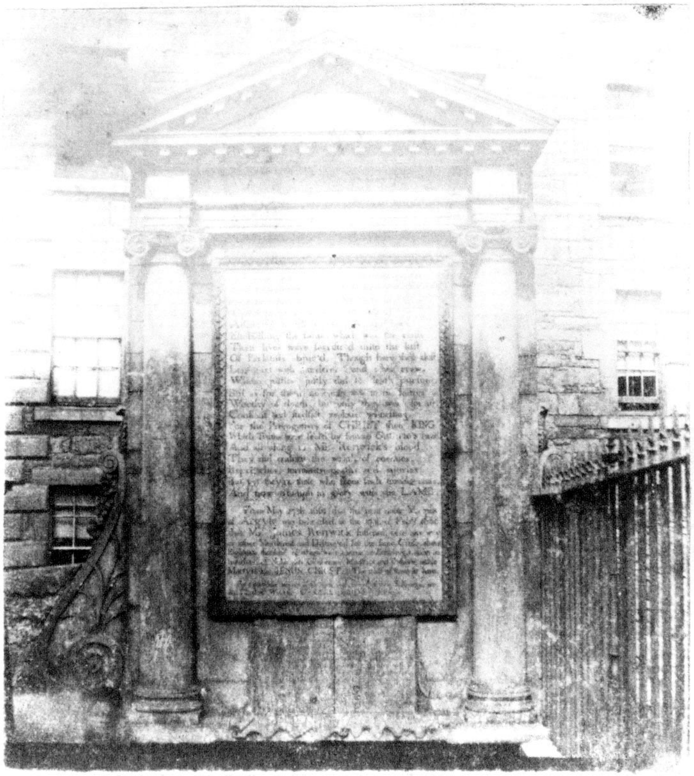

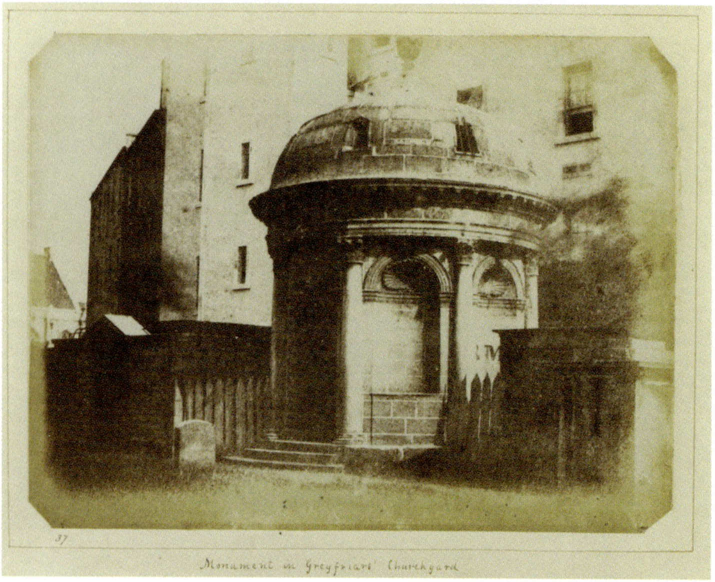

FIG.137
George Moir
Monument to Sir George Mackenzie of Rosehaugh in Greyfriars Churchyard
circa 1844

the repository of memory, Hill divined the power of the new medium and first recognised its destiny.[2]

Naturally, where Hill and Adamson first wandered a host of photographers would follow. Hill's friend George Moir (1800–70), the distinguished lawyer, literary critic, amateur photographer and founder member of the Edinburgh Calotype Club, would undertake a study of Greyfriars as one of his experiments in the technology of the new medium. His *Monument to Sir George Mackenzie of Rosehaugh in Greyfriars Churchyard* [FIG.137], circa 1844, is one of a small group of images he took within the cemetery walls. Similarly, this was a subject that the surgeon Thomas Keith would explore in 1855 when he undertook a photographic survey of the city, partly in the company of his fellow amateur John Forbes White. Keith's works remain amongst the most resonant images of Greyfriars, where he photographed a number of tombs, sometimes within the context of the towering castle, but often focusing on the ornate and melancholic carving. His *Foliage on a Tombstone, Greyfriars (Tomb of John Byres of Coates)* [FIG.138] displays a wild overgrowth of ivy against the fractured architecture of the tomb while sinister carvings, deaths-heads and all, glower from recess and niche. Five years later, in 1860 William Donaldson Clark would move south from his discoveries in the Cowgate to photograph the churchyard with the mist-shrouded castle a distant backcloth.

The examples of Hill and of Keith would be important for the work of the American Pictorialist Alvin Langdon Coburn, who would place a special emphasis on Greyfriars churchyard during his photographic study of Edinburgh in 1905. Coburn was, of course, retracing the journeys of his boyhood hero, the writer Robert Louis Stevenson, and Greyfriars loomed large in the latter's *Edinburgh: Picturesque Notes*, published in 1878. Coburn undertook a number of studies in Greyfriars cemetery and devoted five photographic images to his publication, in 1954, of the photographically-illustrated edition of Stevenson's reminiscences.

Coburn was acutely aware of this connection with Hill, a photographer whom he held in the highest esteem. In a letter to the photo-historian Helmut Gernsheim, dated 1957, Coburn commented on the latter's monograph on Julia Margaret Cameron and enquired, 'Why haven't you done David Octavius Hill, the greatest "Old Master" of the lense [sic]'.[3] Earlier still, in 1915, Coburn had written an article for *The Century Magazine* titled 'Old Masters of Photography'. He began his survey with Hill and noted, 'I have visited his studio on the slopes of the Calton Hill in Edinburgh and have inspected various pieces of his cumbersome apparatus.' He continued:

> And often in the twilight I have walked up to the crest back of his old studio and imagined how Hill must have done so many times while he lived. I can picture him brushing his fine locks back from his forehead as he looked out over the Edinburgh that Stevenson celebrates in his 'Picturesque Notes'... Thus Hill comes to be associated in my memory with Edinburgh and Stevenson.[4]

In this same article Coburn continued his survey of 'old masters' with a review of Thomas Keith. Coburn was certainly prescient in highlighting Keith's contribution to photography and argued that 'it is the "Old Edinburgh" series that stand[s] out as his most remarkable achievement with the camera.'[5] He illustrated Keith's achievement with an image titled *In Greyfriars' Churchyard, Edinburgh*, and this precise monument was photographed by Coburn for illustration in *Edinburgh: Picturesque Notes*, there to be titled with a phrase gleaned from Stevenson's prose, *Costly Monuments of a Very Elegant Proportion*.

Coburn's photographs of Greyfriars Churchyard, then, were part of an important tradition. They were also a kind of testament. Coburn focused on the gravestones and monuments in order to accent notions of mortality. Stevenson had remarked that 'we Scots stand, to my fancy, highest among nations in the matter of grimly illustrating death',[6] but Coburn saw in these memorials a melancholy beauty that touched upon the fugitive nature of human life. Of these images he singled out *A Tree in Greyfriars* [FIG.139] as 'perhaps the most characteristic'.[7] A model of soft-focus Pictorialism, it shows a pathway into the graveyard. The centre and dominant feature of the composition is a leafless tree, while in the background the smoking chimneys and tall façades of the Old Town tenements give way to the spire of the Assembly Hall. It evokes a living Edinburgh, a very hive of human activity, but is foregrounded by nature and the fact of death. This near philosophical contrast was reprised in a further image, again wrought from Stevenson's prose, *Linen on a Clothes Pole Flaps against Funereal Sculpture*. For Coburn this photograph was 'denoting the close proximity of life and death',[8] and in these biographical notes written for Gernsheim he, once again, quotes Stevenson:

> A damp smell of graveyard finds its way into houses where workmen sit at meat. Domestic life on a small scale goes forward visably [sic] at the windows. The very solitude and stillness of the enclosure, which lies apart from the town's traffic, serves to accentuate the contrast.[9]

Hence the juxtapositions of old and new, life and death, time and change, run consistently through Coburn's photographs of Greyfriars. And his image of newly washed linen blowing gently on a breeze, set against the stone of a grave monument, presents a poetic *memento mori*; an epitaph on the inconsequential and transient nature of life itself, but also a homily to a lived history.

From Hill, through Keith and Clark to Coburn, Greyfriars churchyard was presented as a symbolic statement of the nation and its convoluted identity. Nor were these the only photographers to recognize the significance of this memory-place. Charles Kinnear, a distinguished figure in the Photographic Society of Scotland, produced waxed paper images of the site in the late 1850s; John Muir Wood would harvest the scenic symbolism of the locale; and the ubiquitous George Washington Wilson would photograph within the cemetery walls. Of course, wherever Wilson went Valentine would follow and a speciality of both companies was the Martyrs Monument. In the 20th century Robert Moyes Adam, a denizen of Edinburgh, would take a number of evocative panoramas of the cemetery with an eye that reflected the romanticism of Alvin Langdon Coburn. Moreover, in 1990 the contemporary photographer Joe Rock (b. 1948) was commissioned to undertake a

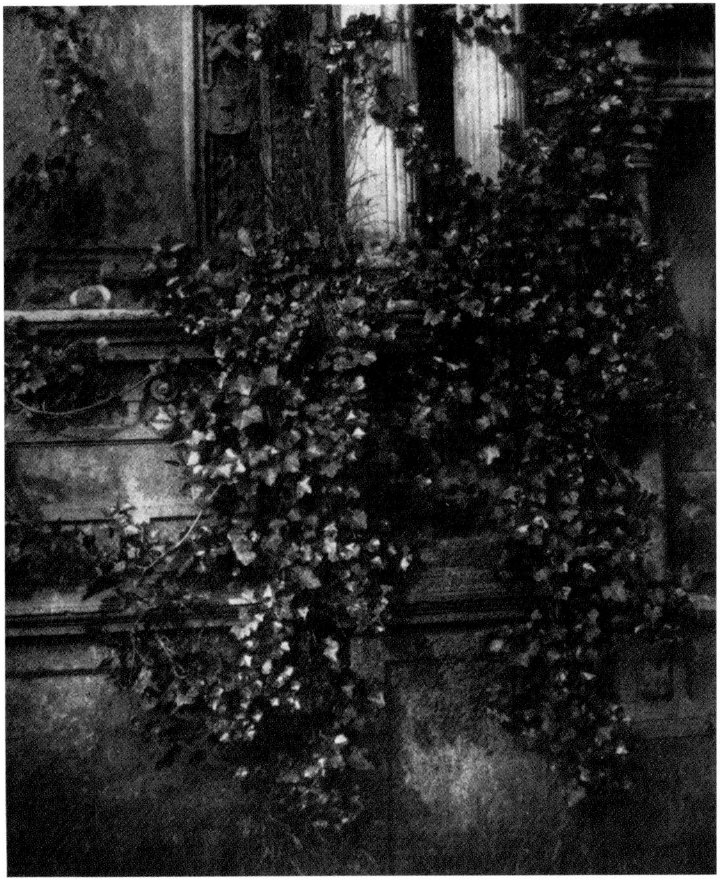

FIG.138
Thomas Keith
Foliage on a Tombstone, Greyfriars (Tomb of John Byres of Coates)
1855

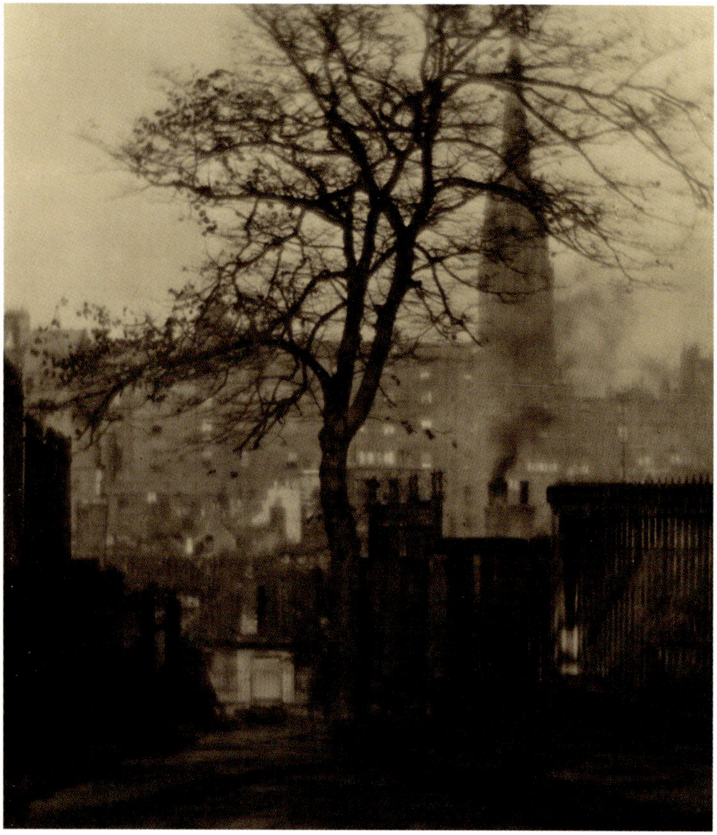

FIG.139
Alvin Langdon Coburn
A Tree in Greyfriars
1905

study of the cemetery by the Greyfriars Kirkyard Trust. The result, a perceptive and sympathetic exploration of the monuments taken with a large format camera, recalls the sense of awe first summoned by those 19th-century pioneers. Indeed, Rock's *Unidentified Tomb* [FIG.140], from 1992, not only invokes the romantic mood of despond and picturesque decay in the graveyard, but subtly evokes the notion of faded glories. And meanwhile the associations of the site, in terms of its history and its significance for photography generally, have meant that every photo-journalist and commercial photographer of note has made a pilgrimage to this melancholy, macabre museum.

The fascination with Edinburgh cemeteries was not confined to Greyfriars, and eminent international photographers, perhaps in search of Hill and Adamson's inspiration, would look to the city's memorial monuments as a subject for meditative reflection. In 1942 Bill Brandt would journey to Scotland in order to complete a photo-essay titled 'The Northern Capital in Winter'.[10] Searching for an ancient cemetery with the castle for a backdrop he took a number of images of St Cuthbert's cemetery at the west end of Princes Street. Similarly, in 1974, Ansel Adams would visit Edinburgh, where Andrea Stillman recalls his interests:

> I was on the trip to Scotland with Ansel, his wife Virginia, [and] his granddaughter Sylvia Mayhew... It was rainy in Scotland so it wasn't ideal conditions for photography... As for the graveyard, I remember it was very close to our hotel, and again it was raining, and Ansel wanted to take some pictures so we strolled across the street where there was a cemetery. He always loved to photograph headstones – starting in the early 1930s – so this was nothing new. There was one very weathered one with little whitish flowers kind of sticking up around the base, and that's what he photographed. When we got home to the US he printed up a few of his European negatives, and... the gravestone from Scotland he even made fine prints of, as I recall. But I don't remember the name of the cemetery – just that it was across the street from our hotel (and I imagine we were staying at the fanciest hotel) and that there was almost a park across from the hotel as well.[11]

Ansel Adams was almost certainly resident in the Caledonian Hotel, across from St Cuthbert's Church and cemetery, and west of Princes Street Gardens. The compelling case is that, in these vistas, the most important photographers of the inter-war period were returning to the very dawn of photographic history, and Hill and Adamson's symbolic theme.

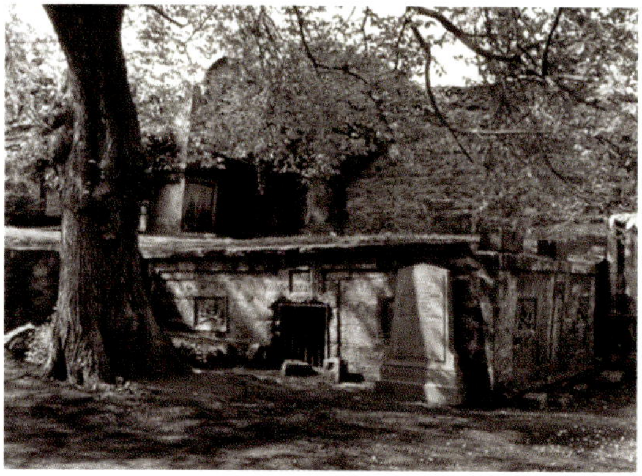

FIG.140
Joe Rock
Unidentified Tomb
1992

Photography from Scotland

While these memory-places and memorials remain a significant feature, helping to define photography from Scotland, it would be wrong to end this narrative in a graveyard. The history of Scottish photography is rich in symbolism, certainly, but it is also abounding in most every variety of nuance and enterprise. Within the limitations of a restricted market and only partial institutional support, Scottish photographers have contributed to the international story of photography in all its diversity. With the technical experiments of David Brewster and those early pioneers in Edinburgh and St Andrews the new medium first found a widespread acceptance. In 1861 it was the Scottish physicist James Clerk Maxwell who first invented a colour photographic process, significantly in the manifestation of a tartan ribbon [FIG.141]. The calotype would be advanced through its use by Scottish photographers, as would the photogravure. And, in the contemporary period, the digital revolution would find a home in Scotland and with young Scottish photographers.

Scientific associations with photography remain important, but it is in the imaginative array of images that photography from Scotland is best expressed. The development of Scottish portraiture, landscape, documentary and fine art photography offers a resplendent history. Rich in variety and intensity, it projects an intricate view of the nation and its people, and demonstrates a positive interaction with the global community. This fundamental commitment was given full voice in a recent project by the young contemporary Claire Wheeldon. Commissioned by the new Scottish Parliament, she was tasked to create a series of photographs to decorate the recently completed parliament building at Holyrood in Edinburgh. Her chosen subject was 'Inclusion' [FIG.142] and she produced a suite of images that gathered diverse groups of people in sparse formal arrangements. These photographs – subtly charged, objective, honest and accessible – accented ideas of association, relationship and a common ground. In many ways these are archetypal works, for like the quintessential photograph from Scotland, they mirror that fundamental democracy at the very core of the culture.

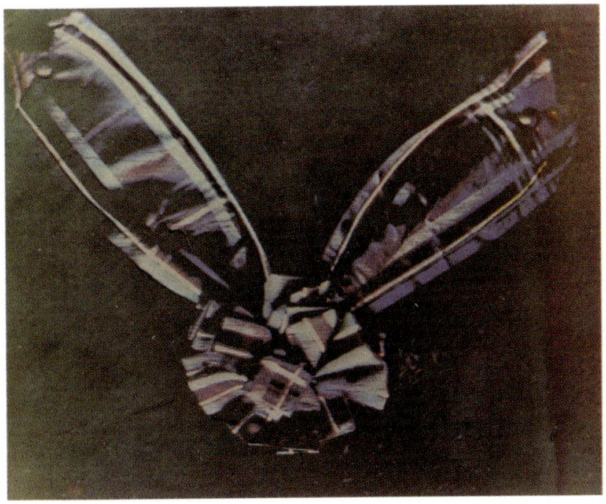

FIG.141
James Clerk Maxwell
The First Trichromatic Colour Photograph, a Tartan Ribbon
1861

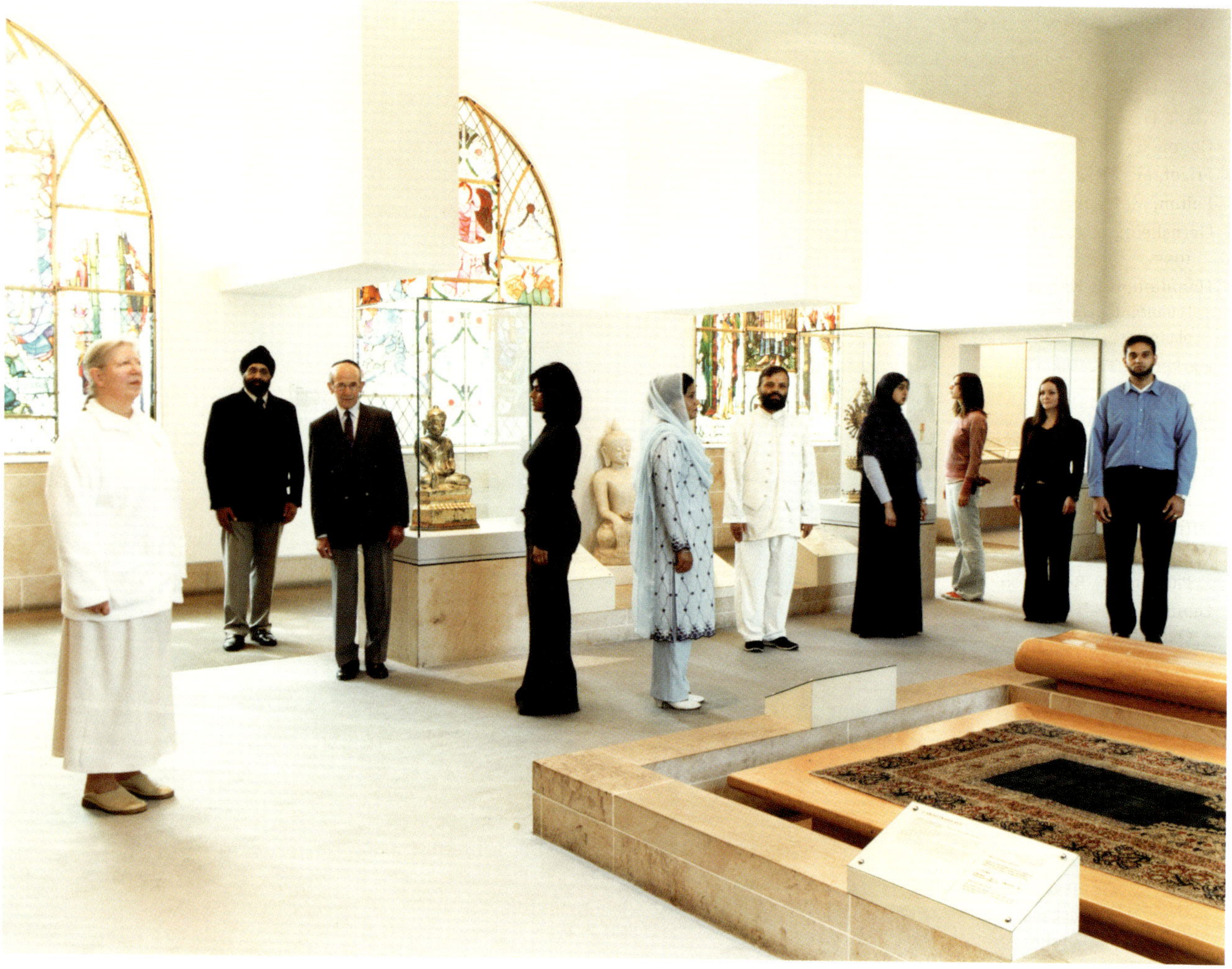

FIG.142
Claire Wheeldon
Inclusion 5 (St Mungo Museum of Religious Life and Art)
from the 'Inclusion' series 2004

Bibliography and Further Reading

General and contextual texts

Campany, D. *Art and Photography*, London 2005.

Clark, G. *The Photograph*, Oxford 1997.

Clark, G. (ed.) The Portrait in Photography, London 1992.

Cotton, C. *The Photograph as Contemporary Art*, London 2004.

Frizot, M. *A New History of Photography*, Koln 1998.

Fulton, M. *Pictorialism into Modernism*, New York 1996.

Gernsheim, H. & A. *The History of Photography*, London 1955.

Hamilton, P. & Hargreaves, R. *The Beautiful and the Damned: the creation of identity in nineteenth century photography*, London 2001.

Harker, M. *The Linked Ring; the Secession Movement in Photography in Britain 1892–1910*, London 1979.

Haworth-Booth, M. *Photography: an Independent Art*, Princeton 1997.

Jeffrey, I. & Mellor, D. *The Real Thing: an Anthology of British Photography 1840–1950*, London 1975.

Jeffrey, I. *Photography: A Concise History*, London 1981.

Lange, A. *On the Bright Side of Life: Contemporary British Photography*, Berlin 1998.

Lenman, R. (ed) *The Oxford Companion to the Photograph*, Oxford 2005.

Lipovetsky, G. *Hypermodern Times*, Cambridge 2005.

Newhall. B. *The History of Photography from 1839 to the Present*, London 1982.

Nora, P. *Realms of Memory*, New York 1992.

Parr, M. & Badger, G. *The Photobook: A History*, vol. 1, London 2004.

Weaver, M. *Alvin Langdon Coburn: Symbolist Photographer*, Oxford 1986.

Weaver, M. *The Art of Photography 1839–1989*, London 1989.

Weaver, M *The Photographic Art; Pictorial Traditions in Britain and America*, London 1985.

Critical texts

Barthes, R. *Camera Lucida; Reflections on Photography*, London 1982.

Barthes, R. *Image, Music, Text*, London 1977.

Brittain, D. *Creative Camera; 30 years of writing*, Manchester 1999.

Benjamin, W. *Illuminations*, London 1970.

Benjamin, W. 'A Small History of Photography', in *One Way Street*, London 1979.

Berger, J. *About Looking*, London 1980.

Berger, J. *Ways of Seeing*, London 1972.

Burgin, V. *Thinking Photography*, London 1982.

Goldberg, V. (ed.) *Photography in Print*, Albuquerque 1981.

Hill, P. & Cooper, T. *Dialogue with Photography*, Manchester 1992.

Sontag, S. *On Photography*, New York 1973.

Tagg, J. *The Burden of Representation*, London 1988.

Wells, L. (ed.) *Photography: A Critical Introduction*, London 2000.

Wells, L. (ed.) *The Photography Reader*, London 2003.

Scottish Photography

General

Brittain, D. & Stevenson, S. *New Scottish Photography*, Edinburgh 1990.

Dougan, R. O. *The Scottish Tradition in Photography*, Edinburgh 1947.

Hannavy, J. *A Moment in Time*, Glasgow 1983.

Kemp, M. *Mood of the Moment*, St Andrews n.d.

Lawson, J. *The Riddell Collection*, Edinburgh 1986.

Smith, G. *Sun Pictures in Scotland*, Ann Arbor 1989.

Stevenson, S. *Light from the Dark Room*, Edinburgh 1995.

Stevenson, S. & Forbes, D. *A Companion Guide to Photography in the National Galleries of Scotland*, Edinburgh 2001.

Strand, P. *Tir A'Mhurain: the Outer Hebrides of Scotland*, New York, n.d.

Selected texts, catalogues and articles

Ashbee, F. & Lawson, Julie. *William Carrick 1827–1878*, Edinburgh n.d.

Bate, D. 'Illuminating Annan', *Portfolio Magazine 3*, 1989.

Berger, J. & Macdonald, P. *Once in Europa*, London 1999.

Berry, J. 'Ron O'Donnell: an interview', *Studies in Photography*, 1996.

Brettle, J. 'Ruth Stirling: an interview', *Scottish Photography Bulletin* 2, 1991.

Bruce, D. 'Oscar Marzaroli: a Tribute', *Scottish Photography Bulletin* 1, Edinburgh 1989.

Buchanan, W. *The Art of the Photographer J. Craig Annan 1864–1946*, Edinburgh 1992.

Buchanan, W. *J. Craig Annan; Selected texts and bibliography*, Oxford 1994.

Buchler, P. 'Owen Logan', *Portfolio Magazine* 26, 1997.

Burnett, J. 'Aesthetes and Engineers: a Carey-on' (Evelyn Carey), *Scottish Photography Bulletin*, Autumn 1987.

Chandler, D. '"Is": Ecstasies I-XXII' (David Williams), *Portfolio Magazine* 4, 1989.

Colvin, C. 'The Alchemical Canvas', *Studies in Photography*, Autumn 1998.

Cooper, T. J. *Between Dark and Dark*, Edinburgh, 1985.

Cooper, T. J. *Dreaming the Gokstadt*, Edinburgh 1988.

Cooper, T. J. 'The Marks of Someone Travelling: Considerations of Patricia Macdonald's Aerial Art', *Portfolio Magazine* 3, 1989.

Davie, A. & Mellor, R. *George Washington Wilson and the Scottish Railways*, Aberdeen 1983.

Daw, R. 'In Solitary Places: Robert Moyes Adam', *Scots Magazine*, vol. 88, 1967–8.

Fisher, A. L. 'Thomas Annan's *Old Closes and Streets of Glasgow*', *Scottish Photography Bulletin*, Spring 1987.

Forbes, D. *An Exile's Eye; the photography of Wolfgang Suschitzky*, Edinburgh 2002.

Forbes, D. 'Situating Realism: an interview with Owen Logan', *Third Text*, vol. 18, issue 4, 2004.

Foster, A. 'Significant Others; the Photographic Portraits of Robin Gillanders', *Portfolio Magazine* 6, 1990.

Foster, A. (et al.) *Fotofeis: Scottish International Festival of Photography*, Edinburgh 1993.

Gilbert, H. 'Scotland's Photographer' (Robert Moyes Adam), *Scotland's Magazine*, March 1947.

Gillanders, R. 'Portraiture', *Scottish Photography Bulletin* 2, 1990.

Gillanders, R. *The Photographic Portrait*, Newton Abbott 2004.

Grant, C. *Relative Values*, Edinburgh 1994.

Gray, M. *George Washington Wilson and the Scottish Fishing Industry*, Aberdeen 1982.

Hamilton, R. 'John Murray (1809–1898): Pioneer Photographer in India', *Scottish Photography Bulletin* 1, 1993.

Hannavay, J. *Thomas Keith's Scotland*, Edinburgh 1981.

Hartley, K. *Dalziel and Scullion: Home*, Edinburgh 2001.

Haworth-Booth, M. 'Maud Sulter; an interview', *History of Photography* 16, 1992.

Hopkinson, A. 'Ron O'Donnell', *Portfolio Magazine* 19, 1994.

Hutchison, A. 'Morocco' (Owen Logan), *Portfolio Magazine* 3, 1989.

Lawson, James. 'Barbie: Photographs by Andy Wiener', *Alba*, 1989.

Lawson, James. 'David Williams: in conversation', *Studies in Photography*, 1996.

Lawson, James. 'Living Scenes: Andy Wiener', *Portfolio Magazine* 7, 1990.

Lawson, James. 'Postscript to Fotofies – Just One Picture', *Scottish Photography Bulletin* 2, 1993.

Lawson, James. 'Robin Gillanders in conversation', *Studies in Photography*, 1996.

Lawson, James. *Sacred and Profane* (Calum Colvin), Edinburgh 1998.

Lawson, James. 'The Problem of Poverty and the Picturesque: Thomas Annan's *Old Closes and Streets of Glasgow 1868–1871*', *Scottish Photography Bulletin* 2, 1990.

Lawson, James. 'The Urban Landscape: between Progress and Decay', *Studies in Photography*, 1998.

Lawson, James. 'To Travel... To Arrive' (David Williams), *Portfolio Magazine* 20, 1994.

Lawson, James. 'Patricia Macdonald: Emergent Landscapes', *Portfolio Magazine* 31, 2000.

Lawson, Julie. *William Donaldson Clark 1816–1873*, Edinburgh 1993.

Lawson, Julie. 'William Donaldson Clark (1816–1873)', *Scottish Photography Bulletin* 1, Edinburgh 1989.

Lawson, Julie. *Women in White* (Clementina Hawarden), Edinburgh 1997.

Lind, M. 'In the margin of the margins, Syrcas by Maud Sulter', *Portfolio Magazine* 19, 1994.

Logan, O. *Bloodlines: Vite allo specchio*, Manchester 1994.

Macdonald, F. 'Paul Strand and the Atlanticist Cold War', *History of Photography*, Winter 2004.

Macdonald, P. *Airworks*, Edinburgh 2001.

Macdonald, P. *Shadow of Heaven*, London 1989.

Macdonald, P. *Order and Chaos: Views of Gaia*, Edinburgh 1990.

Macdonald, P. *The Scenery of Scotland: the Structure Beneath*, Edinburgh 1988.

Macdonald, P. 'To Remain Dissolved: Aspects of Photography and Language', *Studies in Photography*, 1996.

McKenzie, J. *Gorbals Children: A Study in Photographs*, Glasgow 1990.

McKenzie, J. 'Gorbals Children', *Portfolio Magazine* 7, 1990.

McKenzie, J. *Pages of Experience*, London 1987.

McKenzie, R.'"A Long Drawn Out Pleasure" The Art of James Craig Annan', *Scottish Photography Bulletin* 2, 1992.

McKenzie. R. 'A Love Affair with Loch Katrine: Problems of Representation in Early Scottish Landscape', *Scottish Photography Bulletin* 1, 1990.

McKenzie, R. 'By Fin By Wing By Hoof' (Calum Angus MacKay), *Portfolio Magazine* 11, 1991.

McKenzie, R. *Isolate* (Calum Angus MacKay), Edinburgh 1993.

McKenzie, R. 'Raymond Moore', *Portfolio Magazine* 10, 1991

McKenzie, R. 'Thomas Annan and the Scottish Landscape: Among the Grey Edifices', *History of Photography* 16, 1992.

McKenzie, R. 'Thomas Joshua Cooper: an Interview', *Studies in Photography* 1996.

Main, W. 'George Dobson Valentine in New Zealand', *History of Photography* 6, 1982.

Marzaroli, O. *One Man's World: Photographs 1955–1984*, Glasgow 1984.

Marzaroli, O. *Glasgow's People 1956–1989*, Edinburgh 1993.

Mellor, D. 'A Package Flight to the Land of the Dead' (Calum Colvin), *Portfolio Magazine*, 1996.

Mellor, D. 'In Thompson's Forge or Ron O'Donnell meets the Mummy', *Portfolio Magazine* 9, 1990.

Mellor, D. *The Book, the Box, and the Song* (Calum Colvin), Frankfurt 1990.

Mellor, D. *Calum Colvin: Work 1989*, London 1989.

Mellor. D. *The Magic Theatre of Calum Colvin*, Edinburgh 1990.

Normand, T. 'Alvin Langdon Coburn, Robert Louis Stevenson, and Edinburgh', *History of Photography*, Spring 2005.

Normand, T. 'An interview with Calum Colvin', *Transcript*, vol. 1, issue 1, Dec. 1994.

Normand, T. *Calum Colvin's Ossian: Fragments of Ancient Poetry*, Edinburgh 2002.

Normand, T. 'Imagining and Imaging the Land: some ideological formations of landscape photography in Scotland' in F. Cullen & J. Morrison (eds), *A Shared Legacy; Essays on Irish and Scottish Art and Visual Culture*, London 2005.

Normand, T. 'David Williams; one taste: (n)ever changing', *Portfolio Magazine*, 39, 2004.

Normand, T. *The Seven Deadly Sins and the Four Last Things* (Calum Colvin), Edinburgh 1994.

Oliver, G. *Glasgow Portraits by J. Craig Annan*, Glasgow 1968.

Patrizio, A. & Penny, J. *Stephen Lawson; Change by Degrees*, West Virginia 1993.

Patrizio, A. 'Fixing Steel Plates to Glass: Benjamin Baker, Evelyn Carey and the Forth Rail Bridge', *Scottish Photography Bulletin* 1, 1990.

Richon, O. 'Zabat; a Photographic Work by Maud Sulter', *Portfolio Magazine* 8, 1990.

Robertson, J. 'Bloodlines' (Owen Logan), *Portfolio Magazine* 1, 1993.

Robertson, J. 'New Scottish Photography', *Portfolio Magazine* 9, 1990.

Robertson, J. 'Passages; Ruth Stirling', *Portfolio Magazine* 1, 1988.

Russell, M. A. *Different Country; photographs by Werner Kissling*, Edinburgh 2003.

Smart, R. 'Famous Throughout the World' (James Valentine), *Review of Scottish Culture* 4, 1988.

Smith, G. 'Edinburgh Ale by David Hill and Robert Adamson', *Notes in the History of Art* 3, 1983.

Smith, L. M. H. *The Road to the Isles; the Hebrides in Lantern Slides* (George Washington Wilson), Loanhead 1983.

Stevenson, S. 'Catriona Grant: an interview', *Studies in Photography*, 1996.

Stevenson, S. *David Octavius Hill and Robert Adamson*, Edinburgh 1981.

Stevenson, S. 'Edinburgh Ale and the Morning After', *Scottish Photography Bulletin*, 2, 1994.

Stevenson, S. *Facing the Light; the photography of Hill and Adamson*, Edinburgh 2002.

Stevenson, S. *Hill and Adamson's Fishermen and Women of the Firth of Forth*, Edinburgh 1991.

Stevenson S., Lawson, J. & Gray, M. *John Muir Wood 1805–1892: An Accomplished Amateur*, Edinburgh 1988.

Stevenson, S. *Murray Johnston: Landscapes*, Edinburgh 1999.

Stevenson, S. *The Personal Art of David Octavius Hill*, New Haven, 2002.

Stevenson, S. *Thomas Annan 1829–1887*, Edinburgh 1990.

Sulter, M. 'Syrcas', *Portfolio Magazine* 19, 1994.

Sutton-Hibbert, J. 'The Romanies of Sintesti', *Scottish Photography Bulletin* 2, 1994.

Taylor, R. *George Washington Wilson: Artist and Photographer 1823–1893*, Aberdeen 1981.

Waite, L. J. 'Maud Sulter', *Portfolio Magazine* 23, 1996.

Westbrook, C. *Calum Colvin: The Two Ways of Life*, Chicago 1991.

White, S. *John Thomson: Life and Work*, London 1985.

Wiener, A. 'Appearances', *Portfolio Magazine* 1, 1988.

Williams, D. 'One Little Room... An Everywhere', *Scottish Photography Bulletin* 2, 1994.

Williams, D. *Pictures From No Man's Land*, Edinburgh 1985.

Williams, D. 'Self-Portrait', *Studies in Photography*, 1997.

Woods, A. 'The Accepting Lens; the Photography of Joseph McKenzie', *Alba* 8, 1988.

Websites

General

Edinburgh Calotype Club
www.nls.uk/pencilsoflight

National Galleries of Scotland
www.nationalgalleries.org/collections/index.php

National Museum of Photography
www.nmpft.org.uk

Photography in Edinburgh
www.edinphoto.org.uk/index.htm

Portfolio Magazine
www.portfoliocatalogue.com

SSHOP
www.sshop.arts.gla.ac.uk/index.htm

St Andrews University Collection
http://specialcollections.st-and.ac.uk

Stills Gallery
www.stills.org

Street Level Photoworks
www.streetlevelphotoworks.org

Photographers

Jane Brettle
www.janebrettle.com

Calum Colvin
www.calumcolvin.com

Dalziel & Scullion
www.dalzielscullion.com

Patricia Macdonald
www.patriciamacdonald.org.uk

Wendy McMurdo
www.wendymcmurdo.com

Glyn Satterley
www.glynsatterley.co.uk

David Shrigley
www.davidshrigley.com

Iain Stewart
www.iainstewartphotos.co.uk

Jeremy Sutton-Hibbert
www.jeremysuttonhibbert.com

George Washington Wilson
www.visual-evidence.ac.uk/aberdeen

Claire Wheeldon
www.clairewheeldon.com/cv.html

Andy Wiener
www.false.demon.co.uk

David Williams
www.davidwilliamsphotographer.com

End Notes

CHAPTER ONE: Memorial, Document, Object

1 W. G. Sebald, *Austerlitz*, London 2002, p. 258.

2 Roland Barthes, *Camera Lucida*, London 1993, pp. 76–7.

3 *Ibid.*, pp. 31–2.

4 John Berger, 'Uses of Photography', in *About Looking*, London 1980, p. 50.

5 Lawrence D. Kritzman, foreword to Pierre Nora, *Realms of Memory* I, New York 1992, p. ix.

6 Pierre Nora, 'Between Memory and History', in *Realms of Memory* I, New York 1992, p. 3.

7 For a full account of this project see Tom Normand, *Calum Colvin's Ossian*, Edinburgh 2002.

8 Lawrence D. Kritzman, foreword to Pierre Nora, *Realms of Memory I*, New York 1992, p. xii.

9 *Ibid.*, p. xiii.

10 Gilles Lipovetsky, *Hypermodern Times*, Cambridge 2005, p. 67.

11 *Ibid.*, p. 5.

12 Roland Barthes, *Camera Lucida*, London 1993, p. 79.

13 W. G. Sebald, *Austerlitz*, London 2002, p. 259.

14 *Ibid.*, p. 258.

15 Liz Wells (ed.), *The Photography Reader*, London 2003, p. 252.

16 Charles Baudelaire, 'The Salon of 1859', in V. Goldberg (ed.), *Photography in Print*, Alberquerque 1981, p. 125.

17 Elizabeth Eastlake, 'A Review in the London Quarterly Review', in V. Goldberg (ed.), *Photography in Print*, Albuquerque 1981, p. 94.

18 *Ibid.*, p. 96.

19 Allan Sekula, 'The Invention of Photographic Meaning', in V. Goldberg (ed.), *Photography in Print*, Albuquerque 1981, p. 471

20 Martha Rosler, 'In, Around and Afterthoughts' in L. Wells (ed.), *A Photographic Reader*, London 2003, p. 263.

21 *Ibid.*, p. 271.

22 Logan writes of this image: 'The title is *Bob Ballantyne's "Inverted Coalmine", North Sea oil platform, UK Sector*. The image illustrates a metaphor which Bob, a survivor of the Piper Alpha disaster, used to describe his general scepticism about the UK North Sea oil industry. His metaphor of the "inverted coalmine" had several layers of significance. In the first instance it was about the experience of working on UK oil platforms managed and owned by multi-national companies where trade union organisation was suppressed and where a gold rush spirit of adventure was supposed to reign instead. Bob thought the UK oil industry, in contrast to the Norwegian industry, was dominated by the spirit of sheer exploitation. Historically, the metaphor is an accurate description of the economic relationship between oil and coal when UK oil revenues were used to support Margaret Thatcher's reordering of British industry and society.' Email to the author, July 2007.

23 Duncan Forbes, 'Situating Realism: an interview with Owen Logan', in *Third Text*, 18 (4), 2004, p. 274.

24 See, for example, the essays in the two admirable books that Liz Wells has edited; *Photography: a Critical Introduction*, London 1997, and *The Photography Reader*, London 2003.

25 Most obviously, Helmut and Alison Gernsheim, *The History of Photography…*, London 1955, and Beaumont Newhall, *The History of Photography from 1839 to the Present Day*, New York 1958.

26 For a full history of The Edinburgh Calotype Club, and a selection of images by its members, see the National Library of Scotland's website at www.nls.uk/pencilsoflight/history.htm.

27 For a full discussion of this group see M. F. Harker, *The Linked Ring: the secession movement in photography in Britain 1892–1910*, London 1979.

28 See William Buchanan, *The Art of the Photographer J. Craig Annan 1864–1946*, Edinburgh 1992, p. 16.

29 From the first minute book of the Scottish Photographic Federation, reproduced in 'The Scottish Photographic Federation: the first hundred years', Dundee 2003.

30 For information on this group see www.sshop.arts.gla.ac.uk/index.htm.

CHAPTER TWO: Portraits and People

1 Roland Barthes, *Camera Lucida*, p. 79.

2 Elizabeth Eastlake, 'A Review in the London Quarterly Review', in V. Goldberg (ed.), *Photography in Print*, Albuquerque 1981, pp. 92–3.

3 *Jeanne Duval: A Melodrama* by Maud Sulter, Scottish National Portrait Gallery exhibition, 2003.

4 For the definitive account of the partnership see Sara Stevenson, *The Personal Art of David Octavius Hill*, New Haven 2002.

5 Fox Talbot's calotype process, though subject to patent in England, was freely available for use in Scotland. Brewster, a collaborator with Talbot, was enthusiastic to see the process

developed and acted as something of a mentor to Robert Adamson while both were in St Andrews.

6 Sara Stevenson records that '[Hill and Adamson] charted the progress of the new Free Church Assembly Hall, and carried the camera out to Merchiston Castle School, to the south of Edinburgh, where they photographed the family of the Revd Thomas Chalmers, his brother, the headmaster of the school, and a few large groups of the schoolboys', in *Facing the Light: the Photography of Hill and Adamson*, Edinburgh 2002, p. 38.

7 The attribution of this work is not absolutely certain. The catalogue in St Andrews University suggest the photographer is 'Anonymous', however, Rodger's close association with John Adamson would suggest the latter is author of this work.

8 See P. & J. Kinchin, *Glasgow's Great Exhibitions*, Bicester n.d.

9 Linklater's article, accompanying Moser's portrait photographers, was published in both the United States version of *Vogue*, and the British publication, in the summer of 1950.

10 In conversation with the author, May 2004.

11 See *Huff Lane*, Wild Hawthorn Press 2000, and *The Philosopher's Garden*, Edinburgh 2004.

12 Robin Gillanders, 'The Actual Photograph', in *Studies in Photography*, SSHOP, Edinburgh 2000–1.

13 Gilmour was not, however, the first Scottish woman to become involved with photography. The best documented claim to this title is Clementina Hawarden (1822–65), who began taking photographs in 1857. There are also arguments for Lady Mary Jane Matheson (d. 1882), who seems to have been producing photographs as early as 1855; see Quentin Bajac's 'Fragments of Lady Matheson's Work Considered', in *Studies in Photography*, SSHOP, Edinburgh 1999–2000. Moreover, there are interesting claims for the mysterious 'Miss Mann', sometime assistant to David Octavius Hill.

14 Roger Taylor, *George Washington Wilson: Artist and Photographer 1823–93*, Aberdeen 1981, p. 27.

15 *Ibid.*, p. 27.

16 A useful, if incomplete, guide to photographers working in Dunfermline up until 1900 can be viewed at www.fifefhs.org/Records/photographers.htm, where John McDonald, who established a studio in the High Street, Dunfermline in 1856, is the (perhaps appropriately) designated photographer and taxidermist.

17 Walter Benjamin was particularly damning of this development; see his comments in 'A Small History of Photography' as published in *One-Way Street*, London 1979, p. 246.

18 I am grateful to Alastair Dinsmor, Curator, Glasgow Police Museum, for helping locate these images, and for his comment on the photographic 'line-up', 'on the back of the original photo was written: "From left to right – a dirty thief, a card sharper, a pickpocket and a tailor". Where the tailor fits in I don't know except if the other three were his customers and he would have been arrested for Fraud!!'. email, 9 Nov. 2005.

19 Strand identified Stieglitz, alongside David Octavius Hill, as the giants of photography: 'The work of those two men, Hill, the photographic primitive, Stieglitz, who has been the leader in the fight to establish photography... stands out sharply from that of all other photographers.' Paul Strand, 'The Art Motive in Photography', in V. Goldberg (ed.), *Photography in Print*, Albuquerque 1981, p. 284.

20 John Berger, *About Looking*, London 1980, p. 43.

21 For a convincing argument concerning the political context of Strand's work in the Western Isles see F. Macdonald, 'Paul Strand and the Atlanticist Cold War', in *History of Photography*, Winter 2004.

22 John Berger, *About Looking*, London 1980, p. 43.

23 Donald John Campbell in conversation with the author, 20 Dec. 2005.

24 Mary Sinclair (née Campbell) in conversation with the author, 22 Dec. 2005. Interestingly, Mrs Sinclair reports that Strand sent prints of these images to the family, and presumably to all his portrait subjects.

CHAPTER THREE: Land and the Landscape

1 This quote is from the prepublication announcement of the book. For a full discussion of this work see Graham Smith, *Sun Pictures in Scotland*, Michigan 1989.

2 *Photographic Notes*, 1 November 1860, pp. 290–1.

3 Prints, in this procedure, were made by laying the negative directly on to the contact paper and then leaving the print to process in sunlight.

4 See Robert Smart, 'James Valentine', in M. Kemp (ed.), *Mood of the Moment*, St Andrews n.d.

5 The archive of Valentine's company is held in special collections at the University of St Andrews. It is available at www.st-andrews.ac.uk/specialcollections/

6 Robert Moyes Adam began his working life as an assistant gardener in the Botanical Gardens in Edinburgh in 1903. Prior to and simultaneously with this position he studied science at Heriot Watt College, drawing at Edinburgh College of Art and botany at Edinburgh University. In 1914 he was made 'Assistant in Charge of the Studio' at the Botanical Gardens, and in 1915 he was regraded as a botanist. Being in charge of the studio, he was expected to supply drawings of plants for demonstration purposes. He quickly came to use the camera for these activities. This, of course, coincided with his career as a landscape photographer and Adam was recognised as a leading authority on the alpine flora of Scotland. He eventually retired from this position in 1949.

7 Adam was known to destroy any glass plate he considered inferior, and also to keep meticulous notes on the exposure of the negatives. The editor of the *Scots Magazine*, Robert Daw, in a commentary on Adam written in 1968, noted: 'His plates were developed very slowly, perhaps being as long as thirty minutes in the bath... His slow methods of printing enabled him to introduce the gradations of light and shade that were apparent to him when he first decided on a particular viewpoint.' The *Scots Magazine*, 88, 1967–8, p. 462.

8 Adam's entire archive of negatives, with accompanying prints, is now held in the Photographic Collections at the University of St Andrews in Scotland. See note 6.

9 Ansel Adams (1902–84) is generally regarded as one of the greatest of landscape photographers and is an established figure in the canon. He is best known for his images of the Yosemite Valley in California.

10 In respect of this vision it is clear that Robert Moyes Adam manipulated an intense 'depth of field' in his photographs such that foreground and background are equally focused.

11 There is really no substantial literature on Adam's work and most writing tends to be affectionate memoirs. See Hugh Gilbert, 'Scotland's Photographer', in *Scotland's Magazine*, March 1947 Alisdair Alpin MacGregor, 'Robert M. Adam', in *The Enchanted Isles*, Edinburgh 1967; also, the unsigned article by Robert Daw, 'In Solitary Places: Robert Moyes Adam', in the *Scots Magazine*, 88, 1967–8; and the anonymous piece 'Scotland's Pinhole Photographer', in the *Courier and Advertiser*, 14 March 1967.

12 Jeremy Bruce-Watt, 'Photographer of the High Tops', in *Scotland's Magazine*, February 1958. It might be added that the 'Special Correspondent' in the *Courier and Advertiser* of 14 March 1987 has noted 'the sheer weight (some estimates put his equipment at 30lbs)' of Adam's camera and pack, which further turned each journey into a trek.

13 The composite image is created in the darkroom. In the original photograph Adam had a useable image of the cross but the skyline and background were underexposed. He utilised a dramatic sky from an earlier photograph and 'combined' the images in the printing process.

14 In his 1958 interview with Jeremy Bruce-Watt, Adam suggested that his work 'catalogued Scotland's wildlife and its topography as a permanent record against the industrial and other changes of the future'.

15 Adam bought his first camera as a boy of 14; a 'half-plate' model. He began to keep catalogues of his negatives from 1901. In 1908 he was to buy a second camera, a Watson and Son half-plate model, and this he used for the rest of his life. In 1905 he travelled to Mingulay in the Barra group of islands to photograph birdlife, plants and people. His final trip to Mingulay was to the by-then depopulated island in 1922 however, throughout the 20s and 30s he continued to travel on the fringes of Scotland.

16 Rambling groups emerged in the 19th century, with the first being established in York during 1824. In 1892 the West of Scotland Ramblers' Association was created, and by 1905, in England at least, rambling clubs were attempting to persuade the railway companies to offer concessionary rates for organised rambling parties. The early 1930s saw a sharpened political focus in the movement, firstly with the establishment of the National Council of Ramblers' Federation in 1931, and then with the mass trespass on Kinder Scout in Derbyshire during 1932. This

invasion of the private grouse moors resulted in the trial and imprisonment of numerous ramblers. In 1935 the Ramblers' Association was officially registered, with groups throughout the country, which encouraged, in 1949, the National Parks and Access to the Countryside Act to be made law. Ramblers Scotland was established in 1967 but this only formalised an existing momentum for public access to the land. Adam was instrumental in photographing, and therefore publicising, these developments. The eminent landscape photographer Fay Godwin was president of the Ramblers' Association from 1987 to 1990.

17 Jeremy Bruce-Watt, 'Photographer of the High Tops', in *Scotland's Magazine*, February 1958.

18 MS, 'Robert Moyes Adam' by Mary Noble, University of St Andrews Collection. Noble adds: 'Another picture of cowslips at Canty Bay became a poster for the Society for the Preservation of Rural England!'

19 Macdonald has completed a number of large projects using aerial photography. These include *Shadow of Heaven*, 1989, *Views of Gaia*, 1992, *Song of Orpheus*, 1995, and *Airworks*, 2002. Her work is generally undertaken in collaboration with her partner, Angus Macdonald, who acts as pilot.

20 See 'Mark Johnston' in *Studies in Photography*, SSHOP, Edinburgh 1997, pp. 29–31.

21 Macdonald was a trustee of the John Muir Trust from 1995 to 2001, and a member of the main board of Scottish Natural Heritage between 1998 and 2001.

22 Patricia Macdonald, 'To Remain Dissolved: Aspects of Photography and Language', in *Studies in Photography*, SSHOP, Edinburgh 1996, pp. 25–35.

23 *Ibid.*, p. 26.

24 See, in particular, Patricia Macdonald, *Shadow of Heaven: Scotland from Above*, London 1989.

25 Patricia Macdonald, 'To Remain Dissolved: Aspects of Photography and Language', in *Studies in Photography*, SSHOP, Edinburgh 1996, p. 27.

26 *Ibid.*, p. 28.

27 James Lawson, in *Light from the Dark Room*, Edinburgh 1995, pp. 98–9.

28 See, for example, her recent collaboration with John Berger, *Once in Europa*, London 1999, and her exhibition project *Airworks*, Edinburgh 2001.

29 John Taylor, *A Dream of England: Landscape, Photography and the Tourist's Imagination*, Manchester, 1994. It might be added that Patricia Macdonald is fully cogniscant of this discourse and sensitive to its ramifications within her practice; indeed she would view her engagement with ecology and environmentalism as subverting its more acute political connotations.

30 Currently, the only useful monograph on Wood is Sara Stevenson, Julie Lawson and Michael Gray, 'John Muir Wood 1805–1892, an Accomplished Amateur', Edinburgh 1988.

31 'Thomas Joshua Cooper – an Interview with David Bellingham', in *Source*, February 1998.

32 Kathleen Stewart Howe, 'Mapping a Sacred Geography: Photographic Surveys by the Royal Engineers in the Holy Land, 1864–1868', in J. M. Schwartz and J. R. Ryan (eds), *Picturing Place: Photography and the Geographical Imagination*, London 2003, p. 242.

33 Derrick Price, 'Surveyors and Surveyed', in L. Wells (ed.), *Photography: a Critical Introduction*, London 1997, pp. 58–61.

34 *Photographic Notes*, 1 November 1860, p. 290.

35 See John Hannavy, *A Moment in Time: Scottish Contributions to Photography 1840–1920*, Edinburgh 1983.

36 Sara Stevenson and Duncan Forbes, in *A Companion Guide to Photography in the National Gallery of Scotland*, make much of the role of Macpherson's wife, Geraldine Bate, in the partnership that was to produce these photographs; Edinburgh 2001, p. 66.

37 K. Howe in J. M. Schwartz and J. R. Ryan (eds), *Picturing place: photography and the geographical imagination*, London, 2003. pp. 228–9.

38 *Ibid.*, p. 242.

39 See Larry J. Schaaf and Roger Taylor, *British Paper Negatives: 1839–1864*, New York 2001.

40 For some discussion of Murray's response to the uprising see R. Hamilton, 'John Murray: Pioneer Photographer in India', in *Scottish Photography Bulletin*, 1993, pp. 3–9.

41 See also Julie Lawson, 'Fredrick Bremner: a Vision of India', in *Scottish Photography Bulletin*, 1991, pp. 9–16.

CHAPTER FOUR: Documentary

1 There is some evidence that James Robertson photographed preparations for war firstly from his base in Constantinople, and subsequently at Balaklava, during 1854. See B. A. and H. K. Henisch, 'Balaklava 1854', in

Scottish Photography Bulletin, 1, 1993, pp. 10–13.

2 John Falconer, 'Ethnographical Photography in India 1850–1900', in *Photographic Collector*, 5 (1), 1984.

3 John Hannavy, *A Moment in Time: Scottish Contributions to Photography 1840–1920*, Glasgow 1983, pp. 61–2.

4 There were other, significant photographers attached to Brady's studio who would produce some exceptional images of the American Civil War, notably Timothy O'Sullivan (a protégé of Gardner's), George N. Barnard, and Alexander's brother James Gardner (1829–?).

5 See, in reference to this, William Frassanito, *Gettysburg: A Journey in Time*, London 1976.

6 Gardner was also present at the battlefields of Fredericksburg, Gettysburg and Petersburg, and would go on to publish a two-volume edition of his photographs from the American Civil War in 1866, which he disconcertingly titled *Gardner's Sketchbook of the War*. His career blossomed as he was employed to photograph the conspirators in Lincoln's assassination and went on to become an official photographer for the Union Pacific Railroad Company.

7 This is recorded in Elsie Knocker's possession in the Imperial War Museum's records, Photograph Archive, Imperial War Museum, subject list 319. Interestingly the invention of the portable 'snapshot' camera had occasioned an earlier usage within the context of war photography. While serving in the Imperial Yeomanry during the Boer War, the Scottish artist William Skeoch Cumming (1864–1929) had taken informal photographs of the campaign during 1901. These he would use as the basis for paintings; IWM, subject list 200.

8 These are now held in the National Library of Scotland, Acc. 8006.

9 See T. C. Smout, *A Century of the Scottish People 1830–1950*, London 1997.

10 I am indebted, for this information, to Venda Pollock, who has shared with me her exhaustive research on the convoluted publication of Thomas Annan's photographs from resources in the Mitchell Library, Glasgow.

11 Julie Lawson, *William Donaldson Clark 1816–1873*, Edinburgh n.d., p. 7.

12 For a good note on this see Sara Stevenson and Julie Lawson, *Masterpieces of Photography from the Liddell Collection*, Edinburgh 1986, pp. 116–18.

13 Burns published this book in 1868. It was illustrated with 15 of his albumen photographs, which were 'tipped in' to a text written by Thomas Henderson – an early example of the 'photo-book'.

14 See Richard Ovenden, *John Thomson, Photographer*, Edinburgh 1997, pp. 78–88.

15 Duncan Forbes has noted that Hardy was sent to the Gorbals, for the photo-essay 'The Forgotten Gorbals', in order to re-work some material first collected by Bill Brandt. Brandt's images were deemed unconvincing. See S. Stevenson and D. Forbes, *A Companion Guide to Photography in the National Galleries of Scotland*, Edinburgh 2001, p. 154.

16 See D. Forbes, *An Exile's Eye: the Photography of Wolfgang Suschitzky*, Edinburgh 2002.

17 In conversation with the author, March 2006.

18 'Gorbals Children' was originally exhibited at Richard Demarco's Traverse Gallery in Edinburgh, shortly after the completion of the work in 1965, and was published as a documentary photo-book in 1990.

19 This project, exhibited at Aberdeen Art Gallery during 1972, was deemed too partial and created a number of difficulties for McKenzie.

20 See M. Harrison, *Young Meteors*, London 1999.

21 Annan produced his *Views from the Line of the Loch Katrine Water Works* in time for the opening in 1859, with a deluxe publication following in 1877.

22 For some discussion of this see Ray McKenzie, 'A Love Affair with Loch Katrine: Problems of Representation in Early Scottish Landscape', *Scottish Photography Bulletin*, 1, 1990, pp. 3–12.

23 Thomas Bouch's newly constructed Tay Bridge collapsed in a force 10 gale on 28 December 1879. Six carriages from a passing train fell into the river and 75 passengers were killed. A second bridge was completed in 1887.

24 Carey's images were first discussed in Andrew Patrizio's research thesis 'The Ugly and the Useless: Industry as a Theme in Scottish Art and Aesthetics 1880–1980', Edinburgh 1993, where he emphasised the negative reaction of John Ruskin, and also William Morris, to this manifest industrial aesthetic. Subsequently Patrizio has

published 'Fixing Steel Plates to Glass' in *Scottish Photography Bulletin*, 1, 1990, pp. 21–6. See also Sheila MacKay, *The Forth Bridge: a Picture History*, Edinburgh 1990 for a detailed and illustrated study of the history of the bridge.

25 The stereoscope was an early development in photographic history. Sir Charles Wheatstone had proposed the idea at the Royal Scottish Society of Arts as early as 1838. David Brewster helped to develop the idea within the context of photography and it became a common feature of most Victorian living-rooms. Indeed, it remained popular well into the 20th century.

26 This photograph was reproduced in Alfred Stieglitz's *Camera Work* in October 1909, where it was wrongly titled *Newhaven Fisheries*.

27 For a discussion of vernacular and commercial photographs of Scottish emigrants to Canada see Keith Bell, '"Just the Kind of People Canada Wants"; Photographing Hebridean Immigrants for the Canadian Pacific Railway', in *Studies in Photography* 1999–2000, pp. 18–21.

28 These images were discovered by L. M. H. Smith, after Roger Taylor had published his monograph of George Washington Wilson in 1981. They were subsequently published as L. M. H. Smith (ed.), *The Road to the Isles: The Hebrides in Lantern Slides*, by Callum Macdonald Publishing in 1983. A useful article concerning the portrayal of Highland culture and politics in these images was published in 1993; see Martin Padget, 'An Iconography of Difference: Internal Colonialism, Photography, and the Crofters of the Highlands and Islands of Scotland' in *College Literature*, 20 (2), June 1993.

29 Martin Padget, 'An Iconography of Difference: Internal Colonialism, Photography, and the Crofters of the Highlands and Islands of Scotland' in *College Literature*, June 1993, p. 178.

30 L. M. H. Smith, *The Road to the Isles*, p. 32, from the original lecture notes for slide no. 13.

31 *Ibid.*, p. 34 from the original lecture notes for slide no. 14.

32 *Ibid.*, p. 118, from the original lecture notes for slide no. 56.

33 See M. Russell, *A Poem of Remote Lives: Images of Eriskay 1934*, Glasgow 1997, and, *A Different Country: Photographs of Werner Kissling*, Edinburgh 2002.

34 For the key archive of Kent's work see www.orkneylibrary.org.uk/photo gallery/gallindex.htm.

35 Gus Wylie, Preface to *The Hebrides*, Glasgow 1978.

36 See 'Documentary Photography: John Charity in Conversation with James Lawson', in *Scottish Photography Bulletin*, 2, 1990, pp. 47–53.

37 John Thomson, 'Introduction to Illustrations of China and its People', 1873, in V. Goldberg (ed.), *Photography in Print*, Albuquerque 2003, p. 164.

38 *Ibid.*, p. 164.

39 For a discussion of Carrick's life and work see Felicity Ashbee and Julie Lawson, William Carrick 1827–1878, Edinburgh n.d.

40 *Ibid.*, pp. 16–17.

41 Ruth Stirling, interviewed by Jane Brettle, *Scottish Photography Bulletin* 2, 1991, pp. 13–14.

42 Jeremy Sutton-Hibbert, 'Return to Sintesti', in *Black and White Photography*, March 2005.

43 Owen Logan, from 'Pictures of Nigeria in the Digital Age: Owen Logan and Femi Folorunso in Conversation with Pavel Buchler' in the catalogue *A Home of Signs and Wonders*, London 1997, no page numbers.

44 Logan completed his body of work 'Bloodlines, Vite allo Specchio' in 1992. This project examined the close links between Scotland and Italy in the period after the Second World War. Logan's mother was Italian, and so 'In the Italian work I can identify a place, my own place, within the subject. That changes the nature of what's called documentary'; in 'Bloodlines', *Portfolio*, 7, Summer 1993, p. 25.

45 Owen Logan, email to the author, October 2002.

46 Duncan Forbes, 'Situating Realism: an Interview with Owen Logan', in *Third Text*, 18 (4), 2004, p. 268.

47 Owen Logan, email to the author, October 2002.

48 For Cowie's archive see www.st-andrews.ac.uk/special collections/

CHAPTER FIVE: Photography and Art

1 Susan Sontag, *On Photography*, London 2002, p. 143.

2 For an interesting discussion of Whistler and Hawarden see Julie Lawson, *Women in White: Photographs by Lady Hawarden*, Edinburgh 1997, pp. 17–20. See also V. Dodier, 'Clementina, Viscountess Hawarden: Studies from Life', in M. Weaver (ed.), *British Photography in the Nineteenth Century*, Cambridge 1989.

3 Sadly, there is no Hawarden

archive other than the images held at the Victoria and Albert Museum in London.

4 Hawarden exhibited at the Photographic Society of London in 1863 and again in 1864, the year before her death from pneumonia. Her photographs were held in a family album until the 1940s, and exhibited at the Victoria and Albert Museum and in the Scottish National Portrait Gallery in the 1990s. In some degree this paralleled the career of Julia Margaret Cameron, though this latter figure had more widespread recognition in her lifetime. Interestingly Cameron too had a Scottish connection, for she exhibited with the Photographic Society of Scotland in 1864. For a note on this see Roddy Simpson, 'Julia Margaret Cameron and the Photographic Society of Scotland', in *History of Photography*, 28 (1), Spring 2004, pp. 82–7.

5 This famous story may be apocryphal, but it is simply too 'true' to omit. In fact, in 1858 Rejlander exhibited a 'Study from the Two Ways of Life' at the Photographic Society of Scotland, in Edinburgh. It may well be that the study was presented when the full work was proscribed.

6 In fact the quotations from Burns, throughout this suite, come from the bard's collection, *The Merry Muses*. These were themselves collected and 'translated' verse and so Colvin is involved in a double adaptation and is, as it were, appropriating the already appropriated.

7 In fact Emerson would reject his initial hypothesis with his publication of *The Death of Naturalistic Photography* in 1890.

8 William Buchanan in *The Art of the Photographer J. Craig Annan*, London 1992, records that Craig Annan was first in the company of David Octavius Hill when he visited the family home in 1865 and was later introduced to drawing by the esteemed academician in 1869. He goes on, 'After Hill's death in 1870, his widow presented Thomas [Annan] with ninety calotypes which he bound into two volumes. James [Craig Annan] recalled that he looked at them as a schoolboy', p. 12.

9 *Ibid.*, p. 20.

10 Dan Dunlop, 'A Plea for Straight Photography', in *Photo-Era*, xxxiii (5) May 1912, p. 209.

11 *Ibid.*, p. 207.

12 *Ibid.*, p. 209.

13 William Buchanan, *The Art of the Photographer J. Craig Annan*, London 1992.

14 Clive Holland, *Special Summer Number of 'the Studio'*, 1905: *Art in Photography*, edited by Charles Holme, pp. 10–11.

15 *Ibid.*, p. 11.

16 Alexander Allan, and indeed his brother, is amongst the many Scottish photographers whose biography remains in shadow. In 1910 the Trade Directory for Glasgow lists, under 'Photographic Artists', Allan Brothers at 52 West Nile Street, and this listing holds good until 1925.

17 *Ibid.*, p. 11.

18 Coburn showed some nine photographs in 1900 in a salon curated by the symbolist photographer F. Holland Day, in fact a relation.

19 For a discussion of this see Tom Normand, 'Alvin Langdon Coburn, Robert Louis Stevenson and Edinburgh', in *History of Photography*, 29 (1), Spring 2005, pp. 45–59.

20 Helmut and Alison Gernsheim (eds), *Alvin Langdon Coburn, Photographer: an Autobiography*, London 1966, p. 48.

21 R. L. Stevenson, *Edinburgh: Picturesque Notes*, with a preface by Janet Adam Smith, London 1954, p. 23.

22 *Ibid.*, p. 20

23 *Ibid.*, p. 33.

24 Stieglitz would illustrate Coburn's *Weir's Close* in *Camera Work* in July 1906.

25 MS 'Gernsheim/Coburn, Autobiography, Notes', The Gernsheim Collection, Harry Ransom Humanities Research Centre at the University of Texas at Austin.

26 There is an interesting biographical discussion of Watkins by Lori Pauli, 'Margaret Watkins: Making it Home', *Studies in Photography*, 2000–1, pp. 16–23.

27 Bonnie Yochelson, 'Clarence H. White: Peaceful Warrior', in M. Fulton (ed.), *Pictorialism into Modernism: the Clarence H. White School of Photography*, New York 1996, p. 90.

28 Lor Pauli, 'Margaret Watkins: Making it Home', *Studies in Photography*, 2001.

29 The best discussion of Macpherson's Ossian and its influence remains Fiona Stafford, *The Sublime Savage: a Study of James Macpherson and the Poems of Ossian*, Edinburgh 1988. For a discussion of the influence of Ossian on the visual arts see Henry Okun 'Ossian in Painting', *Journal of the Warburg and Courtauld Institutes*, 30, 1967.

30 Macpherson proposed this contentious revision in 'An

Introduction to the History of Great Britain and Ireland' in 1771. It was to become a further aspect in the dispute concerning the veracity of his records thereafter.

31 For a discussion of this series see James Lawson, 'Barbie: Photographs by Andy Wiener', in *Alba*, 1989.

32 See Maud Sulter's 'Blood Money', in the catalogue *Syrcas*, Wrexham 1994, p. 35.

33 'David Williams; Digest of a Conversation with James Lawson', *Studies in Photography*, 1996, p. 22.

34 *Ibid.*, p. 22

35 'Exposure' was exhibited at the Richard Ingleby Gallery in 2005 with an accompanying photobook; *Exposure: Garry Fabian Miller*, text by Ian Warrell, afterword by Richard Ingleby, Edinburgh 2005.

36 Ian Warrell, *Exposure: Garry Fabian Miller*, Edinburgh 2005, p. 10.

37 See David Campay, *Art and Photography*, London 2005, for an international survey of these developments.

38 Satish Padiyar, 'The Luminous Body', in *Portfolio: the Catalogue of Contemporary Photography in Britain*, 32, p. 19.

39 Claire Docherty, 'Give Me a Child When He Is Seven... Wendy McMurdo', in *Portfolio: the Catalogue of Contemporary Photography in Britain*, 30, p. 56.

40 Interview with Neil Mulholland www.davidshrigley.com/articles/nm_interview.html, 2003.

41 *Ibid.*

42 The title is reflective of the single lens of the camera, but also of the fact that Watson is blind in one eye.

43 This experimentation contributed to the fascination with printing methods and chemical options to the extent that a whole school of radical photographic printing emerged in the final decades of the 20th century. See Lyle Rexer, *Photography's Antiquarian Avant-Garde; the New Wave in Old Processes*, New York, n.d.

44 This commission led to the publication Pradip Malde and P. Celina Lunsford, *Imogen Cunningham: the Poetry of Form*, Berkeley 1994.

45 Peter Ride, 'The Dark and the Dead: Isolate by Calum Angus Mackay', in *Portfolio: the Catalogue of Contemporary Photography in Britain*, 19, p. 52.

CONCLUSION

1 Roland Barthes, *Camera Lucida*, London 1993, p. 93.

2 In respect of this idea it is notable that in one study of the churchyard, circa 1845, Hill has included a still-life of the camera itself, juxtaposed against the assembled monuments.

3 MS letter, Coburn to Gernsheim, 27 September 1957, the Gernsheim Collection, Humanities Research Centre, University of Texas.

4 Alvin Langdon Coburn, 'The Old Masters of Photography', in *The Century Magazine*, October 1915, pp. 909–10.

5 *Ibid.*, p. 912.

6 Robert Louis Stevenson, *Edinburgh: Picturesque Notes*, edited by Janet Adam Smith, London 1954, p. 55.

7 Helmut and Alison Gernsheim (eds), *Alvin Langdon Coburn; Photographer*, London 1966, p. 48.

8 MS, Gernsheim/Coburn, Autobiography, Notes, the Gernsheim Collection, Humanities Research Centre, University of Texas.

9 *Ibid*. Coburn is here quoting Robert Louis Stevenson, *Edinburgh: Picturesque Notes*, edited by Janet Adam Smith, London 1954.

10 This photo-essay, with a short text by Sacheverell Sitwell, would be published in the magazine *Lilliput*, Feburary 1942.

11 Andrea Stillman, email to the author, April 2006.

Chronology

1822
Joseph Nicéphore Niépce, a retired French soldier, produced a photographic image using a light-sensitised glass plate.

1826
Niépce's experiments resolved in the creation of images fixed on pewter plates.

1835
Louis Daguerre, a stage designer who had engaged with Niépce in his experiments (from 1827–1833) developed his own method of producing an image using mercury vapours. This was extended into an iodised silver plate method which significantly reduced exposure times.

1839
The French Académie des Sciences was informed of Daguerre's discoveries. Simultaneously, William Henry Fox Talbot's experiments in developing and fixing the latent image came to fruition in England. Talbot had been experimenting with light-sensitive chemicals from the early 1830s, and his method became the common paper-based negative-positive photographic process.

1839
Thomas Davidson opened a shop in Edinburgh which would manufacture photographic equipment including lenses and cameras; he would provide cameras, lenses and reflecting mirrors for Hill and Adamson.

1841
Fox Talbot patented his calotype process, a patent that did not extend to Scotland, so allowing for the free development of the calotype (later the 'Talbotype') in Scotland.

1840s
David Brewster, Principal of the University of St Andrews, engaged in a detailed correspondence with Fox Talbot concerning the science and potential of photography. This knowledge was shared with Brewster's circle, centring upon the University of St Andrews.

c. 1842
The world's first photographic society, the Edinburgh Calotype Club, was founded.

1843
David Octavius Hill, painter, and Robert Adamson, photographer, used the calotype process in their new working partnership.

1844
Fox Talbot published *The Pencil of Nature*, and, having taken various images in Scotland, he published *Sun Pictures in Scotland*.

1848
Robert Adamson died.

1849
David Brewster developed a stereoscopic viewer. Thomas Rodger opened his portrait studio in St Andrews.

1850s
James Valentine redirected his printing firm in Dundee towards a photographic studio specialising in postcards and tourist panoramas. The archive is held in St Andrews University Library Special Collections.

c. 1850
In Edinburgh the photographer and inventor Mungo Ponton experimented with dichromated colloids; work which built upon his interest in photo-sensitive papers, from 1839, and scientific papers on optics.

1851
The Wet Collodian process was developed and further reduced exposure times. Robert Macpherson began his photographic practice in Rome.

1853
The Royal Photographic Society was founded. George Washington Wilson began a short-lived photographic partnership with John Hay in Aberdeen.

c. 1854
Thomas Annan took his first photograph and established his photographic studio in Glasgow in 1857.

1855
Andre Disderi, a French entrepreneur, utilised the photograph in cartes-de-visite and an explosion in photographic portrait studios ensued. At the same time the camera was used to document the Crimean War by Roger Fenton and others, including the Scot James Robertson. In 1861 the American Civil War became a subject for some of the seminal images of war photography. Increasingly the camera was used by artists, while simultaneously the earliest examples of photographic portraiture, images of travel, 'pictorial' photography, manipulated photographs and photographs of objects in motion were developed. In this same year George Washington Wilson opened his commercial photography business in Aberdeen. And the Glasgow Photographic Society was founded.

1856
David Brewster published *The Stereoscope*. This year also saw the founding of the Photographic Society of Scotland, with Horatio Ross as its first vice-president.

1857
Oscar Rejlander exhibited *The Two Ways of Life* in Manchester at the 'Art Treasures Exhibition'. This controversial 'combine photograph' was purchased by Queen Victoria for Prince Albert. This image would be reprised by Calum Colvin in 1991.

1859
The Edinburgh-born William Carrick opened a photographic studio in St Petersburg in Russia.

1861
Founding of the Edinburgh Photographic Society. The eminent Scottish scientist James Clerk Maxwell presented a demonstration of his colour photography to the Royal Institution in London. Here he produced a colour 'photograph' of a tartan ribbon by combining three photographic images separately filtered through a red, blue and green plate. These were projected simultaneously, via lantern slides, to create a colour image.

1861–65
The Scots émigré Alexander Gardner, working for Matthew Brady, photographed episodes from the civil war in the United States of America.

1863
William Notman, having emigrated from Scotland to Canada in 1856 and having established photographic studios throughout Canada, published *Notman's Photographic Selections*, with a second volume in 1865.

c. 1866
Charles Piazzi Smyth, the Astronomer Royal for Scotland, took the first photograph inside the Great Pyramid at Giza.

1868
Thomas Annan began his project photographing slums in the old town of Glasgow, 'The Old Closes and Streets of Glasgow', completed 1871.

1870
David Octavius Hill died; his obituary failed to mention his photographic work. John Thomson travelled in China following photographic sorties in Cambodia and Hong Kong. His landmark publications *Foochow and the River Min* and *China and its People* were published in 1873 and 1874 respectively.

1871
Archibald Burns was commissioned by the Edinburgh Improvement Trust to photograph Edinburgh buildings listed for demolition.

1876–77
John Thompson created some 37 photographs for his photographic study 'Street Life of London', published 1878.

1879
The development of the photogravure by Karl Klic in Vienna; the license to use this new technique was sold to T. & R. Annan and Sons in Glasgow.

1880
George Eastman established his company in the United States, this would become the Kodak Company and would popularise and democratise the camera. The half-tone photographic process was developed and allowed for the publication of photographs in newspapers.

1882
Fred Bremner moved to India, where he established a photographic studio.

1883
James Craig Annan visited Vienna to study the photogravure process with its inventor Karl Klic. Evelyn George Carey, a civil engineer, began photographing the Forth Bridge in construction.

c. 1890
The development of the Oil Pigment Print assisted in the emergence of Pictorialism.

1892
Henry Peach Robinson, a 'Pictorial' photographer and author of *Pictorialism in Photography* and *Picture-taking by Photography*, found the Linked Ring in England. This was a group dedicated to exploring the notion of photography as a 'fine art' with an authentic aesthetic. This was designed to undermine the contention that photography was a branch of the sciences, generally propagated by the Royal Photographic Society. In 1893 this group had its first exhibition, a 'Photographic Salon'.

1894
James Craig Annan was elected into the Linked Ring.

1895
The American photographer E. S. Curtis began his project to photograph Native American Indians; this work, which covered every native American tribe, was completed in 1930; it would have a significant influence on the work of Thomas Joshua Cooper during the middle years of the 1980s.

1897
John Annan, photographer and elder son of Thomas Annan, added a group of new photographic images to his father's 'The Old Closes and Streets of Glasgow'. Craig Annan helped organise and exhibits at the 'International Photographic Exhibition' in Glasgow.

1900
James Craig Annan helped organise an exhibition of photographs for the Glasgow International Exhibition in Kelvingrove Park; works by Hill and Adamson were prominently displayed. The Gum Platinum print was developed.

1902
Following the example of the Linked Ring, and several Continental secessionist organisations, the influential American Alfred Stieglitz founded the Photo-Secession in New York. Stieglitz and his associates, who included America's most eminent and radical photographers, published the influential journal *Camera Work* from 1903 to 1917. This journal would feature the works of Hill and Adamson and the Annans.

1903
Founding of the Scottish Photographic Federation, a national body for the many and expanding local camera clubs.

1904
Alvin Langdon Coburn, the avant-garde photographer based in London, visited James Craig Annan and studied the work of Hill and Adamson. In this year James Craig Annan was elected first president of the International Society of Pictorial Photographers.

1905
Alvin Langdon Coburn photographed in Edinburgh; there he created a series of images in homage to Robert Louis Stevenson.

1905
Robert Moyes Adam photographed the inhabitants of the island of Mingulay. He would later become a significant landscape photographer working exclusively in Scotland; his archive is held in St Andrews University Library Special Collections.

1906
Stieglitz showed Hill and Adamson's work at the Little Gallery of the Photo-secession, founded 1905 in New York City, having been introduced to their work by James Craig Annan.

1907
The first commercial colour film was manufactured in France.

1910
The Albright Exhibition, in Buffalo, New York, presented the apotheosis of American Pictorialism; Hill and Adamson's photographs were exhibited as a group.

1916
Alvin Langdon Coburn began work on his experimental 'vortographs'.

1928
The American Pictorialist Margaret Watkins, an associate of Clarence White in America, moved to Glasgow.

1931
Bill Brandt returned to England, having worked with Kertesz, Brassai, Man Ray, and Atget on the Continent. He began his pioneering documentary photography, including various projects in Scotland.

1932
Ansel Adams, the canonical American landscape photographer, established Group f64 with Imogen Cunningham and Edward Weston. Adams would visit and photograph in Scotland in 1974.

1937
The 'Mass-Observation' project was established in the north of England; this was a sociological attempt to record everyday life which had significant ramifications for documentary photography.

1947
Bert Hardy undertook a documentary project photographing life in the Gorbals in Glasgow.

1949
Lida Moser, a New York-based photographer, was commissioned by *Vogue* magazine to photograph Scotland's cultural and intellectual figures in response to the success of the 'Edinburgh International Festival of the Arts'.

1954
Paul Strand, the great American photographer and finest exponent of 'straight photography', visited South Uist in the Hebrides for his project 'Tir A'Mhurain', published 1962. Strand was an admirer of Hill and Adamson.

1955
Stieglitz's associate Edward Steichen organised the landmark 'The Family of Man' exhibition in New York City.

1959
Oscar Marzaroli founded Studio 59 in Glasgow.

1960s
Marzaroli and Joseph McKenzie undertook extensive documentary studies of ordinary life in the Gorbals in Glasgow, and elsewhere in Scotland.

1977
Stills Gallery in Edinburgh was founded under the directorship of Richard Hough, with Robin Gillanders and Murray Johnston. This gallery exhibited Scottish photographers in an international context and presented the work of Paul Strand.

1982
American-born Thomas Joshua Cooper began a teaching post at Glasgow School of Art, where he was the founding Head of Photography.

1984
Establishment of the Scottish Photographic Archive under the auspices of the National Galleries of Scotland.

1986
The exhibition 'Constructed Narratives', featuring the work of Calum Colvin and Ron O'Donnell, was held at the Stills Gallery in Edinburgh.

1988
The Portfolio Gallery in Edinburgh was founded under the direction of Gloria Chalmers, with Jane Brettle and Mary Ann Kennedy. This gallery exhibited work by Scottish and international photographers and established the magazine *Portfolio*. Murray Johnston became the founding Head of Photography at Edinburgh College of Art.

1989
Street Level Photoworks founded in Glasgow by the Glasgow Photography Group.

1990
The renaissance of Scottish photography was marked with the exhibition 'New Scottish Photography', held in the National Galleries of Scotland, in Edinburgh.

1993
The establishment of 'Fotofeis', a biennial 'Scottish International Festival of Photography'.

c. 1994
Founding of the Scottish Society for the History of Photography.

1995
The landmark exhibition 'Light from the Darkroom: a Celebration of Scottish Photography' was held in the National Galleries, Edinburgh.

2003
The Scottish Society for the History of Photography sponsored an international symposium marking the 200th anniversary of David Octavius Hill's birth.

Index

Luath Press Limited

committed to publishing well written books worth reading

LUATH PRESS takes its name from Robert Burns, whose little collie Luath (*Gael.*, swift or nimble) tripped up Jean Armour at a wedding and gave him the chance to speak to the woman who was to be his wife and the abiding love of his life. Burns called one of 'The Twa Dogs' Luath after Cuchullin's hunting dog in Ossian's *Fingal*. Luath Press was established in 1981 in the heart of Burns country, and now resides a few steps up the road from Burns' first lodgings on Edinburgh's Royal Mile.

Luath offers you distinctive writing with a hint of unexpected pleasures.

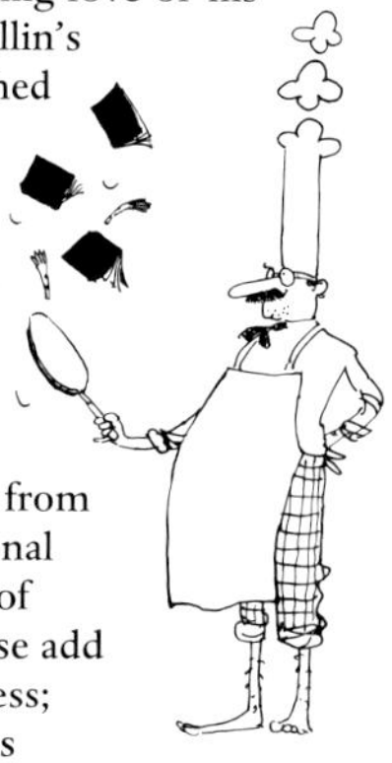

ILLUSTRATION: IAN KELLAS

Most bookshops in the UK, the US, Canada, Australia, New Zealand and parts of Europe either carry our books in stock or can order them for you. To order direct from us, please send a £sterling cheque, postal order, international money order or your credit card details (number, address of cardholder and expiry date) to us at the address below. Please add post and packing as follows: UK – £1.00 per delivery address; overseas surface mail – £2.50 per delivery address; overseas airmail – £3.50 for the first book to each delivery address, plus £1.00 for each additional book by airmail to the same address. If your order is a gift, we will happily enclose your card or message at no extra charge.

Luath Press Limited
543/2 Castlehill
The Royal Mile
Edinburgh EH1 2ND
Scotland

Telephone: 0131 225 4326 (24 hours)
Fax: 0131 225 4324
email: sales@luath.co.uk
Website: www.luath.co.uk